DICTIONARY OF ITALIAN SLANG AND COLLOQUIAL EXPRESSIONS

Daniela Gobetti

Program Associate
Center for European Studies
The University of Michigan, Ann Arbor

BARRON'S

All inquiries should be addressed to:
Barron's Educational Series, Inc.
250 Wireless Boulevard
Hauppauge, NY 11788
http://www.barronseduc.com

ISBN-13: 978-0-7641-0432-9
ISBN-10: 0-7641-0432-2

Library of Congress Catalog Card Number 98-73145

PRINTED IN CANADA
20 19 18 17 16 15 14 13 12 11 10

Contents

Preface

The Italian word *gèrgo,* which translates as both *slang* and *jargon,* derives from the thirteenth-century French word *jergon.* As G. Lotti mentions in *Le parole della gente,* the word *jergon* was used for the first time by the poet Marie de France to identify the language of birds. A *gergo*—or jargon—is a specialized, technical language that makes the group of people (or birds) who use it not easily understandable to outsiders. Jargons have thus been mostly associated with distinct occupational groups, such as bureaucrats and physicians, lawyers and fishermen, sociologists and carpenters. Each of these employs a particular vocabulary, which, in principle, is merely a tool to make communication efficient and accurate. As is well known, however, a professional jargon is also used in the social power game, so as to establish the social and anthropological boundaries of the group, and to exclude "others."

Slang is a synonym of *jargon.* But conventionally, slang has come to indicate one particular jargon: the one that we can all use, independently of professional and technical concerns, when we want to express what official language–and mores–consider taboo, either in content or emotional overtone. Slang has its origins in marginalized social groups, including vagabonds and thieves, students and drug addicts. Technical jargons contribute terms to it, but what sets slang apart is its countercultural and oppositional bent.

A unified slang, accessible to any speaker of a language, presupposes a unified official language that people use in everyday communication, but with which, at times, they may want to "play," or against which they may want to "rebel." This fact explains why it is easier to speak of English slang and French *argot* than of Italian slang. The latter is still in the making, because a unified version of spoken/written Italian, brought about by internal migration, the growth of literacy, and the spread of mass media, above all cinema and television, has established itself only after the Second World War. Before that time, dialects—of which Italian has many—played both the role of everyday language and local slang(s) for most people, as apparent from the presence of dialect words in today's slang.

The growth of a shared, everyday Italian has followed patterns of economic and social development. It will thus not come as a surprise that the process of formation of a unified Italian slang has been faster in the north than in the south, in big cities rather than in small centers, and among literate people—especially young people—rather than among semi-literate and older ones.

Of course, a single unified slang is something of an abstraction. Even when all speakers share the same official language, and thus have the tendency to share the same slang, subgroups remain active. Young people's slang has much in common with the slang of drug addicts, but the two do not overlap completely. The same can be said of the slang of drug addicts and that of criminals—which are both indebted to the older language of the vagabonds and thieves (called *la lingua furbesca*). All these groups lend terms to generic "slang," that is, slang used by the general population, which preserves remnants of (often Italianized) dialect words. Finally, in all kinds of slang we find, morphologically altered, terms borrowed from technical jargons.

These few introductory notes aim at clarifying the criteria used in compiling this dictionary. I have excluded all technical jargons—including those of sports and mass media. I have done so, first, for reasons of size; second, because dictionaries of technical jargons are mostly available; and third but most importantly, because the oppositional and alternative overtone of slang is absent from technical jargons, at least in principle. I have included slang used by four groups: young people/students, drug addicts, criminals, and the general population. The labels— youth, narcotic, criminal, and slang—are meant to indicate the social group that introduces and/or mostly uses a specific word, or sub-meaning of a word. I have only used the label "slang" when I wished to distinguish one sub-meaning from another. Words that are not labeled in any way are those that belong to general slang. "North," "South," and "Center" have been employed to indicate the origin and/or basic area of use of a word.

A caveat is however in order. The identification of the geographical and social origin and/or area of use of a term cannot be considered absolutely valid. Since slang is, to a degree, an underground language, its permutations are more difficult to follow than those of the official language. A dictionary always captures a somewhat obsolete language; even more so in the case of slang. Words pertaining to the young people called *paninari,* for example, are already out of date, as is the social phenomenon to which they refer.

More generally, once a word becomes used by the general population, it tends to lose its slangish tone and function. *Casino,* which means brothel, became "mess, trouble, problem" in general slang, while maintaining its taboo connotation. But it has become such common currency over the last twenty years that it can now be considered a familiar, but inoffensive synonym for "trouble" and "mess." *Puttanaio,* which means "group of whores," and carries the same slang meanings of "mess" and "trouble," still conveys the aggressive tones "casino" used to convey, and it is therefore, if I may say so, "more" slang than casino is.

A typical entry is made of the Italian word or phrase, followed by its translation in official English, by an Italian sentence or phrase that illustrates how the word can be used, and by the English translation. In the latter, I have tried to use slang terms, even though, at times, this has required abandoning the semantic connotation and the context of the Italian word.

Whenever possible, for each word I have given etymology and literal meaning (if one exists independently of the slang meaning). When a slang word appears within the definition of another entry, I have used bold type and the symbol ">" to tell readers that the word has its own entry. I have used parentheses to indicate: a) orthographic variations, meaning that a word appears in two different forms, for example, *lofio* and *lof(f)io:* and b) words that can be left implicit, as in the expression *arrangiarsi (da solo).*

Accents indicate both where stress must fall in pronunciation and whether the vowel is open or closed, even though that distinction is disappearing in the spoken language. Foreign words are not accented in Italian. The reader can assume that the stress will fall on the same syllable as it does in the original language: so Italians will say *jòker,* not *jokèr.* But *Mandrake* becomes *Mandràke.* Vowels are pronounced like Italian vowels, even though there are exceptions. *Flash* becomes *flahsh,* but *sheik* (to shake) remains *sheik.* It is hard to be more specific on this point because pronunciation of foreign words varies greatly, depending on geographical, social, and educational characteristics.

According to the rules of Italian grammar, foreign words are always masculine and invariable. These two principles are, however, widely disregarded by speakers. *Watt* thus becomes a feminine noun, because it is used as a synonym of the Italian word *idea,* which is feminine. When people make the plural of words taken from English, they will (incorrectly) add *s.* So *watt* becomes *watts* (pronounced "vahtz").

The abbreviations should be self-explanatory. I have used "plural" to indicate that the word is used only in that form, as, for example, *calli* in the expresssion *stare sui calli a qualcuno.* I have given the feminine (more rarely the masculine) form of a noun when I thought that readers would not be sure whether the term was used in one of the two genders or in both (for example, *pompinaro* and *pompinara*). I have indicated whether a verb is transitive, intransitive, etc., given that the choice of auxiliary depends, up to a point, on that distinction, as students of Italian will know. Pronominal verbs are verbs that take the reflexive form, but are not true reflexive verbs. *Abbioccarsi* does not really mean that one has put oneself to sleep (!), even though the verb will behave, grammatically, as a reflexive verb and will take the auxiliary "to be."

A final word on contents. Readers will likely be struck by the obsessive reference to sexual matters and their connection to stupidity (especially in the case of the male sexual organ) and cheating and swindling. According to Lotti, in Italian there are about twelve hundred vernacular words for "penis." I have chosen only a few, but there is no denying that sexual innuendo pervades Italian slang. As is true for slang in general, foreign users should be careful with slang words, unless their command of the language and of the social context is excellent. Having said that, I have only labeled "rude" those words which are offensive *even* within a slang context. I have not so labeled all words that would be considered rude if employed in normal conversation: for example, *cazzo* is a strong and aggressive term for penis, whereas *anguilla* is euphemistic, rather than rude.

I am greatly indebted to scholars and writers who have compiled dictionaries and studied the growth of Italian slang over the last fifty years. In particular, I wish to acknowledge the work of Emanuele Banfi, Ivano Bison, Manlio Cortelazzo, Michele Cortelazzo, Lorenzo Coveri, Marino Livolsi, Tullio De Mauro, Ernesto Ferrero, Augusta Forconi, Cesare Lanza, Gianfranco Lotti, Alberto Menarini, Edgar Radtke, and Alberto Sobrero.

I have tried to offer lively sentences and idiomatic translations. All the slang words used in Italian sentences have entries in the dictionary. For English slang, I refer readers to Italo Ferrero, Giorgio Anglesio, and Robert L. Chapman.

LIST OF ABBREVIATIONS

adj. = adjective
C. = center, central
crim. = criminal
Eng. = English
f. = feminine (noun)
indef. = indefinite
interj. = interjection
lit. = literally
Lat. = Latin
m. = masculine (noun)
N. = north, northern
narc. = narcotics
pers. = personal
pl. = plural
polit. = political
pp. = past participle
pron. = pronoun
pronom. = pronominal
recipr. = reciprocal
S. = south, southern
vi. = verb intransitive
vr. = verb reflexive
vt. = verb transitive

ABBIOCCÀRSI, *vi. pronom., C.* To conk out. *Si abbioccò di colpo, russando sonoramente, tra l'imbarazzo generale.* "To everyone's embarrassment, he conked out suddenly, snoring loudly."

ABBIÒCCO, *m., C.* Exhaustion, sudden tiredness. *M'ha preso un abbiocco che manco le cannonate mi svegliavano!* "I got so exhausted that nothing could have awakened me, not even cannon fire."

ABBOFFÀRSI/ABBUFFÀRSI, *vr., S.* To eat excessively, to gorge. *Lui continuava ad abbuffarsi, mentre pezzi di cibo masticati a metà gli cadevano dai lati della bocca.* "He kept on gorging, as bits of half-chewed food fell from the corners of his mouth."

ABBOTTÀRSI, *vr. recipr., C., youth.* (From "botte," blows.) To have a fight, to beat one another up. *Girate alla larga da quel bar, se no vi abbottate un'altra volta con quei teppisti.* "Keep your distance from that bar, otherwise you'll have another fight with those thugs."

ABBOZZÀRE, *vi., C.* To accept meekly a far-from-satisfactory situation. *Si sa, uno parte con tante ambizioni, ma nella vita bisogna abbozzare.* "You know, we begin with great ambitions, then life forces us to lower our sights."

ABBRANCICÀRSI, *vr. recipr., youth.* (From "branche," paws, claws.) **1.** To grab one another in a fight. *I due*

1

pugili si abbrancicavano come due leoni in lotta per una femmina. "The two boxers were grabbing each other like lions fighting over a female." **2.** To embrace passionately. *Va be' che siete innamorati cotti, ma dovete proprio passare tutto il tempo ad abbrancicarvi?* "All right, you're desperately in love, but do you have to be groping each other all the time?"

ABRAMÙCCIO, *m., C., racist.* (Ironic and affectionate diminutive of Abraham, used as a reference to the stinginess attributed to Jews.) Stingy. *A Filippo vuoi chiedere un prestito? Ma lo sai che ha la fama di Abramuccio!* "You want to ask Filippo for a loan? Don't you know he has a reputation for being a Scrooge?"

ACCANNÀRE, *C., youth.* (From > **canna,** cane.) **1.** *vt.* To leave, to dump. *Alla Pucci non gliene va mai bene nessuno; li accanna tutti, uno dopo l'altro.* "Pucci is never happy with anyone; she dumps them all, one after the other." **2.** *vi.* To stop; to let go. *Dai, accanna! Ci hai rotto con le tue lagne!* "Oh, stop it! You're driving us nuts with your whining."

ACCANNÀTO, *m., C., narc.* (From > **canna.**) One addicted to drugs, especially non-narcotic ones. *Mario l'accannato lo chiamano: è sempre lì che tira spinelli.* "They call him Mario the pothead; he spends his entire life smoking joints."

ACCHIAPPÀNZA, *f., C. youth.* (From > **acchiappare,** to catch.) Expedition with the aim of picking up persons of the opposite sex. *Non si vede nessuno in giro stasera; sono andati tutti in acchiappanza.* "No one in sight tonight; they've all gone cruising."

ACCHIAPPÀRE, *vt., C., youth.* (Lit., to catch.) **1.** To pick up, to court someone of the opposite sex. *Allora, hai acchiappato ieri sera in disco o no?* "Well, did you pick anyone up last night at the disco?" **2.** To charm, to attract. *Luisa t'acchiappa forte, eh?* "You really have the hots for Luisa, don't you?"

ACCHITTÀRSI, *vr., C.* To dress up. *Le tre sorelle Buzzi,* *sulla quarantina e nubili, si acchittavano anche per portare a spasso il cane.* "The three Buzzi sisters, about to turn forty and unmarried, got dolled up even to walk the dog."

ACCHITTÀTO, *adj., C.* (From > **acchittarsi.**) Dressed up, elegant. *Uau, come sei tutta acchittata! Sei a caccia di maschioni?* "Wow, aren't you decked out! Are you hunting for beefcake?"

ACCIDÈNTE, *m.* (Lit., accident.) **1.** One of remarkable size and/or stamina. *Io non so come faccia a stare con quell'accidente di Gianna.* "I don't get it. How can he go out with Gianna? She's something else." **2. Un accidente.** Nothing. *Cristo, non si vede un accidente con questa nebbia!* "Hell, I can't see a damn thing in this fog!"

ACCRÒCCO, *m., C.* (From "crocchio," group.) **1.** Pile, heap of things. *Niente discoteca per un mese se quell'accrocco che c'è in camera tua non sparisce prima di sera!* "No disco for a month if you don't clean up that pile of stuff in your room before nighttime!" **2.** Outcome of a badly done job. *E 'sto accrocco per te vorrebbe dire aver ridipinto il garage?* "Do you call this mess painting the garage?"

ACÉTO, *m., C.* (Lit., vinegar.) **Prendere d'aceto.** To get sour. *Non dovrei farmi prendere d'aceto se mio figlio è finito in carcere?* "I'm not supposed to get sour when my son has ended up in jail?"

ÀCIDO, *m., narc.* (Lit., acid.) LSD (lysergic acid diethylamide). **1. Essere in acido.** To be high on LSD. *Lei parlava, parlava, ma lui era in acido e non capiva una parola.* "She was talking and talking, but he was on acid and couldn't understand a word." To be losing one's mind. *Anna è in acido da quando ha saputo di essere rimasta incinta.* "Anna has been out of her mind since she learned she's pregnant." **2. Mandare in acido.** To bewitch, to charm. *Le tettone e il culo possente di Bianca l'hanno mandato in acido.* "Bianca's tits and formidable ass have bewitched him."

ÀCINI, *m. pl., youth.* (Lit., grapes.) **1.** Testicles. **Strizzare gli acini.** (Lit., for one's grapes to get squeezed.) To annoy. *Gino, mi hai proprio strizzato gli acini con le tue proposte di grandi affari.* "Gino, I've had enough of your grandiose business proposals." **2.** Female bosom. *Aveva due acini piccoli ma ben fatti, che si intravedevano attraverso il tessuto leggero della camicetta.* "She had two small, nicely shaped tits, barely visible through the fine fabric of her camisole."

ÀCQUA, *f.* (Lit., water.) **a)** *slang.* **Cambiare acqua alle olive/Cambiare acqua al merlo.** (Lit., to give fresh water to the olives/To give fresh water to the blackbird.) To urinate (referred to men). *Cos'ha Beppe? Ha già cambiato acqua alle olive almeno dieci volte stasera.* "What's wrong with Beppe? He's already watered the olives ten times tonight." **b)** *crim.* **1.** A warning that the police are coming. *Acqua! Acqua! Molla quella cassaforte!* "Watch out! The police! Drop that safe!" **2. Dare acqua alle fave.** (Lit., to water the fava beans.) To do someone in. *"'Hei, sai dov'è finito Giovanni?' "Disse che andava a dar acqua alle fave. Capisci, andò a far fuori Umberto."* "'Hey, where did Giovanni go?' 'He said he was going to water his fava beans. That means he went to kill Umberto, cappeesh?'"

ACÙTO, *adj., youth.* (Lit., sharp.) Sharp, used sarcastically to mean stupid. *Una acuta così non l'ho mai vista: voleva andare a comprare l'acido in farmacia.* "I've never met a girl so sharp; she was planning to go buy acid at the drugstore."

AFFAMÀTO, *adj., N.* (Lit., starved.) Desperately craving sex. *Vittorio è talmente affamato che si farebbe anche una morta.* "Vittorio is so desperate he'd sleep with a corpse."

AFFANBÀGNO, *interj., youth.* See **vaffanbagno.** (Variations: **Affanbyte! Affancuffia! Affanculo! Affanposter! Affantango! Affanturbo!**)

AFFÀRE, *m.* (Lit., thing, gadget.) **1.** Penis. *Il suo affare è* *troppo piccolo per me; peccato, lui è tanto caro!* "His thing is too small for me. Too bad, he's so sweet!" **2.** Love affair. *Il loro affare è durato vent'anni senza che sua moglie ne avesse sentore.* "Their affair lasted twenty years without his wife getting even a whiff of it."

AFGÀNO, *m., narc.* (Lit., Afghan.) Hashish coming from Afghanistan. *È andato in India passando da Kabul ed è tornato carico di afgano.* "He went to India via Kabul and came back loaded with Afghan hash."

AFRICÀNO, *m., N., youth, racist.* (Lit., African.) A person from southern Italy, which is so close to Africa as to be considered culturally part of it (and therefore backward and uncivilized.) *Senti, da Roma in giù non ci si può fidare; sono tutti africani.* "Look, you can't trust anyone south of Rome. They're all Africans."

AGGANCIÀRE, *vt., youth.* (Lit., to hook.) To find an excuse to pick up a person one has a romantic/erotic interest in. *Lei lo ha agganciato all'aeroporto con la scusa di non capire una parola di inglese: adesso se lo sposa.* "She hooked him at the airport pretending she didn't know one word of English; now she's marrying him."

AGGÉGGIO, *m., youth.* (Lit., gadget, instrument.) Penis. *Era chiaramente la prima volta: maneggiava il suo aggeggio senza riuscire a combinare niente.* "No doubt it was his first time. He was handling his tool without getting anywhere."

AGGRAVÀRE, *vt., C., youth.* (Lit., to make worse.) To bother; to become a burden; to harass. *La pianti di aggravare?! Il compito di mate non te lo posso passare.* "Will you stop giving me grief? I can't help you with your math test."

AGNÈLLO, *m., S., crim.* (Lit., lamb.) The victim of theft or extortion. *Tutti agnelli siamo! Se andiamo alla polizia quelli ci bruciano i negozi.* "We're all lambs ready for the slaughter! If we go to the police, those criminals will burn down our stores."

ÀLBA, *f., C., crim.* (Lit., dawn.) The day one leaves prison after serving time. *Tra un mese, anche per lui sorgerà l'alba.* "In a month he'll be out."

ALBÈRGO, *m., crim.* (Lit., hotel.) Police headquarters. *L'antidroga l'ha portata in albergo tre giorni fa. Da allora, più nulla.* "The vice department locked her up three days ago. Not a word since."

ÀLBERI PIZZÙTI, *m. pl., C.* (Lit., bearded trees, i.e., cypresses.) Cemetery (where one finds cypresses). **Andare agli alberi pizzuti.** To die. *Povero Tonino, così giovane, è già andato agli alberi pizzuti.* "Poor Tonino, he was taken so young (to his final resting place)."

ÀLBERO DI NATÀLE, *idiom, m.* (Lit., Christmas tree.) **1.** *slang.* Eighteen-wheeler with all its lights on. *Un enorme albero di Natale veniva giù a tutta birra dalla strada di montagna.* "A huge eighteen-wheeler was crashing down the mountain road at full speed." **2.** *C., narc.* Drug, especially amphetamine. *Non è che hai qualche albero di Natale? Sono in secca da una settimana.* "Do you have any bennies? I've been off for a week."

ALBICÒCCA, *f., S.* (Lit., apricot.) Vagina. *Vende la sua albicocca, ecco cosa fa per campare, quella puttana.* "She sells her peach, that's what that whore does for a living."

ALLEGGERÌRE, *vt., crim.* (Lit., to lighten.) To steal. *Li alleggerirono di tutto—portafogli, valigie, cineprese, automobile—e li abbandonarono sul ciglio della strada.* "They relieved them of everything—wallets, suitcases, cameras, car—and left them stranded on the side of the road."

ALLENTÀRE, *vt.* (Lit., to loosen.) **1.** To give. *Mi allenti un deca?* "Would you give me 10,000 lire?" **2.** To inflict (e.g., blows). *Gli ho allentato due pugni che se li ricorda per un pezzo.* "I landed two blows on his face that he'll remember for a while."

ALLÒCCO, *m., slang.* (Lit., owl.) **1.** Penis, but one which does not work very well. *Lui va fiero del suo uccellone, ma alcune signore bene informate dicono che è un allocco.* "He's very proud of his big dick, but some well-informed ladies say it's a poor thing." **2.** Stupid person, easy to take in. *Il vecchio Salvi ha lasciato l'azienda alla nuora, perché dice che suo figlio è un allocco.* "Old Mr. Salvi left the firm to his daughter-in-law, because he says his son is a fool."

ALLUCINÀNTE, *adj., youth.* (Lit., hallucinating.) **1.** Awesome, dazzling. *Va in giro con un ferro allucinante.* "He drives a marvelous motorcycle." **2.** Horrible. *Hanno avuto una lite allucinante. Mancava poco che si menassero.* "They had an awful argument. They came close to beating each other up." **3.** Crazy, incomprehensible. *Fa discorsi assolutamente allucinanti.* "She says absurd things all the time."

ALLUMÀRE, *vt., youth.* (From > **lumare.**) To stare at, to eye someone. *Puoi allumarla per ore, tanto quella è fuori dalla tua portata.* "You can stare at her for hours, but she's out of your reach."

ALLUNGÀRSI, *vt. pronom., youth.* (Lit., to lengthen.) To eat, to drink, to buy. *T'andrebbe di allungarti una birra e una pizza con me?* "Would you like to come with me for a beer and a pizza?"

ALLUPÀTO, *adj.* (From "a," and "lupo," wolf. To turn into a wolf.) **1.** Ravenous. *Sei proprio allupato! I tuoi ti tengono a pane e acqua?* "You're what's called hungry! Do your folks keep you on bread and water?" **2.** Hungry for sex, after a long period of abstinence. *Dopo sei mesi di prigione è uscito allupatissimo.* "After six months in jail he came out real horny."

ALLUZZÀRE, *vt., C., youth.* (Probably a mixture of "allupare," to turn into a wolf, and "aguzzare," to sharpen.) To excite, to arouse someone's interest. *Il figlio della sora Lella era un ragazzotto di borgata, ma alluzzava Gina un sacco.* "Mrs. Lella's son was a slum boy. Yet, Gina took a fancy to him."

7

ALTERNATÌVO, *adj., youth.* (Lit., alternative, meaning nontraditional.) Young person who behaves like an eccentric, to the point of being antisocial. *Sai com'è lei: un po' strana, quasi alternativa.* (Overheard in the streets of Turin.) "You know how she is: a little weird, almost eccentric."

ALZÀRE, *vt.* (Lit., to lift.) **a)** *crim.* **1.** To steal with dexterity. *Il merlo s'è girato per puntare una tettona e io gli ho alzato la Harley!* "As the fool turned around to stalk big tits, I stole his Harley!" **2.** To earn (in a shady way.) *Se fossi in te non alzerei troppa grana al loro tavolo di poker.* "If I were you I wouldn't make too much money at their poker table." **b)** *youth.* To provoke an erection. *Ugo è un caso clinico. Glielo alza persino la profia di filo!* "Ugo is a desperate case. Even his philosophy teacher gives him a hard-on!"

AMBIDÈSTRO, *adj., m.* (Lit., ambidextrous.) Bisexual. *Beh, sua moglie pare si sia rassegnata al fatto che lui è ambidestro.* "Well, his wife seems resigned to his being bisexual."

AMÌCO, *m., crim.* (Lit., friend.) Knife. *L'ha sgozzata il marito con un amico lungo una spanna.* "Her husband killed her with a blade this big."

AMÌCO DÉGLI AMÌCI, *idiom, m., S.* (Lit., a friend of one's friends.) A person close to, and trusted by Mafia circles. *Il Presidente della Cassa di Risparmio è un amico degli amici, non so se mi spiego.* "The President of the Savings & Loan is a friend of friends, if you get my drift."

AMMANICÀTO, *adj., S.* A person with the right contacts (to get ahead in life.) *Pupetta, che è figlia di un generale, è una bene ammanicata negli alti ranghi dell'esercito.* "Pupetta, whose father is a general, knows the ropes with the high ranks."

AMMÀZZA!, *interj., C.* (From "ammazzare," to kill.) It's a killer! Wow! (Variation: **Ammàppa!**) *Ammazza che macchina ti sei fatto!* "Wow, what a car you've got!"

AMMOLLÀRE, *vt., C.* (Lit., to soften.) **1.** *See* **allentare. 2.** To give, to yield. *Dai, ammollami qualche lira!* "Come on, fork over some money!"

AMMUCCHIÀTA, *f.* (Lit., pile.) **1.** Orgy. Having sex with multiple partners. *Altro che morigerati! Le loro feste finiscono sempre in un'ammucchiata.* "Them? Prudes? Every one of their parties ends up in orgies." **2.** Heterogeneous and confused group. *Quindici partitini nella coalizione governativa: una bella ammucchiata!* "Fifteen small parties in the coalition government: quite a collection!"

ANÀLFA, *m./f., youth.* (Contraction of "analfabeta," illiterate.) The Minister of Public Education. *Studenti! Tutti in piazza contro la riforma proposta dall'analfa!* "Students! Everyone march against the reform bill proposed by the Minister of Public Education!"

ÀNDA! *Interj., youth.* (Old imperative form of "andare," to go.) Move! *Sì, un tizio si è schiantato contro il TIR. Anda! Anda!* "Yes, someone smashed against the eighteen wheeler. Move on! Keep moving!"

ANDÀRE, *vi.* (Lit., to go.) **a)** *crim.* **Andare giù.** (Lit., to fall.) To confess. *La narcotici l'ha malmenato un po' e lui è andato giù subito.* "As soon as the vice squad shook him up a bit, he broke down." **b)** *N., slang.* **Andar giù di brutto/di peso.** To go at it without restraint. *Sei andato giù un po' troppo di peso con la vecchia.* "Didn't you come down a bit too hard on that old bag?" **c)** *N., youth.* **1. Andare sotto.** (Lit., to go under.) To be called on in class. *Porca vacca, devo andare sotto di mate anche oggi!* "Oh shit, the math prof will call on me again today!" **2. Andare in vacca:** *See* **vacca. 3. Andare come una lippa:** *See* **lippa.**

ANDÀTO, *adj.* (Lit., gone.) **1.** *slang.* Lost in outer space; off the wall; having lost one's marbles; out to lunch. *Da quando Roberto l'ha piantata, Mariella va conciata come una barbona: è tutta andata.* "Mariella has been going around like a bag lady ever since Roberto dropped her. She's really lost it." **2.** *narc.* Intoxicated with drugs; stoned. *Non si accorsero neppure dell'arrivo della* *polizia, tanto erano andati.* "They were so stoned they didn't even realize it when the police arrived."

ÀNDI, *m., N.* (From "andare," to go.) Way of proceeding. *Da un po' di tempo in qua, Berto ha presjo un andi che non mi piace.* "Lately, Berto has been acting in a way I don't like."

ÀNFA/ÀNFE, *f., narc.* Contraction of "anfetamina/e," amphetamine/s. *Patrizia vive ad anfe. Non vedi che è magra come un chiodo?* Patrizia lives on amphetamines. Don't you see she's thin as a rail?"

ÀNGELI CUSTÒDI, *m. pl., crim.* (Lit., guardian angels.) The pair of policemen who escort a defendant or a convict. *Il viaggio in treno divenne una tortura, ammanettato com'era ai suoi due angeli custodi.* "The train ride became torture for him, as he sat there shackled to his two guards."

ANGIOLÉTTO, *m.* (Lit., little angel.) Aborted fetus. By extension, abortion. *Suo marito non vuole saperne di prendere delle precauzioni: le ha fatto fare sei angioletti!* "Her husband doesn't want to hear of contraceptives. She's had to have six abortions!"

ANGUÌLLA, *f., N.* (Lit., eel.) Penis. **Pescare anguille.** (Lit., to fish for eels.) To have sexual intercourse with men. *Annina pesca anguille da quando aveva tredici anni: non ha niente da imparare da te.* "Annina has been playing the field since she was thirteen. There's nothing you can teach her."

ÀNNO LÙCE, *m., youth.* (Lit., light-year.) A lot; a long time. *È un anno luce che non ci vediamo!* "I haven't seen you in years!"

ANNUSÀRE, *vt., narc.* (Lit., to sniff.) To sniff cocaine. *Guarda che in quel giro lì annusano tutti.* "I'm warning you. They're all snorters over there."

ANTENÀTI, *m. pl., youth.* (Lit., ancestors.) Older people, parents in particular. *Non vorrai dire agli antenati che sei incinta? Non capirebbero mai.* "You're not going to tell your parents that you're pregnant? They would never understand."

ANTÉNNE, *f. pl.* (Lit., antennas.) Ears. *Lei pare andata, ma in realtà sta sempre con le antenne dritte.* "She may look like she's out to lunch, but she keeps her ears perked."

ANTIBIÒTICO, *m., narc.* (Lit., antibiotic.) Minimum quantity of narcotics, enough for one dose. *Ti arrestano, se ti trovano addosso venti antibiotici.* "They'll arrest you if they find twenty hits on you."

APPARECCHIÀRSI, *vr., C.* (Lit., to prepare oneself.) To do oneself up. *Ma quanto tempo ti ci vuole per apparecchiarti?* "How long does it take you to do yourself up?"

APPICCICÀRSI, *vr. recipr., S.* (Lit., to get glued.) To argue, to quarrel. *Non passava giorno che le due comari non si appiccicassero per qualche sciocchezza.* "Not a single day went by without the two women quarreling over some trifle."

APPOGGIÀRE, *vt., C.* (Lit., to lean, to lay.) **a)** *slang.* Taken from the expression "appoggiare con delicatezza," to lay something down gently; used to mean the opposite: to inflict something bad on someone. *Gli appoggiò una sventola che avrebbe ammazzato un bue.* "He landed a punch on him strong enough to kill an ox." **b)** *youth.* To agree with someone. *"Quel bastardo del prof di italo dovrebbe essere cacciato." "Te lo appoggio."* "'That bastard Italian teacher should be kicked out!' 'I'm with you.'"

APPOLPÀRSI, *vr. recipr., youth.* (Probably from "polpo," octopus). To hug one another tightly, to make love. *Si rotolavano appolpati sul divano.* "They were making out on the sofa, groping like mad."

ARÀRE, *vt., rude.* (Lit., to plow.) To possess sexually. *L'hai arata bene ieri sera?* "Did you screw her well last night?"

ARÀTRO, *m.* (Lit., plow.) Penis. *Stavolta, Dino è andato troppo in profondità con l'aratro e l'ha messa incinta.*

"This time, Dino went too deep with his sword: he got her pregnant."

ÀREA (BOSCHÌVA), *idiom., f., youth.* (Lit., woody zone.) Vagina. **Fare l'area a una ragazza.** (Lit., to work on a girl's woody zone.) To court/to seduce a girl; to possess sexually. *A furia di fare l'area alla Luisa, riuscirai anche a entrare nel bosco!* "If you keep going after Luisa's bush, you'll get into the woods, you'll see."

ARENÀTO, *adj., C.* (Lit., beached; run aground.) Penniless. *Non posso darti neanche un deca: sto proprio arenato.* "I can't even give you ten thousand lire: I'm really strapped."

ÀRIA, *f.* (Lit., air.) **a)** *slang.* **Aria!** Get lost! Vanish! *Aria, ragazzi, aria! Qui c'è anche gente che deve dormire!* "Get lost, boys! There are people here who need their sleep!" **b)** *crim.* **Aria di mare.** (Lit., sea air.) "Forced residence" imposed on a criminal, usually in a small seaside village or on an island. *Meglio andare a prendere un po' d'aria di mare che finire al fresco.* "Better to go get some fresh sea air than to end up in the cooler."

ARISTOCRÀTICA, *f., narc.* (Lit., the aristocratic one.) Cocaine, which is often used by wealthy people because of its high price. *Alle loro feste l'aristocratica era un'ospite d'onore.* "The lady snow was a guest of honor at their parties."

ARMÀDIO, *m.* (Lit., cupboard, closet.) **1.** Tall and imposing man. *Certo che, con un armadio così al tuo fianco, non hai più paura di nessuno.* "I'm sure that with that big fellow at your side you don't have to fear anyone." **2.** Vagina. *Valeria fa entrare tutti nel suo armadio.* "Valeria lets everyone into her closet." **3.** Overcoat. *Ma che fai con quell'armadio addosso? C'è un sole che spacca le pietre!* "Why are you wearing that coat? We're melting under this sun."

ARNÉSE, *m.* (Lit., gadget, tool.) Penis. **Scuotere l'arnese.** (Lit., to shake one's tool.) To possess/To try to possess sexually. *Scuoteva l'arnese a più non posso, ma non* *riusciva a portare a termine il lavoro.* "He was working hard with his tool, but he couldn't finish the job."

ARPIONÀRE, *vt., N., youth.* (Lit., to harpoon.) To do one's best to get another person, especially a girl on the part of a boy. *Ci hanno provato tutti ad arpionare Stefania, ma quella è una che non ci sta.* "They've all tried to catch Stefania, but she's not an easy lay."

ARRANGIÀRSI (DA SÓLO), *vi. pronom.* (Lit., to manage by oneself.) To masturbate. *È una vita che Dino si arrangia da solo; secondo me, non sa più come si fa con una donna.* "Dino has been managing by himself for so long that he no longer knows how to do it with a woman."

ARRAPAMÉNTO, *m., youth.* (From > **arrapare.**) Sexual excitement, being horny. *Lui era in preda a un tale arrapamento che sarebbe salito sui tetti a miagolare coi gatti.* "He was so horny he could have climbed on the roof to howl with the cats."

ARRAPÀNTE, *adj., youth.* (From > **arrapare.**) Very sexy, exciting. *Più arrapante della Paola non ne conosco nessuna.* "I don't know anyone as sexy as Paola."

ARRAPÀRE, *vt., youth.* (From the Italian "rapa," turnip, or the French argot "raper," to grind.) To excite, to turn on. *Non dirmi che quel pirla ti arrapa!* "Are you telling me that jerk turns you on?"

ARRAPÀSCION/ARRAPÀTION, *m., youth.* Pseudo-Anglicism for > **arrapamento.**

ARRAPÀTO, *adj., youth.* (From > **arrapare.**) Horny. *Dài, andiamo in missione, che sono arrapato. Arrapatissimo!* "Let's go cruising. I'm so horny!"

ARRIVÀRE, *vi.* (Lit., to arrive.) To be at the end of one's rope; to be close to dying. *Mi sa che questa macchina è arrivata!* "I'm afraid this car has had it."

ARROTÀRE, *vt.* (Lit., to sharpen.) To be hit by a car (as if it were a blade.) *Ne avrà per sei mesi. L'hanno arrotata mentre andava a scuola.* "She was run over while walking to school; six months in the hospital."

ARSENÀLE, *m., narc.* (English "arsenal.") The entire supply of a drug addict or pusher. *Mentre i poliziotti salivano le scale, lo spacciatore cercò di far fuori tutto l'arsenale.* "While the cops were climbing the stairs, the drug peddler tried to get rid of his entire arsenal."

ARTÈRIA, *f., N., youth.* (From "arteriosclerotica," arteriosclerotic.) Mother of the preppie/yuppie boy or girl identified as a > **paninaro.** *Il figlio porta Timba e Montcler, ma dovresti vedere l'arteria! Solo ed esclusivamente roba firmata.* "Her son wears Timberland and Montcler, and you should see his mom! Only designer labels."

ARTÈRIO, *youth.* (Contraction of "arteriosclerotico," arteriosclerotic.) **1.** *m.* Older man, father. *Luca gira sempre con delle fighe fantastiche perché l'arterio ha un'agenzia di modelle.* "Luca has knockout dates, because his old man runs a model agency." **2.** *f.* Stupidity, mental listlessness. *Alla festa della Titti c'era un'arterio invivibile.* "It was zombie land at Titti's party."

ARTÈRIOS, *m. pl., youth.* (Anglicized plural of > **arterio.**) **1.** Parents of the > **paninaro.** *Ha degli arterios da sballo: pensa che l'hanno portata a sciare in Nuova Zelanda!* "Her folks are awesome. They took her skiing in New Zealand!"

ARTÌCOLO, *m., N.* (Lit., article, item.) **1.** Penis. *Claudio ha un articolo molto richiesto dalle signore.* "Claudio's thing is in great demand among the ladies." **2.** Oddball. *Uno che si chiama Filiberto non può che essere un articolo!* "Someone whose name is Filiberto can only be an oddball."

ARTÌGLI, *m. pl.* (Lit., claws.) Hands of a violent and ruthless person. *Quando i suoi artigli arraffavano qualcosa, non la mollavano più.* "Whenever his paws grabbed onto something, he wouldn't let go."

ASCIÙTTO, *adj., youth.* (Lit., dry.) **All'asciutto.** Without a sexual partner. *Nel giro di una settimana, tutti quelli del giro si erano accoppiati: solo lui era rimasto all'a-*

sciutto. "Everyone in the group paired off within a week: only he was left high and dry."

ÀSOLA, *f.* (Lit., buttonhole.) **a)** *crim.* Knife wound. **Fare un'asola.** To knife someone. *A Vito gli hanno fatto un'asola lunga una spanna, che quasi moriva dissanguato.* "Someone cut a foot-long gash in Vito's body; he nearly bled to death." **b)** *slang.* **1.** Vagina. *Ha un'asola troppo piccola per il mio arnese.* "Her slit is way too small for my tool." **2.** *rude.* Girl, woman. **Farsi un'asola.** (Lit., to make use of a buttonhole.) To possess sexually. *Si fa un'asola diversa ogni sera: forse non trova mai quella giusta.* "He changes tunnels every night. Perhaps he can't find the right one."

ASPÀRAGI, *m. pl., crim.* (Lit., asparagus.) Prison wards; policemen. *È andato a ficcarsi in un campo di asparagi, che l'hanno beccato senza muovere un dito.* "He ended up in the middle of a collar of cops, who thus caught him without raising a finger."

ASPÀRAGO, *m.* (Lit., asparagus.) *slang.* Penis. **Cogliere asparagi.** (Lit., to pluck asparagus.) **1.** (Referred to women.) To sleep with just about anyone. *Luisa coglie qualunque asparago, basta che stia dritto.* "Luisa makes do with any stick, so long as it stays up." **2.** To be a passive male homosexual. *È un asparago, mi spiego? Gli piacciono solo gli asparagi come lui.* "He's a flower, O.K.? He only likes other flowers."

ASPIRÌNA, *f., youth.* (Lit., aspirin.) Contraceptive pill. *Devi allungarti un'aspirina tutte le sere, se no, altro che mal di testa!* "You must take your aspirin every night, otherwise you'll get much worse than a headache!"

ASSATANÀTO, *adj.* (Lit., possessed by the devil.) Extremely horny, uncontrollably excited. *Sta' lontana da Salvatore, che ultimamente è assatanato.* "Keep away from Salvatore. He's been going ape lately."

ASSÓLO, *m., youth.* (Lit., solo performance.) Masturbation. *Meglio farsi dei grandi assoli che cantare in un duetto stonato, no?* "Better to sing solo than an out-of-tune duet, right?"

ASSÙRDO, *adj., youth.* (Lit., absurd.) Incredible, unthinkable. *Spara cazzate su Satana, i polli e le messe nere: cose assurde.* "He's spewing bullshit about Satan, chickens and black masses. Loony stuff."

ATRÒCE, *adj., youth.* (Lit., atrocious.) Very intense, to the point of being unbearable. *Ho una voglia atroce di farmi un po' di neve.* "I'm dying for some snow."

ATTACCÀRE. (Lit., to hang up.) **a)** *vt., slang.* To stick, to be convincing. *Bona pesta sulla stessa storia, ma per me non attacca.* "Bona keeps telling the same story, but it's not sticking." **b)** *youth.* **1.** *vt.* To be enticing, to be pleasing. *Adesso ti attacca anche la polka?* "Now you're taken with polka?" **2.** *vi.* To try an approach with a woman. *Cosa me ne viene se ti dico come attaccare con Betti?* "What's in it for me if I tell you how to win over Betti?"

ATTACCÀRSI (AL TRAM), *vr.* (Lit., to hold on to the street-car.) To be in a desperate, almost suicidal, situation. *E mo' che faccio, m'attacco (al tram)?* "Great. Now I can shoot myself."

ATTIZZÀRE, *vt., youth.* (Lit., to kindle.) To excite, to attract strongly. *T'attizza la Pinuccia? Ma se è un rospo!* "Pinuccia turns you on? She's a toad!"

ATTOPPÀTO, *adj., C.* (From "toppa," drunkenness.) Drunk. *Era così attoppata che non sapeva più quello che diceva.* "She was so loaded she couldn't talk straight any longer."

ATTREZZATÙRA, *f., youth.* (Lit., equipment.) Look; attire. *Ma che ti salta in mente? Hai un'attrezzattura da puttana.* "What do you think you're doing? You're decked out like a whore."

AUTÒNOMO, *m., polit.* (Lit., autonomous.) Member of radical leftist groups, especially active in the 1970s, with anarchic tendencies and willing to use violent tactics. Person who refuses integration into the social mainstream. *Marco è troppo autonomo per i miei gusti; non parla praticamente più con nessuno.* "Marco is way too eccentric for my taste. He barely talks to anyone anymore."

AUTOSTRÀDA, *f., youth.* (Lit., highway.) A very slender girl, without pronounced sexual attributes (lit., without curves, like a highway.) *Lilla è un'autostrada; meglio una bella strada di montagna, come la Barbara.* "Lilla is shapeless; better someone with some curves, like Barbara."

AVEMARÌA, *f., youth.* (Lit., Hail Mary.) Poem. *Tre avemaria devo imparare per domani: quella di italo batte in testa!* "Three poems I have to memorize by tomorrow. The Italian teacher is nuts!"

ÀVI, *m. pl., youth.* (Lit., ancestors.) Parents. *Secondo i suoi avi, dovrebbe rientrare alle dieci il sabato sera!* "According to his parents he should be back at ten on Saturday night!

ÀZZ! ÀZZO! *interj., S. See* **cazzo.**

B

BÀBBIO/BABBIÓNE, *m., C., youth.* Sucker. *Se credono che sia un babbione, si sbagliano di grosso!* "If they think I'm a sucker, they're making a big mistake."

BABBUÌNO, *m.* (Lit., baboon.) **a)** *slang.* Silly, ridiculous person. *Cesare si comporta da babbuino e poi si lamenta che non lo prendono sul serio.* "Cesare, who behaves like a fool, complains that no one takes him seriously." **b)** *youth.* Parent; father. *Dai, fregagli le chiavi della macchina, tanto il vecchio babbuino non capisce una mazza.* "Come on, snatch his car keys. The old fool doesn't understand shit."

BABILÒNIA, *f.* (Lit., Babylon.) Bedlam, mess, racket. *Piantala con 'sta babilonia, non so neanche più di che cosa stavamo parlando.* "Cut out that racket, I can't even remember what we were talking about."

BACCAGLIÀRE. (Probably from Latin "bacchanalia," Bacchanals, or from Roman Hebrew "bahá," to complain.) **a)** *vi., slang.* To argue, to protest, to have a vehement discussion. *In quel bar, non passa sera che non si baccagli.* "In that bar, not one evening goes by without some bickering." **b)** *vt., youth.* To do one's best to seduce someone; to try to pick up someone. *Lorenzo ne baccaglia tre alla volta, e non ne becca mai una.* "Lorenzo goes after three women at a time, and never gets a single one."

BACCALÀ, *m.* (Lit., dried fish.) **1.** Penis. *Ha un baccalà*

18

più morto di uno stoccafisso. "His prick is more dead than dried fish." **2.** Imbecile, idiot; a person taken by surprise. *Che cosa fai lì, fermo come un baccalà? La polizia sta per caricare!* "What are you doing standing there like an idiot? The police are about to charge!"

BACHERÒZZO/BAGARÒZZO, *m.* (Lit., maggot.) **a)** *slang.* Small penis. *T'immaginavi che avesse un bacherozzo, grande e grosso com'è?!* "Would you believe it? Such a big fellow, and his thing is like a string bean!" **b)** *crim.* **1.** Priest. *È sfuggito alla cattura travestendosi da bacherozzo.* "He managed to escape capture by dressing like a priest." **2.** Policeman. *Bacherozzo in vista! Filare!* "The heat's approaching! Scram!"

BACIAPÌLE, *m., youth, rude.* (Lit., bigot.) A person excessive in his devotion; a flatterer. *Puoi scommetterci che la profìa gli cambia il voto. È un tale baciapile!* "You can bet that the prof will change his grade. He's such a kiss-ass."

BACÌLLO, *m., youth.* (Lit., bacterium.) Small, perfunctory kiss. *Mi sono fatto una faticata pazzesca e tutto quello che ho cuccato è stato un bacillo.* "I went out of my way to woo her and all I got was a peck on the cheek."

BACÙCCO, *m./***BACÙCCA,** *f., N., rude.* (From the name of the biblical prophet Habakuk.) An old and weak-minded person, reinforced in the expression **vecchio bacucco,** old imbecile. *Sarà un gioco da ragazzi soffiare il portafoglio a quel vecchio bacucco.* "It will be child's play to snatch that old geezer's wallet."

BÀFFO, *m.* (Lit., moustache.) **a)** *slang.* **Farsene un baffo.** Not to care at all about something. *Vai, vai a spifferare tutta la storia al geronto. A me me ne fa un baffo.* "All right, go tell our old man the whole story. I don't give a damn." **b)** *youth.* **1.** Guy. *Dino è un baffo in gamba, fidati di me.* "Dino is quite a guy, trust me." **2.** Traffic policeman. *Infilati il casco, che quel baffo lì non perdona.* "Put on your helmet; that cop is merciless."

BAG, *Eng., m.* Single dose of heroin. *La pula gli ha trovato*

dieci bag addosso: si farà un bel po' di mesi di collegio.
"The cops found ten bags on him. He'll do time in prison,
that's for sure."

BAGGIÀNA, *f., N.* (Lit., big fava bean.) Vagina. *Una baggiana così non la vedeva da molto tempo.* "He hadn't
seen such a pussy in a long time."

BAGGIANÀTA, *f., N.* (From > **baggiano.**) Nonsense, stupid statement. *Vuoi andare a scalare l'Everest alla tua
età? Ma non dire baggianate!* "You want to go climb
Mount Everest at your age? Don't talk bullshit!"

BAGGIÀNO, *m., N.* **1.** Penis. *Il suo baggiano andava proprio bene per la sua baggiana.* "His bird fit her bird just
right." **2.** Blockhead; fool. *Se dice che può farti
guadagnare cento milioni con quell'affare è proprio un
baggiano.* "If he tells you he can get you a hundred million lire with that deal, he's a fool."

BÀGNA, *f., N.* (Lit., sauce.) Trouble, mess. **Essere nella
bagna.** (Lit., to be in the sauce.) *Le cambiali scadono
domani e non ho una lira: sono proprio nella bagna.* "My
IOUs are due tomorrow and I have zero money. I'm in
real trouble."

BAGNARÒLA, *f., C.* Old car or boat, in bad condition. *La
bagnarola l'ha mollato all'ora di punta; a momenti suc-
cedeva un macello.* "His old wreck let him down at rush
hour; they almost made mincemeat of him."

BAGNÀRSI, *vr.* (Lit., to get wet.) To be sexually excited,
almost to the point of orgasm (for both men and women.)
Le basta che uno le guardi le tette che lei si bagna. "If
someone as much as looks at her tits, she gets all wet."

BÀGNO, *m., rude.* (Lit., bath.) **a)** *jargon.* **Mandare qualcuno ad andare a fare un bagno.** (Lit., to send someone
to take a bath.) To send someone packing. **1.** *Ma va 'a fa'
'n bagno, m'hai rotto.* "I'm fed up with you, get lost." **2.**
Fare un bagno. (Lit., to take a bath.) To be soundly
defeated. *Si è messo a fare a pugni con un ex campione
di pesi massimi: ha fatto un bagno!* "He got into a fist
fight with a former heavyweight champ. He got

creamed!" b) *youth.* **Metterlo a bagno.** (Lit., to get one's penis wet.) To possess sexually. *Se vuoi metterlo a bagno devi andare dietro a Maurizio; quello sì che cucca.* "If you want to get laid, go with Maurizio: he's a big-time operator."

BÀIA DÉI PIRÀTI, *idiom, f., youth.* (Lit., pirates' bay.) Teachers' room. *Sono stata convocata nella baia dei pirati: avranno scoperto che fumiamo nei cessi?* "I was summoned to the teachers' office. Did they find out we smoke in the restroom?"

BAIÒCCHI, *m. pl.* (Lit., old copper coins of the Papal States.) Money. *Ha più baiocchi di zio Paperone.* "He's got more bucks than Uncle Scrooge."

BALCÓNE, *m.* (Lit., balcony.) Bosom. *Ti piacerebbe andare a guardare dal suo balcone, eh?* "You'd like to have a look at her boobs, right?"

BALDÒRIA, *f., youth.* (Lit., merrymaking; spree.) A high-school class where discipline is lax and students can have fun. *Nella baldoria di storia dell'arte ci facciamo la cioccolata con panna.* "During our merrymaking art history class we treat ourselves to hot chocolate with cream."

BALÉNA/BALENÒTTERA, *f.* (Lit., whale.) **a)** *jargon, rude.* Stout girl or woman. *Attenti a non affogare: entra in acqua la balena!* "Watch out for the big waves: the whale is coming in!" **b)** *youth. In culo alla balena!* (Lit., up the whale's ass!) "Break a leg!"

BALÈNGO, *m., rude.* (From "balenga," tottering thing.) Crazy, imbecile, without common sense. *Lascialo passare, è quel balengo di Bobo con la sua Alfa.* "Let him go; it's that screwball Bobo with his Alfa."

BÀLLA, *f., N.* (Lit., bale.) **1.** See **palla. 2. Prendere la balla.** To get drunk. *Quando Lisetta prende la balla dice delle stronzate!* "When Lisetta gets drunk she talks such crap!"

BALLÀRE, *vi.* (Lit., to dance.) **Far ballare qualcuno.**

(Lit., to make someone dance.) **a)** *jargon.* To induce a person to act, one way or another. *Hanno minacciato di rapire mia figlia, così m'hanno fatto ballare.* "By threatening to kidnap my daughter, they had me." **b)** *crim.* To hide part of the loot from one's accomplices. *Dopo che gli ha fatto da basista, quei bastardi l'hanno fatto ballare.* "After he organized the robbery for them, those bastards cheated him out of his share."

BÀLLE, *m. pl., rude.* Northern variant of > **palle.**

BALLÌSTA, *m., rude.* (From "balle," lies.) Liar, braggart. *Adesso si è inventato che suo nonno era un conte. Mai visto un ballista così.* "His latest story is that his grandfather was a count. Never seen such a bullshitter."

BALÓRDE, *f. pl.* (From > **balordo.**) Counterfeit money. *Giravano tante di quelle balorde che nessuno accettava più contanti.* "There was so much phony money around no one took cash any longer."

BALÒRDO, *m./***BALÒRDA,** *f.* **a)** *slang.* Crazy, slow-witted, perceived as dangerous. *Maria la balorda, la chiamano, ma non ha mai fatto male a nessuno.* "Nutty Mary, they call her, even though she never harmed anyone." **b)** *crim.* Gangster, crook. *Hanno ammazzato due caramba in quel bar: ci vanno solo i balordi.* "Two cops got killed in that bar. Only crooks go there."

BALÙBA, *m., N., racist.* (From the African tribe of the Baluba, following a 1950s racist pattern of using names of African populations in derogatory fashion.) Uncouth and uncivilized person; southern Italian. *Sono dei baluba, guarda come hanno ridotto il giardinetto del condominio.* "They're rednecks. Look what they did to the condo garden."

BÀMBA. (From either "bambaccione," or "rimbambito," in one's dotage.) **a)** *f., narc.* Cocaine. *Sniffa bamba come se fosse tabacco.* "He snorts the big C as if it were tobacco." **b)** *m., N.* Stupid or mindless person; sucker. *Non è mica peggiorato con l'età: è sempre stato un bamba.* "He hasn't really gotten worse with age. He was always a sucker."

BÀMBOLA, *f., crim.* (Lit., doll.) Counterfeit key. *Non è più in attività, ma tiene la sua collezione di bambole per ricordo.* "He's no longer working. He keeps his collection of keys for sentimental reasons."

BAMBULÉ! *Interj., narc.* Cheers! Well-wishing formula which precedes the lighting up of a joint (from the invocation of Shiva, the god/goddess of death and resurrection). *Bambulé! A mille spinellate come questa!* "Cheers! To a thousand of these joints!"

BANÀNA, *f.* (Lit., banana.) **a)** *slang.* Penis. *Se glielo chiedi con grazia, magari ti mangia anche la banana.* "If you ask her politely, maybe she'll eat your banana." **b)** *youth.* **Mandare qualcuno ad attaccarsi alla/sbucciare la banana.** (Lit., to send someone hanging from/peeling one's banana.) Invitation to stop being a pain in the neck. *Stai ancora qui a chiedere lira? Attaccati a 'sta banana!* "Still here begging for money? Suck my dick!" **c)** *narc.* **Fumare le banane/Essere in banana dura.** (Lit., to smoke bananas/to be in the condition generated by a banana.) To be stoned. *È in banana dura da tre giorni; per me non ne esce più.* "He's been completely stoned for three days. I'm afraid he won't come out of it."

BANANÀTA, *f., youth.* (From > **banana.**) **1.** Nonsense, idiotic statement. *Perché gli hai dato ancora da bere? Mo' attacca con le sue bananate.* "Why did you give him more to drink? Now he'll start with his baloney." **2.** Drunkenness; stoned condition provoked by narcotics. *Non aveva mai spinellato prima; s'è presa 'na bananata!* "That was her first joint. She really zonked out!" **3.** Nothing. *Primo film in inglese in vita mia: non ho azzeccato una banana.* "First movie in English in my whole life. I didn't get zip."

BANÀNO, *m., youth.* (Lit., banana tree.) **1.** Penis. *Più che un banano, ha un bananone.* "More than a banana, he has a huge banana tree." **2.** Sucker; blockhead. *S'è fatto inchiappettare un'altra volta. Che banano!* "He got screwed again. What a sucker!"

BANCÀTA, *f., N., youth.* **Dare/Prendere una bancata.** To deal/be dealt a hail of blows. *S'è beccato una bancata che lo ha piallato.* "He got such a beating he was flattened."

BANDIÈRA, *f.* (Lit., flag.) **a)** *slang.* Penis. *Avere la bandiera a mezz'asta.* (Lit., to have the flag at half-mast.) To have a weak erection. *Che c'è, sei in lutto, che hai la bandiera a mezz'asta?* "What's the matter? Are you in mourning with your flag at half-mast?" **b)** *crim.* (Probably from "bandire," to outlaw.) **Essere/Stare in bandiera.** To be on the run (from the law). *Ha falsificato la firma di sua moglie su dei grossi assegni; adesso sta in bandiera.* "He faked his wife's signature on some big checks; now he's on the run."

BANDIÈRA CORSÀRA, *idiom., f.* (Lit., corsair flag.) **Battere bandiera corsara.** (Lit., to fly a corsair flag.) **1.** To run away; to flee. *Massimo è un bel vigliacco: come mi ha visto ha battuto bandiera corsara.* "Massimo is what I'd call a coward. As soon as he saw me, he beat it." **2.** To behave as/To be a homosexual. *Non si capiva più se batteva bandiera corsara per finta o per davvero.* "No one knew anymore whether he had gone that way or was just faking it."

BANDIÈRA RÓSSA, *idiom, f., youth.* (Lit., red flag.) Menstrual period. *Niente su e giù stasera, la fanciulla è in bandiera rossa.* "No sex with my girl tonight. The red flag is up."

BANFÀRE, *vi.* To talk, but used mostly in the negative, to mean "to stop talking." *Da quando il capo gli ha dato del millantatore, non ha più banfato.* "He hasn't said a word since the boss called him a liar."

BARÀBBA, *m.* (From the thief Barabbas, spared by Pilate instead of Jesus.) **1.** Vagrant, hobo, rogue. *Girò alla larga dalla piazza, ormai occupata dai Barabba.* "She kept clear of the square, which had been taken over by the bums." **2.** Penis (because it behaves like a rogue.) *Suo marito ha un barabba instancabile.* "Her husband's prick is indefatigable."

BARÀCCA, *f.* (Lit., shed.) **a)** *slang.* Machine or tool in bad condition. *Non finirò mai di tagliare il prato con questa baracca di tagliaerba.* "I'll never finish mowing the lawn with this wreck of a lawnmower." **b)** *crim.* Jail; prison. *Sono finiti tutti in baracca per le scommesse truccate.* "They all ended up in the slammer for rigging the bets."

BARACCHÌNO, *m., N.* (From Piedmontese "barachin," bucket.) **1.** Mess tin. *Tutte le sere la sua vecchia gli preparava il baracchino.* "Every night, his old lady prepared his chow." **2.** Factory worker who eats his lunch out of a can. *Ha fatto il baracchino tutta la vita; Dio solo sa come ha fatto a fare tanta grana.* "He's eaten out of a can all his life. God only knows how he managed to make so much money."

BARBÓNE, *m., youth.* (Lit., hobo.) A person tied to the anachronistic political ideals of his/her youth, now living at the margins of society. *È una barbona impenitente. Pensa che è ancora iscritta al partito marxista-leninista.* "She's a dyed-in-the-wool 60s radical. She's still a member of the Marxist-Leninist party."

BÀRCA, *f.* (Lit., boat.) **a)** *slang.* **1.** Vagina. **Montare in barca.** (Lit., to get aboard.) To have sexual intercourse. *Se siamo fortunati, stasera si monta in barca.* "If we're lucky we'll score tonight." **2.** Car, especially if big. *Con una barca così, ovvio che non riesci a trovare parcheggio.* "With a boat like that, no wonder you can't find any parking." **3. Andare in barca.** (Lit., to go sailing.) To get confused. *Mi fate andare in barca con tutte le vostre ciance.* "You're making me lose my bearings with all your talk." **b)** *crim.* **Comandare la barca.** (Lit., to command a boat.) To lead a criminal organization. *Vedi quell'armadio seduto al tavolo da poker? È lui che comanda la barca.* "See that big fellow at the poker table? He runs the show."

BÀRCHE, *f. pl., youth.* (Lit., boats.) Worn-out shoes. *Girava tutto agghindato, ma ai piedi aveva un paio di vecchie barche.* "He was all spruced up, except for his shoes, which were ugly and worn-out."

BARILÒTTO, *m.* (Lit., keg.) Short and stout person (especially a man.) *Il barilotto ha saltato un metro e venti!* "He's short and fat, and yet he jumped four feet!"

BÀSE, *f., youth.* (Lit., basis.) **Essere di base.** (Lit., to be basic.) Obvious, taken for granted. *"Viene anche la tua squinzia al concerto rock?" "È di base!"* "'Is your chick coming to the rock concert?' 'Obviously!'"

BASÌLICO, *m., narc.* (Lit., basil.) Marijuana. *Ha messo su una piantagione di basilico; fa tanta di quella lira!* "He's started a weed plantation; he's making a bundle!"

BASÌSTA, *m., crim.* (From "base," basis.) Organizer of robberies and thefts (who often doesn't participate in their execution). *Il basista gli organizzò un percorso di fuga degno di un romanzo di fantascienza.* "The brains came up with an escape route that could have come right out of a science-fiction novel."

BÀSSO, *m., youth.* (Lit., short.) Tall and lanky person. *Ehi, basso, che aria tira nella stratosfera?* "Hey, shorty, what's the weather like up there?"

BASTÀRDO, *m., youth.* (Lit., bastard.) Someone who only looks after his/her own interest, even when it would cost him/her nothing to do something for someone else. *Che bastarda che sei! Potevi anche avvertire che la profia era in arrivo.* "You're a scumbag! You could have warned us that the teacher was coming."

BASTÓNE, *m.* (Lit., stick.) **a)** *slang.* Penis. *Mena il bastone piuttosto bene, dicono le signore.* "He uses his stick pretty well, the ladies say." **b)** *crim.* Chief of a Mafia clan. *Salvatore ha ammazzato tutti gli altri bastoni, diventando il bastone solo e unico.* "By killing all the other big shots, Salvatore has risen to the top."

BASTÓNI, *m. pl.* (Lit., sticks.) Legs. *Luigi è tutto bastoni; quando si siede sparisce.* "Luigi is all legs; when he sits down he disappears."

BATÀCCHIO, *m.* (Lit., clapper.) Penis. *Il batacchio gli pendeva moscio tra le gambe.* "His stick hung flat between his legs."

BÀTTERE. (Lit., to strike, to hit.) **a)** *vt./vi., slang.* **1. Battere (il marciapiede).** (Lit., to beat the pavement.) To engage in prostitution on the street. *Batte da quando aveva tredici anni.* "She's been a streetwalker since she was thirteen." **2.** Referred to male homosexuals, to engage in sex for money. *Matteo batte solo con i vecchioni pieni di soldi.* "Matteo only turns tricks for old geezers full of money." **b)** *vt., youth.* **1. Battere i pezzi.** *See* **pezzo. 2. Battere (il chiodo).** (Lit., to hit the nail.) To possess sexually. *Finalmente anche Piero ha trovato una con cui battere il chiodo.* "Finally even Piero found a girl to get it on with."

BÀTTERSELA, *vi., pronom.* (From old military custom of signaling retreat by beating the drums.) To flee; to run away. *Se la sono battuta lasciando il palo a ricevere la madama.* "They beat it, leaving the lookout to greet the cops."

BATTITÀCCHI, *m.* (From "battere i tacchi," to click one's heels, i.e., to come to attention.) Bodyguard. *Il pezzo da novanta era una cosetta da niente, ma coi due battitacchi non ci scherzava nessuno.* "The big shot was a nonentity, but no one dared take on the two gorillas."

BATTÓNA, *f., rude.* (From > **battere**.) **a)** *slang.* Streetwalker. *Ma che prostituta d'alto bordo! Ha fatto la battona tutta la vita.* "High-class lady my ass! She's been a streetwalker all her life." **b)** *youth.* **1.** A girl who is too available for sex. *Un po' battona la Pupetta, eh?* "Pupetta is a bit of a whore, no?" **2.** Batton-girl. (Pseudo-Anglicism formed by mixing "batton(a)" and "girl.") Prostitute. *Ha un esercito di batton-girl che lo mantengono a caviale e champagne.* "He has an army of call girls who keep him in caviar and champagne."

BATTONÀGGIO, *m.* (From > **battere**.) Prostitution. *Miriam dice che sulle pagine gialle dovrebbe anche esserci la voce "battonàggio."* "Miriam says that the yellow pages should have an entry for "'streetwalking.'"

BATTÓNE, *m., rude.* (From > **battere**.) Male homosexual

27

who practices prostitution on the street. *Sei sicuro di voler passare di lì? È la strada dei battoni.* "Are you sure you want to go that way? That's the gay hustlers' street."

BATTÙTA, *f.* (Lit., line; but also from "battuta di caccia," hunting party.) **a)** *crim.* Tip. *Conosco il tipo: ti garantisco che mi ha dato una buona battuta.* "I know the guy. I swear he gave me a good tip." **b)** *youth.* Male group out to find female company. *In battuta bisogna andarci tirati a lucido, se no le squinzie non ti cagano neppure.* "You'd better dress up when you go cruising, otherwise the chicks won't even know you're there."

BAÙSCIA, *m., N.* (Lombard for "saliva.") Braggart, swaggerer. *L'è un gran bauscia; se credi a lui è il padrone di mezza città.* "He's a big braggart; if you believe him, he owns half the city."

BÀVA, *f.* (Lit., slobber.) **1.** Hunger. *Dopo tre settimane di escursioni in Alaska, non ci vedevo più dalla bava.* "After hiking for three weeks in Alaska, I was dying of hunger." **2. Perdere la bava.** (Lit., to be drooling.) To be penniless. *Speriamo che il nonno tiri le cuoia presto, perché abbiamo proprio perso la bava.* "Let's hope grandpa kicks the bucket soon, because we're really down and out."

BAVÓSO, *youth.* (Lit., slobbering.) **1.** *m.* Older man, or considered so by young people. *Vuoi invitare quell'amico dei tuoi alla festa? Ma se è un bavoso!* "You want to invite that friend of your folks to the party? He's a geriatric case!" **2.** *adj.* Show of sexual urge, unbecoming for a man that age. *Suo zio è bavoso; io non gli andrei tanto vicina se fossi in te.* "Her uncle is a dirty old man. I wouldn't go near him if I were you."

BECCAMÒRTO, *m., C., youth.* (Lit., undertaker.) Priest. *Da quando si è pentita dei suoi trascorsi giovanili bazzica solo beccamorti.* "Ever since she repented of her wild youth, she only hangs out with gentlemen of the collar."

BECCÀRE, *vt.* (Lit., to peck.) **a)** *slang.* **1.** To be beaten (literal or figurative). *La nostra squadra di basket le becca sempre.* "Our basketball team takes a beating every time." **2.** To arrest. *Se ti beccano stavolta, non ti fanno più uscire per un pezzo.* "If they nail you this time, you're in for the long haul." **3.** To catch up with; to overcome. *Si è fatto beccare a due giri dalla fine.* "They caught up with him when he had only two laps to go." **b)** *youth.* **1.** To pick up boys/girls; to have success in courting another person. *Beccando pollastre in tanti pollai si è fatto un mucchio di nemici.* "By laying his hands on chicks in so many coops he's made himself a lot of enemies." **2.** To catch in the act; to catch unprepared. *Gli avi lo hanno beccato che scopazzava in camera loro.* "His parents caught him screwing in their bedroom."

BECCÀRSI. (Lit., to peck each other.) **a)** *slang.* **1.** *vt. pronom.* To get (something good). *Quanto si è beccato con quell'affare?* "How much did he rake in in that deal?" **2.** *vt. pronom.* To catch (something bad). *In Africa si sono beccati tutti e quattro la malaria.* "All four of them came down with malaria in Africa." **3.** *vr. recipr.* To tease one another; to wrangle; to argue. *Ma come fanno Anna e Carlo ad essere ancora insieme? Si beccano in continuazione!* "How can Anna and Carlo still be together? They bicker all the time!" **b)** *vr., recipr., youth.* To meet; to get together. *Ci becchiamo domenica al mall, O.K.?* "We'll get together Sunday at the mall, OK?"

BÈCCO, *m.* (Lit., beak.) **a)** *slang.* **1. Becco e bastonato.** Betrayed by one's wife and beaten up, i.e., to add insult to injury. *Becco e bastonato: sua moglie è scappata con suo fratello.* "Betrayed and taken for a ride. His wife ran away with his own brother." **2.** Nerve, brazenness, chutzpah. *Hai chiesto al tuo ex marito di pagarti il viaggio con il tuo nuovo uomo? Hai un bel becco!* "You asked you former husband to pay for your trip with your lover? You've got some nerve!" **3. Il becco (di un quattrino).** Money (usually to indicate lack of). *Va' a cantare in un altro cortile: non abbiamo un becco.* "You came to the wrong address. We don't have a penny." **4. Sotto becco.** On the sly; thanks to a good (but shady) deal. *Beh, sì, la macchina non è un granché, ma l'ho avuta sotto becco.*

"You're right, this car isn't great, but I got it in a shady deal." **b)** *youth.* **Mettere il becco a bagno.** (Lit., to dip the beak.) To possess sexually. *Dice che se non mette il becco a bagno tutte le sere gli si avvizzisce.* "He swears that if he doesn't get it wet every night, it wilts."

BEDUÌNO, *m., racist.* (Lit., Bedouin.) Uncouth and uncivilized person. *Ma chi ti ha dato la patente, beduino?!* "Where did you get your driver's license, idiot?!"

BELÌN/BELÌNO, *m., N.* (From Ligurian "belo," alley.) **1.** Penis. *Non le interessa il tuo belino? E allora cosa ci stai a fare con lei?* "She's not interested in your prick? Then why are you going out with her?" **2.** Nothing. *Questo orologio è di nuovo fermo; non vale un belino.* "This watch has stopped again. It isn't worth shit."

BÈLLA, *f.* (Lit., beautiful.) **a)** *slang, C.* **Alla bella.** Randomly; any old way. *Faceva tutto alla bella, eppure riusciva sempre a ottenere quel che voleva.* "He did everything any old way, and yet he always got what he wanted." **b)** *crim.* **1. Far la bella.** To escape from prison. *Da quando l'hanno messo al fresco il suo unico pensiero è stato come fare la bella.* "From the moment they sent him to the cooler, he's been thinking only about how to leap over the wall." **2. Andar per bella.** To succeed in running away after committing a theft. *Andarono per bella con i gioielli nascosti sotto il cappello.* "They got away with the jewelry hidden under their hats."

BELLESPÓNDE, *epithet.* (Lit., nice banks.) Sexy girl, whose most attractive feature is her bottom. *Quando arriva bellesponde tutti i colleghi si precipitano a ossequiarla.* "When buttercup walks in, all her male colleagues rush to pay her homage."

BÈLLO, *adj.* (Lit., beautiful.) **a)** *crim.* **1.** Legal, clean. *'Sti gioielli son belli, vero? Se no, non li compro.* "This jewelry is clean, right? Otherwise, no deal." **2.** Person with no criminal record. *Per fare il colpo con i titoli al portatore bisogna trovare un socio bello.* "If we want to cash those bearer's bonds we must find a clean partner."

b) *youth.* Intelligent, interesting, stimulating. *Gira con della bella gente, ma devi avere un sacco di grana.* "He hangs around some spiffy people, but you need a lot of money to do that."

BÉLVA, *f., youth.* (Lit., beast.) One with outstanding skills in a particular field. *Non capisce un cazzo di donne, ma in greco è una belva.* "He knows zilch about women, but he's a wizard in Greek."

BENEMÈRITI, *m. pl.* (From the carabinieri, called "Arma benemerita," meritorious corps.) Policemen. *Ha avuto l'alto onore di essere stato beccato da due benemeriti.* "He's had the high honor of being picked up by two cara-binieri."

BENGÒDI, *m., youth.* (Legendary land of plenty.) Extraordinary pleasure, intense psychic and physical enjoyment. *Un bengodi con lei, mi fa fondere.* "Such kicks with her, I lose it."

BÈNZA, *f.* **a)** *youth.* (Contraction of "benzina," gasoline.) Any "fuel" necessary in order to go on living. *Sono rimasto con il carro senza benza, e niente benza neanche nel portafoglio: sono tornato a piotte!* "No gas in my car, and no money in my wallet: I came back on foot!" **b)** *narc.* (Contraction of "benzedrina," benzedrine.) Heroin; any narcotic. *Questa benza è super; chi te la allunga?* "This dope is great. Who's the provider?"

BENZÌNA, *f.* (Lit., gasoline.) **a)** *C., slang.* Alcoholic beverage, especially wine. **Fare il pieno di benzina.** (Lit., to fill up the tank with gasoline.) To drink a lot. *Fa il pieno di benzina tutti i sabati, non ne sgarra uno.* "He tanks up every Saturday, without exception." **b)** *narc. See* **benza.**

BÉRE, *vt.* (Lit., to drink.) **a)** *crim.* **1.** To arrest. *Se continui a perseguitarla, ti farai bere.* "If you keep stalking her, you'll get nailed." **2. Bevuto di brutto.** (Lit., drunk in a bad way.) Caught in the act by the police. *Questa volta dieci anni non glieli toglie nessuno, l'hanno bevuto di brutto.* "This time, he'll do ten years without parole. They caught him in the act." **3. Bevuto di bello.** (Lit., drunk in a nice way.) Charged with no evidence. *Il mio avvocato mi ha promesso di tirarmi fuori in dieci giorni: m'hanno bevuto di bello.* "My lawyer promised he'd get me out in ten days. They have no hard evidence." **b)** *youth.* **Pagare da bere alla moto/macchina.** To refuel. *Ci pensi tu a pagare da bere alla macchina? Io sono all'asciutto.* "You're filling up the tank, aren't you? I'm broke."

BERNÀRDA, *f., N.* Vagina. *Non sai cos'è la bernarda alla tua età?* "At your age, you don't know what a cunt is?"

BERNARDÓNI, *m. pl., C.* Eyeglasses. *Porta dei bernardoni che le nascondono mezza faccia.* "She wears enormous glasses that cover half her face."

BÈRTA, *f.* (Lit., pocket.) **Mettere in berta.** (Lit., to put in one's pocket.) **1.** To pocket; to save. *Un milione qui, uno là; alla fine ha messo in berta due miliardi.* "A million here, a million there; in the end he pocketed two billion." **2.** To endure an offense without responding. *Metti sempre in berta! Ma che uomo sei!* "You're always letting people have their way with you! What kind of man are you?" **3.** *rude.* To possess sexually. *Vuoi che te lo metta in berta?* "Would you like me to stick it in?"

BÉSTIA, *f.* (Lit., beast.) **a)** *slang.* **1.** Uncivilized and/or violent man. *Quella bestia di suo marito l'ha menata un'altra volta.* "Her husband is an animal. He beat her up again." **2.** Extremely strong man. *Se chiedi aiuto a Renato facciamo in un amen: è una tale bestia!* "If you ask Renato for help, we'll do it in no time: he's such a bull!" **3.** *rude.* **Da bestia.** Fit for a beast. *Abbiamo tagliato tutti gli alberi vecchi, un lavoro da bestie.* "We cut down all the old trees, a beastly job." **b)** *youth.* **1.** Big motorcycle. **Digli di farti fare un giro sulla sua bestia: godurioso!** "Ask him for a ride on his bike: out of this world!" **2.** Friend, guy. *Ehi, bestia, come ti va la vitaccia?* "Hey, motherfucker, what's the word?"

BESTIÀLE, *adj., youth.* (Lit., beastly.) Amazing, unbelievable, exceptional, awesome (in both positive and negative sense). *Hai avuto un culo bestiale. Due minuti dopo che* *te l'eri filata è arrivata la pula.* "You're fucking lucky. The cops got here two minutes after you sneaked out."

BESTIÓNE, *m., youth.* (Lit., big beast.) Youth or adult male with exceptional sexual organs. *Lasciala perdere, per lei ci vuole un bestione.* "Forget about her, what she needs is a bull."

BEVERÀGGIO, *m.* (Lit., concoction.) **a)** *youth.* Any kind of drink. *Chi porta i beveraggi alla festa?* "Who's bringing the drinks to the party?" **b)** *crim.* Roundup. *Un bel beveraggio di battone ed il lavoro della nottata era fatto.* "They rounded up a few streetwalkers, and their night's work was done."

BEVÙTO, *adj.* (Lit., pp. of to drink.) **1.** Drunk. **2.** Arrested. *See* **bere.**

BIÀNCA, *f.* (Lit., white.) **a)** *narc.* Cocaine; also in the expression **Bianca Signora.** (Lit., white lady.) *Frequenta solo la Bianca Signora.* "He only does coke." **b)** *youth.* Blunder. *L'ultima bianca di Gianni: ha fatto delle proposte oscene alla madre di Marina, prendendola per sua sorella.* "Gianni's latest blunder: he made advances to Marina's mother, mistaking her for her sister."

BIANCHÈTTO, *m., crim.* (Lit., white shoe polish.) Money, silver. *Abbiamo rischiato la pelle per entrare nella villa, ma ci abbiamo trovato solo del bianchetto.* "We risked our necks to get into that villa, and all we found was a little silver."

BIÀNCO, *adj.* (Lit., white.) **a)** *crim.* **1. Essere giù di bianco/Stare in bianco.** To be low on cash. *Era giù di bianco, ma per fortuna gli offrirono di partecipare al colpo in banca.* "Just when he was so low on cash, they offered him to take part in that bank robbery." **2.** To have a clean record. *Luisa è bianca, è per quello che porta lei i soldi oltre confine.* "Luisa is clean, that's why she's smuggling the money across the border." **b)** *slang.* **1. Andare in bianco.** (Lit., to go white.) In romantic and/or sexual endeavors, to get nowhere with another person. *È la decima volta che usciamo insieme, ma mi sa che anche* *stasera vado in bianco.* "It's the tenth time that we will have gone out together, but I'm afraid I'll get nowhere this time too." **2. Mandare qualcuno in bianco.** (Lit., to cause someone to go white.) To prevent someone from doing what he/she is intending to do. *Nicola m'ha mandata in bianco dicendo a Luca che uscivo già con un altro.* "Nicola messed up my plans by telling Luca I'm already seeing someone else." **c)** *youth.* **Vedere bianco qualcuno.** (Lit., to see someone white.) To have a low opinion of someone's skills. *La banca avrà anche sganciato qualche lira per la tua società, ma ti vedo bianco.* "The bank may have forked over a little money for your firm, but I don't think you're going far." **d)** *crim.* **Lupara bianca.** *See* **lupara. Morte bianca.** *See* **morte.**

BÌBI, *m., children.* (From Latin "bibere," to drink.) **Fare bibi. 1.** To drink. *Fa' bibi, che l'aranciata ti fa bene.* "Drink up, orange juice is good for you." **2.** To hurt. *Lo so che fa bibi, ma vedrai che passa presto.* "It's true, it hurts, but it'll be gone in a second."

BÌBLIO, *m., youth.* (Abbreviation of "biblioteca," library.) Library. *È inutile invitare Vittorio, lui passa la vita in biblio.* "It's no use inviting Vittorio; he practically lives in the library."

BICARBONÀTO, *m., narc.* (Lit., bicarbonate.) Cocaine. *C'è una svendita di bicarbonato. Sei del giro?* "There's a sale of dust going on. Are you game?"

BICCHIÈRE, *m.* (Lit., glass.) **1. Fondi di bicchiere.** (Lit., glass bottoms.) False jewelry; glass. *I famosi gioielli di sua zia si sono rivelati fondi di bicchiere.* "Her aunt's famous jewelry turned out to be glass." **2.** Vagina. **Arrotare il bicchiere.** (Lit., to sharpen glass.) To possess sexually. *Se arrota il bicchiere ancora un po', va a finire che lo rompe.* "If he works on her cunt some more, he'll end up breaking it." **3.** Buttocks. **Farsi arrotare il bicchiere.** (Lit., to let someone else sharpen one's glass.) To allow oneself to be taken in. *Credeva di essere tanto furbo, invece si è fatto arrotare il bicchiere.* "He thought he was really shrewd; instead they did quite a job on him!"

BIDONÀRE, *vt.* (From > **bidone.**) To swindle. *Ti hanno bidonato anche stavolta? Non mi stupisco.* "You got screwed this time too? I'm not surprised."

BIDONÀTA, *f.* (From > **bidone.**) **1.** Swindle, trick. *È la seconda volta che il motore della lavapiatti va k.o.: che bidonata ci siamo presi!* "The dishwasher motor has gone bust a second time. We really got screwed!" **2.** Washout. **Dare una bidonata.** To swindle/to take someone in. *Dà bidonate alle vecchie signore vendendo assicurazioni fasulle.* "He cheats old ladies out of their money, selling them false insurance policies."

BIDÓNE, *m.* (Lit., tank.) Cheat. **Tirare un bidone a uno.** To stand someone up (in any kind of engagement, including a romantic date). *"Al treno delle sette,"* gli ha detto, e poi gli ha tirato il bidone! "At the seven o'clock train," she told him, and then she stood him up.

BIDONÌSTA/BIDONÀRO, *m.* (From > **bidone.**) Swindler. *Professione: bidonista di vecchietti.* "Profession: swindler of old people."

BIÈCO, *m., youth.* (Lit., grim.) **1.** Guy who tries to swindle others, mistakingly believing himself to be very cunning. (Also **bieko.**) *Solo tu sei riuscita a farti incastrare da quel bieco.* "You're the only one who managed to get screwed by that twerp." **2.** Friendly way of addressing another guy who has the reputation of being astute. *Allora, bieco, come va lo smercio dei giornaletti porno?* "Hey, motherfucker, how are your sales of porno magazines?"

BÌGI, *m. pl., youth.* (Lit., grey ones.) **I bigi.** Parents. *I bigi non sono malvagi, solo un pozzo noiosi.* "My old folks aren't evil, but boy, are they boring."

BIGIÀRE, *vt., N., youth.* (From German "biegen," to bend, through Lombard "bigià," to avoid, to go around.) To skip class. *Per bigiare, si bigia, ma alla fine sarà grigia.* "For now we play hooky, but at the end there's hell to pay."

BIGIÀTA, *f., youth.* (From > **bigiare.**) The action of skipping class. *Una bigiata collettiva pazzesca!* "A great collective class-skipping expedition!"

BIGÌNO, *m., youth.* (From > **bigiare.**) Cliff's Notes; crib. *"Hai scritto che la Prima Guerra Mondiale è scoppiata nel 1913?" "Era nel Bigino!"* "'So you wrote that World War I broke out in 1913?' 'I found it in my Cliff's Notes!'"

BIGNÀMI, *m., youth. See* **bigino.**

BÌGOLO, *m.* (Lit., kind of long pasta.) **1.** Penis. *Alla Renata il bigolo piace bello duro, al dente.* "Renata likes her hot dogs nice and hard." **2.** Blockhead. *Non cercare di spiegargli come funziona il telefonino: è un bigolo.* "Don't try to explain to him how to use the cellular phone: he's a blockhead."

BIGOLOGÌA, *f., youth.* (Mixture of > **bigolo,** and "biologia," biology.) Profound knowledge of male anatomy and physiology. **Laureata in bigologia.** (Woman with a degree in "bigologia".) Sexually experienced woman. *Trenta ne devi aver avuti per laurearti in bigologia.* "You must have had at least thirty guys to get a degree in 'dickology.'"

BILANCÌNO, *m., C.* (Lit., trace horse.) **Andare a bilancino.** To live off others; to sponge. *Va a bilancino da sempre, ma è ora che cambi aria. Qui lo conoscono tutti.* "He's been living off other people since day one, but it's time he moved on to new pastures."

BÌMBA, *f., N., crim.* (Lit., baby girl.) Counterfeit key. *Non portarti dietro la bimba. Può darsi che ci sia pula in giro.* "Don't carry that false key on you. There may be cops around."

BIODEGRADÀBILE, *adj., youth.* (Lit., biodegradable.) Said of a girl or boy who falls in love easily and often. *Un lento con lui e sei cotta? Sei proprio biodegradabile.* "One cheek-to-cheek dance and you're wild about him? You're really easy to get."

BIÓNDA, *f., crim.* (Lit., blonde.) Cigarette made with blonde tobacco. **Traffico delle bionde.** Cigarette smuggling. *Da quando hanno tolto la tassa sulle cigarette, il traffico delle bionde è crollato.* "Cigarette smuggling has plunged ever since they did away with the cigarette tax."

BÌPEDE, *adj., youth.* (Lit., two-footed.) Equipped with a car (which has wheels as humans have feet.) *Ah, la vita da bipede è un'altra cosa!* "Life with four wheels is something else!"

BÌRRA, *f.* (Lit., beer.) **1.** Vigor, energy. **A tutta birra.** With great energy; very fast. (Probably by analogy with the bubbling of beer froth.) *Il drago era famoso per fare sempre tutto a tutta birra.* "That go-getter was famous for doing everything at full speed all the time." **2. Farci la birra.** To find something utterly useless. *Cosa ci faccio con quel ferrovecchio? La birra!* "What's that old wreck good for? Nothing." **3. Dare la birra a qualcuno.** To leave someone behind in the dust. *Il piccolino ha dato la birra a Tonio, che nessuno aveva mai battuto.* "Shorty left Tonio behind in the dust. Tonio, who'd never been beaten!"

BÌSCA, *f., crim., S.* (Lit., illegal gambling joint.) Counterfeit key, which is as illegal as a gambling casino. *Chi t'ha fatto 'sta bisca? Non aprirebbe neanche una porta aperta.* "Who made you this fake key? It wouldn't open an open door."

BISCHERÀGGINE, *f., C.* Stupidity, imbecility. *Puoi accusarlo di tutte le nefandezze, ma non di bischeraggine.* "You can accuse him of all kinds of things, but not of dumbness."

BÌSCHERO, *m., C.* (Lit., peg of a stringed instrument.) **1.** Penis. *Quando è in ballo il suo bischero, lui si comporta da bischero, non so se mi spiego.* "When his manhood is at stake, he behaves like a prick, do you see what I mean?" **2.** Stupid person. *Solo un bischero può credere a tutto quello che scrivono i giornali.* "Only an idiot believes everything he sees in the papers."

BISCÒTTO, *m., youth.* (Lit., cookie.) Penis. **Mettere a bagno/Intingere/Inzuppare il biscotto.** (Lit., to dip the cookie.) To possess sexually. *Lei lasciava che lui mettesse a bagno il suo biscotto, ma per il resto non collaborava.* "She graciously let him dunk it; otherwise, she didn't cooperate much."

BIT, *Eng., m., youth.* Moment; small amount of time. *Hai un bit per me? Ho bisogno urgente di consigli.* "Do you have a moment for me? I need some good advice, now."

BLABLABLÀ, *m., youth.* (From the verb "blaterare," to blather.) Yakety-yak. *Ed è la classe media che paga sempre per tutti, e gli immigrati rubano il lavoro a noi, e bla bla bla.* "And it's the middle class that's always paying for everyone else, and immigrants take our jobs, and blah blah blah."

BLINDÀRE, *vt., N., youth.* (Lit., to armor.) **1.** To beat up. *T'hanno blindato a dovere, eh?* "They really did you over, didn't they?" **2.** To arrest. *Scendi dal motorino, che se no ci blindano.* "If you don't get off the moped, they'll nab us." **3.** To ground someone. *Mio caro, hai preso la macchina di papà senza permesso? Sei blindato per un mese.* "My dear, you took dad's car without asking? You're grounded for a month." **4.** To call on someone in class. *Che stronzo quello di mate: m'ha blindato due volte di seguito.* "The math teacher called on me twice in a row. What a fuckhead!"

BLITZ, *m., youth.* (From German "Blitz," lightning.) Fast person. *Già qui? Sei veramente un blitz.* "Here already? You're like a lightning bolt!"

BLOCCÀRE, *vt., youth.* (Lit., to block; to stop.) To approach a person with romantic/sexual goals. *Oh, no, c'è Umberto. Quello mi blocca e non si scolla più.* "No, not Umberto! If he corners me he'll stick with me the whole night."

BOCCHINÀRO, *m./***BOCCHINÀRA,** *f., rude.* (From > **bocchino.**) A person who performs fellatio. *"Hai la bocca da bocchinara," lui continuava a dirle, ma lei face-*

va finta di non capire. "'You have a sucker mouth,' he kept on telling her, but she pretended not to get it."

BOCCHÌNO, *m., rude.* (Lit., pouting mouth.) Fellatio. *A dire il vero, un bocchino fatto bene può essere il massimo.* "To be perfectly honest, a blow job, well done, can be just great."

BÒCCIA, *m., N.* (Lit., bowl.) **a)** *slang.* **1. Essere una boccia persa.** (Lit., to be a lost bowl.) To be an untrustworthy, incompetent person. *Non vuole più lavorare con noi? Meglio così, tanto era una boccia persa.* "He doesn't want to work with us any longer? It's just as well, he's a lost cause." **2.** Head. **Scopare la boccia.** To have a haircut. *Quando vai militare, la prima cosa che fanno è scoparti la boccia.* "The first thing they do to you in the army is they shave your head." **b)** *youth.* Molotov cocktail. *Attento con quel sacco: ci sono dentro cinque bocce.* "Be careful with that bag. There are five Molotov cocktails in it."

BOCCIÀRE, *vt.* (Lit., to hit with a bowl/to reject.) **a)** *youth.* To hold someone back at the end of the school year. *M'han bocciato. L'unica consolazione è che non vedrò più il profio di italo.* "They've held me back. The only good thing about it is that I won't see the Italian teacher ever again." **b)** *slang.* To hit another vehicle. *Ho bocciato con la BMW di mio padre: adesso sono cazzi acidi.* "I crashed my father's BMW. Now I'm in deep shit."

BÒCIA, *m., N., youth.* (From regional military jargon for > **boccia.**) **1.** Fresh recruit. *Ai bocia fanno fare tutti i lavori più schifosi in caserma.* "The worst chores in the army are reserved for the new recruits." **2.** Greenhorn, inexperienced young person. *Ma perché non gli dai un po' di tempo? È un bocia.* "Give him some time, won't you? He's a rookie."

BÒIA. (Lit., executioner.) **a)** *m., crim.* **1.** Spy, informer. *Non fidarti di lui; ha già fatto il boia in passato.* "Don't trust him. He's spilled the beans before." **2.** Loan shark, fleecer. *Il boia non gli ha dato un'altra dilazione e lui si* *è sparato.* "The loan shark didn't give him any more time, so he shot himself." **b)** *intensifier, N., slang. Fa un freddo boia.* "It's fucking cold!"

BOIÀTA, *f., N., youth.* (From > **boia.**) **1.** Nonsense, rubbish. *Che boiate vai dicendo? Armando non è un magnaccia.* "What's this rubbish? Armando is not a pimp." **2.** Vile and shameful action. *L'ha menata in mezzo alla strada: una boiata degna di lui.* "He beat her up right on the street: only a bastard like him would do that."

BÓLLA, *f., youth.* (Lit., bubble.) Haughty and arrogant person. *Fa la bolla con tutti, ma quando avvista il preside diventa un agnello.* "He plays God with everyone, but as soon as he sees the principal he turns into a lamb."

BÒMBA, *f.* (Lit., bomb.) **a)** *slang.* **1.** Amazing news. *Il primo ministro sta per essere accusato di corruzione: domani scoppierà la bomba.* "The prime minister is about to be indicted for corruption. The news will break tomorrow." **2.** Loud fart. *Nessuno vuole mai sedersi vicino a lui perché è famoso per le sue bombe.* "No one ever wants to sit next to him. He's famous for his loud farts." **b)** *youth.* **1.** Amazingly good person or thing. *Per me la Lilla non è quella gran bomba che si dice.* "If you ask me, Lilla isn't as great as they say." **2.** Very fast car or motorcycle. *La nuova Suzuki è una bomba.* "The new Suzuki is a rocket." **3.** Very strong alcoholic beverage. *Beve solo bombe.* "He only drinks highballs." **c)** *narc.* **1.** Any stimulant. *Se non si fa almeno due bombe, non si alza neanche dal letto.* "Without at least two hits he doesn't even get up from bed." **2.** Drug addict. *Quella bomba di Enrico? Io ci metterei una croce sopra.* "I would forget about Enrico; he's a junkie if there ever was one."

BOMBARDÀRE, *vt., youth.* (Lit., to shell.) To court someone assiduously and annoyingly. *È da tre mesi che lo bombarda: come la luma, gira al largo.* "She's been after him for three months. As soon as he catches sight of her, he vanishes."

BOMBÀRE, *vi., youth.* (From > **bomba.**) **1.** For music to have an exciting beat. *Era da tanto che un concerto rock non bombava così.* "I can't remember the last time a rock concert blew me away like that." **2.** To work great. *La mia vecchia Cinquecento lusso bomba ancora che è un piacere.* "My old Cinquecento deluxe is still purring like a pussycat." **3.** To have vehement sexual intercourse, stimulated by drugs or music. *Dopo la fumata si bomba.* "First we smoke, then we fuck."

BOMBÀRSI, *vr., narc.* (From > **bomba.**) To take narcotics. *Si sono bombati di brutto e sono finiti tutti al pronto soccorso.* "They overdosed and ended up in the emergency room."

BÒNA/BONÀZZA, *adj., C.* (Lit., good.) Sexy and well-endowed girl. *Pe' bona è bona, ma non si fa mica cuccare.* "She's a knockout, I grant it, but I doubt she'll even let you get near."

BÒNGO, *m., N., racist.* (Metaphor for African, taken from a 1960s song.) Foreigner; person who is slightly off. *Quel bongo salta su per le cose più strane. Deve venire da Marte.* "That weirdo loses it for the most amazing reasons. He must come from Mars."

BÒNO/BONÀZZO/BONÓNE, *m., C.* (Lit., good.) Handsome and very attractive boy. Hunk. *Si sa, i boni vanno solo con le bone.* "You know how it is. Hunks only go with dolls."

BÓNZO, *m., youth.* (Lit., Buddhist monk.) One who acts too old for his/her age, and is too attached to old ideas (as a Buddhist monk is supposed to be). *Stefano è un bonzo totale: passa tutte le domeniche dallo zio.* "Stefano is an old-timer. He spends all his Sundays at his uncle's."

BORÀZZO, *m., youth, N.* One of poor intelligence and ability, not liked by the other members of the group. *Con noi in disco non ci viene più, se si porta dietro quel borazzo.* "She isn't coming dancing with us anymore, if she drags that clod along with her."

BORBÓNE, *m., N./C. youth.* (Lit., belonging to the

Bourbon dynasty, which ruled parts of the South until the unification of Italy in 1861.) A professor who is a died-in-the-wool conservative. *Sta' attento a quello che scrivi nel tema di storia: al borbone, Mussolini piace ancora.* "Be careful what you write in your history essay. The teacher still likes Mussolini."

BORDÈLLO, *m.* (Lit., whorehouse.) Mess, brawl, racket. *Dai, aiutatemi a ripulire 'sto bordello prima che torni la vecchia.* "Come on, help me clean up this mess before my old lady comes back."

BOREÀLE, *adj., youth.* (Lit., borealis.) Awesome, magnificent. *L'ultimo CD degli Aura? Boreale!* "The last CD by the Aura group? Awesome!"

BORGHESÌA, *f.* (Lit., bourgeoisie.) Soldiers close to being discharged, and therefore about to become civilians again. *Beato te, che fai parte della borghesia.* "Lucky you; you're close to being a civilian again."

BÓRSA, *f.* (Lit., scrotum.) A pain in the neck. *Io alle riunioni di partito non ci vado più: sono delle borse incredibili.* "I won't go to party meetings ever again. They're an incredible pain in the neck."

BÒTTA, *f., youth.* (Lit., blow.) **1.** Unusual and exciting event. **Una botta di vita.** (Lit., a moment of high life.) *Ho passato Capodanno nel loro castello in Tirolo: è stata una botta di vita.* "I spent New Year's Eve in their castle in Tirolo. What a kick!" **2.** One-night stand. *Secondo me, le hai dato una botta solo perché era bevuta.* "Look, she got drunk. That's why you had your one-night stand with her."

BOTTÉGA, *f.* (Lit., shop.) **a)** *slang, rude.* **1. Avere la bottega aperta.** To have the fly of one's trousers open. *È completamente sfatto: gira con la bottega aperta.* "He's completely lost his mind; he wanders around with his fly open." **2.** Vagina. *Vivien ha una bella bottega, ma un po' troppo cara.* "Vivien has a nice snatch, but it's a bit expensive." **b)** *crim.* Reformatory. **Essere a bottega.** (Lit., to be learning a craft.) *Essere stato a bottega gli è* *servito per imparare a rubare meglio.* "He improved his stealing technique thanks to reform school."

BÒTTO, *m.* **a)** *slang.* (Lit., shot.) Fireworks. *Ah, senza i botti di Capodanno Napoli non sarebbe più la stessa.* "Without fireworks on New Year's Eve, Naples wouldn't be Naples anymore." **b)** *crim.* (Lit., blow.) Mugging, bag-snatching. *Lui fa i botti e il suo complice si becca la metà del bottino.* "He does the mugging, and his accomplice gets half the loot."

BOTTÓNE/BOTTONCÌNO, *m.* (Lit., button.) Clitoris. *Mi sono stufata di lui; non pigia mai il bottone giusto.* "I got fed up with him; he never pushes my love button right."

BRANDÓNE, *m., C.* (Lit., big chunk.) One-thousand-lire banknote. *Non ci crederai, ma tiene tutti i suoi soldi in brandoni.* "You're not going to believe me, but he keeps all his money in one-thousand-lire notes."

BRÀVA, *f., crim.* (Lit., the good one.) Ironic for police. *La brava è venuta ad arrestare i cattivi.* "The nice cops came to arrest the naughty boys."

BRÈGNA, *f., N., youth. See* **brogna.**

BRICOLAGE, *French, m., youth.* (Lit., do-it-yourself.) **1.** A lot of (things/people); mess; chaos. *Bel bricolage di pivelle in quel caffè. Ci buttiamo?* "Nice bunch of chicks in that café. Shall we give it a try?" **2.** Excellent thing or situation. *Il suo nuovo PC? Un bricolage di elettronica!* "His new PC is an outstanding piece of machinery."

BRÌGA, *m., crim.* (Abbreviation of "brigadiere.") First-rank officer in the carabinieri (police). *È rimasto briga tutta la vita.* "He never made it beyond *brigadiere.*"

BRÒCCA, *f., youth.* (Probably modification of > **boccia,** head.) **1. Perdere la brocca.** To lose one's head. *Ha perso la brocca per Paola, che non lo caga nemmeno.* "He lost his head for Paola, who doesn't give a damn about him." **2.** Buttocks. *Ha una bella brocca, ma per il resto . . .* "She's a got nice tush, otherwise . . ."

BRÒCCOLI, *m. pl.* (Lit., broccoli.) **a)** *slang.* Testicles. *Da capo a piedi l'hanno maciullato, compresi i broccoli.* "They smashed him from head to toe, his nuts included." **b)** *narc.* Marijuana. *Michele è sempre fornito perché coltiva broccoli in giardino.* "Michele is never out of stock. He grows grass in the garden."

BROCCOLÌSTA, *m., N., crim.* (From > **broccoli.**) Police informer. *Chiudi il becco: c'è quel broccolista di Silvio con le antenne dritte.* "Shut up. There's Silvio, the snitch, with his ears perked."

BRÒDA, *f.* (Lit., slops, watered-down coffee.) **a)** *youth.* Gasoline. *Sta bagnarola beve più broda di un cammello assetato.* "This wreck guzzles more gas than a thirsty camel." **b)** *narc.* Drug taken orally. *Va avanti a broda.* (Lit., to run on slops.) "He runs, poorly, on pills."

BRÒDO, *m.* (Lit., broth.) **a)** slang. Sperm. *È bastato che lei lo slumasse di striscio perché lui facesse il brodo.* "All she did was glance at him sideways, and he creamed." **b)** *crim.* Cash earned through illegal activity. *Grazie al colpo al furgone postale hanno brodo per il resto dei loro giorni.* "They can live in splendor for the rest of their lives thanks to that heist of the postal van." **c)** *youth.* See **broda.**

BRÓGNA/BRÙGNA, *f., N., youth.* (Northern variant of "prugna," plum.) Vagina. *Secondo me ha una brogna bella matura, ma non la lascia cogliere a nessuno.* "If you ask me, her pudding is just about ready, but she doesn't let anyone get a taste of it."

BRÒNZO, *m., youth, rude.* (Lit., bronze.) **1.** Policeman (because in American movies policemen usually wear a bronze badge.) *Il bronzo era in borghese, così ci sono cascato.* "He was a plainclothes cop, so I fell for it." **2.** Skunk, bastard. *Si era fatto la fama di bronzo fregando i complici dopo il colpo.* "He acquired the reputation of a skunk, because he cheated his accomplices after the robbery." **3.** Tan. **Farsi il bronzo.** To get a tan. *Ma che ci vai a fare al mare? Tanto ti sei già fatto il bronzo con la* *lampada.* "Why are you going to the beach? You got yourself that nice artificial tan."

BROWN, *Eng., m.* (From the expression "brown sugar," a kind of heroin.) Any heavy drug. *Quando può, si fa del brown; quando manca la lira, sfumazza.* "When she can, she does heavy stuff. When she's out of cash, she smokes."

BRÙCIO, *m., youth.* (Lit., scald, burn.) **Al brucio. 1.** Very quickly, like a shot. *"Questo tema fa schifo!" "Beh, sai, ho dovuto farlo al brucio."* "'This essay is garbage!' 'Well, I had to do it in no time.'" **2.** Thrilling, intriguing. *Le spedizioni notturne con Paolone sono sempre al brucio.* "Our nightly expeditions with big Paolo always give me a kick."

BRUSCOLÌNI, *m. pl., C.* (Lit., small pieces.) Small thing, trifle, especially from a financial point of view. *Ehi, cinquecento milioni non sono mica bruscolini!* "Hey, five hundred million lire isn't peanuts!"

BRÙTTA, *f.* (Lit., the ugly thing by definition.) Hunger. *Aveva una brutta da non vederci più.* "He was starving."

BRÙTTO, *adj.* (Lit., ugly.) **a)** *crim.* **1.** Cunning, experienced in crime. *Bisogna essere brutti per svaligiare quella villa.* "It takes real sharks to burglarize that villa." **2.** *Fa brutto!* "Watch out! The police!" **b)** *youth.* **Di brutto.** (Lit., in an ugly way.) Cunningly; by force. *L'hanno buttato fuori dal locale di brutto.* "They threw him out of the joint head first."

BÙCA, *f.* (Lit., hole.) **a)** *slang.* **1. Mandare/Mettere in buca.** (Lit., to hole out.) To corner someone in an unfavorable position. *Vuole indietro i soldi che mi ha prestato; mi ha messo proprio in buca.* "She wants back the money she lent me right away. She's put me in a bad spot." **b)** *youth.* **Dare buca.** To stand someone up. *Era la terza volta che Elena gli dava buca; perché si era fissato con lei?* "It was the third time Elena stood him up. Why did he have this fixation about her?"

BUCAIÒLA, *f., C., rude.* (From > **buca/buco.**) Prostitute. *Stanotte fa troppo freddo persino per le bucaiole.* "It's too cold even for streetwalkers tonight."

BUCAIÒLO, *m., C., rude.* (From > **buca/buco.**) Male homosexual. Also used as a generic insult. *Guarda che quello è un locale per bucaioli.* "I'm warning you, that's a joint for faggots."

BUCÀRE, *vt.* (Lit., to make a hole.) **a)** *crim.* To make an opening in a building, so as to be able to carry out a robbery. *Sono entrati nel salone delle cassette di sicurezza bucando in collo.* "They got into the safe deposit box room by boring through the floor." **b)** *youth.* **1.** To skip class. *Buchiamo stamattina?* "How about playing hooky with me this morning?" **2.** *rude.* To deflower a girl. *Dì, l'hai bucata poi l'altra sera?* "Well, did you pop her cherry the other night?"

BUCÀRSI, *vr., narc.* (Lit., to pierce oneself.) To be a habitual user of heavy drugs. *Ha le braccia che sembrano un colabrodo, eppure i suoi non sanno che si buca!* "His arms look like a sieve, and yet his folks don't know he shoots up."

BUCÀTA. a) *adj., youth, rude.* (From > **bucare, b) 2.**) Deflowered, no longer a virgin. *Per me, Adele ti fa un mucchio di robe, ma non è bucata.* "I believe Adele is available for a lot of stuff, but she still has her cherry." **b)** *f., narc.* (From > **bucarsi.**) Group injection of heavy drugs. *La bucata di ieri non m'ha preso per niente.* "Yesterday's shoot-up didn't do anything for me."

BÙCO, *m.* (Lit., hole.) **a)** *slang.* **1.** Financial deficit. *Quando sono andati a vedere i libri contabili hanno trovato un buco da due miliardi.* "When they checked the books they found two billion missing." **2.** *rude.* Passive male homosexual. *Marianna s'è presa una sbandata per Vito! Ma lo sa che è un buco?* "Marianna has a crush on Vito. Does she realize he's a faggot?" **3.** Miserable dwelling. *Non vorrai mica portarti quella modella da copertina nel tuo buco?* "You're not taking that cover girl to your hole in the wall!" **b)** *youth.* **1.** Buttocks. **Avere un buco pazzesco.** *See* **culo. 2. Fare buco.** (Lit., to make a hole.) *See* **andare in > bianco. 3. Fare un buco.** (Lit., to make a hole.) To fail when called on in class. *Mamma Santa, che buco ho fatto in filo!* "Holy Mother, I flunked the philosophy test real bad." **4.** Vagina. **Riempire/ Tappare il buco.** (Lit., to fill the hole.) To possess sexually. *Vai in giro a tappar buchi anche stasera?* "Are you going in search of snatch tonight too?" **c)** *narc.* **1.** Drug injection; syringe mark; dose. *Smercia buchi, per quello s'è fatto la Porsche.* "He sells hard stuff, that's how he got a Porsche." **2. Essere in buco.** (Lit., to be in a hole-like situation.) To be intoxicated with narcotics. *Tu sei in buco anche senza bucarti.* "You're zonked out even without shooting up."

BUCÒMANE, *m., narc.* (From > **buco.**) Drug addict. *C'è chi è mitomane, chi ninfomane, chi piromane. Lui è un bucomane.* "In this world there are megalomaniacs, nymphomaniacs, pyromaniacs. He's a 'shotmaniac.'"

BÙFALA, *f., C.* (Lit., she-buffalo.) **a)** *crim.* **1.** Meat ration distributed in jail (so called because of its toughness). *Di nuovo bufala? Oh, no! Meglio il pastone delle galline.* "Not this rubber again! Better the chicken hash." **2.** Swindle, trick. *Dopo tutte le bufale che ha organizzato, gliene hanno fatta una a lui.* "After all the tricks he did to others, they did one to him." **b)** *slang.* **1.** Blunder. *È andata a farle le condoglianze, invece il marito era scappato con la segretaria. Che bufala!* "She went to pay her condolences, only to discover her husband had run away with the secretary. What a goof!" **2.** Rubbish; movie or book of very low quality (and therefore a swindle for the consumer, from Roman butchers' practice of selling buffalo meat pretending it to be veal). *Il film era una tale bufala che siamo usciti a metà.* "The movie was such rubbish that we left halfway through."

BÙFFO, *m., crim.* (Lit., funny.) **1. Fare buffi/Essere pieno di buffi.** (Lit., to be full of funny [things].) To have a lot of debts. *Tu ridi, ma non è buffo essere pieno di buffi.* "You may laugh, but it's no fun being loaded with debts." **2. A buffo.** Without paying. *È una vera volpe il Lello: mangia sempre a buffo.* "Lello is a real fox. He manages to get all his meals for free."

BUGGERÀRE, *vt.* (English "to bugger," to sodomize.) **1.** *rude.* To practice sodomy. *Quando è venuto il momento buono, lui non ce l'ha fatta a buggerarla.* "When the right moment came, he couldn't bring himself to bugger her." **2.** To swindle. *Faccia d'angelo m'ha buggerato ben bene.* "Pretty face screwed me just fine."

BUGGERATÙRA, *f.* (From > **buggerare.**) Swindle. *Mi hanno inflitto tante buggerature che m'hanno fatto fallire.* "I got screwed so many times I went under."

BUNKER, *m.* (From German "Bunker," air-raid shelter.) **a)** *slang.* Courtroom used for terrorist and mafia trials, equipped with exceptional security systems. *Per il processo alla cupola mafiosa hanno dovuto ingrandire l'aula bunker.* "For the trial of the mafia big shots, the high-security courtroom had to be enlarged." **b)** *youth.* Group, gang. *Gira esclusivamente con quelli del suo bunker.* "He hangs around with the members of his gang and no one else."

BUÒNA, *youth.* (Lit., good.) **1.** *adj.* Said of a girl who is presumed ready for sexual intercourse. *Io mi porterei dietro i goldoni, per me la Sandra è buona.* "I would bring along some rubbers; I think Sandra is ready." **2.** *interj.* **Buona!** Expression of agreement and understanding among friends. *"Tutti in vasca domani!" "Buona!"* "'Everyone downtown tomorrow!' 'Fine!'" **3.** *interj.* Enough! *Buona! Le tue storie hanno rotto!* "Cut it out! We've had enough of your stories!"

BURÌNO, *m./***BURÌNA,** *f., rude.* Uncouth person; redneck. *Sputacchia dappertutto: che burino!* "He spits all over the place. What a redneck!"

BÙRRO, *m.* (Lit., butter.) **Dare del burro.** (Lit., to spread butter.) To flatter, to appease. *Credi di ottenere il posto di* *lavoro dandole del burro?* "Do you really think you can get that job by buttering her up?"

BUSCÀRE, *vt.* (From Spanish "buscar," to look for, to provide.) **1.** To catch something unpleasant. *Mi sono buscato un raffreddore di quelli!* "I caught a terrible cold!" **2.** To be defeated. *Con te a tennis non ci gioco più: le busco sempre.* "I'll never play tennis with you again. I take a beating every time."

BUSÓNE, *m.* (From Bolognese dialect term "buso" for "buco," hole.) **1.** *rude.* Passive male homosexual. *Tutti credono che sia uno stallone, invece è un gran busone.* "People think he's a great stud; on the contrary, he's a faggot." **2.** Extremely lucky man. *Va' con lui alle corse, è un gran busone.* "Go to the races with him. He's really lucky."

BÙSTA/BUSTÌNA, *f.* (Lit., envelope.) **a)** *narc.* Single dose of a heavy drug, especially heroin, because it is sold in small envelopes. *Se non sganci le svanziche, niente busta.* "No money, no hit." **b)** *youth.* Bed. *Ha passato tutta la domenica in busta.* "She spent all Sunday in the sack."

BUSTARÈLLA, *f.* (Lit., small envelope.) Money (which used to be handed over in an envelope) with which a public official or a politician is bribed. *"Siamo nelle sue mani per quella legge sull'inquinamento," piagnucolò l'industriale, spingendo la bustarella verso l'uomo politico.* "'We're in your hands for that law on pollution!' the industrialist whined, while pushing the envelope toward the politician."

BUTTADÉNTRO, *m.* (Lit., the one who throws you in.) Person in charge of choosing those who will get into a disco. *Conosco il buttadentro del Blu Notte: vedrai che ci fa entrare.* "I know the bouncer at the Blue Night; he'll let us in, you'll see."

BUTTAFUÒRI, *m.* (Lit., the one who throws you out.) Bouncer. *Metti via l'amico che arriva il buttafuori!* "Hide the knife; the bouncer is coming!"

BUTTÀRE. (Lit., to toss, to throw.) **a)** *vi., crim.* **1. Buttare dentro.** (Lit., to throw in.) To burglarize a house. *Il vostro piano è interessante, ma noi buttiamo solo dentro.* "Your plan is interesting, but we only do burglaries." **2. Buttare il fagotto.** *See* **fagotto. b)** *vt., youth.* **1.** To yield a gain. *Quanto ti ha buttato il lavoro di géo al Club Méditerranée?* "How much did you make last summer as an entertainer at Club Med?" **2.** *Come ti butta?* How's it going?

BUTTÀRE SU, *vi., youth.* (Lit., to toss up.) **1.** To inflict, to impose. *Mi ha buttato su un giaccone che secondo me è di seconda mano.* "He tricked me into buying a coat that looks second-hand to me." **2.** To possess sexually. *Oggi si è persino fatto la doccia. Evidentemente vuole buttare su.* "He even showered this morning. He must be looking to get laid."

BUTTÀRSI, *vr., youth.* (Lit., to plunge.) To find the courage to approach a girl. *Ieri sera Giorgio s'è buttato e, sorpresa sorpresa, ha caricato.* "Last night Giorgio screwed up his courage, and, lo and behold, he picked up a girl."

BÙZZO, *m., youth.* (Probably a contraction of "buzzurro.") Uncouth and badly mannered boy. *Un buzzo, ecco quello che sei, a dirle che lui le mette le corna.* "You're a skunk. Why tell her that he sleeps around?"

BYTE, *m., youth.* (From computer jargon.) **Va' a fa' 'n byte.** *See* **bagno.**

C, C., C..., *m., rude.* The letter "c" used euphemistically instead of the following words, which are all rude. **1.** *See* **cazzo. 2.** *See* **coglione, coglioni. 3.** *See* **culo. 4.** *See* **cane.**

CA', abbreviation of > **cazzo.**

CABRIOLET, *m., crim.* (Lit., convertible.) A check that will bounce, or that will turn out to be stolen. (In Italian such a check is called "scoperto," uncovered, a term also used for a convertible car, or a coupe.) *Le hanno rifilato un cabriolet da dieci milioni.* "They palmed off a bad check for ten million lire on her."

CACÀRE, variant of > **cagare,** in dialects of central Italy.

CACARÈLLA, variant of > **cagarella,** in dialects of central Italy.

CACÀTA, variant of > **cagata,** in dialects of central Italy.

CÀCCA, *f., rude.* (Lit., shit.) **a)** *slang.* **Avere la cacca al culo.** To be scared shitless. *Ghignavano e facevano i gradassi, ma si vedeva che avevano la cacca al culo.* "They were sneering and bragging, but they were obviously scared shitless." **b)** *narc.* Generic for drug. *Ti vende tutta la cacca che vuoi, basta che sganci.* "He'll sell you all the shit you want. All you have to do is to fork over the money."

CACCAVÈLLA, *f., S.* (Lit., clay pot.) Prostitute. *No, non si è mai sposato, ma si è fatto tutte le caccavelle della zona.*

"No, he never married, but he's had all the hookers in this area."

CACCIABÀLLE, *m., N.* (Lit., ball kicker.) Liar, boaster. *Non vorrai mica credergli? Il suo soprannome è caccia-balle.* "You don't believe him, do you? His nickname is bullshitter."

CACCIÀRE, *vt., N.* (Lit., to hunt.) **a)** *slang.* To steal. *Bella quella pelliccia! Dove l'hai cacciata?* "Nice fur coat. Where did you lift it?" **b)** *youth.* **Cacciare su. 1.** To cough up. *Caccia su il centone che mi devi o ti denuncio!* "Cough up the hundred you owe me, or I'll turn you in!" **2.** To do, to cause (something negative). *Mi ha cacciato su una fregatura di prim'ordine.* "He did me in real fine."

CACCIAVÌTE, *m.* (Lit., screwdriver.) Penis. *Non sa parlar d'altro che del suo cacciavite.* "All he talks about is his tool."

CÀCCOLA, *f.* **a)** *youth.* A hideous person or thing. *Al concorso delle caccole, Maria vincerebbe.* "Maria would be the winner in the ugliness contest." **b)** *narc. See* **caccolo.**

CÀCCOLO, *m., narc.* (From either > **cacca,** or "calcolo," gallstone.) Small piece of hashish. *Silvia gira sempre con le tasche piene di caccole. Un giorno o l'altro finisce dentro.* "Silvia goes around with her pockets full of bits of hashish. One of these days she'll end up in jail."

CACIÀRA, *f., C.* Noise, racket. *Hanno fatto una caciara da svegliare anche i morti.* "They made a racket that was enough to waken the dead."

CACÓNE, *m., rude.* Variant of > **cagone,** in dialects of central Italy.

CACTUS, *m., youth.* (Lit., cactus.) Penis. *Quando Max le ha domandato se voleva vedere il suo bel cactus la Lilli, mongola, ha pensato che lui parlasse di una pianta.* "When Max asked her if she wanted to see his cucumber, Lilli, who is really dumb, thought he was talking about a vegetable."

CADREGHÌNO, *m., N.* (Lit., small chair, from the Latin

"cathedra.") Prestigious position that yields power and money. *Sta seduto su quel cadreghino da vent'anni; non sarai certo tu a farglielo mollare.* "He's been holding that position for the last twenty years; you won't be the one who forces him to quit it."

CAFFETTIÈRA, *f.* (Lit., coffee pot.) **a)** *crim.* The tall hat of traffic police. *Rallenta, c'è una caffettiera all'angolo!* "Slow down! There's a policeman at the corner!" **b)** *slang.* Old and rattling car. *La sua caffettiera è inconfondibile: fa più casino di un aeroplano.* "You would recognize his old wreck anywhere: it makes more noise than an airplane."

CAGACÀZZO, *m./f., N., youth, rude.* (From > **cagare,** and > **cazzo.**) A person who is a pain in the neck. *Se la sono squagliata perché è arrivato quel cagacazzo di Gino.* "That dumbass Gino just arrived, so they all cleared out."

CAGÀRE, *N., rude.* (Lit., to defecate.) **a)** *slang.* **1.** *vi. Va' a cagare!* "Go shit in your hat!" **2.** *vi. pronom.* **Cagarsi sotto.** To be scared shitless. *Tre brutti ceffi mi hanno circondato nel garage sotterraneo. Tu non ti saresti cagato sotto?* "Three ugly mugs surrounded me in the underground garage. You wouldn't have shit in your pants?" **b)** *vi., crim.* To confess; to squeal. *Di Salvatore non ti puoi fidare. Lo sai che ha già cagato altre volte.* "You can't trust Salvatore; you know he's squealed before." **c)** *vt., youth.* **1.** To give, to fork out. *Dai, cagami la lira.* "Come on, fork out the money." **2. Cagare/cagarsi qualcuno o qualcosa.** To pay attention to, to be interested in, used especially in the negative form. *Poveretta, quella lì non se la caga proprio nessuno.* "Poor thing, no one gives a damn about her." **3.** *vr. recipr.* To have an intimate relationship with another person. *Ma dove vivi? Sono mesi che non si cagano più.* "Where have you been? They haven't been an item for months." **4.** *vt.* **Far cagare (il cazzo.)** (Lit., to make someone's prick shit.) *See* **cagacazzo.**

CAGÀTA, *f., N., rude.* (Lit., defecation.) Rubbish, nonsense. *Vuole farmi sborsare due milioni per un quadro che, detto fra noi, è una cagata pazzesca.* "He wants me to cough up two million lire for a painting that, to tell you the truth, is a piece of crap."

CAGHÉTTA, *f., N., rude.* (Lit., diarrhea.) Fear. *Basta che il proffo di filo la guardi e le viene la caghetta.* "If the philosophy teacher as much as looks at her, she shits in her panties."

CÀGNA, *f., N., crim.* (Lit., bitch.) Outstanding promissory note; money troubles. *Se a fine mese non pago quella cagna, finisco in collegio.* "If I don't pay that IOU by the end of the month, I'll end up in the can."

CAGÓNE, *m., rude.* (From > **cagare.**) A cowardly person, someone who shits in his/her pants. *Sono finiti tutti nel crepaccio perché quel cagone di Mario ha mollato la corda.* "They fell into the crevice because that coward Mario let go of the rope."

CAIMÀNO, *m., youth.* (Lit., caiman.) Unscrupulous, tough guy. *Se chiedi aiuto a Berto, che è un caimano, li sistema lui.* "If you ask help from Berto, who's a toughie, he'll straighten them out."

CALÀRE. (Lit., to decrease.) **a)** *vi., slang.* To decrease; to go limp. Proverb. *La malattia dell'agnello: cresce la pancia, cala l'uccello.* "Lamb's disease: the belly grows, the dick shrinks." **b)** *youth.* **1.** *vt.* To give; to lend; to pay. *Stasera cali tu.* "Your turn to fork out tonight." **2.** *vi. Cala, cala!* "Stop bragging!"

CALDÙCCIO, *m., youth.* (Lit., warm and cozy.) **Al calduccio.** In the vagina. *Voleva starsene un po' al calduccio, ma i suoi sono rientrati all'improvviso e ha dovuto tirarlo fuori in fretta.* "He enjoyed staying inside her, but suddenly his folks arrived and he had to take it out real quick."

CALIÀRE, *vt., youth.* To skip class. *Caliano un giorno sì e uno no.* "They skip class every other day."

CALÌFFA, *f., N.* (Lit., woman caliph.) **a)** *crim.* Madam of a brothel. *Una califfa grande e grossa come un peso* *massimo aprì loro la porta del bordello.* "The door of the brothel was opened by a madam as huge as a heavyweight champion." **b)** *N., slang.* Strong and emancipated woman. *Era conosciuta da tutti come "la califfa." Nessuno si ricordava più il suo vero nome.* "She was known as 'la califfa.' No one remembered her real name anymore."

CALÌFFO, *m., N.* (Lit., caliph.) **a)** *slang.* Owner and/or manager of a nightclub; boss. *Sta' attento con quella coca; il califfo non vuole roba nel suo locale.* "Be careful with that coke; the boss doesn't want that stuff in his nightclub." **b)** *crim.* Person charged with pocketing bribes. *Ha passato la bustarella a un califfo, ma non sa chi ci stia dietro.* "He handed the bribe to a taker, but he has no idea who is behind it." **c)** *youth.* **1.** A strong and skillful person without many moral scruples. *Vedi quel ferro? L'ha avuto per due soldi da Bruno, che nel campo delle moto è un califfo.* "See that motorcycle? I got it for nothing from Bruno. When it comes to motorbikes, he's the man." **2.** A boy who has success with girls. *Pietro ha fama di califfo, ma con Giuliana gli è andata buca.* "Pietro has a reputation as a ladies' man, but he got nowhere with Giuliana."

CÀLLI, *m. pl.* (Lit., corns.) **Stare sui calli a qualcuno.** (Lit., to stand on someone's corns.) To be very annoying to someone. *Se viene anche Maurizio a quella cena, io non ci vengo: è uno che mi sta veramente sui calli.* "If Maurizio comes to your dinner, I won't. He's a real pain in the neck."

CALMÀRSI, *vr., youth.* (Lit., to calm down.) To come off one's high horse; to lower one's sights. Also in the expression: **Darsi una calmata.** *Ma chi ti credi di essere? Ma datti una calmata!* "Who the hell do you think you are? Cool it!"

CÀLO, *m., narc.* (Lit., decrease.) The ending of a drug experience; comedown. *E piantala! Non vedi che è in calo?* "Let him be. Don't you see he's coming down from a high?"

CÀLVI, *m. pl., youth.* (Lit., the bald ones.) Old and anti-quated parents (grandparents; relatives in general.) *Gli ho parlato per ore a ufo: me lo dovevo immaginare che i calvi erano anche arterio.* "I spoke for hours without getting through to them. Not surprising that besides being ancient, they have arteriosclerosis."

CALZÈTTA, *f., n.* (Lit., sock.) **Una mezza calzetta.** A nonentity. *"Non sei altro che una mezza calzetta,"* dissero sghignazzando, *"neanche capace a tirarti su le braghe da solo."* "'You're a nonentity' they said sneering at him, 'you can't even pull up your pants by yourself.'"

CAMOMILLÀRSI, *vr., youth.* (From "camomilla," camomile.) To calm down. *Non pensi che la sbarbina farebbe bene a camomillarsi un po'?* "Don't you think that kid ought to chill out a little?"

CAMPÀNA, *f., N., crim.* (Lit., bell.) **Stare in campana.** To be on the lookout. *"Tu ti fidi di Beppe?" "Beh, è un po' scimunito, ma non ci vuole un genio per stare in campana."* "'You're not telling me you trust Beppe!' 'Well, he's somewhat dumb, but it doesn't take a genius to be the lookout.'"

CAMPORÈLLA. (From "campo," field.) **Andare in cam-porella,** *idiom, N.* **a)** *slang.* To go to a secluded spot in the fields/countryside to neck or to make love. *Quando eravamo giovani noi, se si voleva stare in pace con l'innamorato bisognava andare in camporella.* "When we were young the only way to be alone with your boyfriend was to head for the open fields." **b)** *crim.* To get out of jail after doing one's time. *È andato in camporella, beato lui.* "He got out, lucky him."

CAMÙFFA. Stare in camuffa, *idiom, N., youth. See* **stare in > campana.**

CANARÌNO, *m.* (Lit., canary.) **a)** *slang.* Penis. **Cambiar l'acqua al canarino.** (Lit., to give fresh water to the canary.) To urinate. *"E Franco dov'è finito?" "A cambiar l'acqua al canarino."* "'Where did Franco go?' 'He's changing the canary's water.'" **b)** *crim.* Police informer, who "sings" like a canary. *Lui crede di cavarsela facendo il canarino, ma anche i canarini finiscono in gabbia!* "He thinks he can get out of trouble by playing the canary, but canaries end up in cages too!"

CANCÈLLI, *m. pl., C./S.* (Lit., gates.) Jail; prison. *Ha trucidato marito e suocera a colpi d'ascia: dai cancelli non esce più.* "She murdered her husband and mother-in-law with an axe; she'll never get out of prison."

CÀNCRO, *m., youth, rude.* (Lit., cancer.) Ugly person, especially female. *Ma come fa Angela, che, diciamoci la verità, è un cancro, ad avere tanti uomini?* "To tell you the truth, Angela looks like cancer to me. How come she gets so many men?"

CANDÉLA, *f.* (Lit., candle.) **1.** Penis. **Spegnere la candela.** (Lit., to blow out the candle.) To possess sexually. *Umberto mi cerca solo quando vuole spegnere la candela.* "Only when he wants to have sex does Umberto come looking for me." **2.** Mucus. **Avere ancora la candela.** (Lit., to have mucus dripping from one's nose.) To be a greenhorn. *Non vorrai portarti tuo fratello all'occupazione dell'università?! Ha ancora la candela!* "You aren't thinking of taking your brother to the sit-in at the university?! He's a greenhorn."

CANÈSTRO, *m., N.* (Lit., basket.) **1.** Buttocks. *Bella non è, ma ha uno di quei canestri!* "She is no beauty, but she has quite a cake." **2.** Vagina. **Fare canestro.** (Lit., to score a basket.) To possess sexually. *Roberto sembra una mezza calzetta, eppure fa sempre canestro.* "Roberto looks like a nonentity, and yet he scores every time."

CÀNI, *m. pl., C., rude.* (Lit., dogs.) **Cani e porci.** (Lit., dogs and pigs.) Everyone, with no discrimination. *I miei vicini hanno tanti soldi e si danno tante arie, ma a casa loro invitano cani e porci.* "My neighbors have a lot of money and are very snobbish, but they invite just about everyone."

CÀNNA, *f.* (Lit., cane, stick.) **a)** *slang, rude.* Penis. *Era un ragazzo piccolo e mingherlino, ma aveva una canna* *poderosa.* "The boy was short and slim, but he had a thick rod." **b)** *crim.* Gun. *Gino non va mai in giro senza canna, chi ha orecchie per intendere . . .* "Gino goes nowhere without his cane, if you get my drift . . ." **c)** *narc.* Joint. **Fare/Pippare/Farsi una canna.** To smoke a joint. *Ah, che meraviglia! Erano mesi che non mi pippavo una bella canna.* "This is great! It's been months since I smoked a good joint."

CANNÀRE, *N.* **a)** *youth.* **1.** *vi.* To flee (from > **canne, a1**). *Meglio cannare prima che la vecchia befana veda il vetro rotto.* "We'd better clear out before the old witch sees the broken window." **2.** *vi.* To plan a sexual encounter. *Mario vorrebbe tanto cannare con te. Che gli dico?* "Mario would really like to work out with you. What should I tell him?" **3.** *vi.* To floor it. *Cannava giù per la discesa a cento all'ora.* "He was flooring it, coming down the hill at one hundred kilometers an hour." **4.** *vt.* To leave one's boyfriend/girlfriend. *L'ho cannato: mi faceva le corna con Giuliana.* "I ditched him. He was betraying me with Giuliana." **5.** *vt.* To fail someone at the end of the school year. *Quella stronza l'aveva detto all'inizio dell'anno che mi avrebbe cannato.* "That bitch said at the beginning of the year that she'd hold me back." **6.** *vt.* To fail a test. *Mia sorella ha cannato un altro compito di chimica, e adesso vuole che lo dica io al grigio.* "My sister flunked another chemistry test. Now she wants me to break the news to our old man." **7.** *vt.* To swindle. *Sono riusciti a venderti quel ferrovecchio? T'hanno cannato un'altra volta!* "They managed to sell you that pile of junk? You got screwed once again." **b)** *vi., narc.* To smoke joints. *Mai cannato così! Dove hai preso 'sta roba?* "Never smoked so good. Where did you buy that stuff?"

CANNÀTO, *adj.* **a)** *narc.* Stoned. *Sono cannati persi.* "They're completely stoned." **b)** *youth.* **1.** Off the wall. *La Giovanna è sempre stata un po' cannata.* "Dear Giovanna's always been slightly off the wall." **2.** Taken in. *Se ne andava in giro smaniando: "So' cannato! So'* *cannato!*" "He wandered about town ranting and raving, 'I got screwed! I got screwed!'"

CANNATÙRA, *f., youth.* Swindle, bad result in general (from > **cannare** 7). *Che cannatura 'sto ferro! Adesso anche la frizione è kaputt!* "They really screwed me with this piece of junk! Now the clutch is gone."

CÀNNE, *f. pl.* (Lit., sticks.) **a)** *slang.* **1.** Legs. *È tutto canne: quando si siede sparisce.* "He's all legs; as soon as he sits down he disappears." **2.** Throat. *L'ispettore studiò il cadavere immerso in una pozza di sangue: la causa della morte era stato un bel taglio alle canne.* "The inspector studied the body, which was immersed in a pool of blood. The cause of death was a clean cut through the throat." **b)** *youth.* **1. Essere nelle canne.** To be in trouble and to have to fix it quickly. *Gli devo restituire i soldi domani, se no mi manda dietro i suoi scagnozzi. Sono proprio nelle canne.* "If I don't give him his money back by tomorrow, he'll send his gorillas after me. I'm in deep shit." **2. Fare aria alla canne.** (Lit., to fan the canes.) Not to mind, not to be fazed. *Lascialo sbraitare: tanto, a me fa aria alle canne.* "Let him rant and rave: he can't faze me."

CANNONÀTA, *f.* (Lit., cannon shot.) Blast (positive). *Hai visto l'ultimo film di Kevin Costner? È una cannonata!* "Did you see Kevin Costner's latest movie? It's a blast!"

CANNÓNE, *m.* (Lit., cannon.) **a)** *crim.* Revolver. *Nessuno lo contraddisse: era ovvio dal rigonfiamento sotto l'ascella della giacca che si portava dietro un bel cannone.* "No one dared argue with him. You could tell he was packing a big cannon from the bulge in the armpit of his jacket." **b)** *narc.* Big stick. *Sgancia, sgancia. Vuoi mica che ti venda un cannone così per due lire?* "Fork out the money. You don't seriously believe that I would sell you such a big stick for a pittance." **c)** *slang.* **1.** Buttocks. *Sta seduto sul suo cannone tutto il santo giorno; cosa vuoi che combini?* "He spends the day sitting on his ass. Of course he'll never get anything done." **2.** Penis. *Secondo Maria, che se ne intende, Gianni ha uno di quei* *cannoni* . . . "According to Maria, who is an expert, Gianni has quite a cannon." **3.** A top performer. *Vero, è solo un ferrovecchio, ma nel suo campo è un cannone.* "True, he's only a scrap dealer, but in his field he's tops."

CANNÙCCIA, *f., narc.* (Lit., straw.) Sniffing cocaine or amphetamines with a straw. *Te ne fai delle cannucce, eh, marpione?* "You do sniff a lot, right, wise guy?"

CANTÀRE, *vi., crim.* (Lit., to sing.) To spill the beans. *Da ragazzo voleva fare il tenore. Adesso canta coi poliziotti, certo non alla Scala!* "As a child he wanted to become a tenor. Now he's singing to the police, not at La Scala!"

CÀPA, *f., S.* Head. **Fare una capa tanta.** To make someone's head spin (because of too many demands, complaints, etc.) *Ho lasciato andare mia figlia in vacanza con il suo ragazzo. M'ha fatto 'na capa tanta!* "My daughter was driving me crazy, so in the end I let her go on vacation with her boyfriend."

CAPÒCCIA, *f.* (From "capo," head.) Overseer, supervisor, boss. *Il capoccia non è malvagio, solo un po' tonto.* "Our boss isn't bad, just slightly dumb."

CAPOLÌNEA, *f., N.* (Lit., terminal.) **Arrivare al capolinea.** (Lit., to arrive at the terminal of a bus line.) To be at the end of one's life. *Non c'è più niente da fare per il povero Adolfo: è arrivato al capolinea.* "There is nothing we can do for poor Adolfo; he's at his last stop."

CAPPÈLLA, *f.* (Lit., mushroom cap.) **a)** *slang.* **1. Fare una cappella.** To make a blunder. *Mi è sfuggito che l'avevo visto a cena con la segretaria: mi sono fatta una cappella!* "I let on that I saw him dining with his secretary. I really blew it!" **2. Prendersi una cappella.** To fall in love. *Massimo si prende almeno una cappella alla settimana.* "Massimo falls in love at least once a week." **b)** *youth.* Hat, cap. *Guarda che buffo il Marco con quella cappella in testa.* "Look how funny Marco looks with that cap on."

CAPPELLÀRE, *vi. See* **cappella, a1.**

CÀPPERO, *m.* (Lit., caper.) **a)** *slang.* **1.** Penis. *Ci sono capperi di tutte le misure, come ben sai.* "Bananas come in all sizes, as you well know." **2.** *Capperi!* "Wow!" **b)** *youth.* **Del cappero.** Euphemism for **del > cazzo.**

CAPPÒTTA, *f., C./S.* (Italianization of the French "capote," hood.) Breasts, tits. *Le toccò timidamente la cappotta che era bella grande, morbida morbida.* "He timidly touched her large, soft jugs."

CAPPÒTTO, *m.* (Lit. coat.) **a)** *slang.* Slam. Winnning all the points of a deal in a card game. **Dare/Fare cappotto.** To inflict a total defeat. *La nostra squadra gli ha dato cappotto: qui non li rivedremo, te lo assicuro.* "Our team inflicted a total defeat on them; we'll never see them again, rest assured." **b)** *crim.* The cement envelope in which a corpse is buried. *Quelli di Cosa Nostra hanno fatto un cappotto così bello a Michelino che non se lo toglierà mai più.* "Cosa Nostra made such a nice coat for Michelino that he'll never take it off."

CAPPÙCCIO, *m.* (Lit., hood.) Foreskin and condom. *Il suo cappuccio non si bagna mai, perché lui gli mette sempre il cappuccio!* "His head never gets wet, because he always puts on a shower cap."

CARÀMBA, *m.* Distortion of the police corps called "carabinieri." *Coi caramba non ci puoi ragionare. Se li vedi, dattela a gambe.* "You can't reason with "carabinieri." If you see them, run."

CARAMÈLLA, *f.* (Lit., candy.) **a)** *crim.* **1.** Bullet. *La notte di San Valentino sono fioccate più caramelle che chicchi di riso a un matrimonio.* "On St. Valentine's night it was raining more bullets than rice at a wedding." **2.** Counterfeit key. *Come facciamo a entrare senza la caramella?* "How can we get in without the key?" **b)** *youth.* Penis. *Vuoi succhiare la mia caramella?* "Do you want to suck my lollipop?"

CARAMÈLLE, *f. pl.* (Lit., candies.) **1.** Money. *Queste qui sono tutte le caramelle che hai? Non andrai lontano.* "These are all the beans you have? You won't go far." **2.**

Testicles. *Non so tu, ma io ho solo due caramelle.* "I don't know about you, but I only have two marbles."

CARAMPÀNA, *f., N., rude.* (Probably from the name of a group of Venetian houses, Ca' Rampani, where prostitutes used to live in the thirteenth century.) Old prostitute; old and bitchy woman. *Gino ha un bel coraggio a portarsi a letto quella vecchia carampana.* "Gino sleeps with that old bag; he has guts."

CARBÓNA, *f., N.* (Probably abbreviation of "carbonaia," charcoal kiln.) Small and dark dwelling. *La sua carbona gli serve solo per scopare.* "He uses his den only for screwing."

CARBURÀRE, *vi.* (Lit., to carburet.) To function well; to feel well. *Non so, stasera non carburo.* "I don't know, tonight I'm out of sorts."

CARBÙRO, *m.* (Lit., carbide.) **1.** Wine, alcoholic beverage. *Siamo tutti così mosci! Dai, facciamoci un po' di carburo.* "We're all so lifeless! Come on, let's have some booze." **2.** Money. *L'arterio si rifiuta di sganciare il carburo per far aggiustare la mia vecchia trappola.* "My old man refuses to fork out the money to repair my wreck."

CARCÀSSA, *f.* (Lit., carcass.) **1.** Human body in bad shape. *Gira per le strade trascinandosi dietro la sua vecchia carcassa.* "He wanders about dragging his tired bones." **2.** Wreck (said of a vehicle). *Questa non è una macchina, è una carcassa!* "This isn't a car; it's a wreck!"

CÀRDIO, *m., youth.* (Contraction of "cardiocircolatorio," cardiovascular.) Shock. *Se sputo quello che so vi viene un cardio.* "If I tell you what I know, you'll be shocked."

CARIÀTIDE, *f., youth.* (Lit., caryatid, a type of classical Greek statue used as a pillar in temples.) Deadweight (said of a person). *Anche stasera Giovanna si è portata dietro quella cariatide di sua cugina.* "Even tonight Giovanna showed up with her cousin in tow, a deadweight if there ever was one."

CARIÀTIDI, *m. pl., youth.* (Lit., caryatids.) Old people, grandparents, too old to understand anything. *Cosa vuoi che capiscano i tuoi? Sono delle cariatidi.* "What do you want your grandparents to understand? They're as good as dead."

CARICÀRE, *vt.* (Lit., to load.) **a)** *slang.* To pick up girls or boys. *"Allora, avete caricato in discoteca?" "Macché, è andata buca."* "'Well, did you pick up anyone at the disco?' 'Heck, no, we got nowhere.'" **b)** *youth.* To be overloaded with homework. *Il profio di mate ci ha caricato di roba per lunedì.* "The math teacher loaded us with homework for Monday."

CÀRLO IL CÀLVO/CÀRLO MARTÈLLO, *idiom, m., youth.* (Lit., Charles the Bald, Charles the Hammer (Charles Martel), two Frankish kings.) Penis. *Ho soprannominato il mio aggeggio "Carlo Martello," perché non ha mai perso una battaglia.* "I nicknamed my dick 'Charles the Hammer,' because it has never lost a battle."

CARÒTA, *f., youth.* (Lit., carrot.) Penis. *Ha una bella carota, dura dura.* "He's got a nice, hard stick."

CARRÈTTA, *f.* (Lit., two-wheeled cart.) Old vehicle (boat, car, etc.) which can barely move. *Non capisco perché sia così affezionato a quella vecchia carretta.* "I don't understand why he's so attached to that old wreck."

CARRIÒLA, *f.* (Lit., wheelbarrow.) *See* **carretta.**

CARRÒZZA, *f.* (Lit., coach.) Car. *Finalmente è riuscito a farsi la carrozza!* "Finally he managed to buy a car!"

CARROZZÀTA, *adj.* (From "carrozzare," to build the body.) **Ben carrozzata; carrozzata di lusso.** Woman endowed with noteworthy sexual attributes. *Gambe lunghe, ben carrozzata, con gli occhioni grandi grandi: la Loren spiccicata.* "Long legs, well endowed, big eyes: a Sophia Loren look-alike."

CARROZZERÌA, *f.* (Lit., car body.) Feminine sexual attributes (usually abundant). **1. Essere giù di carrozzeria.** Not too shapely a woman; unattractive woman. *La Lilli sarà anche intelligente, simpatica, ecc., ma è pro-*

prio giù di carrozzeria. "Lilli may be intelligent, nice, etc., but she isn't at all attractive." **2. Rifarsi la carrozzeria.** (Lit., to redo one's body, referred to a woman.) *È andata dal chirurgo plastico più caro di Roma a rifarsi la carrozzeria.* "She went to the most expensive plastic surgeon in Rome to have her body redone head to toe."

CARROZZÓNE, *m.* (Lit., caravan.) An inefficient and wasteful government office or administrative agency. *Giuro, il governo ha stanziato altri soldi per un carrozzone che si occupa degli orfani della Prima Guerra Mondiale!* "I swear, the government has set aside more funds for an agency that looks after World War I orphans."

CARRÙBA/CARÙBBA, *m. See* **caramba.**

CÀRTA, *f., youth.* (Lit., paper; card.) **Una carta.** A thousand lire. *Dieci carte è tutto quello che vuoi sganciare?* "Ten thousand lire is all you want to cough up?!"

CÀRTE, *f., pl.* (Lit., cards.) Documents; papers. *Ma le carte sono in ordine? Se no, niente prestito.* "Are your papers in order? Otherwise, no loan."

CARTÈLLA, *f., crim.* (Lit., briefcase.) Punch; blow. *Gli ho dato una cartella che gli ha fatto saltare due denti.* "I gave him a wham that knocked two teeth out of his mouth."

CARTELLÀRE, *vt.* (From > **cartella.**) To beat someone up. *Sta' attento a come parli, che quelli non ci pensano su due volte a cartellarti ben bene.* "Be careful what you say because they won't think twice about beating you up."

CÀRTOLA, *f., youth.* (Contraction of "cartolina," postcard.) **1.** Face. *Ha una cartola che non mi va.* "I don't like her face." **2.** Exuberant girl. *È una cartola simpatica, ma troppo vivace per i miei gusti.* "She's a nice girl, but way too lively for my taste."

CARTONÀRE, *vt., N., youth.* (From > **cartone, a.**) To beat someone up. *See* **cartellare.**

CARTÒNE, *m.* **a)** *youth.* Blow; punch. *See* **cartella. b)**

narc. Joint. *Dai, fammi dare una tirata al cartone.* "Come on, let me take a puff from your joint." **c)** *N., crim.* A high-denomination note. *Berto vuole cinque cartoni per quell'impianto CD rubato? Tanto vale comprarlo in negozio.* "Berto wants five hundred thousand lire for that stolen CD player? It's just as well to buy it in a store."

CASCÀRE, *vi., crim.* (Lit., to fall.) To get as a profit; to earn. *Cosa ci casca per noi se teniamo la bocca chiusa?* "What's in it for us if we clam up?"

CASÈRMA, *f., youth.* (Lit., barracks.) School. *Hanno suonato il campanello; devo rientrare in caserma.* "They rang the bell. I must go back to class."

CASINÀRO, *m./***CASINÌSTA,** *m./f., youth.* (From > **casino.**) Troublemaker. *Hai perso i soldi che dovevi versare sul conto di tua madre? Che casinista che sei!* "You lost the money you were supposed to deposit in your mother's account? What a screw-up you are!"

CASÌNO, *m.* (Lit., brothel.) **a)** *slang.* **1.** Mess; racket; fuss. *Quando la polizia ha cercato di caricarli sulla nave, i clandestini si sono messi a piantare casino.* "When the police tried to force them to board the ship, the clandestine refugees started to raise a big racket." **2.** Difficult situation; trouble. *Ti sei fatta arrestare alla manifestazione? Ma come fai a metterti sempre nei casini?* "You got arrested at the demonstration? How come you always get into trouble?" **b)** *youth.* **1.** *adv.* A lot. *O.K., concedo, la Barbara mi piace un casino.* "OK, I grant that much; I like Barbara a lot." **2.** *m.* Great quantity. *C'era un tale casino di gente al concerto rock che non siamo riusciti a sentire nulla.* "There were so many people at the rock concert that we couldn't hear anything."

CASTÀGNA, *f., youth.* (Lit., chestnut.) **1.** Vagina. *Ti lamenti sempre che lui della tua castagna non sa che farsene. Piantalo!* "You complain all the time he has no use for your peach. Leave him!" **2.** Violent punch. *Lo mise fuori gioco con una bella castagna sul naso.* "He knocked him out with a punch in the nose." **3.** Blunder;

mistake. **Prendere qualcuno in castagna.** To catch someone in the act. *La maestra l'ha presa in castagna mentre cercava di copiare.* "Her teacher caught her in the act while she was trying to cheat."

CASTAGNÀRE, *vt.* (From > **castagna.**) **a)** *crim.* To beat someone up violently. *Si misero in quatto contro uno e lo castagnarono a dovere.* "The four of them joined forces and let him have it." **b)** *slang.* To defeat another team decisively. *Abbiamo castagnato il Milan per la terza volta di fila.* "We plastered the Milan soccer team for the third time in a row." **c)** *youth.* To be caught unprepared when called on in class. *Quello di fisica l'ha castagnata.* "The physics teacher called on her in class and she got clobbered."

CASTÀGNE, *f. pl.* (Lit., chestnuts.) Testicles. *Ehi, sta' attenta! Mi stai pestando le castagne!* "Watch out! You're squashing my nuts!"

CASTAÑETAS, Spanish, *f. pl.* (Lit., castanets.) *See* **castagne.**

CASTÈLLO, *m.* (Lit., castle.) **a)** *slang.* Vagina. *Dici che stasera ce la fa a entrare nel castello?* "Do you think that tonight he'll be admitted into the castle?" **b)** *crim.* Jail; prison. *Lascia perdere, lo sai che da questo castello non si riesce a uscire.* "Come on, you know it's impossible to get out of this icebox."

CATERPILLAR, *Eng., m., youth.* (Perhaps from the company Caterpillar, which makes bulldozers and other heavy machinery.) Strong, aggressive, irresistible person. *Inutile cercare di fermare Massimo: è un caterpillar.* "Don't even think of stopping Massimo: he's a powerhouse."

CATÒIA/CATÒIO, *f., m., S., crim.* (From the Greek "katógeion," underground room or passageway.) Jail; prison. *Sante? È di nuovo in catoia.* "Sante? He's in the slammer again."

CATÒRCIO, *m.* **1.** A car in very bad condition but still working. *M'hanno venduto un bel catorcio!* "What a lemon they sold me!" **2.** *rude.* Ugly and graceless girl. *Esce con quel catorcio?* "He's going out with that horse?"

CAVALCÀRE. (Lit., to ride a horse.) **a)** *vt., slang, rude.* To possess sexually. *Pensi che lei si lascerebbe cavalcare?* "Do you think she'd let me ride her?" **b)** *vi., narc.* To be under the influence of heroin. *Non sprecare il fiato, sta cavalcando.* "Don't waste your breath; she's floating."

CAVÀLLO, *m.* (Lit., horse.) **a)** *youth.* Motorcycle. *Lo si vedeva arrivare da lontano, in sella a un immenso cavallo nero.* "You could see him from afar, riding a huge black motorcycle." **b)** *slang, rude.* Penis. **Mettere il cavallo nella stalla.** (Lit., to put the horse in the stable.) To possess sexually. *"Vuoi mettere il cavallo nella stalla?" Gli domandò ammiccando.* "'Would you like to horse around with me?,' she asked him invitingly." **c)** *crim.* **1.** Accomplice. **Cavallo da corsa.** (Lit., racehorse.) Good and fast accomplice. *Se vuoi fare il colpo alla gioielleria, chiedi aiuto a Max, che è un cavallo da corsa.* "If you want to rob the jewelry store, ask Max for help, he's first class." **2.** Gun. *Non vorrete mica svaligiare la banca senza cavalli?* "You don't want to rob the bank without guns, do you?" **d)** *narc.* **1.** Heroin. **Essere a cavallo.** (Lit., to be on horseback.) To be under the influence of heroin. *Era a cavallo da tre giorni e pareva che non ne sarebbe sceso mai più.* "He was high for three days and it looked like he would never come down again." **2.** A narcotics peddler or distributor. *Chiedi al cavallo, magari ha un po' d'erba da darti.* "Ask the pusher, maybe he's got some grass for you."

CAVATÌNA, *f., youth.* (From "cavare," to pull out.) Quick and unplanned sexual act. *Nell'intervallo, Alberto e Lilla si sono fatti una cavatina nel cesso dei maschi.* "During recess Alberto and Lilla squeezed in a quickie in the boy's washroom."

CAVÈRNA, *f.* (Lit., cave.) **a)** *slang.* **1.** Mouth. *Con una* *caverna così, si mangia anche un bue intero.* "With a mouth like that he could swallow an ox whole." **2.** *rude.* Vagina. *Alla fine gli bastò sborsare due soldi per avere accesso alla sua caverna.* "In the end, a little money was all he had to fork out to get access to her cunt." **3.** *rude.* Buttocks. *Avrebbe voluto esplorare la sua caverna, ma lei non ne volle sapere.* "He would have liked to explore her ass, but she refused vehemently." **b)** *youth.* Dwelling; place. *Andiamo nella tua caverna?* "Shall we go to your hovel?"

CAVOLÀTA, *f.* Euphemism for > **cazzata.**

CÀVOLO, *m.* Euphemism for > **cazzo.**

CÀXO, *m., youth.* Euphemism for > **cazzo.**

CAZZÀRO, *m., C., rude.* (From > **cazzo.**) **a)** *slang.* Busybody. *Piantala di ficcare il naso dappertutto: non vorrai farti la fama del cazzaro.* "Stop nosing around; you don't want to get a reputation as a busybody." **b)** *crim.* A person who acts as lookout on behalf of his/her accomplices. *Di professione? Fa il cazzaro, ma la pula non l'ha mai beccato.* "His profession? He's a lookout, but the police have never caught him."

CAZZÀTA, *f., rude.* (From > **cazzo.**) **1.** Nonsense. *Ma non dire sempre cazzate!* "Don't give your usual bullshit!" **2.** Stupid act. *Ho perso tutta la liquidazione alle corse. Mi sono fatto la cazzata più grossa della mia vita.* "I lost all my severance pay at the racetrack. I really fucked up." **3.** Badly done thing; rubbish. Said of books, films, shows, etc. *Ma perché non uscite con noi, invece di stare a vedere quella cazzata alla tele?* "Why don't you come out with us, instead of watching that crap on TV?" **4.** Easy thing to do (also in the diminutive, **cazziatella**). *Salire al rifugio è una cazzata, non ascoltare quel fifone di Paolo.* "Climbing to the shelter is a breeze. Don't listen to Paolo; he's a coward."

CAZZEGGIÀRE, vi., youth, rude. (From > **cazzo.**) To waste time saying or doing silly things. *Abbiamo passato la serata facendo a gara a chi cazzeggiava meglio.* "We spent the evening competing for first prize in bullshitting."

CAZZÉGGIO, *m., youth, rude.* (From > **cazzo.**) Spending one's time saying and doing silly things. *L'estate passò, in un modo o nell'altro, di cazzeggio in cazzeggio.* "The summer went by, one way or another, as we wasted our time with nonsense."

CÀZZI, *m. pl., rude.* (From > **cazzo.**) **1.** Business, affairs. *Fatti i cazzi tuoi!* "Mind your own business!" **2. Cazzi acidi/amari.** (Lit., sour/bitter pricks.) Serious problems; big trouble. *Hanno ipotecato la casa per tre volte il suo valore. Adesso sì che sono cazzi acidi.* "They mortgaged their house for three times its market value. Now they're in deep shit."

CÀZZO, *m., rude.* (Probably variant of "cazza," ladle, from the late Latin "cattiam" or "captiam," possibly from "capere," to pick up.) **1.** Penis. (Used in several idiomatic phrases.) **Gloriare il cazzo.** (Lit., to glorify one's penis.) To possess sexually. *Non ha ancora gloriato il cazzo a vent'anni. Non lo vedo bene.* "Twenty years old and he hasn't dunked his prick yet. Something's wrong." **Levarsi/Togliersi dal cazzo.** (Lit., to get off someone's prick.) To go away; to free someone of one's presence. *Togliti dal cazzo e lasciami lavorare!* "Fuck off and let me do my work!" **Mangiarsi il cazzo**. (To eat one's own prick.) To kick oneself. *Ho prestato dei soldi a quel farabutto di Umberto! Mi mangerei il cazzo.* "I lent money to that jerk Umberto! I'd like to kick myself." **Rompere il cazzo.** (Lit., to break someone's prick.) To be extremely annoying. *Con tutte le tue lamentele mi hai proprio rotto il cazzo.* "I've had it with you and your whining!" **Scendere dal cazzo (e andare a piedi).** (Lit., to get off one's prick [and walk].) To cool it. *Gli ho detto di scendere dal cazzo, che non era mica l'unico ad essere rimasto fregato.* "I told him it was time to cool it. He wasn't the only one who got screwed." **Stare sul cazzo a qualcuno.** (Lit., to stand on someone's prick.) To be extremely displeasing to someone. *A me la Giovanna sta sul cazzo in maniera atroce.* "A pain in the ass, that's what I think Giovanna is." **2.** Nothing. *Non me ne importa un cazzo.* "I don't give a fuck." *Questo battitappeto non serve a un cazzo.* "You can't do shit with this vacuum cleaner." **3.** In various derogatory and sarcastic expressions. **Alla cazzo di cane.** Any which way; no matter how. *Ma fai sempre le cose così? Alla cazzo di cane?* "Do you always do things this way, using your prick instead of your brain?" *Col cazzo!* "My ass!/Your ass!" **Del cazzo.** Stupid, senseless. *È un'idea del cazzo.* "It's a fucked-up idea." **Grazie al cazzo!** "How smart of you!" **Testa di cazzo.** Dickhead. *Il tuo amico è una bella testa di cazzo.* "Your friend is a true dickhead." **4.** Used as an intensifier. *Vado dove cazzo mi pare.* "I'll go wherever the hell I want." **5.** As an interjection. *Cazzo, che bella figa!* "Shit, what a piece of ass!" *Frena, cazzo! C'è un TIR!* "For Christ's sake, stop! That's an eighteen-wheeler!"

CAZZÓNE, *m., rude.* (From > **cazzo.**) Shithead. *Se le scopa e poi va in giro a vantarsene: un vero cazzone.* "He fucks them and then goes around bragging about it. A real shithead."

CAZZÒSO, *adj., youth, rude.* (From > **cazzo.**) Difficult; annoying. *Il giorno prima di partire per le vacanze, la mia macchina si è rotta. Che problema cazzoso!* "My car broke down the day before I left on vacation. What a pain!"

CAZZÙTO, *adj., rude.* (From > **cazzo.**) **a)** *slang.* Cunning; with it. *Non c'è che dire, Luigi è uno cazzuto. Ha venduto la sua vecchia carriola per il doppio del valore di mercato.* "Undeniably Luigi is a fox. He sold his old wreck for twice the market price." **b)** *youth.* **1.** See **cazzoso. 2.** Endowed with remarkable sexual organs (of a man.) *Mi sono stufata di Piero, non è abbastanza cazzuto per me.* "I got fed up with Piero; poorly endowed, you know what I mean?"

CÉCIO, *m., C., crim.* (Lit., bean.) Big diamond. *Non si stancava mai di ammirare il cecio, che mandava sprazzi di luce in tutte le direzioni.* "She never tired of looking at her big stone, which beamed rays of light in all directions."

CÈFALO, *m., rude.* (Lit., gray mullet.) **a)** *slang.* **1.** Penis. *Era alla ricerca di un cefalo vispo, grande o piccolo non importava.* "She was looking for a lively fish; big or small, it didn't matter." **2.** Stupid person. *Di cefali è pieno il mondo; di aquile ce ne sono ben poche.* "The world is full of fools; geniuses are few and far between." **b)** *youth.* Ugly and uninteresting person. *In montagna ci vanno solo i cefali; i belli vanno al mare.* "In the mountains you find only eyesores; the ones who knock your eyes out go to the beach."

CELERÌNO/CELERÒTTO, *m.* (From "celere," rapid, attribute of the emergency squad of the police.) Ironic for policeman. *Non ti preoccupare, che quel celerino lì non beccherà mai nessuno.* "Don't worry, that beagle will never catch anyone."

CEMENTÀTO, *adj., youth.* (Lit., cemented.) **Restare cementato.** (Lit., to get cemented.) To be stuck in a place or an activity; to do nothing new or interesting. *Restate sempre lì cementati. Ma perché non andate almeno a giocare a calcio?* "You're stuck there. Why don't you go play soccer, at least?"

CÉNERE, *f., S., narc.* (Lit., ash.) Narcotics in powder form. *Che cazzo fai? Quella cenere m'è costata un occhio della testa.* "What the fuck are you doing? That dust cost me an arm and a leg."

CENTÓNE, *m., N.* (From "cento," one hundred.) One-hundred-thousand-lire banknote. *Tira sempre fuori qualche centone dalle tasche. Un giorno di questi lo borseggiano.* "He's always fishing big bills out of his pockets. One of these days he'll get mugged."

CERÌNO, *m, C./S., crim.* Knife. *Ehi, guagliò, metti via quel cerino!* "Hey, wise guy, stash that knife!"

CÈRO, *m.* (Lit., tall candle.) Penis. *Dai, spegnimi 'sto cero.* "Come on, play with my thing."

CERÓNE, *m., youth.* (Lit., grease paint.) Excessive make-up applied on one's face. *Chissà che faccia ha, sotto tutto* *quel cerone.* "Who knows what her face looks like under all that make-up."

CESELLATÓRE, *m., N.* (Lit., engraver.) **Cesellatore della zolla/di zolle.** (Lit., clodhopper.) Tacky person. *Si è messo due cherubini dorati sopra il letto: degno di un vero cesellatore di zolle.* "He decorated his headboard with two golden cherubs; that's what I call tacky."

CESPÙGLIO, *m., youth.* (Lit., bush.) **1.** Hair. *Ah, sei tu. E chi ti riconosceva dietro quel cespuglio?* "Oh, it's you. Who could guess, under that mop?" **2.** Pubic hair. *Lei è il tipo che si depila pure il cespuglio.* "She's the type who shaves her bush too."

CÈSSO, *m., youth, rude.* (Lit., restroom; toilet.) Ugly thing or person (mostly female.) *Sua sorella è proprio un cesso!* "Her sister is a blot on the landscape."

CÉSTO, *m., youth.* (Lit., basket.) **Fare cesto.** (Lit., to score a basket; to dunk.) To possess sexually. *Ha fatto cesto dieci volte ieri sera, dice lui.* "Last night he scored ten times, so he says."

CHARLIE BROWN, *Eng., m.* (Name of Charles Schultz's Peanuts character, used to mean heroin.) Heroin. *Hai del charlie brown per la festa? Se no, non mi lumi.* "Will you have any stuff at the party? Otherwise, I won't show up."

CHÉCCA, *f., rude.* (Probably a diminutive of "Francesca," Frances.) Passive male homosexual, whose attitude and manners are very feminine. Queer. *Era la checca ufficiale del paese; persino il prevosto lo salutava con affetto.* "He was the village's official queer; even the priest greeted him with affection."

CHIÀPPE, *f., pl., rude.* (Lit., buttocks.) **1. Alzare le chiappe.** (Lit., to lift one's buttocks.) To stand up; to move on. *Alzate le chiappe, ragazzi, che se no morite incollati qui.* "Move your asses, boys, otherwise you'll die right where you are." **2. Stringere le chiappe a qualcuno.** (Lit., for someone to have one's buttocks squeezed.) *Vedendoli schierati ad aspettarlo, gli si strinsero le chiappe.* "The sight of them lined up waiting for him scared his pants off."

CHIAVÀRE, *rude.* (From late Latin "clavare," to nail.) **1.** *vi.* To have sexual intercourse. *Non fanno nient'altro che chiavare, come i conigli.* "They do nothing but fuck like rabbits." **2.** *vt.* To possess sexually. *Era tanto che aveva voglia di chiavarla. Stasera forse era la volta buona.* "He had wanted to fuck her for a long time. Perhaps tonight would be his lucky night." **3.** *vt.* To swindle. *Non m'hanno preso in giro, m'han chiavato a dovere!* "They didn't pull my leg, they screwed me just right."

CHIAVÀTA, *f., rude.* (From > **chiavare.**) **1.** Sexual act. *Una bella chiavata prima di cena non farebbe mica male, eh?* "A nice fuck before dinner would do us good, don't you think?" **2.** Swindle. *Ti stupisci che t'abbia rifilato un centone falso? Mastro di chiavate lo chiamano.* "You can't believe he palmed off a phony hundred-thousand-lire note on you? 'Cocksmith' is what they call him."

CHIAVATÓRE, *m., rude.* (From > **chiavare, 1.**) Boy or man of outstanding sexual powers and endeavors. *Per me, se lei si trova un bel chiavatore si calma un po'.* "If she can find a good stud, she'll calm down."

CHIÀVICA, *f., S., rude.* (Lit., sewer.) **1.** Prostitute. *Samanta te la dà anche per poco, ma resta 'na chiavica.* "Samanta will give it to you for next to nothing, but she's still a whore." **2.** Disgusting person. *Si lava una volta al mese e ha l'alito che puzza. Che chiavica!* "He takes a shower once a month and his breath stinks. What a disgusting person!"

CHIAVÓNE, *m., rude, youth.* (From > **chiavare, 1.**) A boy who is very successful with girls. *C'è chi ha tutte le fortune! Lui sembra nato per fare il chiavone.* "Some people are born under a lucky star! He was born to be a great screwer."

CHIÈSA, *f., N., crim.* (Lit., church.) Tavern. *Da bravi cristiani, santificano il giorno del Signore andando in* *chiesa.* "Being good Christians, they celebrate the Lord's day by going to the bar."

CHÌLO, *m., N., crim.* (Lit., kilogram.) One-thousand-lire banknote. *Vuole solo cento chili per quella borsa di coccodrillo? Per me è rubata.* "He's only charging a hundred thousand lire for that crocodile bag? It must be stolen."

CHIODÀTA, *f., youth.* (Lit., nailing.) **Darsi una chiodata.** (Lit., to give oneself a nailing.) To let something be; to give up. *E datti una chiodata! Non sarai l'unico ad essere stato piantato dalla ganza.* "Get real! You're not, and will never be, the only one dumped by his girlfriend."

CHIÒDI, *m. pl.* (From > **chiodo.**) Debts. **Piantar chiodi.** (Lit., to drive nails.) To acquire debts. *Di chiodi ne ha piantati tanti nella sua variegata carriera di uomo d'affari!* "During his checkered career as a businessman, he racked up quite a few debts."

CHIÒDO, *m.* (Lit., nail.) **a)** *crim.* Knife. *L'unico gingillo che si portava dietro era una bel chiodo.* "The only weapon he carried was a big knife." **b)** *slang.* **1.** *rude,* Penis. **Piantare il chiodo.** (Lit., to drive a nail.) To have sexual intercourse; to stick it up someone's ass. *A lui interessa solo piantare il chiodo, non importa dove.* "All he cares about is sticking it into something, no matter what." **2.** Obsession. **Avere un chiodo nel cervello.** To have a bee in one's bonnet. *Ha avuto un solo chiodo nel cervello fin da bambino: diventare fantino.* "He's had a bee in his bonnet since he was a child: to become a jockey." **Battere il chiodo.** (Lit., to strike the nail.) To be very insistent. *Batti e ribatti il chiodo, Guglielmo ha fatto riaprire l'inchiesta.* "By not taking no for an answer, Guglielmo got the inquiry reopened." **3.** Business. **Non battere chiodo.** (Lit., to strike no nails.) Not to get any business. *Ha bussato a molte porte con la sua idea di aprire una Disneyland casereccia, ma non ha battuto chiodo.* "He knocked on many doors in the attempt to open a local Disneyland, but he got nowhere." **c)** *youth.* **1.** Wreck (said of a car or motorcycle). *Ha poca lira, si* *accontenta di un vecchio chiodo.* "He doesn't have much money. He'll make do with an old wreck." **2.** A person who is a pain in the neck. *Che chiodo Lalla! Quasi una crocifissione.* "Lalla is such a pain! Almost a crucifixion."

CHÌSSENE!, *interj.* (Lit., who gives [a damn]!) *See* **fregarsene.**

CHITÀRRA/CHITARRÌNA, *f.* (Lit., guitar.) Vagina. **Suonare la chitarrina.** (Lit., to play the guitar.) To have sexual intercourse. *Facevano dei bei duetti tutte le sere, suonando la chitarrina.* "They played nice duets in bed every night, playing the guitar."

CIABÀTTA, *f., N.* (Lit., slipper.) **a)** *slang.* **1.** Mouth. *Dalla sua vecchia e sdentata ciabatta uscivano solo insulti.* "Out of his old and toothless mouth came only insults." **2.** *rude.* Prostitute. *È una vecchia ciabatta, che ogni tanto s'intenerisce e la dà via gratis.* "She's an old slut. If she feels sorry for you, she'll give it to you for free." **b)** *C., crim.* High-denomination banknote. *Ciabatte in quantità ci vogliono per quel cecio, non qualche chilo!* "You need lots of big notes for that stone, not just a few tens."

CIAMPÒRGNA, *f., rude.* (From northern term for "zampogna," pipes.) **1.** Prostitute. *See* **ciabatta. 2.** Gossip. *Sss, abbassa la voce, che c'è quella ciamporgna a portata d'orecchio!* "Sh, lower your voice, that old gossip can hear you."

CIÀPA-CIÀPA, *m., N.* (From "ciapé," to catch.) **1.** Trinket; useless gadget. *S'è fatta convincere a comprare un dosatore di dentifricio elettrico: bel ciapa-ciapa!* "They sold her an electric toothpaste dispenser: what a useless gadget!" **2.** Policeman. *Ehi, sta' in guardia, i ciapa-ciapa sono scesi sul sentiero di guerra.* "Be on the lookout, the cops are on the warpath."

CIAPPÌNO, *m., N.* Chore. *Saranno anche tutti ciappini da niente, ma alla fine della giornata sono distrutta.* "They may all be mindless chores, but at the end of the day I'm beat."

CIBÀRE, *vt., N., youth.* (Lit., to feed.) To steal. *"Allora, hai* *cibato la macchina?"* *"No, c'era troppa pula in giro."* "'So, did you steal that car?' 'No, too many cops around.'"

CIBÌ CIÈRRE, *idiom, youth.* (Acronym of "C.B.C.R.," "Cresci Bene Che Ripasso." If you still look like that when you've grown up, I'll stop by.) (Said by a boy to a girl.) *"Dai, portami in moto con te!"* *"Non quest'anno: cibì cierre."* "'Come on, give me a ride on your motorcycle!' 'Next year, maybe; you do show promise.'"

CÌCCA, *f.* **1.** (From the French "chique," cigarette butt.) Cigarette. *La sua faccia spariva dietro al fumo della cicca che gli pendeva da un angolo della bocca.* "His face disappeared behind the smoke of the cigarette that hung from the corner of his mouth." **2.** (Probably from the brand Chiclets, in northern Italian variant "cicles.") Chewing gum. *Cicche, scarpe da tennis e rock and roll: i mitici anni cinquanta.* "Gum, tennis shoes, and rock-and-roll: the mythical 1950s."

CICCÀRE, *vt.* (From > **cicca, 1.**) **a)** *youth.* **1.** To smoke. *La filona è così rimba che riescono a ciccare in classe.* "Their philosophy teacher is so out of it that they can smoke in class." **2.** To give someone a blow job. *Lei ti ciccherebbe anche, ma vuole qualcosa in cambio.* "She'd consider giving you a blow job, if you pay her back." **3.** To fail. *Ma come si fa a ciccare l'esame di ginnastica?!* "How can you flunk a gym test?" **b)** *narc.* To smoke dope. *Io con te non cicco più: a momenti ci restavo.* "I won't smoke with you ever again. I came this close to croaking."

CICCÀTO, *adj., narc.* (From > **ciccare, b.**) Stoned. *Non so se sia per l'alcol o l'hashish, ma Danilo è ciccato due giorni sì e uno no.* "Who knows whether it's alcohol or hashish, but Danilo is conked out every other day."

CICCHÈTTO, *m., N.* (From the French "chiquet," bit.) **1.** Shot of liquor. *Cominciano alle sette di mattina col primo cicchetto.* "They start with their first shot at seven in the morning." **2.** (From the military jargon.) Reproach from one's boss. *Il suo capo l'ha beccata che telefonava al suo bello: le ha fatto un cicchetto!* "Her boss caught her cooing on the phone with her beau. He almost fired her!"

CIÈCO, *m., youth.* (Lit., blind.) Shortsighted person. *Guarda che se guida il cieco vi schiantate.* "I'm warning you. If that blind bat is at the wheel, you'll get creamed."

CIELLÌNO, *m., youth.* (Member of the Catholic group "Comunione e Liberazione," Communion and Liberation.) Slow; stupid. *Un ciellino così non l'avevo mai visto: ha scambiato il suo piumino per una camicia di jeans.* "Never seen a dope like that; he traded in his down jacket for a jeans shirt."

CIÈLO, *m.* (Lit., sky.) **a)** *crim.* Ceiling; roof. *Sono entrati nell'attico dal cielo.* "They broke into the penthouse from the roof." **b)** *narc.* Effect caused by narcotics. *Sono volati in cielo due ore fa, beati loro.* "They zoned out two hours ago, lucky them."

CIENNETÌ, *adj., youth.* (Acronym of "C.N.T.," "Centrale di Nervi in Tensione," nervous system plant at high voltage.) Extremely nervous; hyper. *O.K., non dico più una parola. Stasera sei veramente ciennetì.* "Fine, I'll keep my mouth shut. Tonight you're a nervous wreck."

CÌFRA. (Lit., figure, digit.) **a)** *f., slang.* A big amount of money. *Per andare in vacanza alle Seychelles devi sganciare una cifra.* "You'll need a lot of dough to go to the Seychelles for vacation." **b)** *adv., youth.* **Una cifra/Una cifra al periodico.** (Lit., a number to the nth power.) A lot. *Se non scassa una cifra, non è contento.* "If he doesn't bug you to the nth degree, he isn't happy."

CÌMA, *f., youth.* (Lit., peak.) Person of outstanding intelligence and ability. *Grande scopatore e una cima: ovviamente è imbattibile.* "Great stud and a genius: clearly unbeatable."

CINGHIÀLE, *m., youth.* (Lit., boar.) **1.** Very strong person. *Quella disco sarà anche il massimo, ma io non ci vado senza il cinghiale.* "That disco may well be the best, but

I'm not going without our friend the hulk." **2.** A person who lives on the outskirts of town, in the backwoods, and who is therefore uncouth, uncivilized, and provincial. *L'ultimo grillo di Barbarella è di scopazzare con un cinghiale.* "Barbarella's latest passing fancy is to get it on with a backwoods boar."

CÌNGHIOS, *m. pl., youth, rude.* (Pseudo Hispanism, variant of > **cinghiale.**) **Los cinghios**. Among the well-off, up-to-date Milan teenagers, Italians from the south, who are considered uncivilized and uncouth. *Los cinghios si assomigliano tutti: tarchiatelli, scuri e pronti allo scontro fisico.* "'Los cinghios' look all the same: stout, dark, and always ready for a fight."

CINQUEFÉTTE/CINQUEPIÒTTE, *f., youth.* (Composed of "cinque," five, and "fette/piotte," feet.) The "FIAT Cinquecento" car. *Tu non ci crederai, ma abbiamo anche caricato sei persone nella mia vecchia cinquefette!* "You won't believe it, but we even squeezed five people in my old 'five-footer!'"

CINQUÓNE, *m., C.* (From "cinque," five.) Five-thousand-lire note. *Due cinquoni al chilo la lattuga? Ma siamo matti?* "Ten thousand lire a kilo for lettuce? Have they lost their minds?"

CIOCCÀRE, *N.* (Probably from "ciocca," log.) **a)** *vi., slang.* To argue; to have a loud row. *Cioccano in continuazione: poi lui esce sbattendo la porta e lei ulula tutta la notte.* "They bicker all the time; then he walks out slamming the door, and she cries all night." **b)** *vt., youth.* To beat up someone. *"Che t'è successo?" "M'hanno cioccata quando han trovato solo diecimila lire nel portafoglio."* "'What's wrong with you?' 'They thrashed me when they found only twenty thousand lire in my wallet.'"

CIOCCÀTA, *f.* (From > **cioccare, a.**) **1.** Racket. *Dopo l'ultima cioccata tra noi è finita.* "After the last row, it's over between us." **2.** Reproach. *Ma chi si crede di essere quello lì che mi fa sempre delle cioccate?* "Who the hell does he think he is that he's always reproaching me?"

CIÒCCO, *m.* (Lit., log.) **a)** *slang.* Penis. *È un armadio: non poteva che avere un bel ciocco.* "Being such a big dude, he had to have a big stick too." **b)** *youth.* **1.** Hit; crash. *Abbiamo sentito un ciocco fortissimo e ci siamo ritrovati nel fosso.* "We heard a loud crash and found ourselves in the ditch." **2. Di ciocco.** Suddenly. *Te la squagli così di ciocco?* "Are you sneaking away just like that?" **c)** *narc.* The moment the effect of a narcotic hits. *Ah, quando viene il ciocco, che sballo!* "When the blast comes, what a kick!"

CIÒSPO, *adj., N.* (From a dialect term meaning "old, in bad shape.") **1.** *rude.* Ugly (especially referred to women). *Si capisce che sono tutte disponibili, sono tutte ciospe!* "Of course they're all available, they're all eyesores." **2.** Old womanizer (or someone pretending to be one). *Il ciospo l'aveva seguita fin sotto casa, ma non sembrava pericoloso.* "The old philanderer had followed her home, but he didn't seem dangerous."

CIP, *m., youth.* **1.** (Italianization of English "chip," as in poker chip.) Money. *Niente cip, niente roba.* "No money, no dope." **2.** (Italianization of English "cheap," inexpensive.) Cheap. *Ai saldi mi sono cuccata delle scarpe cip che sono uno schianto.* "I found some great shoes on sale that were really cheap."

CÌPRIA, *f., narc.* (Lit., powder.) Cocaine. *Sono tipi sofisticati, non restano mai senza cipria.* "They're sophisticated types, never out of dust."

CIQUÌTA, *f., youth.* (From the brand name of a banana producer.) Penis. *È nervosetta, io le prescriverei una cura di ciquita.* "She's hyper. I would prescribe banana therapy for her."

CÌRO, *m., youth.* (First name of a nineteenth-century patriot, Ciro Menotti, whose last name reminds one of the verbal form "menarla," to annoy, to bore.) **1.** A pain in the neck. *Cazzo, non fare il ciro!* "Shit, don't be a pain!" **2.** One whose behavior and attire are outdated and unrefined. *Al giorno d'oggi il capello lungo lo portano solo i ciri.* "Nowadays long hair is only for old-timers."

CISSÀRE, *vt., N., youth.* **1.** To incite, to provoke. *Se hon la pianti di cissarmi ti riduco in polpette!* "If you don't stop psyching me out I'll make hamburger meat out of you!" **2.** To excite, to titillate. *Ti cissa la sbarbina, eh?* "That twist turns you on, doesn't she?"

CISSÀRSI, *vr., N., youth.* To get a swelled head. *Si è cissata solo perché lui l'ha slumata in disco.* "She thinks she's Marilyn Monroe because he glanced at her in the disco."

CÌSTE, *f., youth, rude.* (Lit., cyst.) Ugly girl. *Sarà anche una ciste, ma al buio non te ne accorgi.* "She may be a scarecrow, but who sees that in the dark?"

CITRÀTO, *m.* (Lit., citrate, which, dissolved in water, produces a frothy effervescence.) **a)** *youth.* Slow, inadequate. **Andare a citrato.** (Lit., to run on citrate.) To be slow on the take, as if functioning with poor fuel. *Vai a citrato stamattina? Ti sto passando il compito di mate!* "Are you slow on the take this morning? I'm passing you the answers to the math test." **b)** *narc.* Cocaine; drug in general. *È ridotta a un vegetale: non va neanche più a citrato.* "She's a vegetable. Even doped she can't function any longer."

CIÙCCA, *f., N.* Drunkenness. *Si prese una bella ciucca e cercò di dimenticarsi di lei.* "He got drunk as a lord and tried to forget her."

CIUCCIÀRE. a) *vt., slang.* **1.** To suck. *Ciuccia il latte, cocco di mamma, che ti fa crescere alto e robusto.* "Drink your milk, honey, so you'll become a big boy." **2.** To gulp down. *Ciucciano whisky come se fosse acqua.* "They soak up whisky as if it were water." **3.** *rude.* To give a blow job. *Per ciucciare, ciuccia, ma si vede che non le piace.* "She sucks it, if you ask her, but she doesn't enjoy it at all." **b)** *youth.* **1.** *vi.* To kiss. *Se ciucciate ancora un po' restate incollati.* "If you smooch any longer you'll get stuck." **2.** *vt.* To steal. *Si è fatto ciucciare lo zaino.* "He managed to get his backpack stolen."

CIÙCCO, *adj., N.* **1.** Drunk (said of a person.) *Lascialo perdere, non vedi che è ciucco perso?* "Leave him alone, can't you see he's dead drunk?" **2.** Malfunctioning (of a machine/car.) *È tre settimane che la macchina è ciucca, ma stamattina non parte proprio.* "The car has been out of kilter for three weeks, but this morning it's dead."

CIUF-CIUF, *m.* **a)** *children.* Train. *"Allora, bambini, cos'è che fa ciuf-ciuf?" "Il treno!"* "'Kids, tell me, what makes choo-choo?' 'The train!!!!'" **b)** *slang.* Sexual intercourse. *Attraverso la sottile parete della camera d'albergo ascoltò il loro ciuf-ciuf per tutta la notte.* "He could hear their lovemaking all night through the thin wall of the hotel room."

CIUFÈCA/CIUFÈGA, *f., S.* **1.** Repulsive liquid or drink. *Non vorrai offrire questa ciufega perché è fatta in casa?!* "Don't tell me you're going to serve this concoction because it's homemade?!" **2.** *rude.* Ugly old woman. *A lui piacciono le ciufeghe, che ti devo dire?* "He likes old bags, what can I tell you?"

CIUFFÀRE, *vt., N., youth.* (Variation of "acciuffare," to grab.) **1.** To catch. *Il direttore del supermercato m'ha ciuffato con il CD che avevo intascato.* "The supermarket manager caught me with the stolen CD in my pocket." **2.** To steal. *Se si accorgono che abbiamo ciuffato i soldi dalla cassa finiamo in collegio!* "If they realize we pocketed the till money we'll end up in the slammer."

CIÙLA, *f., N., rude.* **1.** Penis. *È tonto, ma sa menare la ciula.* "He's dumb, but he knows how to use his dick." **2.** Dumb-ass. *Sei una ciula a credere che lui ti darà una mano.* "You're an idiot if you believe he'll help you out."

CIULÀRE/CIULLÀRE, *N.* (From > **ciula,** 1.) **a)** *slang, rude.* **1.** *vt.* To have sexual intercourse. *Ehi, bellona, vuoi ciulare?* "Hey, baby, wanna fuck?" **2.** *vt.* To steal. *Gli ho ciulato il portafoglio mentre dormiva.* "I stole his wallet while he was sleeping." **3. Ciulare nel manico.** *See* **manico. b)** *youth.* To hold someone back at the end of the school-year (unfairly.) *M'ha ciulato solo perché ho sballato l'ultimo compito in classe!* "She's holding me back a year only because I flunked the last in-class test!"

CIULÀTA, *f., N., rude.* (From > **ciula, 1.**) **1.** Sexual intercourse. *Una bella ciulata ti fa stare di buon umore per una settimana.* "A nice fuck puts you in a good mood for a week." **2.** Swindle. *Ce l'ha scritto in faccia che è il tipo da prendersi solo delle ciulate.* "He has it written all over his face: he's a candidate for getting screwed."

CLOÀCA, *f., rude.* (Lit., sewer.) **1.** Person of excessive and disgusting appetite. *Se inviti Pietro devi farne il doppio. Lo sai che è una cloaca.* "If you invite Pietro, make double helpings. You know he's a bottomless pit." **2.** Corrupt and evil person. *Vuoi fotterla con la forza? Io non t'aiuto. Va' da Tonio, che è una cloaca.* "You want to take her by force? Don't ask me for help. Ask Tonio, he's a scumbag."

COÀTTO, *m., youth.* (Lit., forced.) Youth who follows the dictates of fashion with no discrimination, and who's therefore unrefined and tacky. *Seguire la moda ve bene, ma fare il coatto no, eh!* "To follow fashion is okay, but to be a slave to it, no."

CÒBRA, *m., youth.* (Lit., cobra.) Great womanizer. *Stasera abbiamo chiuso: è in arrivo Max il cobra.* "Our chances are zero tonight. Here comes Max, the great stud."

CÒCA, *f.* **a)** *youth.* Abbreviation of Coca-cola. *Ci allunghiamo una bella coca ghiacciata?* "How about an ice-cold Coke?" **b)** *narc.* Abbreviation of "cocaine." *Carlo tornava da tutti i suoi viaggi d'affari in Bolivia con della coca di prima.* "Carlo returned from all his trips to Bolivia with top-level coke."

CÒCCO/COCCOLÓNE, *m.* Sudden need to sleep; falling asleep unexpectedly. *È andata a sbattere contro un albero perché le è preso un coccolone.* "She crashed against a tree because she suddenly conked out."

COCKTAIL, *Eng., m., narc.* Cigarette made of tobacco and marijuana. *Si fa un bel cocktail ogni sera, per quello è così rilassata.* "Every night she rolls herself a nice cocktail; that's why she's so relaxed."

COCÓMERO, *m.* (Lit., watermelon.) **a)** *slang.* Head. *Ma che ci sta dentro quel tuo cocomero? Segatura?* "What do you have inside that noggin? Sawdust?" **b)** *youth.* Stupid person. *Albertone è un cocomero, ma torna utile quando si devono menare le mani.* "Albertone is really slow, but he comes in useful in a fistfight."

COCORÌTA, *f., rude.* (Lit., parakeet.) Mature woman who dresses and behaves like a young girl. *Tutte le sere, alla scuola di ballo liscio, ci trovava l'Adriana, conciata come una cocorita.* "Every evening, at the ballroom-dance school, there was Adriana, decked out like a teenager."

COCÙZZA, *f.* (Variation of "cucuzza," pumpkin.) One million lire. *Sgancia le dieci cocuzze, se no ti faccio dare lo sfratto.* "Cough up the ten million, otherwise I'll have you evicted."

CÓDA, *f., rude.* (Lit., tail.) Penis. **Far andare il codino.** (Lit., to wag the tail.) To possess sexually. *Non fa andar male il codino, ma è così noioso!* "He's quite good at wagging his tail, but he's so boring!"

CÒFANA, *f., C./S.* Great quantity of food. *Pesa cento chili perché mangia cofane di spaghetti da quando è nato.* "He's grown to weigh two hundred and twenty pounds by eating loads of spaghetti ever since he was born."

COGLIONÀTA, *f., rude.* (From > **coglione**) Big mistake; stupid act. *Non avevi assicurato i gioielli? Ma come si fa a fare una coglionata così?* "You never insured your jewels? How could you do such a dumb thing?"

COGLIÓNE, *m., rude.* (From late Latin "coleonem," testicle.) Incredibly stupid person. *Ha fatto cinquanta milioni di debiti per comprarsi il fuoristrada? Un vero coglione.* "He got in debt for fifty million to buy the four-wheel drive? What a moron."

COGLIONERÌA, *f., rude.* (From > **coglione**.) Stupidity; idiocy. *Se parla ancora con quel poliziotto dei suoi affarucci poco puliti, le daranno una laurea in coglione-*

ria. "If she goes on talking about her shady deals with that cop, she'll be awarded a degree in assholery."

COGLIÓNI, *m. pl., rude.* (From > **coglione.**) **1.** Testicles. (Used in several idiomatic phrases.) **Avere i coglioni in giostra.** (Lit., to have one's balls on the merry-go-round.) To be really pissed off. *Non ti ci mettere anche tu, che oggi ho già i coglioni in giostra.* "Don't get started; today I'm already royally pissed off." **Avere i coglioni pieni di/Averne i coglioni pieni.** (Lit., to have one's balls full of (whatever bothers one).) Not to be able to stand someone/something any longer. *E piantala di piagnucolare perché lui t'ha piantato! Ne ho i coglioni pieni!* "Stop whining because he left you! I've had enough!" **Essere uno coi coglioni.** To have balls. *Ha fatto scappare quei tre brutti ceffi da solo: è uno coi coglioni.* "He chased away those three goons all by himself. He has some balls." **Levarsi/Togliersi dai coglioni.** (Lit., to get off someone's balls.) To make oneself scarce. *Se fossi in te mi toglierei dai coglioni, prima che si accorgano che ti sei fatto fregare la roba.* "If I were you I'd make myself scarce before they find out the stuff is missing." **Rompere i coglioni a qualcuno.** To break someone's balls. *Perché, quando c'è un problema, venite tutti a rompere i coglioni a me?* "Why on earth are you all breaking my balls whenever you have a problem?" **Stare sui coglioni a qualcuno.** (Lit., to stand on someone's balls.) To be a nuisance for someone. *Lo so che non mi ha mai fatto niente, ma a me lui sta sui coglioni.* "True, he never did me any wrong, but I can't stand the sight of him." **2.** Implicit, in the expression: *Oggi mi/ti/gli girano (i coglioni).* (Lit., today my (your/his) balls are turning.) "I'm really cross today."

COLLASSÀRE, *vt., youth.* (Lit., to collapse.) To impress someone deeply; to shock someone. *È arrivata alla festa con una scollatura da far collassare anche un morto.* "She showed up at the party showing enough cleavage to shock a dead man."

COLLASSÀTO, *adj.* (From > **collassare.**) **a)** *youth.*

Shocked; dazed. *Sono totalmente collassato: ho appena visto Elena impastarsi con il motorino.* "I'm in a daze. I just saw Elena get smashed up on her moped." **b)** *narc.* Intoxicated with narcotics. *Miagolava in un angolo, collassato e beato.* "He was moaning in a corner, blissfully smashed."

COLLÈGIO, *m., crim.* (Lit., boarding school.) Jail; prison. *Vado in collegio per sei mesi, ma quando esco ne riparliamo.* "I'm going to the slammer for six months. When I get out, we'll start where we left off."

COLÓMBA, *f.* (Lit., dove.) **a)** *crim.* Clandestine note exchanged between convicts. *Sta' in guardia, dopo il pasto arriverà in volo una colomba.* "Be ready, there's a message arriving for you after lunch." **b)** *slang.* Vagina. *Se non l'acchiappi stasera, la sua colomba volerà via.* "If you don't make a move tonight, her bird will fly away."

COLÓMBE/COLOMBÈLLE, *f. pl.* (Lit., doves.) Tits. *Nel sogno era circondato da un gruppo di giovani donne, felici che lui giocasse con le loro colombelle.* "In his dream he was surrounded by a group of young women, happy to let him toy with their apples."

COLÓMBO, *m.* (Lit., pigeon.) Penis. *Beh, lui non è certo un Adone, il suo colombo becca dove può.* "Well, he's far from being an Adonis, his bird pecks wherever it can."

CÓLPI, *m. pl.* (Lit., blows.) **a)** *slang.* Testicles; sexual energy. *Si arrese dopo il quinto amplesso, i colpi finalmente esauriti.* "He gave up after the sixth ejaculation, finally out of power." **b)** *youth.* **Dare colpi.** (Lit., to hit.) **1.** To have sexual intercourse. *La mena sulle sue prodezze erotiche. In realtà, non ha mai dato colpi.* "He goes on and on about his erotic endeavors; as a matter of fact, he's never done it." **2.** To be successful; to be good at what one does. *Vero, è arrogante, ma è uno che dà colpi.* "True, he's arrogant, but he's so good at what he does." **3. Perdere colpi.** (Lit., for a car to lose strokes.) For one's performance to worsen. *Se incomincio a perdere colpi a vent'anni, cosa farò a sessanta?* "If I start going downhill at twenty, what will I do at sixty?" **c)** *narc.* **Dare dei colpi.** To get a few puffs from a joint. *Abbiamo dato colpi in venti allo stesso spinello; era meglio lasciar perdere.* "Twenty people puffing from the same joint; better to forget about it."

CÒMA, *m.* (Lit., coma.) **a)** *narc.* Exhaustion due to excessive use of narcotics. *Non riesce neanche a trascinarsi al cesso, tanto è in coma.* "She can't even go pee, she's so fried." **b)** *youth.* Extremely boring thing or situation. *Che coma quella festa!* "Gee, that party was for zombies!"

COMÀRE, *m., C., crim.* (Lit., woman neighbor.) **1.** Safe. *Questa comare qui si scassa solo con la dinamite.* "Only dynamite will crack this safe open." **2. La com(m)are secca.** (Violent) death. *Quando viene a farti visita la comare secca, sei arrivato al capolinea.* "When the grim reaper comes to visit you, you're at the last stop."

COMATÓSO, *adj., youth.* (Lit., comatose.) **1.** Exhausted. *Che casa diavolo avete fatto per essere in questo stato comatoso?* "What the hell did you do to look like zombies?" **2.** Boring, listless; bored. *Non vorrai passare la sera al club dei comatosi?* "Don't tell me you want to spend the evening at the Comatose club?"

COMBÌNO, *m., C., youth.* (From "combinare," to arrange.) Meeting among close friends; date. *Sono secoli che non ho un combino; m'hanno attaccato la lebbra?* "I haven't had a date in ages. Am I a leper?"

COM'È?, *idiom, youth.* (Lit., what is it like?) How are you? How are things going? *Com'è? Si dice in giro che convoli.* "How are things going? The news is that you're tying the knot."

COMPILATION/COMPILÉSCION, *f., youth.* (English "compilation," and a pseudo-Anglicism modeled on it.) **1.** List. *Ho una compilescion di cose da fare incredibile.* "I've got a list of things to do you wouldn't believe." **2.** Great quantity. *La raccolta degli LP dei Beatles ti costerà una compilescion di svanziche.* "The collection of Beatles LPs will cost you a pile of money." **3.** Attire. *Al* *vernissage Luisa sfoggiava una compilation anni cinquanta.* "At the opening Luisa was decked out in a 1950s outfit."

CONFÈTTO, *m.* (Lit., almond-based candy.) Bullet. *Io, da solo, gli ho ficcato in corpo dieci confetti!* "I plugged him with ten bullets, all by myself!"

CONQUÌBUS, *m.* (Variant of Latin expression "cum quibus nummis," with what money.) Money; wherewithal. *Se non trovi il conquibus, non farti neanche vedere.* "If you can't find the wherewithal, don't even show up."

CONTABÀLLE, *m., rude.* (From "contare," to recount, and > **balle,** lies.) Liar. *Per me è un contaballe, ma possiamo metterlo alla prova.* "I think he's a bullshitter, but we can put him to the test."

CONTRABBÀSSO, *m., rude.* (Lit., contrabass.) **1.** Buttocks. **Suonare il contrabbasso.** (Lit., to play the bass.) To practice anal sex. *Umberto è a favore delle pari opportunità: suona il contrabbasso con i maschietti e con le femminucce.* "Roberto is in favor of equal opportunity. He buggers both men and women." **2.** Girl with big buttocks. *È tutta magrina, senza tette, ma guarda che contrabbasso si porta dietro.* "She's so thin, with no tits, but she has such a big ass." **3. Fare il contrabbasso.** To snore loudly. *Cos'è questo rumoraccio? È mio marito che fa il contrabbasso.* "What is this noise? It's my husband playing bass."

CONTRÀTTO, *m., youth.* (Lit., contract.) Progress report in school. *Se faccio vedere quel contratto al vecchio, sono un uomo morto. Me lo firmi tu?* "If I show that progress report to my old man, I'm history. Would you falsify his signature?"

CONTROPÀRTE, *f., youth.* (Lit., counterpart.) Teacher; professor. *Ho negoziato una riduzione del carico di lavoro con la controparte di storia.* "I negotiated a reduction of the workload with our history teacher."

CONVÌTTO, *m., crim.* (Lit., boarding school.) Jail; prison.

Mi hanno mandata al convitto perché ho rubato sei mele! "They sent me to the joint because I stole six apples!"

COPÈRTA, *f.* (Lit., blanket.) **a)** *crim., rude.* A woman who, in hotels of low repute, "warms the bed" of guests willing to pay for her services. *Portiere, pensa che potrei avere una bella coperta in più stanotte?* "Concierge, do you think I could have a spare blanket tonight?" **b)** *youth.* Motor vehicle insurance. *Sono a piotte: mio padre non forca più la lira per la coperta.* "I'm a pedestrian. No more money from my father for my car insurance."

COPERTÓNE, *m., narc.* (Lit., tire.) **Essersi fatto un copertone/Essere fatto come un copertone.** To be drugged up. *La sua vecchia è entrata d'improvviso in camera sua, ma non ha nemmeno capito che Clelia si era fatta un copertone!* "Her mother barged into her bedroom, but she didn't even realize that Clelia was drugged up."

CÒPPIA, *f., youth.* (Lit., couple.) **Strana coppia.** Parents. (From the American film, *The Odd Couple.*) *La strana coppia va al ballo liscio tutti i sabato sera.* "My folks go ballroom dancing every Saturday night."

CÒPPOLA, *f.* (Lit., cap.) **a)** *crim.* **Coppola storta.** (Lit., tilted cap.) Mafioso. *Non fare uno sgarbo a coppola storta, che ti stende.* "Don't be rude with that wise guy: he'll kill you." **b)** *youth.* Hat. *Va' che coppola s'è messa sulla zucca, con i nastrini e le piume!* "What a hat she's wearing! With bows and feathers!"

COPRÌRE, *vt., slang, rude.* (Lit., to cover.) To possess sexually. *Il vecchio marito non la copre più, così lei si consola con il giardiniere.* "Her old husband doesn't cover her any longer. She found consolation with the gardener."

CÒRDA, *f.* (Lit., rope.) The police, because they tie the person they have apprehended. *Persino la corda si fa vedere poco da queste parti.* "Even the police don't show up much around here."

CÒRNA, *f. pl.* (Lit., horns.) **1. Avere/Portare le corna.** (To wear horns.) To have been betrayed by one's spouse or partner. *Lui porta le corna da anni, però lo fa con dignità, devo dire.* "He's been wearing horns for years, but he does it with dignity, I must say." **2. Avere sulle corna.** (Lit., to have someone on one's horns.) To dislike someone intensely. *Lui ha Renata sulle corna da quando lei ha convinto Valeria a piantarlo.* "He's had it in for Renata ever since she convinced Valeria to dump him." **3. Fare/Mettere le corna a qualcuno.** (Lit., to make someone else wear horns.) To betray one's spouse or partner. *Cosa crede, di essere lui l'unico bravo a mettere le corna?* "Does he think he's the only one good at cuckolding?" **4. Fare le corna.** To knock on wood. *"Corre voce che quegli spacciatori potrebbero essere rilasciati." "Facciamo le corna!"* "'Rumor has it that they might let those drug pushers out.' 'Let's knock on wood.'"

CORNÀCCHIA, *f., rude.* (Lit., crow.) Talkative and gossipy person, often in the expression, **vecchia cornacchia.** *Non ti preoccupare di quella vecchia cornacchia, tanto non le crede più nessuno.* "Don't worry about that old gossip, no one believes her any more anyway."

CORNIFICÀRE, *vt., rude.* (Lit., to make someone else wear horns.) *See* **fare/mettere le > corna.**

CÒRNO, *m.* (Lit., horn.) **1.** Penis. *Lui chiama il suo arnese "il corno," perché ce l'ha sempre, ma dico sempre, duro.* "He calls his gadget 'the horn,' because he has a hard-on all the time, I swear." **2. Un corno.** Nothing. *Te ne vai in vacanza senza di me? Non me ne importa un corno!* "You're going on vacation without me? I don't give a damn!" **3.** A single act of conjugal betrayal. *Quante scenate per un misero cornetto!* "What a scene over a little hanky-panky!"

CÒRPO, *m., crim.* (Lit., body.) One-thousand-lire note. *Cosa vuoi che siano cinquanta corpi al giorno d'oggi?* "What's fifty thousand lire these days?"

CORRÈNTE, *m., S., crim.* (Lit., running, flowing.) Theft accomplished from a vehicle in motion. *Se ci mettiamo a* *fare correnti, è più difficile che ci cucchino.* "If we take up motorized mugging, it'll be easier not to get caught."

CÓRTE MARZIÀLE, *idiom, f., youth.* (Lit., court martial.) Teachers' board. *La corte marziale decide domani se ciularmi per il secondo anno di fila.* "The court martial decides tomorrow whether to hold me back a second year in a row."

CÒSA, *f.* (Lit., thing.) **a)** *slang.* **1.** Vagina. *Resti tra noi, ma tu l'hai almeno vista la sua cosa?* "Between us, have you at least seen her thing?" **2.** Penis. *See* **coso. b)** *youth.* **1. Le mie cose.** Menstrual period. *Sto come un cane oggi: ho le mie cose.* "I feel horrible today; I've got my period." **2. Fare quella cosa/certe cose.** (Lit., to do those things.) To have sexual intercourse. *Ma tu l'hai già fatta quella cosa?* "Have you done it already?" **3. Una cosa veloce.** (Lit., a quick thing.) A quick and unplanned sexual act. *Meglio una cosa veloce che niente, lui disse, ma non ci fu verso di convincerla.* "Better a quickie than nothing, he pleaded, but there was no way to convince her."

CÒSCIA, *f., S., crim.* (Lit., thigh.) **La coscia di cavallo/prosciutto.** (Lit., horse leg; pork leg.) Machine gun. *L'avresti mai pensato che gli albanesi esportassero cosce di prosciutto?* "Would you believe that the Albanians export machine guns?"

CÒSMICO, *adj., youth.* (Lit., cosmic.) Awesome. *"Hai visto la sua piscina coperta?" "Cosmica!"* "'Have you seen his covered swimming pool?' 'Awesome!'"

CÒSO, *m.* (Variant of "cosa," thing.) **a)** *slang.* Penis. *Aveva appoggiato distrattamente la mano sul suo coso.* "She laid her hand on his thing nonchalantly." **b)** *youth.* Moped. *Non scende mai dal suo coso: tra poco si trasforma in un centauro.* "He never gets off his moped. He'll end up a centaur."

COSTRUÌRE. (Lit., to build.) **a)** *vi., narc.* To roll a joint. *Era molto ricercato perché costruiva da dio.* "He was in high demand because of his skill at rolling joints." **b)** *vi. pronom., youth.* **Costruirsi qualcuno.** (Lit., to make someone up.) To take someone in. *Me la sono costruita piano piano, fino a quando non l'ho convinta a darmi i titoli di stato.* "I worked her up slowly, until I persuaded her to give me her bonds."

COTÈNNA, *f., N., youth.* (Lit., hide.) Head. **Perdere la cotenna/Andar fuori di cotenna/Uscire di cotenna.** To lose one's mind. (Also in the sense of falling in love.) *L'hanno trovata con i polsi tagliati. Ma cos'è che l'ha fatta uscire di cotenna?* "They found her with her wrists slashed. What on earth made her lose her mind?"

CÒZZA, *f., C./S.* (Lit., mussel.) **a)** *slang.* Vagina. *Lei gliel'ha data una volta: adesso lui pensa solo alla sua cozza.* "She did it with him once. Now all he thinks about is her pussy." **b)** *youth, rude.* **1.** Ugly and unpleasant girl. *Perché ti sei fissato con quella? Di cozze così ce n'è un fottio!* "Why are you stuck on that one? The world is full of scarecrows just like her!" **2.** Person in a dark mood (similar to the color of a mussel.) *Ehi, sei proprio una cozza oggi; mordi se mi avvicino?* "Wow, you're in a bad mood today. Will you bite if I get close?" **3. Fare la cozza.** (Lit., to play the mussel.) To be the odd man out. *Volete che esca con voi e poi mi fate fare la cozza!* "You ask me out, and then you make me play the odd-man out!"

CRÀNIO, *m.* (Lit., skull.) **a)** *slang.* **A cranio.** (Lit., per head.) Per person. *Il biglietto della finale costa un centone a cranio: o prendere o lasciare.* "The ticket to the championship game will cost you a hundred dollars: take it or leave it." **b)** *crim.* The person who organizes a criminal act. *Il resto della banda va bene, ma senza un cranio non andate lontano.* "The rest of the gang is OK, but without a brain you won't go far." **c)** *youth.* Very intelligent person, deserving respect and admiration. *Vuoi un'udienza col cranio? Due mesi di preavviso, peggio del papa.* "Do you want an audience with our genius? Two months' notice, worse than the pope."

CRAVÀTTA, *f., N., crim.* (Lit., tie.) **1.** Shadowing, tailing.

Era piccolo e senza segni particolari, ideale per le cra- vatte. "He was short and without particular marks; ideal for shadowing." **2. Essere una fabbrica di cravatte.** (Lit., to be a tie factory.) To be a loan shark (because they both "choke" their victims.) *Visse bene grazie alla sua fabbrica di cravatte, finché un giorno non lo ammaz- zarono.* "He lived quite well as a loan shark, until one day they killed him."

CRAVATTÀRO, *m., N., crim.* (From > **cravatta, 2.**) Loan shark. *Se vai da un cravattaro respiri oggi, ma soffochi domani.* "If you go to a loan shark, you breathe today, but you'll choke tomorrow."

CREATÙRA, *f., crim.* (Lit., creature.) Handgun; revolver. *Accarezzava la creatura che teneva nascosta in tasca, come se avesse paura che sparisse.* "He stroked the small piece he had hidden in his pocket as if he were afraid it would disappear."

CREPÀRE, *vt., C.* (Lit., to die.) To rob someone; to be robbed. *M'han crepato sul quindici: è la terza volta 'sto mese!* "They robbed me on the number fifteen bus; it's the third time this month!"

CRÌBBIO!, *interj., N.* (Euphemism for "Cristo," Christ.) Damn! *Cribbio, i vigili m'han portato via la macchina!* "Jesus! They towed away my car!"

CRISANTÈMO, *m., youth.* (Lit., chrysanthemum.) Middle-aged person. *Per essere un crisantemo è ancora in gamba: è arrivato in cima con me.* "Even though he's on the wrong side of forty, he's good; he climbed to the top with me."

CRÌSTO, *m.* (Lit., Christ.) **a)** *youth.* **Un cristo d'uomo.** Tall, vigorous man, prone to anger. Also **cristone.** *Sta' attenta a quello che dici: è un po' un cristone.* "Mind your words with him; sometimes he gets angered easily. **b)** *N., slang.* **Fare un cristo.** To trip; to fall. *Ho fatto un cristo e mi sono rotto due denti.* "I fell flat on the floor, breaking two teeth."

CRÒSTE, *f. pl.* (Lit., scabs.) **Star sulle croste a qualcuno.** (Lit., to sit on someone's scabs.) To be very annoying for someone else; to impose oneself on others. *"Perché ti sta tanto sulle croste?" "Perché passa tutte, dico tutte, le serate da noi."* "'Why does she get so much on your nerves?' 'Because she comes over every single night.'"

CÙBO, *m., narc.* (Lit., cube.) A piece of hashish. *Ehi, sta' attento, ti è caduto un cubo dalla tasca!* "Hey, watch out, you lost a cube!"

CUCADÒR/CUCCADÒR (*pl.* **cucadores/cuccadores**), *m., youth.* (Pseudo-Hispanism from > **cuccare, b3.**) **1.** Boy with the reputation of a Casanova. *Parlano di lui come del grande cucador, ma io non sono mica convinta.* "Rumor has it he's a great lover-boy, but I have my doubts." **2.** Boy. *Ehi, cuccadores, ci facciamo una partita?* "Hey, guys, how about a game?"

CUCCÀRE, *vt., N.* (From the Milanese "cücca," to swindle, to pull someone's leg.) **a)** *slang.* To steal. *M'han cuccato la pelliccia al ristorante.* "Someone stole my fur coat at the restaurant." **b)** *youth.* **1.** To catch a disease. *Ha cuccato la malaria in Africa.* "He caught malaria in Africa." **2.** To be inflicted a punishment, time in prison, etc. *S'è cuccato tre anni di riformatorio per quella rissa.* "He got three years of reform school for that brawl." **3.** To get something positive. *Ho cuccato cinque milioni per quella consulenza.* "I made five million lire for that consulting job." **4.** To be beaten up. *Le ha cuccate da Aldo, che non si può dire un peso massimo.* "He got beat up by Aldo, who isn't exactly a heavyweight." **5.** To be defeated. *La nostra squadra di pallavolo le ha cuccate per la prima volta in due anni.* "Our volleyball team got beaten for the first time in two years." **6.** To arrest. *T'han cuccato con le carte di credito addosso? Che volpe!* "They found the stolen cards on you when they caught you? What a fox!" **7.** To eat or drink. *Ci cucchiamo una spaghettata di mezzanotte?* "How about some midnight spaghetti?" **8.** To win over a person in whom one has an erotic/sentimental interest. *Crede di essere indifferente al mio fasci-*

no, ma prima o poi lo cuccherò, vedrai! "He thinks he's indifferent to my charms, but sooner or later I'll catch him, mark my words!"

CÙCCIA, *f.* (Lit., pet's basket.) **1.** Bed. *Stiamocene ancora un po' a cuccia, fa così freddo stamattina.* "Let's lie in the sack a little longer. It's so cold this morning." **2.** Vagina. *Non posso venire a cuccia?* "Would you let me into your pussy?" **3.** Garage. *Non lascia mai la sua Mercedes nuova fiammante fuori dalla cuccia.* "He never leaves his brand-new Mercedes outside the garage."

CUCÌTO, *adj., crim.* (Lit., sewn.) To keep one's mouth shut; to be cool. *Sta' cucito, che prima sentiamo cos'han-no da offrire.* "Keep your mouth shut. First we listen to their offer."

CUCÙZZA, *f. See* **cocuzza.**

CULÀTA, *f., rude.* (From > **culo, a3.**) Stroke of luck. *Cento milioni alla lotteria. Ammazza, che culata!* "A hundred million lire in the lottery! Wow, what a stroke of luck!"

CULÀTTA, *f., N.* (Lit., breech of a gun; rump.) **a)** *crim.* Trousers back pocket (where men usually keep their wallets.) *Era un artista a palpeggiare le culatte delle sue vittime senza che se ne accorgessero.* "He was an artist at feeling his victim's back pocket without getting caught." **b)** *slang.* Buttocks. *La sua culatta poderosa ingombrava tutto il campo visivo.* "Her mighty ass took over the entire visual field."

CULATTACCHIÓNE, *m., youth, rude.* (From > **culatta, b.**) Passive male homosexual. *Famoso culattacchione, il Nicola, molto apprezzato.* "Famous faggot, Nicola, highly appreciated."

CULATTIÈRE, *m., youth, rude. See* **culattacchione.**

CULATTÓNE, *m., rude.* (From > **culatta, b.**) Passive male homosexual. *See* **culattacchione.**

CÙLO, *m., rude.* (Lit., ass.) **a)** *slang.* **1. Alzare il culo.** (Lit., to lift one's ass.) To get moving. *Alza il culo, che dobbiamo dipingere tutta la staccionata prima di sera.* "Move your ass. We have to paint the whole fence by sunset." **2.** (With a negative connotation.) **Fare il culo a qualcuno.** To scold someone; to swindle someone. *L'arterio m'ha fatto un culo così quando ha trovato l'hashish nell'armadio.* "The old man let me have it when he found hashish in my closet." **Farsi il culo/Farsi un culo così.** To go all out. *Mi sono fatto un culo della madonna, però sono riuscito a salvare la ditta.* "I almost killed myself to save the firm." **Leccare il culo a qualcuno.** To lick someone's ass. *È stato licenziato anche se ha leccato il culo al padrone per anni.* "He was sacked, even though he's licked the boss's ass for years." **Metterla nel culo a qualcuno.** To sodomize someone; to swindle someone. *Gliel'hai messa in culo ben bene rifilandogli quella vecchia carretta a quel prezzo.* "You really screwed him by selling him that old lemon at that price." **Prendere qualcuno per il culo.** To pull someone's leg. *Parli sul serio o mi stai prendendo per il culo?* "Are you serious or are you taking me for a ride?" **Prenderlo/la nel culo.** (Lit., to take it in the ass.) To be sodomized; to be a passive male homosexual; to get screwed. *Povero Lorenzo, lo prende in culo letteralmente e mataforicamente!* "Poor Lorenzo, he gets it in the ass literally and metaphorically." **Stare sul culo a qualcuno.** (Lit., to stand on someone's ass.) To be disliked intensely. *Dillo che ti sto sul culo perché ho avuto la promozione e tu no!* "Why don't you admit that it drives you nuts that I was promoted and you weren't?!" **Strizzare il culo.** (Lit., to feel one's ass pinch.) To be scared shitless. *Gli ha fregato quella partita di roba, e adesso gli strizza il culo solo a vederli.* "He cheated them out of their share of the stash. Now he shits in his pants just at the sight of them." **3.** (With a positive connotation.) **Essere culo e camicia.** (Lit., to be like ass and shit.) To be two peas in a pod; to be in cahoots. *Si detestano, ma se si tratta di fregare gli altri sono culo e camicia.* "They can't stand each other, but when it comes to cheating other people they're like two peas in a pod." *Che culo!* How lucky! **Avere un colpo di culo.** To have a stroke of luck. *Ha avuto un colpo di culo incredibile: alla matura hanno*

dato un problema di matematica che conosceva già.
"She had an amazing stroke of luck. At the licensing test they gave a math problem she had done before." **4.** Passive male homosexual, also in the expressions **culo allegro** (lit., cheerful ass), and **culo rotto/culorotto** (broken ass). *Non ci vanno più i vecchietti a giocare a carte: adesso è la piola dei culi del quartiere.* "You no longer see old guys playing cards in that joint. It's become the local faggots' hangout." **b)** *youth.* **1. Rotto in culo.** (Lit., with a torn ass.) Really unlucky. *Rotto in culo, sono: ho inciampato nella profia mentre compravo la maria.* "I was so unlucky I bumped into the prof while buying dope." **2. In culo alla balena!** *See* **balena.**

CULÓNA, *f., youth, rude.* (From > **culo.**) Girl or woman endowed with large buttocks. *Dovrai spostarti, lo sai che la culona ha bisogno di due posti.* "You'll have to make room for big-ass. You know she needs two seats."

CUMQUÌBUS, *m. See* **conquibus.**

CÙPIO, *m., rude.* Passive male homosexual. *Non mi chiamare più cupio, se no ti spacco il muso!* "If you call me faggot once more, I'll smash your face!"

CURÀRE, *vt., youth.* (Lit., to cure.) To keep an eye on; to watch carefully. *Ti ha fatto delle proposte oscene? Adesso ce lo curiamo noi.* "He's harassing you? Don't worry, we'll keep an eye on him."

CÙRVE, *f. pl.* (Lit., curves.) Breast and buttocks. *Era tutta curve, ma quando apriva bocca ti toglieva qualunque voglia.* "She was all curves, but as soon as she opened her mouth, what a letdown."

CÙZZA, *f., youth.* (Contraction of > **cocuzza.**) Boy who gets many girls. *Rinaldo è una cuzza, anche se non lo diresti a guardarlo.* "Rinaldo is a lover boy, even though he doesn't look like one."

CUZZÀRE, *vt., youth.* (From > **cuzza.**) To conquer girls. *Per cuzzare ci vuole becco.* "If you want to pick up girls, you must have chutzpah."

DÀMA, *f.* (Lit., lady.) **a)** *slang.* Passive male homosexual. *Come dama non c'è male, ma come cavaliere è meglio lasciarlo perdere.* "As a queen he isn't bad; forget about him as a rooster." **b)** *crim.* Safe, also in the form **damigella.** *Lascia fare a me. Con quella dama bisogna procedere delicatamente.* "Let me do it. You have to be gentle with that safe."

DAMIGIÀNA, *f.* (Lit., wine vat.) **1.** Buttocks. *Si portava a spasso la sua damigiana con orgoglio.* "She walked around swaying her big behind with pride." **2.** Large-hipped woman. *A Nino piacevano le damigiane: soffici, rassicuranti, avvolgenti.* "Nino liked large-hipped women; soft, reassuring, who wrapped all around you."

DÀRCI DÉNTRO, *idiom, vi.* (Lit., to insist.) **1.** To pitch in. *Ci abbiamo dato dentro e abbiamo finito in tempo per la consegna.* "We pitched in, so we finished right on the deadline." **2.** To have sex intensely. *In gioventù era una che ci dava dentro, ma ormai . . .* "In her youth she went at it furiously, but now . . ."

DÀRE, *vt., slang.* (Lit., to give.) **1. Dare dei metri.** *See* **metro. Dare la paga.** *See* **paga. Dare delle tacche.** *See* **tacca. 2.** *rude.* **Darla (via).** (Lit., to give it [one's cunt] away.) To be sexually available (referring to a woman). *La dà via un po' troppo facilmente, per i miei gusti.* "She gives it away a little too easily, if you ask me." **3.** *rude.* **Darlo.** (Lit., to give it.) To possess sexually. *Guarda che lui lo dà* *a tutte, basta fargli un po' di moine.* "Look, he'll give it to any woman; all you have to do is soap him up a bit." **4. rude. Darlo.** To be an active male homosexual. *Per me lui è uno che lo dà.* "I think he's a homo." **5. rude. Darlo via.** (Lit., to give it [one's ass] away.) To be a passive male homosexual. *Non si direbbe a guardarlo, ma lui lo dà via.* "You wouldn't say it by the looks of him, but he's a queer." **6. Darle.** (Lit., to give those.) To beat someone up. (Also used metaphorically, meaning to defeat.) *Non ti molesteranno più: gliele abbiamo date di santa ragione.* "They won't harass you anymore. We beat the shit out of them."

DARK, *Eng., m./f., youth.* A boy/girl who adopts a funereal look and attire. *Enrico le ha detto: "Se non la pianti di fare la dark, puoi anche scordarti di me."* "Enrico told her: 'If you don't knock off that Addams family look, you can forget about me.'"

DÀRSELA, *vt. pronom.* (Lit., to give oneself to it.) **a)** *slang.* **Darsela (a gambe).** To take to one's heels. *Quando vide la guardia giurata del supermercato, il ragazzo se la diede a gambe.* "As he saw the store guard, the boy took to his heels." **b)** *youth.* To be a snob. *Se la dà da morire, non diresti mai che fa il benzinaio.* "He's so snobbish, you'd never know he works at a gas station."

DATA (BASE), *Eng., m. pl., youth.* Name and address. *Allora, gli hai sganciato i data?* "So, did you give him your data?"

DAVÀNTI, *adv., rude.* (Lit., in front.) **1.** On one's genitals. *Io non gli stringerei la mano, se la tiene sempre davanti.* "I wouldn't shake his hand; he keeps it down there all the time." **2.** Up the vagina. *Lei vuole farlo solo davanti.* "She doesn't want to do it through the back door."

DÈCA, *m.* (From the prefix meaning "ten"). Ten thousand lire. *Il geronto ti ha dato solo un deca per la pizza?!* "Your old man gave you only ten thousand for pizza?!"

DEDRÌO, *m., N., rude.* (Lit., behind.) Buttocks. *La ganza ha un bel dedrio, non c'è che dire.* "That chick has a nice tush, no question about it."

DEMENZIÀLE, *adj., youth.* (From "demente," demented.) Unbelievable, crazy. *Ascolta solo musica demenziale.* "He listens only to crazy music."

DÉNTRO, *adv.* **a)** *crim.* (Lit., inside.) In jail; in prison. *È dentro da dieci anni.* "He's been in the slammer for ten years." **b)** *narc.* **Esserci dentro.** (Lit., to be in it.) To be a drug addict. *Se vuoi aiutarla, portala dal medico: ormai c'è dentro.* "If you want to help her, take her to the doc. She's hooked."

DEPRESSIÓNE, *f., youth.* (Lit., depression.) Everything that is boring, oppressive, monotonous. *Oddio, non mi trascinerai di nuovo a teatro. Che depressione!* "You're not taking me to see another play. What a bore!"

DIDIÈTRO, *m., rude.* (Lit., behind.) Buttocks. **Prendere per il didietro.** (Lit., to grab someone's behind.) To take someone for a ride. *M'ha preso per il didietro con quella storia della malattia di sua madre.* "He took me for a ride with that story about his mother's illness."

DIGIÈI, *m., youth.* (Italian pronunciation of English acronym "DJ," disc jockey.) Handsome and easygoing boy. *Positivo, il Carlo, un digiei notevole.* "Thumbs up for Carlo, quite a guy."

DINÈROS, *m. pl., youth.* (Pseudo-Hispanism from the song "No tengo dinero," I have no money.) **Los dineros.** Money. *Lui cucca le fighette solo perché ha los dineros.* "He gets the girls only because he has dinero."

DÌO, *m., youth.* (Lit, God.) **1. Da dio.** Exceedingly well; giving a high performance. *Questo ferro va da dio.* "This motorcycle flies." **2.** Outstanding person. *Sei un dio.* "You're a great dude."

DÌRE, *vi., C.* (Lit., to say.) *"Come ti dice?" "Mi dice sfiga."* "'How are things going for you?' 'Like shit.'"

DÌSCO, *m.* (Lit., record.) **a)** *slang.* **Voltare il disco.** (Lit., to flip over the record.) To change position during sexual intercourse. *Perché non vuoi mai voltare il disco?* "Why don't you ever want to do it another way?" **b)** *youth.* **1.**

Topic of conversation. **Cambiare disco.** (Lit., to change the record.) To change the subject. *Di nuovo lì con la storia dei suoi tradimenti? Cambia disco!* "Still talking about his betrayals! Stop harping!" **2.** Disco. *Tutti in disco sabato sera!* "Everyone at the disco Saturday night!"

DISCÙLO, *m., youth, rude.* (The opposite of > **culo,** ass, meaning luck.) Misfortune. *Ti è caduto il Rolex nel fiume? Come disculo non c'è male.* "You dropped your Rolex into the river? That's what I call being unlucky."

DITÀLE/DITALÌNO, *m., rude.* (Lit., thimble.) Female masturbation. *Povera Giulietta, è ridotta al ditalino.* "Poor Giulietta, she's reduced to playing with herself."

DÌTO, *m., youth, N.* (Lit., finger.) One hundred thousand lire. **Alzare un dito.** (Lit., to lift one finger.) To earn one hundred thousand lire. *Vuoi alzare un dito facile?* "Do you want to make a hundred thousand lire real easy?"

DOC, *adj., youth.* (Acronym for "denominazione di origine controllata," certified name of origin.) Excellent; of high quality. *Quelle fanghe sono care, ma sono doc.* "Those shoes are expensive, but they're top quality."

DO IT YOURSELF, *Eng., idiom, youth.* Masturbation. *E un fautore del do it yourself.* "He's a do-it-yourself advocate."

DÒLCE, *adj., crim.* (Lit., sweet.) Easy to steal. *Ti interessa il colpo alla vecchia villa? È una cosetta dolce.* "Are you interested in doing the old villa? It's an easy job."

DOWN, *Eng., adv.* **a)** *m., narc.* **Essere in down.** See **essere in > calo. b)** *adv., youth.* **Essere down.** (Lit., to be down.) To feel depressed and listless. *Mai vista una serata così. Eravamo tutti down.* "Never seen an evening like that. We were all zombies."

DRÀGA, *f.* **1.** (Lit., she-dragon.) Strong and daring woman. *Era veramente una draga, temuta persino dai bulli del quartiere.* "She was quite an Amazon, feared even by the local thugs." **2.** (Contraction of "dragatori," sweepers.) Plainclothes policemen. *Le provano tutte, ma si vede* *lontano un miglio che sono draga.* "They try all their tricks, but you can see from a mile away that they're cops."

DRAGÀRE, *vt., N., youth.* (From French argot "draguer," lit., to dredge.) To try to pick up girls/boys; to cruise. *Dragare o morire! Era il loro motto.* "Cruise or die! That was their motto."

DRÀGO, *m.* (Lit., dragon.) **a)** *slang.* Man of exceptional strength, daring, and ability. *Preso da una rabbia incontrollabile, sfidò Berto, detto anche il drago, a fare a botte.* "Seized by an uncontrollable anger, he challenged Berto, known as the Dragon, to a fistfight." **b)** *youth.* Moped. *Ehi, bellina, ti andrebbe un giro sul drago?* "Hey, sweetie, would you like a ride on my horse?" **c)** *narc.* **Vedere draghi.** (Lit., to see dragons.) To feel angst. *Un caso pietoso: vede draghi anche quando non è fatta.* "A terrible case. She sees monsters even when she's not high."

DRAGUEUR, *m., youth.* (From French argot: a male who is persevering and successful at picking up women.) *In gioventù aveva fama di dragueur.* "As a young man he had a reputation as a womanizer."

DRÌTTA. (Lit., right hand.) **a)** *crim.* **1.** *f.* A good tip. *Mi hanno dato una buona dritta: la vecchia vive sola ed è sorda.* "They gave me a good tip; the old bag lives alone and she's deaf." **2.** *f.* Tip. *Ehi, ispettore, io ti ho dato una buona dritta; sei tu che hai piantato un casino.* "Hey, inspector, I gave you a good tip. You messed things up!" **3.** *m.* Police informer. *Arrotondava il bilancio facendo il dritta.* "He feathered his nest by being a tipster." **b)** *f., narc.* Stock of narcotics available on the market. *C'è una dritta di cenere senza acquirente: interessato?* "There's some star dust sitting around waiting for a buyer: interested?"

DRÌTTO, *adj.* (Lit., straight.) **1.** Referred to the penis: erect, turgid. *Povero Danilo, riesce a tenerlo dritto solo per pochi secondi!* "Poor Danilo, he can't keep it up for more than a few seconds!" **2.** Referred to a person: cunning, astute, able to get what he/she wants, not always with honest means. *Lui si crede un dritto, ma gliela faccio vedere io!* "He thinks he's a fox, but he hasn't met me!"

DRIZZÀRE, *vt., N., crim.* (Lit., to straighten.) To identify; to recognize. *Hanno fatto un identikit incredibile: stavolta lo drizzano di sicuro.* "They did an amazing composite. This time they'll nail him for sure."

DRIZZÀRSI, *vi. pronom., rude.* (Lit., to rise.) To get an erection. *Le ha provate tutte. Niente da fare, non gli si drizza più.* "He's tried everything, to no avail. He can't get it up any longer."

DRÒGA, *f., youth.* (Lit., drug.) **1.** Consumer goods. *Ha sempre droga di lusso: l'ultimo pezzo è uno zaino Chanel.* "She's always got luxury stuff: the latest item is a Chanel backpack." **2.** Television. *Sei ancora lì a guardare la droga alle tre di mattina?* "Are you still watching the boob tube at three in the morning?" **3.** Religion (from the expression: "Religion is the opiate of the people.") *La droga le ha dato la serenità, dice.* "Religion gave her peace, she says."

DROGÀTO, *m., youth.* (Lit., drugged.) TV addict. *Anche Luciano diventa un drogato quando ci sono i campionati del mondo di calcio.* "Even Luciano becomes a tube-addict when the World Cup Soccer championship is on."

DROGOLÓSO, *narc.* (From "droga," drug.) **1.** *m.* Drug addict. *Appartiene alla tribù dei drogolosi, sguardo spento e corpo a buchi.* "He belongs to the doper tribe, zombie look and sievelike body." **2.** *adj.* Stoned. *Bavoso, piagnucoloso e drogoloso: che bamba!* "Drooly, whiny, and dopey: what a weenie!"

DRÙGO, *youth.* (From Russian "drug" (friend) used as a slang word in Stanley Kubrick's film, *A Clockwork Orange.*) **1.** *m.* Daring, arrogant youth. *L'ultimo vero drugo si è visto nei lontani anni settanta.* "The last cool guy was seen in the now-distant 1970s." **2.** *adj.* With it, tough. *Non sei poi così drugo, eh?* "You're not such a tough guy in the end, huh?"

DRÙIDO, *m., youth.* (Lit., druid.) Alien; old-fashioned person. *Uscite insieme da sei mesi e non t'ha neanche toccata? Beh, ha la fama di druido.* "You've been going out for six months and he's never touched you? Well, he does have a reputation for being old-fashioned."

DÙE, *m., crim.* (Lit., two.) **1.** Feet. *Viene col due; la carretta è kaput.* "He comes on foot; his old wreck is out of commission." **2.** Jail/prison, by definition (because of the address of a prison in Milan, Via Filangieri 2). *Non si trova poi così male al due, pensa te.* "He says life is not so bad in the can, would you believe it?" **3.** In blasphemous expressions, a metaphor for "Dio," God. *Due cane, che paura!* "Holy shit, what a scare!" **4.** Testicles. *Non mi rompere i due!* "Don't break my balls!"

DÙE PÀLLE, *idiom, f. pl., rude. See >* **palle.**

DÙE RÌGHE, *idiom., f. pl. See* **righe.**

DÙE RUÒTE, *idiom, f. pl., youth. See* **ruote.**

DUESPÓNDE, *m., f., youth.* (Lit., two banks.) Bisexual. *Pensa un po': fratello e sorella, tutti e due duesponde.* "Brother and sister, both AC/DC. Amazing."

DÙRA, *f., N., crim.* (Lit., hard, tough.) **1.** Strong-armed robbery. *Il colpo lo faccio, ma non se è una dura.* "I'll come in on it, but not if it's armed robbery." **2. In dura.** (Lit., in a tough spot.) To be penniless. *Un drago come lui non sta in dura a lungo.* "A go-getter like him doesn't stay broke for long."

DÙRO. (Lit., hard, tough.) **a)** *adj., slang.* **1.** Erect. To have a hard-on (metaphorically, to be a tough, angry guy). *La Lega ce l'ha duro!* (Political slogan.) "The League has a permanent hard-on!" **2.** Dead. *È inutile chiamare l'ambulanza: è duro.* "It's no use calling an ambulance. He's cold." **b)** *adv., youth.* **1.** Completely. *Sei fatta dura; il down sarà da piangere.* "You're bombed out real bad; coming down won't be a joke." **2.** *m.* Tough guy. *Guarda quel duro come coccola il suo micetto!* "Look at that toughie cuddling his kitten!" **c)** *m., crim.* One who does not confess to the police. *Hanno beccato Salvatore? Non preoccuparti, è un duro.* "The police got Salvatore? Not to worry, he's tough."

E A ME/TE/NÓI (CHE ME/TE/CE NE FRÉGA)?, *idiom, rude.* What do I (you/we) care? *See* also **fregarsene.** "*Esci con Luciana, però vuoi uscire anche con sua sorella.*" "*E a te?*" "'On top of going out with Luciana you want to date her sister.' 'What do you care?'"

ECSTASY, *Eng., f.* Hallucinogenic drug. *Sono tornati dall'America con la fissa dell'ecstasy.* "They came back from the States with a bug for ecstasy."

ÈFFE, (the letter "f.") **1.** *m.* (Abbreviation of "effeminato," effeminate.) Passive male homosexual. *Lui è un effe, capito?* "He's a faggot, got it?" **2.** *adj.* Fucked up. *Se ho perso la chiave della cassaforte sono davvero effe.* "If I lost the key to the safe I'm really fucked up."

EINSTEIN, *m., youth.* (From the name of the great physicist.) **1.** Professor of mathematics and/or physics. "*Cos'ha spiegato l'Einstein ieri?*" "*Boh? Dormivo.*" "'What did the Einstein explain yesterday?' 'Who knows? I was asleep.'" **2.** Student who excels in those subjects. *Fagli un sorrisino, che l'einstein ci passa il compito di mate.* "Smile at him, so Einstein helps us with the math test." **3.** Scientist. *Sballa tutti i compiti di mate, ma dice che da grande vuole fare l'einstein.* "She flunks every math test, but she says that when she grows up she wants to be a scientist."

ELARGÌRE, *vt.* (Lit., to give generously.) **a)** *youth.* To give (tell, do) negative things with largesse. *Elargisce bidonate a destra e a manca.* "He hands out dirty tricks left and right." **b)** *narc.* To deal drugs. *Da quando in qua elargisci pasticche?* "How long have you been pushing pills?"

ELÀSTICO, *m., rude.* (Lit., rubber band.) Hymen. **Avere l'elastico rotto.** (Lit., to have a torn rubber band.) Not to be a virgin anymore. *Non ho ben capito se lei l'elastico ce l'ha rotto o no.* "It's unclear to me if she's still all in one piece or not."

ELÈTTRICO, *adj., youth.* (Lit., electric.) Said of anything that gives intense emotions. *Ti interessa un giornale porno veramente elettrico?* "Are you interested in a porno magazine that's out of this world?"

ELMÉTTI, *m. pl., youth.* (Lit., helmets.) Policemen. *Hai nascosto la roba? Gli elmetti bazzicano nella zona un pozzo.* "Did you hide the stuff? The cops have been hanging around a lot."

ÈMMA, *f., narc.* (Female name.) **Miss Emma.** Heroin. *Frequenta solo più Miss Emma.* "He sees no one but Miss Snow."

ÈMME, *f., rude.* (The letter "m" for "merda.") Shit. *Ma che ti ha messo quell'idea di emme in testa?* "Who the hell put that shitty idea in your mind?"

EMMEGÌ, *m., youth.* (Acronym of M.G., "movimento gambe," leg movement.) *Preferisce stare a casa piuttosto che venire emmegì.* "She prefers staying at home rather than coming on foot."

ÈPA, *f., narc.* (Abbreviation of "epatite.") Hepatitis. *Di epa si guarisce, ma di AIDS . . .* "You can get rid of hepatitis, but AIDS . . ."

ÈRBA, *f.* (Lit., grass.) **a)** *narc.* Marijuana and hashish. *Tienti quell'erba, non la vorrebbero neanche le capre.* "Keep that grass, not even goats would eat it." **b)** *crim.* **1. Mandare/Andare a mangiar l'erba.** (Lit., to send someone to/to go eat grass.) To kill/To die. *L'hanno mandato a mangiar erba perché ha cantato.* "They sent him to push up daisies because he sang." **2. Fare erba.** (Lit., to make hay.) To make money. *Fa erba, non c'è dubbio, Dio solo sa come.* "He makes a lot of money, no doubt, God only knows how." **3. Dare l'erba a qualcuno.** (Lit., to give someone grass.) To give someone a life sentence. *Credeva di farla franca, invece gli han dato l'erba.* "He thought he would get away with it, but instead they gave him life without parole."

EREMÌTA, *m., f., youth.* (Lit., hermit.) A youth without a romantic/sexual partner. *Fa l'eremita per forza, ma se le trovi un combino non piange.* "She plays the hermit, but if you find her a date she won't complain."

ÈRO, *f., narc.* (Abbreviation of "eroina.") Heroin. *No, con l'ero non ho più niente a che fare.* "I have nothing to do with big H any longer."

ESÌSTERE, *vi., crim.* (Lit., to exist.) To be possible. *Farti da palo? Non esiste.* "Play the lookout for you? Don't even think about it."

ÈSSERCI, *vi.* (Lit., to exist.) To be or play dumb. *Ci fai o ci sei?* "Are you playing dumb, or are you that dumb?"

ESTRÈMA UNZIÓNE, *idiom., f., youth.* (Lit., last rites.) End-of-year oral test that determines whether one gets promoted or is held back. *Se non passo l'estrema unzione, i grigi mi lucchettano il drago per un mese.* "If I flunk the last test, my old folks will lock up my motorcycle for a month."

ÈTERO, *adj.* (Abbreviation of "eterosessuale.") Heterosexual (said by a homosexual). *Per essere un etero è ancora sopportabile.* "For a stud he's almost bearable."

FA', *adj., rude.* Abbreviation of "falso," false, in the expression **Dio fa'!** *Dovevi andare a raccontargli della diossina nel pozzo, Dio fa'!* "You had to tell him about the dioxin that seeped into the well, Christ!"

FABBRICÀRE, *vt., N., crim.* (Lit., to make.) **1.** To swindle, to take in. *L'abbiamo fabbricato bene con quella partita di carne avariata!* "We did a number on him making him buy that rotten meat!" **2. Fabbricare il mazzo.** To stack the deck (of cards). *Non era possibile che infilasse tante carte buone una dopo l'altra, a meno che non avesse fabbricato il mazzo.* "He couldn't have got so many good cards, unless he had stacked the deck."

FÀCCIA, *f.* (Lit., face.) **1. Faccia (di tolla).** (Lit., tin face.) Nerve; chutzpah. *Hai una bella faccia (di tolla) a chiederle di uscire con te dopo che le hai messo le corna con sua sorella.* "You've got some nerve asking her out after you cheated on her with her sister." **2.** *rude.* **Avere la faccia peggio del culo.** (Lit., for one's face to be worse than one's ass.) To be shameless. *Vive sfruttando le prostitute di colore, ma fa le campagne anti-immigrati. Ha la faccia peggio del culo.* "He lives off working girls from Africa, but he's big in anti-immigrant campaigns. He's a shameless bastard." **3.** *rude.* **Faccia da coglione/culo/ pirla.** To be a shithead, a dumbass. *Ha una faccia da coglione incredibile, eppure dicono che sia un mezzo genio.* "He looks like an asshole, but people say he's a genius."

FAGIÒLO, *m.* (Lit., bean.) *See* **cecio.**

FAGNÀNO, *m., adj.* (From Piedmontese "fagnan," like French "fainéant," good-for-nothing.) Lazy, good-for-nothing. *Ci ha messo un'intera giornata a dare il bianco a una parete: è proprio un fagnano.* "It took him all day to paint one wall. He's a real good-for-nothing."

FAGOTTÀRO, *m., C.* (From "fagotto," bundle.) Sunday-only vacationer who goes on picnics with the entire family and all his cooking paraphernalia. *Appena parcheggiata la macchina sul lato della strada, i fagottari si precipitarono a cucinare spaghetti e braciole.* "Having parked their car on the side of the road, the Sunday excursionists rushed to cook spaghetti and pork chops."

FAGÒTTO, *m. rude.* (Lit., bundle.) **1.** Fetus. **Buttare il fagotto.** (Lit., to throw away the bundle.) To have an abortion. *Ho dovuto buttare il fagotto. Se mio padre si accorgeva che ero incinta m'ammazzava.* "I had to get an abortion. If my father knew I was pregnant he would kill me."

FANÀLI, *m. pl.* (Lit., beams.) **1.** *slang.* Eyes. **Fanali balordi.** Defective eyesight. *Guida senza occhiali nonostante i suoi fanali balordi: è un pericolo pubblico circolante.* "He drives without glasses despite his poor eyesight; he's a public menace." **2.** *youth.* Eyeglasses. *Quanto vuoi per questi fanali?* "How much do you want for these glasses?"

FANÀTICO, *m., adj., C.* (Lit., fanatic.) Excessive; someone who has too high an opinion of what he/she does. *D'accordo, sarà anche in gamba come barista, ma non lo trovi un po' fanatico?* "Okay, he may be the king of bartenders, but don't you think he goes on a bit too much about it?"

FÀNGHE, *f. pl., youth.* (From "fangoso," muddy.) Shoes (because they get dirty easily). *"Fanghe nuove?" "No, riciclate da mia sorella, che cambia tutti i momenti."* "'New footgear?' 'No, recycled by my sister, who changes her stuff all the time.'"

FANGÓSE, *f. pl. See* **fanghe.**

FANZINE, *Eng., youth.* Magazine for teenagers. *Hai visto il nuovo look di Madonna sull'ultimo numero di Fanzine? Boreale!* "Did you see Madonna's new look in the latest issue of *Fanzine*? Awesome!"

FÀRE, *vt.* **a)** *crim., rude.* **1. Fare la festa (a qualcuno).** *See* **festa. 2. Fare fuori (qualcuno)/Fare fuori una donna.** *See* **fuori. 3. Fare su.** *See* **su. b)** *slang.* **Fare su e giù.** *See* **su.**

FARFÀLLA, *f.* (Lit., butterfly.) **a)** *slang.* Prostitute. *Sei a caccia di farfalle?* "Are you looking for an easy lay?" **b)** *crim.* **1.** *See* **colomba. 2.** Promissory note. *Ho una grossa farfalla in scadenza, non avresti qualche lira?* "I've got a big IOU coming up. Could you lend me some money?" **c)** *narc.* **Vedere farfalle.** (Lit., to see butterflies.) To be in great shape. *Adesso che non si buca più vede farfalle.* "Now that he's kicked the habit he's in great shape."

FARFALLÀRE, *vt., crim.* (From "farfalla," butterfly.) To steal part of the loot from one's accomplices. *Non si sa chi, ma qualcuno li ha farfallati.* "No one knows who, but someone cheated them of the loot."

FÀRI, *m. pl.* (Lit., beams.) *See* **fanali.**

FARÌNA, *f., narc.* (Lit., flour.) Cocaine; heroin. *Conosci Renzo, detto il mugnaio? Lui non è mai senza farina.* "Do you know Renzo, a.k.a. the 'gold digger'? He's always well supplied with gold dust."

FARLÒCCO, *m., N., youth.* Naive person, easily taken in. *Matteo è un tale farlocco che si beve persino le tue fandonie.* "Matteo is so gullible that he even swallows your stories."

FÀRSI. (Lit., to do to/for oneself.) **a)** *vt. pronom., youth.* **1.** *rude.* To possess sexually. *Me ne sono fatte ben cinque in una sera!* "I had five in one night." **2. Farsi qualcosa.** To buy, to consume, to use something. *Fatti un valium e sgasati un po', OK?* "Take some Valium and cool it, OK?" **3. Farsi una pelle.** *See* **pelle. 4. Farsela sotto.** (To do it in one's pants.) To be terrified. *È bastato che lui lanciasse qualche vaga minaccia che tu te la sei fatta sotto!* "All he had to do was to make some vague threats to make you piss in your pants!" **b)** *vi. pronom., narc.* To inject drugs. *Si fa, te lo dico io, anche se lo nasconde bene.* "He shoots up, believe me, even though he hides it well."

FÀSCIO, *m., youth.* (Lit., fasces, the symbol of ancient Rome adopted by the Fascist movement.) **1.** Fascist. *Negli anni settanta era un fascio, adesso si atteggia a conservatore illuminato.* "In the seventies he was a Fascist. Now he plays the enlightened conservative." **2.** Authoritarian person, tied to past mores and ideas. *Il generale del terzo piano dice che se continuiamo a fare casino con le moto ci denuncia. Che fascio!* "That retired general, who lives on the fourth floor, warned us that if we keep making a racket with our motorcycles he'll turn us in. What an old fogy!"

FASÙLLO, *adj., slang.* (From a Hebrew word adopted by the Roman underworld.) **1.** False, not authentic. *Quel fagiolo lì è fasullo.* "That diamond is false." **2.** A worthless but pretentious person. *Si riempie la bocca di paroloni, ma è uno fasullo.* "He talks like a book, but he's a phony."

FÀTTO, *adj.* (Lit., done, made.) **a)** *narc.* Stoned. *È fatto duro.* "He's stoned." **b)** *youth.* **1.** Beat up; exhausted. *Io sono fatta; in cima ci vai tu.* "I'm beat. You go up to the top." **2.** In love. *È veramente fatta, anche se non capisco cosa ci veda in lui.* "She's really head over heels. What does she see in him?"

FÀVOLA, *f.* (Lit., fairy tale.) **a)** *slang.* Lie, tall tale. *Incantava tutti con le sue favole.* "He charmed everyone with his tall tales." **b)** *youth.* Fascinating, extremely attractive person or thing. *Lo farei anch'io un giro con Francesca: è una favola!* "I wouldn't mind a ride with Francesca myself. She's fabulous!"

FEMMIN(I)ÉLLA, *f.*/**FEMMIN(I)ÈLLO,** *m., S., rude.*

(From "femmina," female.) Transsexual; passive male homosexual. *Sua madre non ci può credere che suo figlio è una femminella.* "His mother can't make peace with the fact that he's a pansy."

FERRÀTA, *f., youth.* (From "ferro," iron.) Car crash. *Sono morti in sei nella ferrata sul cavalcavia.* "Six people died in the car crash on the overpass."

FÈRRI, *m. pl.* (Lit., irons.) **1.** Handcuffs. *Quando si rese conto che doveva affrontare la folla con i ferri ai polsi, scoppiò in pianto.* "She broke down crying as she realized that she'd have to face the crowd in handcuffs." **2.** Shoes. *Ma come fai a camminare con quei ferri ai piedi?* "Tell me, how can you walk with those shoes?"

FÈRRO, *m.* (Lit., iron.) **a)** *youth.* Car; moped. *Se mi presti il ferro metto una parola buona per te con Luisa.* "If you lend me your iron, I'll put in a good word for you with Luisa." **b)** *crim.* Gun. **Ferrolungo.** Submachine gun. *Ma che colpo vuoi fare, che hai bisogno di un ferrolungo? Non ti basta un ferro?* "Why do you need a submachine gun for the robbery? A gun isn't enough?"

FÉSSA (and the diminutive **fessarella**), *f., S., rude.* (Pp. of "fendere," to split.) Vagina. *I due ragazzi si appostavano ogni sera dietro le latrine, sperando di vedere qualche fessa.* "The two boys lay in wait behind the outhouse every night, hoping to get a glimpse at some slits."

FÉSSO, *m., S., rude.* (Pp. of "fendere," to split.) **1.** Dumbass. *M'hai preso per fesso che cerchi di rifilarmi quel rottame?* "Do you take me for such a dumbass that you're trying to palm off that wreck on me?" **2. Fare fesso qualcuno.** To betray one's spouse/partner. *Tua moglie t'ha fatto fesso un'altra volta? E falla fessa a tua volta!* "Your wife cheated on you one more time? Do the same to her!"

FESSÙRA, *f.* (Lit., slit.) *See* **fessa.**

FÈSTA, *f.* (Lit., party.) **1. Far la festa a qualcuno.** To kill someone. *Gli hanno fatto la festa a mezzanotte dietro la vecchia fabbrica.* "They bumped him off at midnight, behind the old factory." **2.** *rude.* **Far la festa a una donna.** To possess sexually; to rape. *Si sono messi in cinque a farle la festa.* "The five of them got together and gang-banged her."

FETÈNTE, *m./f.*, **FETENTÓNE,** *m.*/**FETENTÓNA,** *f. S., rude.* (Lit., stinking.) Vile person. *Se quel fetente ti mena un'altra volta, gli spacco il muso.* "If that skunk beats you up again, I'll break his face."

FÉTTA, *f., crim.* (Lit., slice.) **1.** Banknote. *Solo fette pulite per il riscatto, se no lo fanno fuori.* "Only clean bills for the ransom, otherwise they'll kill him." **2.** Counterfeit key. *Cristo, 'sta fetta non gira! Chi apre la cassaforte adesso?* "Christ, this key isn't working! How do we open the safe now?"

FÉTTE, *f. pl.*/**FETTÓNI,** *m. pl.* (Lit., slices.) **1.** *slang.* Feet. **Alzare le fette.** To split. *Alziamo le fette, gente? Ci sta crescendo la muffa addosso.* "Let's split, folks. We'll grow moss if we stay here any longer." **2. Farlo a fette.** (Lit., to slice it [one's penis].) To be a pain in the neck. *Gliel'ha fatto a fette al vecchio fino a quando non gli ha mollato le chiavi dello yacht.* "He harassed his old man until he handed over the keys to the yacht."

FÌCA, *f., rude.* **1.** Vagina. *Da una donna Giacomo vuole solo la fica.* "All that Giacomo wants from a woman is her cunt." **2.** Girl, woman, usually very sexy. **Una fica bestiale/imperiale/mostruosa/spaziale. Un tocco/un pezzo di figa.** (Also in the augmentative and superlative forms **figona** and **fighissima.**) *Loredana è una fica mostruosa, ma inavvicinabile.* "Loredana is a great chick, but you can't get near her." **3. Niente fica.** No sexual activity. *Niente fica, povero Aldo: sua moglie è in sciopero.* "No screwing for poor Aldo. His wife is on strike."

FICAIÒLO, *m., youth.* (From > **fica, 2.**) A boy who is successful in getting girls. *Il cucador massimo è finito dentro; adesso la palma di ficaiolo ce l'ha Filippo.* "The king of studs has wound up in the slam. Filippo is now the big operator on the block."

FICCÀRE. (Lit., to thrust.) **a)** *vt., slang, rude.* To possess sexually. *Se la ficca, vedrai che si calma!* "If he fucks her, he'll cool down, you'll see." **b)** *vi., youth.* To find attractive; to like. *Mick Jagger è uno che mi ficca un sacco.* "Mick Jagger turns me on, I can't tell you how much."

FICCÀRSI, *vr., rude.* (Lit., to get into something.) **1.** To manage to get access to a group of people so as to reap advantages from them. *È qui solo da due mesi, ma s'è già ficcato.* "He's been here only two months, but he's already well connected." **2.** To start a sentimental relationship. *Si è ficcata con Elio per disperazione.* "Better Elio than nothing, that's why she's going out with him."

FICCÀTO, *adj.* (Lit., stuck.) Well-placed socially or professionally, and therefore able to get fringe benefits for oneself or others. *Dice di essere ficcato a Bruxelles, ma io ho i miei dubbi.* "He says he's in the loop in Brussels, but I have my doubts."

FÌCO, *adj., m., rude.* (Lit., fig.) **1.** Handsome youth, sexually promising. (Also in the augmentative and superlative forms **figone** and **fighissimo.**) *Per figo, è figo; non un einstein, però.* "He's a hunk, I grant it; not a rocket scientist, though." **2.** *m.* **Un fico.** Nothing; not at all. *Vuoi uscire con mio fratello, non con me? Non me ne importa un fico.* "You want to date my brother instead of me? I couldn't care less."

FIÈNO, *m., narc.* (Lit., hay.) Light drug, especially hashish and marijuana. *Ho del fieno fresco. Ti va di bruciarne un po' con me?* "I have some fresh hay. Would you like to have a smoke with me?"

FÌGA, *f., rude.* See **fica.**

FIGÀIO, *m., youth.* (From > **figa.**) Large group of girls (hopefully available for sex). *La terza B è un gran figaio, ma l'ingresso è riservato ai superdotati.* "A lot of nice cunts in that history class, but entry is reserved for the studs."

FIGÀTA, *f., youth.* (From > **figa.**) Well-done, positive situation or thing. *Belle ganze, un pozzo da bere, persino un po' d'erba. Il party è stato una gran figata.* "Beautiful gals, lots to drink, even some pot. The party was a smashing success."

FIGHÉTTA, *f.* (Diminutive of > **figa.**) **a)** *crim.* Spy in a prison. *Nicola rischia grosso a fare la fighetta.* "Nicola may pay dearly for playing the canary." **b)** *youth.* Attractive, up-to-date girl, who belongs, or pretends to belong, to the upper class. *Laura si dà arie da fighetta, ma suo padre vende frutta e verdura.* "Laura plays the fancy chick, but her father runs a grocery store."

FIGHETTERÌA, *f., N., youth.* To behave as a > **figo.**

FIGHÉTTO, *m., youth.* (From > **figo.**) Handsome, up-to-date boy who belongs, or pretends to belong, to the upper class. *A me i fighetti mi lasciano fredda; preferisco un bel maschione.* "I don't like cute preppies; I prefer a big macho."

FIGHETTÓNE, *m., youth.* (From > **fighetto.**) Boy who exaggerates his attempt at being well-groomed and sophisticated. *Lo chiamano il fighettone della Magliaia: va in giro tutto leccato, tra sorci e immondezza.* "They call him the dude of the ghetto. He wanders the streets all spruced up, skirting around rats and garbage."

FÌGLIO, *m., rude.* **Figlio di puttana/Figlio di mignotta.** (Lit., son of a bitch.) A person one is forced to admire and respect, though with mixed feelings. *Io non so se bari. So solo che quel figlio di puttana ha vinto di nuovo a poker.* "I don't know if he cheats. All I know is that that son of a bitch won again at the poker table."

FÌGO, *m., rude. See* **fico.**

FILÀRE. (Lit., to spin.) **a)** *vi., slang.* To flee. *Filate! C'è la madama in arrivo!* "The police are coming! Scram!" **b)** *vt., youth.* **1.** To court; to date (a boy or a girl). *Sono mesi che la filo, non ho cuccato neanche un bacillo.* "I've been after her for months: not even a peck on the cheek." **2.** To have had enough of something. *Sei di nuovo qui a* *piangere miseria? Chi ti fila!* "Are you in dire straits again? Who gives a damn!"

FILARÌNO, *m., youth.* (From > **filare, b1.**) A fling between two teenagers. *Sono così teneri: hanno solo dodici anni ed è il loro primo filarino.* "They're so sweet! Twelve years old and having their first fling."

FILIBÈRTA, *f., N.* (Female name.) Vagina. *Non dice mai la parola figa, solo filiberta, filiberta.* "Rather than using the word cunt, he talks about 'that thing.'"

FILÌPPA/FILIPPÌNA, *f., N.* (Female name.) *See* **filiberta.**

FÌLO, *m., youth.* (Lit., thread.) **Fare il filo a qualcuno.** To court someone. *Gli faceva il filo sfacciatamente, anche in presenza della moglie.* "She pursued him brazenly, even with his wife there."

FÌLO, *f., youth.* (Contraction of "filosofia," philosophy.) *Che razza di profia di filo vi siete beccati, che non sa neanche chi è Derrida?* "You got a philosophy teacher who doesn't know who Derrida is? Who is she?"

FILÓNE, *n.* (From > **filare.**) **a)** *slang.* Cunning flatterer. *Ti ha spillato un bel po' di quattrini? Eh, è un gran filone!* "He squeezed a lot of money out of you? Well, he's a great asskisser." **b)** *S., youth.* **1. Far filone.** To skip classes. *Stavolta non vengo: se ci beccano ancora a far filone siamo fottuti.* "This time I'm not coming. If they catch us cutting class again we're cooked." **2.** Professor of philosophy. *Adesso anche il filone vuole farci fare i compiti scritti!* "Now even the philosophy teacher wants to assign written tests!"

FÌNA, *f., crim.* Contraction of "finanza," from the name of the Italian customs police ("Guardia di Finanza"). *La fina ha avuto una soffiata che la roba sarebbe arrivata stanotte.* "The Customs police had a tip that the stuff would arrive tonight."

FÌNE (DEL MÓNDO), *idiom, f., youth.* (Lit., the end of the world.) Extraordinary person, thing, or situation; awesome. *Il concerto di Bruce Springsteen è stata la fine del mondo!* "The Bruce Springsteen concert was incredible!"

FINÒCCHIA, *f., rude. See* **finocchio.**

FINOCCHIERÌA, *f., rude.* (From > **finocchio.**) **1.** The condition of passive male homosexuality. *Si è convertito alla finocchieria dopo essere stato piantato dalla moglie.* "After he was left by his wife, he converted to faggotry." **2.** Bar frequented by gays. *Hanno dato fuoco a quel bar perché è il punto di raduno della finocchieria.* "They set fire to that bar because it's the local faggots' meeting place."

FINÒCCHIO, *m., rude.* (Lit., fennel.) Passive male homosexual. *Io non dico che lui sia antipatico, ma resta comunque un finocchio.* "I'm not saying I don't like him. I'm saying he's a faggot."

FIÒCA, *f., N., narc.* (From the northern dialect word for "neve," snow.) Cocaine; heroin; narcotics in general. *Ha fioca di tutti i tipi, basta pagare.* "He's got snow of all kinds. All you have to do is pay."

FIOCCÀRSI, *vr. recipr., N., youth.* To kiss, especially among very young teenagers. *Vi siete fioccati tu e Paolo? No? Ma cosa aspettate?* "So, any smooching between you and Paolo? No? What are you waiting for?"

FIOCCHÉTTA/FIOCCHETTÌNA, *f., youth.* (From "fiocco," meaning wad.) Young preppie girl who follows the latest dictates of fashion, especially those typical of a > **paninaro.** *Da quando è in quel giro lì si è trasformata in una fiocchettina.* "Ever since she joined that circle, she's become a preppie."

FIÒCCO, *m.* **a)** *slang, rude.* (Probably from the term for "jib," meaning ass.) Buttocks. *Voleva fregarli e invece se l'è presa nel fiocco.* "He was trying to trick them, and he got tricked instead." **b)** *youth.* Kiss. *Dai, dammi almeno un fiocco!* "Come on, give me at least a kiss!"

FIOCINÀRE, *vi., N., youth.* (Lit., to harpoon.) To go all out in the attempt to conquer a boy or a girl; to pick up girls/boys. *In quella scuola lì si fiocina bene, devono essere a corto di galli.* "There's lots of available chicks in that school; they must be short on roosters."

FIONDÀRSI, *vr.* (Lit., to sling oneself.) To rush somewhere, as fast as a stone thrown from a sling. *"Gli elmetti stanno portandoti via il ferro." "Fermali, che mi fiondo!"* "'The cops are towing away your motorcycle.' 'Hold them! I'll zip right over!'"

FISARMÒNICA, *f., crim.* (Lit., accordion.) Wallet. *Una grossa fisarmonica spuntava invitante dalla tasca posteriore dei calzoni.* "A fat wallet peeped out enticingly from the back pocket of his trousers."

FÌSSA, *f., youth.* (Abbreviation of "fissazione," obsession.) **1.** Mania, obsession. **Prendere la fissa di qualcosa/ Andare in fissa per qualcosa.** *L'ultima di Anna è che è andata in fissa per la macareña.* "Anna's most recent fixation is the macareña." **2.** Something one likes very much. *Lo so che è assurdo, ma Rodolph Valentino per me è una fissa.* "I know it's absurd, but Rudolph Valentino is an obsession for me."

FÌSSO. (Lit., fixed.) **a)** *adj., narc.* Stoned; exhausted. *Si droga di brutto. Guarda com'è fisso.* "He's into heavy stuff. Don't you see how stoned he is?" **b)** *adv., youth.* **1.** Without scruples; decisively. *Per fare affari con Leonardo devi andare giù fisso.* "If you want to do business with Leonardo, you have to come down hard." **2. Di fisso.** For sure. *Alessandro ti dà una buca. Di fisso.* "Alessandro will stand you up. Count on it."

FIXÀRSI, *vi., narc.* (From English "to fix.") To take drugs, especially by injection. *Vogliono passare tutto il weekend a fixarsi.* "Their plan for the weekend: to shoot up."

FLANÈLLA, *f.* (Lit., flannel.) **a)** *slang.* **Far flanella.** (Lit., to make lint.) To waste one's time. *Invece di stare a far flanella, perché non tagliate l'erba?* "Why don't you mow the lawn, instead of standing there twiddling your thumbs?" **b)** *crim.* To frequent a brothel, but without having sex. *A sedici anni lo portarono al bordello, ma solo a far flanella.* "They took him to the brothel when he was sixteen, just to get a feel for it." **c)** *youth.* To neck. *Hanno passato la serata nascosti dietro il divano a far flanella.*

"They spent the evening necking behind the sofa."

FLASH, *Eng.,* **a)** *m., narc.* Peak moment of the effect of narcotics. *Vive solo per i flash, per il resto è uno zombie.* "He lives to get blasted; the rest of the time he's a zombie." **b)** *m., youth.* **1.** Great idea. *Stavo lì a sguazzare nella vasca quando mi è venuto il flash del secolo.* "I was splashing around in the bathtub, when I got the idea of the century." **2.** *adv.* **Da flash.** Awesome. *Te lo appoggio: suo padre è da flash.* "Granted, her father is awesome."

FLAUTÌSTA, *m./f.* (Lit., flutist.) Person who performs blow jobs. *Se sei così arrapato telefona a Mariella: lei fa anche la flautista.* "If you're that horny, call Mariella. She plays the flute too."

FLÀUTO, *m.* (Lit., flute.) Penis; also called **flauto a pelle. Suonare il flauto a pelle.** (Lit., to play the skin-flute.) To give someone a blow job. *La signora suonava il flauto a pelle con grande maestria.* "The lady played the skin-flute with great dexterity."

FLÈBO. (Abbreviation of "fleboclisi," phleboclysis.) **a)** *f., narc.* **1.** Drug injection. *Io la flebo con te me la faccio, ma con una siringa pulita.* "OK, I'll shoot up with you, but with a clean needle." **2. Farsi una flebo.** To get on one's feet again, physically and psychologically. *Se non si fa una flebo può anche scordarsi la vela quest'estate.* "If she doesn't get back on her feet, she can forget about sailing this summer." **b)** *youth.* **1.** *f.* Boring person or thing. *Dobbiamo zupparci Adriana anche stasera? È una tale flebo!* "Do we have to put up with Adriana tonight too? She's such a bore!" **2.** *Fatti una flebo!* "Mind your own business!" **3.** *adv.* **Da flebo.** So strong as to remain stoned. *Ho fatto un volo da flebo con gli sci.* "I got knocked out when I fell with my skis." **4.** *adv.* Marvelous, awesome. *Lalla non è solo boreale, è da flebo.* "Lalla isn't just marvelous, she's a knockout."

FLIPPÀRE, *vt., youth.* (From English "to flip.") **1.** To swindle. *Ti sei fatta flippare da su fratello, che ha tredici anni?* "You were taken in by his brother, who's thirteen?"

2. To steal. *Le ho flippato il telefonino mentre sbavava davanti alla vetrina di Armani.* "While she was drooling in front of the Armani shop, I lifted her cellular."

FLIPPÀRSI, *vr.* (From English "to flip out.") **a)** *youth.* To get a swelled head; to get excited. *Non è il caso di flipparsi così: magari va tutto a monte.* "Don't get too hyper: things may still go wrong." **b)** *narc.* To take drugs, referring to the danger of taking an overdose. *Guarda che se flippi male sono cazzi acidi.* "If you flip out badly you'll be in deep shit. Be careful."

FLIPPÀTO, *adj.* (From > **flipparsi, b.**) **a)** *narc.* Flipped out after taking drugs. *Quand'è flippato fino a quel punto gli puoi anche rubare le mutande.* "When he's flipped out that far, you can even steal his underwear." **b)** *youth.* **1.** Bombastic. *Da flippata qual è, Barbarella racconta in giro di aver avuto una storia con Alberto di Monaco.* "Shows what a boaster Barbarella is. She talks about having had an affair with Albert of Monaco." **2.** Out of one's mind. *Vuoi tuffarti da trenta metri d'altezza? Sei completamente flippato?* "You want to dive from thirty meters? Are you out of your mind?"

FLOPPÀRE, *vi., youth.* (From English "floppy," and "to flop.") For a male, not to be able to complete the sexual act. To be impotent. *Con lei floppo sempre, non so perché.* "I always flop with her, I don't know why."

FÒCA, *f., youth.* (Lit., seal.) **1.** See **fica. 2.** Silly, naive, especially referring to a girl. *Non ha messo il lucchetto alla bici, così gliel'hanno rubata. Che foca!* "She didn't lock the padlock, so her bike was stolen. What a silly goose!"

FOCOMÈLICO, *adj., youth.* (Lit., affected by cerebral palsy.) Disabled, handicapped, even if physically healthy. *Ho cercato di spiegargli le equazioni di secondo grado tre volte. Focomelico totale.* "I tried three times to explain second degree equations to him. A real spastic."

FÓGNA, *f., slang, rude.* (Lit., sewer.) **a) Essere una fogna.** (Lit., to be a sewer.) To have a stomach (and swallow everything, both literally and metaphorically). *È una tale fogna che si è mangiato tutto il pesce, inclusa la testa.* "He's such a pig he ate the whole fish, head included." **b)** *f.*, youth, rude. **1.** Anus/Vagina. *Bianca è disposta a darti tutte e due le fogne—se paghi.* "Bianca would be willing to let you use both her holes—if you cough up." **2.** Very ugly girl. *Vi siete presi il meglio e a noi avete lasciato solo le fogne, eh?* "You got the best ones and left the eyesores for us, right?" **3.** *adv.* **Da fogna.** Real bad. *Non posso farti un prestito: mi va letteralmente da fogna.* "I can't lend you any money. I'm in the pits."

FOGNÀTO, *adj., youth.* (From > **fogna.**) Extremely dirty; filthy. *Mai visto un buco così fognato; ma come fai a respirare?* "Never seen such a stinkhole. How can you breath?"

FONDÈLLI, *m. pl.* (Lit., bottoms.) Buttocks. **Prendere per i fondelli.** (Lit., to seize someone by his/her buttocks.) To take someone for a ride. *In camera da letto sua moglie non c'era, tanto meno con un amante. L'avevano preso per i fondelli.* "The bedroom was empty: his wife wasn't there, let alone a hypothetical lover. They had played a trick on him."

FONDÈLLO, *m.* (Lit., bottom of various objects.) Buttocks. **Avere fondello.** To be lucky. *Il giorno prima che scadessero le cambiali ha vinto alla lotteria: ma come si fa ad avere tanto fondello?* "The day before his IOUs expired, he won the lottery. How come he's so lucky?"

FÓNDERE, *vi., youth.* (Lit., to melt.) **1.** To get extremely bored. *Ma perché m'hai trascinato a 'sta conferenza? C'è da fondere!* "Why did you drag me to this lecture? It's so boring!" **2.** To be strongly attracted to someone; to get excited. **Fondere (la cotenna).** For one's head to be spinning. *Se quella figona mostra un altro po' di coscia mi fonde la cotenna.* "If that broad shows another piece of thigh, I'll lose it." **3.** **Essere/Avere fuso.** To be burned out. *Un altro passo io non lo faccio. Ho fuso!* "I'm not moving another inch. I'm beat!"

FÓNDO (DÉLLE NÀTICHE/DÉLLE RÉNI/DÉLLA SCHIÈNA), *m.* (Lit., bottom [of one's back].) *See* **fondello.**

FORAGGIÀRE, *vt.* (Lit., to supply with fodder.) To subsidize someone in order to get an advantage. *Lei va a letto col principale, che la foraggia senza badare a spese.* "She sleeps with her boss, who keeps her in splendor."

FORÀGGIO, *m.* (Lit., fodder.) Food, meals. *Ricordava ancora con orrore il foraggio che gli avevano ammannito in collegio.* "He still remembered with horror the slop they used to feed him in boarding school."

FÒRBICE, *f., crim.* (Lit., scissors.) **1.** Act of pickpocketing accomplished by inserting the index and middle fingers into the victim's pocket, as if they were scissors. *La tecnica della forbice non è difficile, però bisogna avere delle dita agili.* "The scissor-pinching technique is not difficult, but you need quick fingers." **2. Fare una forbice.** Not to pay a prostitute for the service she has provided. *La donna, scarmigliata e seminuda, lo rincorse gridando: "M'ha fatto una forbice!"* "'The woman, unkempt and half-naked, ran after him shouting: 'He stiffed me!'"

FÓRCA, *f., N.* (Lit., gallows.) **a)** *crim.* Spy, traitor. *Salve, forca, stavolta hanno fatto la forca a te, eh?* "Hello, turncoat, this time you got turned in, eh?" **b)** *youth.* **Fare forca.** To skip classes. *Dalle mie parti, saltare la scuola per una settimana senza giustificazione si chiama "fare forca."* "In my book, not going to school for a week for no reason is called playing hooky."

FORFAIT, *French, m., narc.* Potpourri of light drugs. *Se vi accontentate vi posso preparare un bel forfait.* "If it's okay with you, I can put together a nice mix."

FÓRNO, *m.* (Lit., oven.) Mouth. *Nel suo forno ci entra anche un bue.* "He could get an ox into his mouth."

FÒRTE, *youth.* (Lit., strong.) **1.** *adj.* Original, eccentric, positive (said with a bit of envy). *Ti sei presentato alla visita militare con le stampelle? Sei forte!* "You showed

121

up for the army medical on crutches? You're something else!" **2.** *adv.* Much. **Andare forte.** (Lit., to go fast.) To have success. To be in fashion. *A uomini sei andata forte ultimamente.* "You've been picking up a lot of men lately."

FORTÉZZA, *f.* (Lit., fortress.) **a)** *crim.* Safe. *La fortezza possiamo prenderla con la forza o con l'inganno.* "We can take the safe by force or by cunning." **b)** *slang.* Vagina. *La sua fortezza non è molto ben difesa.* "Her fortress is not well defended."

FÒRZA, *f.* (Lit., strength.) **a)** *crim.* The police. *Chi ha fatto la soffiata alla forza?* "Who blew the whistle to the police?" **b)** *youth.* Outstanding person or thing. *Non l'avrei mai detto, ma tuo zio è una forza!* "I didn't expect it. Your uncle is quite a guy!"

FÒSFORO, *m.* (Lit., phosphorus.) Intelligence; memory; brain. *Queste parole incrociate sono per gente con più fosforo di me.* "This crossword puzzle is for someone smarter than I am."

FÒSSILE, *m., youth.* (Lit., fossil.) Elderly person; parent. *Non mi dire che in cima sono arrivati prima i fossili!* "Don't tell me that the fossils got to the top first!"

FÓTTERE, *vt., rude.* (From Latin "futuere," to copulate.) **a)** *slang.* **1.** To possess sexually. *Diceva che moriva se non la fotteva, ma è stata una gran delusione.* "He kept saying that he would die if he didn't fuck her, but afterwards he was mightily disappointed." **2.** To swindle. *Non è che Tommaso ci stia fottendo con sta 'storia del socio misterioso?* "Do you think Tommaso is shitting us with this story about a mysterious partner?" **3.** To steal. *Cosa me ne viene a me, se ti aiuto a fotterle la pelliccia?* "What's in it for me, if I help you walk away with her fur coat?" **4.** *Va' a farti fottere!* "Go fuck yourself!" **b)** *youth.* To hold someone back at the end of the school year (unfairly). *La corte marziale mi ha fottuto perché ho firmato la petizione per far fuori il kaiser. Incredibile!* "The court martial held me back at the end of the year because I signed a petition to get rid of the principal. Incredible!"

FÓTTERSENE, *vi. pronom., rude.* (From > **fottere.**) Not to give a damn about something. *Io me ne fotto di te, dei tuoi soldi, della tua famiglia!* "I don't give a fucking damn about you, your money, or your family!"

FÓTTERSI, *vr., rude.* (From > **fottere.**) To cause one's own ruin. *Credendo alle sue promesse si sono fottuti da soli.* "They did themselves in by believing his promises."

FOTTÌO, *m., rude.* (From > **fottere.**) A lot. *C'era un fottio di gente alla partita di basket.* "There was a huge crowd at the basketball game."

FOTTITÓRE, *m., youth, rude.* (From > **fottere.**) Stud. *Sarà anche un gran fottitore, però a me non mi fa venire nessuna voglia.* "He has a reputation as a great stud, but he doesn't turn me on."

FOTTITÙRA, *f., rude.* (From > **fottere.**) **1.** Sexual intercourse. *È rimasto secco nel bel mezzo di una fottitura.* "He kicked the bucket in the middle of a nice fuck." **2.** Swindle. *La fottitura del secolo, l'han chiamata, riuscire a vendere alla mafia calce al posto di cocaina.* "The sting of the century, they called it, selling lime to the mob instead of coke."

FOTTÙTO, *adj., rude.* (From > **fottere.**) **a)** *slang.* Taken in; done in. *Quando vide i due energumeni sbarrargli l'uscita dal vicolo, pensò, "son fottuto."* "As he saw the two thugs blocking the end of the alley he thought, 'I'm dead.'" **b)** *youth.* **1.** Held back at the end of the school year. *Il verdetto della corte marziale? Fottuto, mia cara, fottuto.* "The verdict of the teachers? Damned, my dear, damned." **2.** Damned; darned. (Also in the superlative form **fottutissimo.**) *Che fottutissima cazzata vai dicendo? Non ti ho ciulato io il telefonino!* "What the fuck are you talking about? I did not steal your cell phone!"

FRÀC(CO), *m., N., rude.* (Term referring to the tails of a tailcoat.) **1.** Buttocks. **Prendersela nel fracco.** (Lit., to take it in the behind.) See **culo. 2.** A lot (of blows); a thrashing. *Se mi scopre a fumare, mio padre me ne dà un* *fracco.* "If my father finds out that I smoke, he'll give me a thrashing."

FRÀCICO/FRÀCIDO, *adj., C., narc.* (Lit., soaking wet.) Full of alcohol or drugs. Stoned. *Ammazza, come puzzi! Sei proprio fracido.* "Gee, you stink! You're loaded."

FRÀNA, *f., youth.* (Lit., landslide.) **1.** Failure, referring to a person. *Che frana che sei. Ti sei lasciata fregare l'ultimo biglietto del concerto sotto il naso.* "How dumb can you be? They swiped the last ticket to the concert right out from under your nose." **2.** Also its opposite: incredibly able person. *Uno che entra sempre senza pagare è una bella frana!* "Someone who always manages to get in for free is tops!"

FRANCOBOLLÀRE, *vt., youth.* (From "francobollo," stamp.) **1.** To (try to) seduce, conquer another person. *Sono mesi che cerca di francobollarmi; mai visto uno così testone.* "He's been after me for months; never seen anyone that stubborn." **2.** To possess sexually. *S'è fatta francobollare anche da te? Mamma santa, è insaziabile.* "You screwed her too? Gee, she's insatiable."

FRÀTTE, *f. pl., C.* (Lit., thicket.) **Andar per fratte.** *See* **andare in > camporella.**

FREAK, *Eng., youth.* **1.** *adj.* Extravagant in manners and attire; antisocial. *Ehi, amico freak, non vuoi dirmi dove hai preso quella palandrana? No? Anche oggi fai lo sciopero della parola?* "Hey, freak, you don't want to tell me where you found that cloak? You're not talking today either?" **2.** *m./f.* Person who uses, or is in favor of using, drugs. *Parla da freak, ma non ha spinellato una sola volta in vita sua.* "He talks like a junkie, but he hasn't smoked a single joint all his life."

FREGÀRE, *vt., rude.* (Lit., to rub.) **a)** *slang.* **1.** To possess sexually. *See* **ciulare. 2.** To have anal intercourse. *See* **inculare. 3.** To swindle someone. *T'ha fregato? Ti sta bene, così impari a non ascoltarmi.* "He screwed you? Fine, next time you'll listen to me." **4.** To steal. *Dio cane, mi han fregato un'altra volta l'orologio.* "Shit, they stole my watch again." **b)** *youth.* To flunk. *See* **fottere.**

FREGÀRSENE, *vi. pronom., rude.* (From > **fregare.**) Not to give a damn. *Vai in vacanza col tuo amante? Me ne frego.* "You're going on vacation with your lover? I don't give a damn."

FREGÀTA, *f., rude.* (From > **fregare.**) **1.** Sexual intercourse. *E comprale un altro drink, che poi una bella fregata non ce la toglie nessuno.* "And buy her another drink, so we get a nice fuck for sure." **2.** Swindle. *See* **fregatura.**

FREGATÙRA, *f., rude.* (From > **fregare, a3.**) Swindle. *La vita è piena di fregature, ma la più grossa è venire al mondo.* "Life is full of hose jobs, but the biggest one is having been born."

FRÉGNA, *f., C., rude.* **1.** Vagina. *See* **bernarda. 2.** Nonsense, trifle. *T'ha mollato una sberla? E non fare tante storie per una fregna così.* "He slapped you? Don't go on and on about such nonsense." **3. Avere le fregne.** To be in a bad mood. *E va bene, ho le fregne. E allora?* "All right, I'm grumpy. So what?"

FREGNÀCCIA/FREGNACCIÀTA, *f., C., rude.* (Pejorative of > **fregna.**) Lie, nonsense, stupid thing. *E chi gli crede più a quello? Dice solo fregnacce.* "No one believes a word he says. He bullshits all the time."

FREGNACCIÀRO, *m., C., rude.* (From > **fregnaccia.**) A person who tells tall tales. *Noto a tutti come il fregnacciaro della borgata, riusciva comunque a trovare una vittima ignara.* "Well known as the trickster of the neighborhood, he still managed to find innocent victims."

FREGNÓNE, *m., rude.* (From "fregno," penis.) Person easy to swindle; blockhead. *Rideva di tutto cuore, il fregnone, mentre gli altri due gli portavano via la moto pezzo a pezzo.* "He was laughing wholeheartedly, that dumbass, while the two of them made off with his cycle piece by piece."

FRÉGO, *m., C.* (From > **fregare.**) A lot. *Alessandra ti piacerà anche un frego, ma non fa per te.* "You may like

Alessandra a lot, but she's not your type."

FRÉGOLA, *f., rude.* (Lit., reproductive heat.) **1.** Sexual urge. *Si aggirava per le strade deserte, in preda a una fregola incontenibile.* "He wandered the deserted streets, prey to an insatiable desire for sex." **2.** Craving. *Sai come sono le donne incinta; le è venuta la fregola per una torta alla cioccolata alle tre di mattina.* "You know what pregnant women are like; she got a sudden craving for chocolate cake at three in the morning." **3.** Restlessness. *Ma cos'è 'sta fregola che non puoi star fermo un minuto?* "What's wrong with you that you can't stay still one minute?"

FREGOLÌNA, *f., youth.* (Diminutive of > **fregola, 2.**) Sexy girl who craves sex. *Una fregolina così è pronta per essere colta.* "She's a cherry ready to be popped."

FRÉSCA, *f., C., rude.* (From > **fregna** plus "frasca.") **a)** *slang. See* **bernarda. b)** *youth.* Banknote; money. *Gira molta fresca in quel night, non tutta pulita.* "A lot of money, and I didn't say clean money, changes hands in that nightclub."

FRESCÀCCIA, *f., C., rude. See* **fregnaccia.**

FRÈSCO. (Lit., fresh, cool.) **1.** *adj.* Brazen; shameless. *Con quella faccia fresca ottiene tutto quello che vuole.* "He's so brazen he gets everything he wants." **2.** *m.* Jail; prison. *Ehilà, pallidone, sei stato al fresco?* "Hello there, paleface, have you been in the cooler?"

FRESCÓNE, *m., C., rude. See* **fregnone.**

FRICCHETTÀRO, m., **FRICCHETTÀRA**, *f.*, **FRICCHETTÓNE**, *m.* **FRICCHETTÓNA**, *f., C.* (From English > **freak.**) **a)** *youth.* One who freaks out, loses it. *Stefano è un po' un fricchettone. Meglio stare attento a quello che gli racconti.* "Stefano is something of a freak. Be careful what you tell him." **b)** *narc.* Drug addict. *È un fricchettaro pluriennale. Non lo sapevi?* "He's a long-term freak. Didn't you know that?"

FRITTÀTA, *f.* (Lit., Italian-style omelette.) **Fare una frit-**

tata. (Lit., to make an omelette.) **a)** *slang.* To make a mess of things. *Hai rotto il vaso cinese della nonna? Hai fatto una bella frittata!* "You broke your grandmother's Chinese vase? That's a fine mess!" **b)** *crim.* To kill someone. *Volevano solo dargli una lezione, invece di Piero hanno fatto una frittata.* "They wanted to teach Piero a lesson; instead they iced him."

FRÌTTO, *adj.* (Lit., fried.) **Mangiare il fritto.** (Lit., to eat fried stuff.) To possess sexually. *"Sei ancora all'antipasto?" "Oh, no, ho mangiato anche il fritto."* "'Are you still having appetizers?' 'Oh, no, I've moved on to the main course.'"

FRITTÙRA, *f., crim.* (Lit., dish made of fried meats/various kinds of fish/vegetables.) Loot. *Ha nascosto così bene la frittura che adesso non la trova più.* "He hid the loot so well even he can't find it any longer."

FROCIÀGGINE, *f., C., rude.* (From > **frocio**.) **1.** Being a passive male homosexual. *S'è preso la frociaggine durante i suoi anni di collegio.* "He turned into a faggot during his years in the slammer." **2.** A group of homosexuals. *La frociaggine si trova tutta a Mikonos per le vacanze.* "Faggots, queers, and inverts: they all show up on Mykonos at vacation time."

FRÓCIO, *m., C., youth, rude.* Passive male homosexual. *Dici davvero, è un frocio? Ma se si fa sempre vedere in giro con delle stangone pazzesche!* "Him, a faggot? You can't be serious! He's always in the company of amazing broads."

FRULLÀTO, *m., youth.* (Lit., milk/fruit shake.) **1.** Cocktail. *Non temere, alla loro festa ci sarà un casino di frullati.* "Not to worry. There will be lots of booze at their party." **2.** Necking. *Un po' di frullato è meglio che niente.* "Better a little necking than nothing." **3.** Oral sex. *Le piacciono molto, dico molto, i frullati.* "She likes to suck a lot, and I mean a lot."

FRÙLLO, *m., youth.* (Lit., whir.) A gaggle of girls. *Che c'è stasera, il coprifuoco, che non vedo frulli?* "Are we under curfew tonight? Is that why I don't see any girls around?"

FRÙTTA, *f.* (Lit., fruit.) **Alla frutta.** (Lit., for dessert.) **a)** *slang.* At the end of one's tether. *"Che aspetto orribile hai!" "Sono veramente alla frutta."* "'You look terrible!' 'I'm really finished.'" **b)** *youth.* Original, exciting, brilliant. *Geniaccio, simpatico; niente da dire, è uno alla frutta.* "Brilliant, nice; granted, he's super."

FRÙTTA E VERDÙRA, *idiom., m.* (Lit., fruit and vegetables.) Male homosexual. *Si è offeso perché Gianni gli ha fatto un'avance? Ma lo sanno tutti che è un frutta e verdura.* "He got offended because Gianni made an advance to him? But everyone knows he's a fruit."

FUGHÌNO, *m., N., students.* (Diminutive of "fuga," flight.) **Far fughino.** To skip classes. *Cosa mi date per non spifferare che vi ho visto far fughino?* "I saw you skip classes. What will you give me to buy my silence?"

FUMÀRE, a) *vt., narc.* (Lit., to smoke.) To smoke marijuana. *È uno che fuma un casino.* "He smokes pot a lot." **b)** *vi., slang, rude.* **Fumare i coglioni a qualcuno.** (Lit., for someone's balls to be burning.) To be beside oneself. (Also with the subject left implicit: **Mi (ti/gli) fumano . . .)** *Vuole che paghi io i suoi debiti di gioco. Dammi un estintore, che mi fumano i coglioni!* "He wants me to pay his gambling debts. Give me a fire extinguisher, my balls are burning!"

FUMÀRSELA, *vi. pronom., crim.* (Lit., to smoke away.) To flee. *Sento puzza di bruciato. Meglio fumarsela.* "I smell a rat. We'd better scram."

FUMÀTO, *adj., narc.* (Lit., smoked.) Under the influence of light drugs. *"Che ha da ridere a un funerale?" "È fumata persa."* "'Why is she laughing at a funeral?!' 'She's flying.'"

FUMETTÀRO, *m., youth.* (From "fumetto," comic strip.) Comic strip writer. *Ha sempre detto che da grande avrebbe fatto il fumettaro.* "He always said that when he grew up he would be a comic strip writer."

FUMÉTTO, *m., youth.* (Lit., comic strip.) Idea. *M'è venuto un fumetto megalattico, ma se non sganciate me lo tengo per me.* "I've got a marvelous idea, but if you don't cough up some money I'll keep it for myself."

FUMIÉLLO, *m., C./S.* See **spinello.**

FUMÌFERO, *m., youth.* (Lit., smoke producer.) Smoker of joints. *Non so se quest'erba è buona. Domanda al fumifero.* "I don't know if this grass is any good. Ask the pothead."

FÙMO, *m.* (Lit., smoke.) **a)** *narc.* Marijuana; hashish. *Questo è il prezzo di mercato del fumo: o prendere o lasciare.* "This is the market price for smoke: love it or leave it." **b)** *crim.* **1. Fare fumo.** (Lit., to make smoke.) To run away. *Hanno dovuto far fumo a mani vuote.* "They had to run away empty-handed." **2. Dare il fumo a qualcuno.** To beat someone; to leave someone in the dust. *Non gareggio più con lui: mi dà il fumo ogni volta.* "I'm not racing with him anymore. He leaves me behind in the dust every time."

FUNGÀRE, *vi., youth.* (From > **fungo, a.**) To have sexual intercourse. *Dice che in barca si funga meglio, cullati dalle onde.* "He says it's nicer to do it on a boat, rocked by the waves."

FÙNGO, *m.* (Lit., mushroom.) **a)** *slang.* Penis. *Sei una potente, guarda come hai fatto crescere il mio fungo!* "Oh mighty one, look how you've made my mushroom grow!" **b)** *youth.* **1. Cercare funghi.** (Lit., to go looking for mushrooms.) Said of a woman who wanders about aimlessly, available for sexual adventures. *Come vedi, passa tutte le sere al bar a cercar funghi.* "You can find her every night in that joint, looking for sex." **2.** Umbrella. *Prendi il fungo che piove!* "Take the umbrella. It's raining."

FUÒCO, *m., N., youth.* (Lit., fire.) **Far fuoco.** See **far fughino** under **fughino.**

FUÒRI, *adv.* (Lit., out, outside.) **a)** *crim.* **1.** Out of prison, free. *Per lui è più pericoloso fuori che dentro.* "He's in greater danger outside than inside." **2. Far fuori qual-cuno.** To do someone in. *Non ha avuto tempo di dire "bah," che l'hanno fatto fuori.* "They did him in before he could even open his mouth." **3.** *rude.* **Far fuori una donna.** (Lit., to do a woman in.) To possess sexually. *L'ha fatta fuori solo per vendicarsi di Giovanni.* "He wanted to make Giovanni pay. That's why he banged her." **4. Essere fuori di testa.** To be out of one's mind. *Teresa è fuori di testa da quando suo figlio si è ucciso.* "Ever since her son committed suicide Teresa has been out of her mind." **5. Essere uno/una del fuori.** (From the acronym for the Italian gay organization FUORI.) To be gay. *Non vuole che si sappia, ma è una del fuori.* "She doesn't want it to be known, but she's gay." **b)** *narc.* **1.** Not to be a drug addict any longer. *Perché continui a offrirle la roba? Ormai lei è fuori.* "Why do you keep on offering her stuff? She's kicked the habit." **2.** Intoxicated with narcotics. *Non è mica scemo, solo che è fuori sei giorni su sette.* "He's not stupid, you know, just bombed six days out of seven."

FUSIÓNE, *youth.* (Lit., fusion.) **1.** *idiom.* **Essere in fusione.** (Lit., to be melting.) To be close to orgasm. *Quando ballo con Enrico sono praticamente in fusione.* "When I dance with Enrico I almost come." **2.** *adv.* **Da fusione.** (Lit., so as to make one melt.) Wonderful. *Dio, canta da fusione.* "God, his singing is out of this world."

FÙSO, a) *m., slang.* (Lit., spindle.) Penis. *Ha il fuso che gira bene, è molto richiesto.* "He's got a fine-working tool, in high demand." **b)** *adj., youth/narc.* (Lit., melted.) **1. Essere fuso.** To be beat, stoned. *Tu non guidi, sei troppo fuso.* "You're not driving. You're too stoned." **2.** As an intensifier, meaning "beyond hope." *È gelosa fusa.* "She's consumed by jealousy."

FÙSTO, *m.* (Lit., trunk.) Handsome (young) man. Stud. *Nonostante avesse passato la trentina, era ancora un bel fusto.* "Even though he was well beyond thirty, he was still quite a hunk."

GÀBBIA, *f.* (Lit., cage.) **a)** *slang.* **1.** Jail; prison. *L'hanno messo in gabbia per la terza volta.* "They put him in the slammer for the third time." **2.** Lunatic asylum. *Pazza da gabbia, eppure il medico non vuole ricoverarla.* "She's cuckoo. Why doesn't her physician send her to the hospital?" **b)** *youth.* School. *Ancora un'ora di gabbia. Che palle!* "One more hour of school. What a bore!"

GÀBOLA, *f., N.* (Northern dialect word for "cabala.") Intrigue; machination; device. *Abbiamo trovato una gabola per non pagare le tasse di successione.* "We found a gimmick for not paying any inheritance tax."

GÀGNO, *m., N.* (From Piedmontese "gagnolare," to whine.) Baby; toddler. *Non puoi venire con noi, sei solo una gagna.* "You're not coming with us, you're just a baby."

GALÀTTICO, *adj., youth.* (Lit., galactic.) Fabulous. *"Che ne dici del mio nuovo computer?" "Galattico!"* "'So, what do you think of my new computer?' 'Phenomenal!'"

GALÈRA, *f., youth.* (Lit., prison.) School. *È cominciato un altro anno di galera!* "Another year of school has just begun!"

GÀLLA, *f., youth.* (Feminine of > **gallo.**) A girl one is dating. *Claudia è ancora la tua galla o è di nuovo in pista?* "Is Claudia still your chick or is she available again?"

GALLÀGGINE, *f., youth.* (From > **gallo.**) Behavior and lifestyle of young people who are handsome, well-off, and up-to-date. *Sulle piste da sci il massimo della gallaggine quest'anno sono i berretti con le piume.* "On the ski slopes feathered caps are *the* look of the year."

GALLÀTA, *f., youth.* (From > **gallo.**) An enticing event or situation. *Quest'estate va in canoa sul Colorado: che gallata!* "He's going canoeing on the Colorado River this summer. What a treat!"

GALLÌNA, *f., rude.* (Lit., hen.) **1. Vecchia gallina.** Old woman. *Una vecchia gallina, piena di soldi e di voglie, magari sarebbe riuscito a concludere qualcosa.* "She was an old hen, full of money and whims—there was a chance he would get somewhere with her." **2.** Stupid woman. *Io da lei avrei già divorziato. È una gallina incredibile.* "I would have divorced her years ago. She's such a hen."

GÀLLO, *m., youth.* (Lit., rooster.) **1.** A man who is aggressive and almost harassing toward women. *Tieni le mani a posto! Non hai ancora capito che i galli non vanno più?* "Keep your hands where I can see them! Haven't they told you that cavemen are out of fashion?" **2.** A lady killer. (Also in the diminutive and ironic form **galletto,** and in the superlative form **gallo di dio.**) *"Dove sono finite le bellone?" "Al bar della spiaggia. È arrivato Augusto, gallo di dio."* "'Where did all the broads go?' 'To the bar on the beach. Augusto the great lady killer is here.'"

GALLÒSO, *adj., youth.* (From > **gallo.**) **1.** Enticing, pleasant. *Un safari in Kenia? Galloso!* "A safari in Kenya? Fabulous!" **2.** Said of a youth, especially male, with sex appeal. *Galloso il tuo ganzo. Mi fai fare un giro?* "Your man is quite sexy. Can I have a ride?"

GALVANIZZÀTO, *adj., youth.* (Lit., galvanized.) Excited, exhilarated. *"Perché è così galvanizzato?" "Ha appena saputo che non deve andare militare."* "'Why is he so hyper?' 'He just found out he's not going to be drafted.'"

GÀMBA, *f., N., youth.* (Lit., leg.) **1.** One hundred thousand lire. **Alzare una gamba.** (Lit., to lift a leg.) To earn one hundred thousand lire. **2. Mezza gamba.** (Lit., half a leg.) Fifty thousand lire. *"Allora, hai alzato una gamba o mezza?" "Ne ho alzate due!"* "'So, did you make a hundred thousand or fifty thousand lire?' 'I made two hundred!'"

GAMBIZZÀRE, *vt.* (From "gamba," leg.) **a)** *slang, polit.* To shoot someone in the legs. *Quando fa certi discorsi da fascio, mi viene voglia di gambizzarlo.* "When he starts talking like a Fascist, I get a strong urge to go for his kneecaps." **b)** *youth.* To flunk a student. *T'ha gambizzato di greco?* "Did she flunk you in Greek?"

GÀNCIA, *f., N.* (Perhaps from "gancio," hook.) Hooker. *Non vale granché neanche come gancia.* "She's not worth much even as a hooker."

GÀNCIO, *m., S.* (Lit., hook.) **a)** *crim.* **1.** A theft carried out with dexterity (by using one's hands as a hook.) *Non riesce più a fare ganci, ha l'artrosi.* "He can't do his old sleight-of-hand thefts any longer. He has arthritis." **2.** Thief; accomplice. *Se vuoi ti faccio da gancio, ma una gioielleria io non l'ho mai fatta.* "If you want I'll join you in the burglary, but I've never done a jewelry store before." **3.** Daring man, willing to go to any lengths to get what he wants. *Come tutti i veri ganci, è un tipo affascinante.* "Like all daredevils, he's a charming type." **b)** *youth.* Date, appointment. *Se non gli davo il gancio, non me lo toglievo più di torno.* "I had to give him a date just to get rid of him."

GÀNZO, a) *m., slang.* Lover, paramour. *Fornisce ganzi alle signore sole.* "He provides studs to lonely ladies." **b)** *youth.* **1.** *adj.* Shrewd. *Sei stata ganza a fingere di non sapere che esce con lui.* "You pretended not to know she's going out with him. That was foxy!" **2.** *m.* The person one is dating. *Donatella appartiene alla categoria delle possibili ganze.* "Donatella belongs to the category of possible dates."

GAS, *Eng., m., youth.* Power; speed; rhythm. *Ne ha del gas* *per essere così mingherlino.* "You wouldn't believe he's got so much pep from the looks of him."

GASÀRSI, *vr., youth.* (From > **gas.**) **1.** To get a swelled head. *Da quando fa il master in scienze aziendali si è gasato un fottio.* "He's been on an ego trip ever since he began his MBA." **2.** To get excited; to be turned on. *Adesso non gasarti perché ti ha detto che hai dei begli occhioni.* "Now, don't get all hyped-up because he said you have great eyes."

GASÀTO, *adj., youth.* (From > **gasarsi.**) **1.** Bigheaded. *Gira con Filofax, cellulare e portatile. È tutto gasato!* "He never leaves home without Filofax, cellular, and laptop. He thinks he's it." **2.** Excited; hyper. "*Hai idea come mai è così gasato?*" "*Dev'essere riuscito ad accalappiare la Nicoletta.*" "'Why on earth is he so hyper?' 'He must have scored with Nicoletta.'"

GATTÀRA, *f., C.* (From "gatta," she-cat.) A woman, often old and lonely, who devotes herself to stray cats (which are numerous in Rome). *Non dirai sul serio! Elvira ha fondato un club di gattare?* "You can't be serious! Elvira's founded a cat-lovers' club?"

GATTÌNI, *m. pl.* (Lit., kittens.) **Fare i gattini.** To vomit. *Ho bevuto schifezze tutta la sera, così ho passato la notte a fare i gattini.* "I drank a lot of crap all evening, so I spent the night puking."

GÀTTO, *m., crim.* (Lit., cat.) **1.** Pickpocket; thief. *Fai ancora il gatto? Non avevi deciso di cambiar vita?* "Are you still a thief? Didn't you say you wanted to mend your ways?" **2.** Cop. *Fammi entrare che ho un gatto alle calcagna.* "Let me in, I've got a cop on my heels."

GATTONÀRE, *vt., C.* (from "gatto," cat.) **a)** *youth.* To court a girl. *A me piace farmi gattonare, mica concludere subito.* "I like a long courtship, rather than getting into the sack right away." **b)** *crim.* To steal. *Gattona nelle case dei suoi amici, ecco cosa fa per campare.* "He goes around cleaning out his friends' homes, that's what he does for a living."

GAZZÈLLA, *f.* (Lit., gazelle.) Police car, called "gazelle" because of its speed. *Si precipitarono sul luogo del furto con la gazzella, ma la preda era già scappata.* "The police rushed to the premises, but their prey had already flown away."

GELATÌNA, *f., narc.* (Lit., jelly.) Feeling of exhaustion that overcomes a drug addict at the end of a drug trip. *"Secondo te è morto?" "Ma no, è solo in gelatina."* "'Do you think he's dead?' 'Not to worry; he's only coming down.'"

GENGÌVE, *f. pl., youth.* (Lit., gums.) **1. Fare le gengive colorate.** (Lit., to make gums change color.) To punch someone in the face (until the gums turn red). *"Ma che le è successo?" "Ah, il suo ganzo le ha fatto le gengive colorate."* "'What happened to her?' 'Her lover-boy beat her black and blue.'" **2. Sulle gengive!** Forget it! *Vieni da me dopo avermi fregato con quella farina? Sulle gengive!* "You're asking for my help after cheating me with that dust? Forget it!"

GERÓNTO, *m., youth.* (From Greek "old.") Any person who looks old to youngsters. *Il mondo è pieno di geronti, e chi gli paga la pensione? Noi!* "The world is full of old geezers, and who pays for their retirement? We do!"

GESSÉTTO, *m., N./C.* (Lit., piece of chalk.) A traffic policeman wearing the white summer uniform. *D'estate i gessetti saranno anche eleganti, ma ti danno la multa lo stesso.* "The traffic police have a spiffy summer uniform. That doesn't prevent them from giving you a ticket."

GÈSSO, *m., N.* (Lit., chalk.) **a)** *crim.* **Far del gesso.** (Lit., to produce chalk.) To beat, to thrash. *Per carità, non fategli del gesso, non è lui che ha cantato.* "For heaven's sake, don't thrash him. He's not the one who talked." **b)** *narc.* Heroin. *Alla dogana te la vedi tu col gesso.* "You're the one who is going to get that stuff through customs."

GETTONÀRE, *m., youth.* (From "gettone," token.) To call someone by phone, but with the connotation that a popular person is called often. *È una molto gettonata.* "She's in high demand." (Perhaps by analogy with a record played often in a jukebox.)

GHÈI, *m., N.* (From German "Geld," money.) Money. *"Come stai a ghei?" "Perché, vuoi un prestito?"* "'How are you doing in the green stuff department?' 'Why? Do you want a loan?'"

GHÈNGA, *f., youth.* (Misspelling of English "gang.") The group of young people to which one belongs. *Come mai tu non fai parte di nessuna ghenga?* "Why aren't you one of the boys? Something wrong with you?"

GHIÀCCIO, *m., narc.* (Lit., ice, from English "ice cream," which in slang means "drugs in the shape of small crystals.") *Se vuoi farti, ordina del ghiaccio.* "You want to get a high? Ask for some ice."

GHÌGNA, *f., youth.* (Lit., grimace.) Face. *Ehi, non c'è bisogno di fare quella ghigna. Basta dire di no.* "OK, OK, don't make that face. All you have to do is say no."

GHIGNÀRE, *vi.* (From > **ghigna.**) **a)** *slang.* To laugh. *Adesso ghigna, poi ci pensa il principale a metterlo a posto.* "He's laughing now, but wait until the boss finds out." **b)** *narc.* Hysterical laughing, a sign that narcotics are having a pleasant effect. *Da come ghigna, si direbbe che il viaggio stia andando bene.* "Judging from her laughter, I'd say her trip is going well."

GHIGNÀTA, *f.* (From > **ghignare.**) Laughter. *A momenti morivamo della ghignate.* "We almost died laughing."

GIÀNNI/GIAN, *m., crim.* (Contraction of "giannizzero," janissary.) Member of the carabinieri police corps. *Dice che vuole fare il gianni per mettere dentro quel bastardo di suo padre.* "He's going to become a cop, he says, so he can put away that bastard, his father."

GIGÉTTO, *m.* Whim. *Mi è preso il gigetto di vedere se sta ancora con lui.* "I've got a whim. I want to find out if she's still with him."

GÌGI, *m.* (Diminutive of "Luigi," Louis.) Menstrual period. *Stai sempre così male quando ti viene il gigi?* "Do you feel that sick every time you get your period?"

GÌGIO, *adj.* Defective, damaged, malfunctioning. *Non correre, che ho una gamba gigia.* "Don't rush, my leg is hurting."

GINÀTA, *f., youth.* (From the name "Gino.") Stupid idea, thing, or action worthy of a > **gino,** ugly and boring by definition. *Hai avuto tu l'idea di dipingere la tua camera rosa confetto? Un'altra delle tue ginate.* "Was it your idea to paint your room baby-pink? Another of your stupid ideas."

GINGÌLLO, *m.* (Lit., knickknack.) Revolver. *Non giocare troppo con quel gingillo, è carico!* "Don't toy around with that piece! It's loaded."

GÌNO, *m., N.* (Masculine name.) **a)** *slang.* Penis. *Si prende molta cura del suo gino.* "She takes good care of his dick." **b)** *youth.* A simpleton, a dupe who would like to be a > **paninaro,** but is not up to it. *Guardi Beppe, che è un gino, e sai subito come non devi vestirti.* "You take one look at Beppe, who is a simpleton, and you know at once what not to wear."

GIOBBÀRE, *vt., N./C.* (Either from "Giobbe," Job, the much-abused character in the Bible, or from the English "job," as in "to do a job on someone.") To swindle, to take in. *Sta seduto tutto il giorno nel parco, in attesa di un poveretto da giobbare.* "He spends his days on a park bench, waiting for some poor soul he can take in."

GIOIÈLLI DI FAMÌGLIA, *idiom., m.* (Lit., family jewels.) Male sexual organs. *Per lui il sesso è una tale ossessione che ha fatto un'assicurazione sui gioielli di famiglia.* "He's so obsessed with sex that he insured his private parts."

GIOVANNÌNA, *f., C.* (Diminutive of "Giovanna," Joan.) Vagina. *See* **filiberta.**

GIRAMÉNTO, *m., rude.* (Lit., turning.) **Giramento di coglioni/di palle/di scatole;** (lit., the turning of testicles). Annoyance, impatience. *Non so cos'abbia Anna che non* *va, ma mi fa venire certi giramenti . . .* "I don't know what's wrong with Anna, but she drives me nuts . . ."

GIRÀRE, *vi., rude.* (Lit., to turn.) **1.** *Ma ti gira (il cervello)?* (Lit., "Is your brain turning?") "Are you nuts?" **2. Girare (i coglioni/le palle/le scatole.)** *See* **coglioni.**

GÌRO, *m.* (Lit., turn.) **a)** *slang.* **1.** Gang, social environment. *Chi è quella là? Non è una del giro.* "Who is that girl? She's not one of us." **2.** *rude.* **Un giro di buchi.** A circle of faggots. *Puoi stare tranquilla che quelli non ti toccano. È un giro di buchi!* "Rest easy, those guys will never touch you. They're a bunch of faggots." **3.** Love affair. *Visto com'è azzimata ultimamente? Deve averci un giro.* "Have you noticed how she's dressing lately? She must be having an affair." **b)** *narc.* Drug traffic. *Hai del giro, o devo rivolgermi a qualcun altro?* "Do you have any stuff, or should I ask someone else?"

GÌTA, *f., narc.* (Lit., excursion.) **Fare/Farsi una gita.** (Lit., to go on an excursion.) To shoot drugs in the company of others. *Triste storia: sono andati a fare una gita e non sono più tornati.* "Sad story; they went on a group trip and never came back."

GIÙLIO, *m., N./C.* (Masculine name.) Crowbar used for break-ins. *Cosa credi di fare con quel giulio lì? Quella porta peserà cinquanta chili!* "What do you think you're doing with that crowbar? That door must weigh fifty kilos!"

GIÙSTO, *adj., youth.* (Lit., right.) Said of one who acts in conformity with the rules and tastes of the group. *È troppo giusto quel tuo amico!* "That friend of yours—he's too much!"

GIUSTÓNE, *m.*/**GIUSTÓNA,** *f., youth.* (From > **giusto.**) A person who gets the approval of the group. *Vuoi entrare nel loro giro? Ascolta le sue dritte, è una giustona.* "Do you want to hang around with them? Listen to her tips, she's an insider."

GNÒCCA, *f., N.* (Lit., bump.) **a)** *slang.* Vagina. *Ha una gnoc-*

ca smisurata. "Her pussy is huge." **b)** *youth.* Well-endowed, sexy girl. *Che dici, ci proviamo con quelle due gnocche?* "How about giving it a try with those two chicks?"

GNÒCCO, *N.* (Lit., potato dumpling.) **a)** *m., slang.* Blockhead, thickhead. *Non lo capisci, gnocco, che se continui ad accelerare ci impantaniamo per sempre?* "Don't you understand, thickhead, that if you keep on flooring it we'll get stuck in this mud forever?" **b)** *adj., youth.* Virile; handsome. *Per lei nessuno è mai abbastanza gnocco.* "No rooster is ever good enough for her."

GNÓLA, *f., N., youth.* (From the northern dialect verb "gnauler," to whine.) Whine. *Stai attaccando un'altra gnola?* "Are you starting a new kvetching session?"

GNÒMO, *m., N., youth.* (Lit., gnome.) Thickhead. *Non potevate mandarne uno un po' meno gnomo alla riunione?* "Didn't you have anyone less dense to send to the meeting?"

GNÙGNU, *m., N.* Fool. *L'hai pagata prima di scoparla? Sei proprio un gnugnu.* "You paid her before screwing her? You're a real doodle."

GÒBBA, *f.* (Lit., hunchback.) Good luck. **Avere una bella gobba.** (Lit., to have a nice hunchback.) To have remarkably good luck. *Hai avuto una bella gobba a non farti beccare alla dogana.* "You had a stroke of luck with customs not catching you."

GODÈRE, *vi., N., youth.* (Lit., to enjoy, above all sexually.) To feel great pleasure, not necessarily sexual; to be pleased. *Godevano come dei matti, spiando tra le canne Tonino che cercava disperatamente i suoi vestiti.* "They had the time of their lives peeping through the reeds, while Tonino searched frantically for his clothes."

GODÙRIA, *f., N., youth.* (From > **godere.**) **1.** Pleasure, enjoyment. *Sbronzi e un po' fatti, si buttarono in piscina tutti vestiti. Una vera goduria.* "Drunk and slightly stoned, they jumped fully clothed into the swimming pool. What a kick!" **2.** Pain, suffering. *Ho passato il* *weekend a studiare latino. Sai che goduria!* "I spent the weekend studying Latin. What a pain!"

GODÙTA, *f., N., youth.* (From > **godere.**) Intense pleasure, sexual and nonsexual. (Also in the diminutive **godutina.**) *Che ne dici di una seduta nel Giacuzzi con me? Potrebbe venirne fuori una bella godutina.* "How about a Jacuzzi session with me? We might get a nice kick out of it."

GOLDÓNE, *m.* Condom. *Ha bisogno di goldoni speciali, fuori misura.* "He needs special rubbers, size XX-Large."

GÓNDOLA, *f.* (Lit., gondola.) Vagina. **Andare in gondola.** (Lit., to ride a gondola.) To have sex. *Era dolce andare in gondola, scordandosi il mondo.* "How sweet it was to roll in the hay, the world forgotten."

GRÀNA, *f.* **1.** (Lit., grain.) Money. **Scucire la grana.** To cough up money. *Non ha scucito la grana della protezione e quelli gli hanno dato fuoco al negozio.* "He refused to pay protection money, so those thugs burned down his store." **2.** (Lit., clogging grain.) Trouble. *Cosa vuoi anche tu da me? Sono già pieno di grane.* "Now you want something from me too? Leave me alone, I have enough headaches already."

GRÀNDE, *adj., youth.* (Lit., big.) **Alla grande.** In a big way. *"Ve la siete goduta?" "Alla grande!"* "'Did you have a good time?' 'Super!'"

GRANFÌGA, *f., N.* (Lit., great cunt.) A sexy and beautiful woman. *Te la dà solo se implori. Si crede una granfiga.* "If you want her you must beg her. She thinks she's Venus."

GRÀNO, *m.* (Lit., grain; wheat.) *See* **grana.**

GRANÓSO, *adj.* (From > **grana.**) Full of money. *Monica bazzica il club del golf perché ci vanno tanti tipi granosi.* "Monica hangs around the golf club because it's full of fat cats."

GRANTÙRCO, *m., C.* (Lit., corn.) *See* **grana, 1.**

GRÀTTA, *m., C., crim.* (From "grattare," to scratch, to grate.) Thief. *Paolo, il gratta, ti vuole vedere. Avrà un* *colpo in mente.* "Paolo the thief wants to see you. He must be planning a heist."

GRATTACHÉCCA, *f., C., crim.* (From > **grattare,** and "Checcha," diminutive of "Francesca," Frances.) Stolen goods; loot. *Il grattacheccha lo lasciamo dov'è per almeno sei mesi. Chiaro?* "The loot stays put for at least six months. Got it?"

GRATTAGRÀTTA, *m.* (Lit., scratch-scratch.) Politician (because he/she supposedly steals at the first occasion). *Il grattagratta ha promesso mari e monti, ma chi ci crede?* "The greedy politician has promised the moon and the stars. Do you believe him?"

GRATTÀRE, *vt.* (Lit., to scratch, to grate.) To pinch. *Fammi invitare alla villa. Ci penso io a grattare i gioielli.* "Get me an invitation to that villa. I'll snatch the jewelry."

GRATTUGIACÀZZI, *f., youth, rude.* (From "grattugiare," to grate, and "cazzo," prick.) A particularly ugly and aggressive girl. Ballbuster. *Dev'essere masochista. Si è ficcato con quella grattugiacazzi di Renata.* "He must be a masochist. He's going out with Renata, Ms. Ballbuster."

GRÈZZA, *f., C.* (From the adjective "grezzo," rough.) **Fare una grezza.** To make a blunder. *Se mandi un regalo di Natale al professore, per me ti fai una grezza.* "You want to send a Christmas present to your teacher? I think you're making a big mistake."

GRÌCCIO, *adj., N.* Stingy. *Non è povera, è griccia.* "She isn't at all poor; she's stingy."

GRI(F)FÀRE, *vi., youth.* **1.** To skip classes. *Abbiamo grifato per guardare i mondiali di sci alla TV.* "The world skiing championship was on TV; that's why we skipped classes." **2.** To make a blunder. *Lo vedrebbe anche un cieco che lei si è fatta la plastica! Grifi per vocazione?* "Even a blind bat could see she had plastic surgery. How come you always goof?"

GRÌFO, *m., C.* (Lit., snout.) **a)** *slang.* **1.** Face. *Non mi piace* *il suo grifo, e i suoi modi tanto meno.* "I don't like his mug, and his manners even less." **2. Fare un grifo.** To fall heavily onto the floor. *È inciampata nello strascico e ha fatto un bel grifo.* "She tripped on her gown and fell flat on the floor." **b)** *youth.* **Prendere un grifo.** To make a blunder. *See* **grifare.**

GRÌGIA, *f.* (Lit., grey.) **Fare una grigia.** *See* > **grezza.**

GRÌGIO, *m.*/**GRÌGIA,** *f., youth.* (Lit., grey.) Father/Mother. (Reference to hair color.) *Vatti a fidare dei grigi. Hanno annunciato che divorziano.* "Would you believe it? My old folks have announced they're getting a divorce."

GRÌLLA, *f.* (Feminine of > **grillo.**) Vagina. *Ha una grilla vispa.* "She has a lively pussy."

GRILLÉTTO, *f.* (Lit., trigger.) Clitoris. *Mi sono stufata di lui, non trova mai il mio grilletto.* "I got fed up with him. He never finds my love button."

GRÌLLO, *m.* (Lit., cricket.) Penis. *È tanto depresso, poverino, ha il grillo che non salta più.* "He's so depressed, poor darling; his cricket doesn't sing anymore."

GUAGLIÓNE, *m.*/**GUAGLIÓNA,** *f., S.* **a)** *slang.* Boy/Girl. *E che bella guagliona vi siete trovato, Don Peppì.* "What a beautiful girl you've found, Don Peppì." **b)** *crim.* Member of a Mafia gang. *Parlane con quel guaglione: è uno dei nostri.* "Talk to that guy about your problem. He belongs to our clan."

GUÀNTO, *m.* (Lit., glove.) Condom. *La sera non esce mai senza guanti.* "He never goes out on the town without his rubbers."

GUÀPPO, *m., S.* A member of the Camorra, Naples' version of the Mafia. *Da borsaiolo è passato a guappo. Bella carriera.* "He went from pickpocket to member of the Mob. Great career move."

GUBBIÀRE, *vi., N., youth.* To sleep. *Fossi in te gubbierei un po', prima di andare in disco.* "If I were you I'd catch forty winks before going dancing."

GÙBBIO, *m., N.* (From > **gubbiare.**) Sleep. *Fate venire un gubbio pazzesco coi vostri discorsi.* "You'll put me soundly to sleep with all your talk."

GUFÀRE, *vi., N., youth.* (From "gufo," owl.) **1.** To laugh, to sneer (similar to an owl's call.) *Che avete da gufare in quel modo?* "Why are you laughing like hyenas?" **2.** To bring bad luck. (Possibly because the owl is a bird of ill omen.) *Io il suo nome non lo dico. Ha la fama di essere una che gufa.* "I won't say her name. She's known for giving you the evil eye."

GUFÀTA, *f., N., youth.* (From > **gufare, 1.**) Laughter, sneering. *Ci siamo fatti una bella gufata quando gli sono caduti i pantaloni.* "We had a lot of fun when he dropped his pants."

HAMBURGER, *Eng., m.* Fool. *Io non ci sto a vendere libri usati con Paolo. È un tale hamburger!* "I'm not getting into the used books business with Paolo. He's such a beefhead!"

HANDICAPPÀTO/HÀNDY, *adj., m., youth.* (From the English "handicap.") To be unskilled, almost disabled, even if physically all right. *Quando lei gli si è buttata addosso, è rimasto lì come un salame. Come si fa a essere così handy?* "When she threw herself at him, he stood there like a statue of salt. How can anyone be so gaga?"

HARDWARE, *Eng., m., youth.* Body; physical characteristics. *La grigia è andata a Los Angeles solo per rifarsi l'hardware.* "My mother went to Los Angeles just for some body work."

HARRY, *Eng., m., narc.* Heroin. *Non ne ha mai abbastanza di harry. Un giorno di questi fonde.* "He never has enough of harry. One of these days he'll melt."

HENRY, *Eng., m., narc.* Heroin. *See* **harry.**

HIGH, *Eng., m., narc.* State of euphoria caused by narcotics or alcohol. **Essere in high.** To be high. *Non ha capito niente di quello che hai detto. È in high.* "She didn't get one word of what you said. She's high."

HIPPY, *Eng., m./f., adj., youth.* A youth who dresses and behaves like a 1960s hippy. *Fa l'hippy, ma in garage ha*

144

una Mercedes e una Porsche. "He plays the hippy, but he has a Mercedes and a Porsche in his garage."

HOP, *Eng., m.* Opium; narcotic in general. *È passato all'hop perché ha un buon fornitore.* "He moved on to hop because he has a good supplier."

HOSTESS, *Eng., f.* Prostitute. *L'ho vista a un convegno a Londra; lo sapevi che faceva la hostess?* "I saw her at a conference in London. Did you know she was a hooker?"

I

'IÀO, *interj., youth.* Contraction of "ciao," hello. *"Non ci fai la grazia di salutare neanche stamattina?" "Iao."* "'You're not honoring us with a greeting this morning either?' 'Hi.'"

IBERNÀRSI, *vi. pronom., youth.* (Lit., to hibernate.) **1.** To get chilly. *Chiudi quella porta che qui ci stiamo ibernando.* "Shut that door. We're freezing." **2.** To seclude oneself at home. *"L'hai più vista in giro?" "No, dev'essersi ibernata."* "'Have you seen her lately?' 'No, she must have gone into hibernation.'"

IÈLLA, *f., S.* Bad luck. *Hai scassato anche la sua macchina? Che è, porti iella?* "You crashed his car too? What's the matter with you, do you bring bad luck?"

IMBALLÀRSI, *vi. pronom., youth.* (From "imballare il motore," to race the engine.) To be overcome by such excitement as to get stuck. *Dio, se quel figo mi sorride un'altra volta mi imballo.* "Gee, if that hunk smiles at me one more time, I'll melt."

IMBALLÀTO, *adj., narc.* (From > **imballarsi.**) Drugged out; out to lunch. *Dai, prendigli i soldi; è così imballato che non se ne accorge nemmeno.* "Let's take his money now. He's so junked he won't even notice."

IMBARCÀRSI, *vi. pronom., N., youth.* (Lit., to board.) To get a crush on someone; to start a love affair with someone. *Lo so che Cesare non fa per me, ma mi sono imbar-*

cata persa. "I know Cesare isn't right for me, but I've fallen head over heels in love with him."

IMBARCÀTA, *f., N., youth.* (From > **imbarcarsi.**) Crush. *La segue come un cagnolino: s'è preso una bella imbarcata.* "He follows her like a dog. He's got a big crush on her."

IMBARCÀTO, *adj., N., youth.* (From > **imbarcarsi.**) **1.** In love. *Ridevi tanto di me; adesso sai cosa vuol dire essere davvero imbarcato.* "You used to make fun of me; now you see what it means to be really in love." **2.** Drunk. *Attento al palo! Mamma mia, sei imbarcato sul serio.* "Watch out for that pole! Wow, you're soaked."

IMBELINÀRSI, *vi. pronom., N., rude.* (From > **belino.**) To get into trouble. *Convocato di nuovo in commissariato? Ma come fai a imbelinarti in continuazione?* "Called down to the police station again? How come you're always getting into trouble?"

IMBONÌRE, *vt., youth.* (Lit., to coax.) To court. *Credi a me, ci stanno tutte se le imbonisci a dovere.* "Believe me, no woman will say no if you stroke her the right way."

IMBOSCÀRSI, *vr., N., youth.* (Lit., to take to the woods, to shirk.) To retreat to a secluded place in order to neck. *Si imboscano sempre in biblio durante l'ora di fisica. Tanto la profia è orba.* "Every time there's physics, they hide in the library and neck. Their teacher is that blind."

ÌMBRA/IMBRANÀTO, *adj., N.* (From the jargon of the Alpini, a mountain military corps.) **1.** Clumsy. *Dammi quel casco che te lo metto io. Sei imbra totale.* "Here, let me help you put on that helmet. You're so clumsy." **2.** Greenhorn; novice. *Ehi, tu, la macchina fotografica è da questa parte. Che imbranata!* "Hey, you there, the camera is on this side! What a nerd!"

IMBRANATÙRA, *f., N., youth.* (From > **imbranato.**) Behavior typical of a clumsy person. *Potresti dar lezioni di imbranatura; faresti un sacco di soldi.* "You could give lessons in 'nerdiness'; you'd make a ton of money."

IMBUFALÌTO, *adj.* (From "bufalo," buffalo.) As angry as an enraged buffalo. *Eh, se sei imbufalita! Hai poi aspettato mezz'ora!?* "Gee, you're fit to be tied! I made you wait what—half an hour!?"

IMPACCHETTÀRE, *vt., crim.* (To wrap up.) To arrest. *Li hanno impacchettati all'uscita della bisca clandestina.* "The cops nabbed them as they were coming out of the illegal casino."

IMPADELLÀRSI, *vr., N.* (From "padella," pan, stain.) To stain one's clothes. *Ogni volta che si mette un vestito nuovo puoi giurarci che s'impadella.* "Every time she wears a new dress she stains it, you can count on it."

IMPALÀRE, *vt., N., youth, rude.* (Lit., to impale.) To possess sexually. *S'è lasciata impalare, ma era come farsi una morta.* "She let me stick it in, but it was like making love to a corpse."

IMPALLONÀRSI, *vi. pronom., N.* (From "pallone," balloon.) To dull one's senses with narcotics/alcohol so as not to think about anything. *Lasciami stare! Voglio solo impallonarmi per non pensare più a lui.* "Leave me alone! All I want is to get wasted, so I can stop thinking about him."

IMPASTÀRSI, *vi. pronom., youth.* (From "pasta.") To turn into pasta (dough) in a traffic accident. *Si è impastato contro un TIR, è vivo per miracolo.* "He smashed against an eighteen-wheeler. It's a miracle he's alive."

IMPASTICCÀRSI, *vi. pronom., narc.* (From > **pasticca.**) To use narcotics of any kind. *Se vuoi smettere di impasticcarti, piantalo.* "If you really want to kick the habit, dump him."

IMPASTICCÀTO, *adj., narc.* (From > **pasticca.**) Intoxicated with narcotics. *Non credevo che ce la facesse a tornare a casa, impasticcato com'era.* "He was so smashed, I was afraid he wouldn't make it home."

IMPÀZZA, *f., youth.* (From "impazzare," to whoop it up.) A party bordering on an orgy; drug party. *Uh, che lagna,* *solo perché non ti ho detto che sarebbe stata un'impazza!* "What a whiner, just because I didn't tell you there would be dope at the party."

IMPEDÌTO, *adj., youth.* (From "impedire," to prevent.) Stupid. *Gli vogliamo tutti bene, anche se è un po' impedito.* "We all love him, even though he's not all there."

IMPERMEÀBILE, *m., youth.* (Lit., raincoat.) Condom. *Mariuccia è incazzata nera. Salvatore non vuole saperne di usare l'impermeabile.* "Mariuccia is beside herself. Salvatore refuses to use raincoats."

IMPESTÀTO, *adj., youth.* (From "impestare," variant of "appestare," to infect.) Hard, complicated. *Il compito di mate era impestatissimo.* "The math test was impossible."

IMPÌCCIO, *m., C.* (Lit., fix.) **Fare l'impiccio.** To make a woman pregnant; to get pregnant. *Oh, Gesù, m'ha fatto l'impiccio. Cosa dico a mio marito?* "Jesus, he got me pregnant. What will I tell my husband?"

IMPIOMBÀRE, *m., C.* (Variant of "piombare," to cover with lead.) To shoot someone dead. *L'hanno impiombato così bene che da morto pesava il doppio.* "They pumped so much lead into him he weighed twice as much."

IMPI(P)PÀRSENE, *vi. pronom.* (From > **pip(p)a.**) Not to give a damn. *Me ne impippo di te e dei tuoi casini.* "I couldn't care less about you and your problems."

IMPOLLASTRÀTO, *adj., N.* (From > **pollastro/pollo.**) Reduced to impotence; daft. *Impollastrato, fissava la cassaforte vuota a bocca aperta.* "Frozen, he stared at the empty safe with his mouth wide open."

IN, *Eng., adv.* **a)** *slang.* Up to date. *I tacchi alti sono di nuovo in, ma Dio sa se sono scomodi.* "High heels are in again. God, they're uncomfortable." **b)** *narc.* Intoxicated with narcotics. *È in, ma lo nasconde bene.* "He's on, even though he hides it well."

INASCÒLTABLE, *adj., youth.* (Pseudo Anglicism for "inascoltabile," unbearable to listen to.) *Da quando in qua ti piacciono le canzoni degli anni cinquanta? Sono* *inascoltable.* "Since when have you developed a liking for 1950s songs? They're unbearable."

INCACÀRSENE, *vi. pronom., youth, rude.* (From > **cacca.**) Not to give a damn. *Io me ne incaco di loro. Se hai paura, stattene a casa.* "I don't give a shit about them. If you're afraid, stay home."

INCANNÀRE, *vt., N., youth.* (From > **canna, a.**) **1.** *rude.* To possess sexually. *Dice che nella sua vita ne ha incannate almeno cinquecento.* "Throughout his life, he's fucked at least five hundred women, he says." **2.** To trick. *Vuoi incannarlo per vendicarti che ti ha portato via la ragazza, giusto?* "You want to trick him because he took your girl, don't you?"

INCANNÀTA, *n., N., youth.* (From > **canna, a.**) **1.** *rude.* An act of sexual possession. *Lalla è disponibile per incannate di gruppo.* "Lalla is available for group fucks." **2.** Trick; rip-off. *Per fare la sua ultima incannata si è travestito da Hara-Krishna.* "For his last sting he disguised himself as a Hare Krishna."

INCANNÀTO, *adj.* (From > **cannare.**) **a)** *narc.* Stoned. *Diventa pericoloso quando è incannato.* "When he's stoned he becomes dangerous." **b)** *youth.* Stupid; daft. *Non raccontargli tante panzane su di lei, che poi ci crede, incannato com'è.* "Don't tell him so much crap about her. He believes it, being the shit-for-brains that he is."

INCANNATÓRE, *m., N., youth, rude.* (From > **canna.**) Great lover. *Cosa vuoi, anche il più grande degli incannatori fa cilecca ogni tanto.* "What can you do? It happens even to the greatest stud in the world once in a while."

INCAPPUCCIÀTO, *adj., youth.* (Lit., hooded.) Said of a penis covered with a condom. *Hai paura dell'AIDS, adesso, per quello lo metti a bagno incappucciato?* "Now you're afraid of AIDS, is that why you're wearing a shower cap?"

INCARTÀRSI, *vi. pronom.* (Lit., to be left holding unmatched cards.) **1.** To get confused, mixed up. *Ma non siamo già passati di qui? Devo essermi incartato.* "Didn't we drive through this place before? I must have got mixed up." **2.** To hit a vehicle. *Guidava lei, naturale che ci siamo incartati.* "She was at the wheel, that's why we smashed the car."

INCARTOLÀRSI, *vr., youth.* (From > **cartola, 1.**) To make oneself up; to get a tan with an ultraviolet lamp. *Dove sei andata a incartolarti così? Sei carbonizzata.* "In what salon did you get that tan? You're burned to a crisp."

INCASINAMÉNTO, *m.* (From > **casino.**) Fix; mess. *Lui le ha detto di venire qui, mentre io le ho detto di andare a casa. Che incasinamento!* "He told her to come here. I told her to go home. What a mess!"

INCASINÀRE, *vt.* (From > **casino.**) To make a mess; to get someone else in trouble. *Mi incasini portandomi a casa due drogati e non dovrei incazzarmi?* "You put me on the spot by bringing home two drug addicts, and I'm not supposed to lose it?"

INCASINÀTO, *adj., youth.* (From > **casino.**) **1.** Said of a person whose life is messy and problematic. *È sempre stata incasinata, ma nessuno pensava che si sarebbe suicidata.* "She was in a jam all her life, but no one thought she'd kill herself." **2.** Hard to understand. (Also in the superlative **incasinatìssimo.**) *Ha un problema incasinatissimo con la banca.* "He's got an incredibly messy problem with his bank." **3.** Busy; stretched too thin. *Non ho neanche tempo di parlarti, oggi; sono troppo incasinato.* "I don't even have time to talk to you today. I'm in too much of a mess."

INCAVOLÀRSI, *vi. pronom.* (From "cavolo," cabbage.) Euphemism for > **incazzarsi.**

INCAVOLÀTO, *adj.* (From > **incavolarsi.**) Euphemism for > **incazzato**.

INCAVOLATÙRA, *f.* (From > **incavolarsi.**) Euphemism for > **incazzatura.**

INCAZZÀRE, *vi., rude.* (From > **cazzo.**) **Fare incazzare qualcuno.** To make someone very angry. *Non fatelo incazzare con le vostre cretinate, ci sono già gli operai in* *sciopero.* "Don't drive him up the wall with your non-sense. He's got enough to do with the workers on strike."

INCAZZÀRSI, *vi. pronom., rude.* (From > **cazzo.**) To get very angry. *Tu t'incazzi per niente. Ti ho solo detto che quel ragazzo non fa per te.* "You fly off the handle over nothing. All I said was that that boy is not for you."

INCAZZÀTO (NÈRO), *adj., rude.* (From > **cazzo.**) Very angry. *Sono incazzato nero: quelli del fisco vogliono altri dieci milioni.* "I'm really pissed off. The tax bureau wants another ten million lire from me."

INCAZZATÙRA, *f., rude.* (From > **cazzo.**) Fit of anger. *Suo figlio le fa prendere delle incazzature!* "Her son gives her so much grief!"

INCAZZÓSO, *adj., rude.* (From > **cazzo.**) A person who is prone to anger. *Non mi piace lavorare con lui. È un tipo incazzoso.* "I don't like working with him. He's on such a short fuse."

INCHIAPPETTÀRE, *vt., N., rude.* (From "chiappetta," diminutive of "chiappa," buttock.) **a)** *slang.* **1.** To sodomize. *L'ha inchiappettata malamente ed è finita in ospedale.* "He stuck it up her ass so bad she ended up in the emergency room." **2.** To cheat, to rip off. *Certo che ho assunto un investigatore privato: non voglio mica farmi inchiappettare.* "Of course I hired a private eye. I don't want to get fucked." **b)** *youth.* To catch a student unprepared so as to flunk him/her. *Se il professore ha deciso di inchiappettarti, ti inchiappetta. Rassegnati.* "Look, if the teacher has his mind set on flunking you, he'll find a way to flunk you. Stop worrying."

INCHIODÀTO, *adj., N.* (Lit., nailed.) **a)** *slang.* **1.** Full of debts. *Lui ha perso il lavoro; adesso sono inchiodati seriamente.* "He lost his job. Now they're up to their ears in debt." **2.** A woman who got herself pregnant. *Basta che mi guardi e mi ritrovo inchiodata.* "All he has to do is look at me and I get pregnant." **b)** *youth.* Clumsy youth, not up to date, disliked by his/her peers. *Non invitarla più; è una inchiodata.* "Don't invite her again. She's a nerd."

INCIUCCÀRE, *vt.* (From > **ciucco.**) To get everything wrong. *Ho inciuccato i conti; non ci capisco più niente.* "I got all my calculations wrong. I can make neither head nor tail of them."

INCIUCCÀRSI, *vi. pronom.* (From > **ciucco.**) To get drunk. *Eravamo così felici di averla scampata che ci siamo inciuccati ben bene.* "We were so glad to have come out unscathed that we went on a nice drinking spree."

INCIÙCIO, *m., C., polit.* (Lit., involuntary rubbing against one another.) Under-the-counter alliance between politicians who belong to rival parties. *L'inciucio tra i leader della maggioranza e dell'opposizione non è più un segreto per nessuno.* "The dirty deal between the leaders of the majority and the opposition is no longer a secret to anyone."

INCOCCIÀRE, *C.* (From "coccia," head) **1.** *vt.* To bump into someone. *Li ho incocciati al cinema.* "I bumped into them at the movies." **2.** *vi.* To get the right (or wrong) person. *Guarda che con me incocci male.* "I warn you. You've come to the wrong address."

INCOLLÀTO, *adj., N., youth.* (Lit., glued.) Listless; lazy; unimaginative. *Quello sarebbe il grande drago? Ma se è più incollato di un morto.* "That's the great go-getter? He looks flatter than a dead man to me."

INCROCCHIÀRSI, *vr., C.* (From "crocchio," group.) To crowd together. *Si erano incrocchiati tutti sul luogo dell'incidente.* "They had all crowded near the place of the accident."

INCULÀRE, *vt., rude.* (From > **culo.**) **a)** *slang.* **1.** To sodomize. *La prima notte che ha passato in prigione l'hanno inculato.* "They stuck it up his ass the first night he spent in jail." **2.** To cheat, to rip off. *Per chi mi prendi, per uno che si fa inculare senza dire ba?* "Who do you think I am? One of those guys who gets fucked without saying a word?" **b)** *youth.* **1. Inculare i professori.** (Lit., to stick it up one's teacher's ass.) To get promoted to the next grade (without deserving it). *Dammi una mano* *nell'ultimo compito in classe di chimica, che per una volta lo inculo io.* "Help me out with the last chemistry test. At least I'll get him this time."

INCULÀTA, *f., rude.* (From > **inculare.**) **1.** Sodomization. *Il ricordo peggiore degli anni passati in prigione erano le inculate che aveva dovuto subire.* "His worst memory of his years in prison was of the times he had to take it up his ass." **2.** Rip-off, sting. *Hai degli scrupoli, dopo tutte le inculate che ti ha dato lui?* "You have scruples, after all the times he's ripped you off?" **3.** Running into a car. *Dovresti vedere com'è ridotta la mia Mercedes nuova dopo quell'inculata.* "You should see what my new Mercedes looks like after they ran into me."

INDIÀNI, *m. pl., crim.* (Lit., Indians.) Members of the Italian Customs and Internal Revenue Police Corps (who try not to draw attention to themselves). *È nei pasticci: gli indiani hanno scoperto che truccava gli incassi.* "He's in trouble. The tax agents found out he was doctoring his cash receipts."

INFÀME, *m., S., crim.* (Lit., wicked person.) Spy, traitor. *Non può più farsi vedere da queste parti, lo sanno tutti che è un infame.* "He can no longer show his face around here. Everyone knows he's a turncoat."

INFISCHIÀRSENE, *vi. pronom., rude.* (Probably from the French, "Je m'en fiche," I couldn't care less.) I don't give a damn. *Me ne infischio se te ne vai. Per quello che mi servi quando ci sei!* "I don't give a damn if you leave. You're of no use to me anyway."

INFOGNÀRSI, *vi. pronom.* (From "fogna," sewer.) **1.** To get angry. *Non infognarti tanto, che ti viene un infarto.* "Don't get so worked up. You'll get a heart attack." **2.** To fall in love (and therefore to be in trouble). *Anna s'è infognata in un amorazzo con un tizio che ne ha già altre due.* "Anna's having an affair with a guy who's already seeing two other women." **3.** To get into trouble. *Si infognarono in un giro dove giravano soldi sporchi.* "They got mixed up with people who handle dirty money."

INFOGNÀTO, *adj.* (From > **infognarsi, 3.**) In trouble; in debt. *Infognato com'è, uno di questi giorni finirà per commettere una sciocchezza.* "He's so heavily in debt that one of these days he'll do something silly."

INFORCÀRE, *vt., rude.* (From "forcone," pitchfork, meaning penis.) **1.** To possess sexually. *Lei si fa inforcare, e poi lo va a dire al marito.* "She gets laid, and then goes home and tells her husband." **2.** *See* **fare > forca.**

INFRATTÀRSI, *vr., C. See* **imboscarsi.**

INFROCIÀRE, *vt., C.* To hit something. *Hanno infrociato il muretto del ponte con la moto.* "They hit the parapet of the bridge with their motorcycle."

INFUMÀ(NA)TO, *adj., N., youth.* Extremely annoyed; angry. *Si può sapere che cosa t'han fatto che sei così infumato?* "Would you mind telling me what they did to get you fuming like that?"

INGANNAPÒPOLO, *m./f.* (Lit., one who cheats the people.) Member of parliament. *Tu ti fidi di quell'ingannapopolo perché è una donna. Staremo a vedere.* "You trust that politico because she's a woman. We'll wait and see."

INGARELLÀRE, *vi., youth.* (From "gara," race.) To race, to compete. *Visto la mia nuova moto da cross? Ti va ancora di ingarellare con me?* "Seen my new cross-country cycle? Are you still thinking of racing me?"

INGHÌPPO, *m., C./S.* (From a Roman word, probably of Hebrew origin.) Snag. *Siamo in un bell'inghippo, con i soldi sotto sequestro in banca.* "We're in a jam, with our assets frozen."

INGORGÀRSI, *vt. pronom.* (Lit., to get clogged.) To get drunk. *Gli è bastata mezz'ora per ingorgarsi.* "Half an hour was all it took to send him under the table."

INGRANÀRE, *vi.* (Lit., to put into gear.) To be on a good start with people or with a new activity. *La mia socia mi ha mollato proprio quando gli affari incominciavano a ingranare.* "My partner ditched me just when the business was taking off."

INGRIFÀRSI/INGRIGNÀRSI, *vi. pronom., S.* To get turned on. *Leggeva* Playboy, *ma ha smesso perché non si ingrifa più.* "He used to read *Playboy*, but he gave it up because it doesn't turn him on any longer."

INGUATTÀRSI, *vr., C.* (Variation of "acquattarsi," to squat so as to hide.) To hide. *Bisogna inguattarsi per un po', finché le acque non si siano calmate.* "We'd better go in hiding for a while, until the dust settles."

INSACCÀRE, *vt.* (Lit., to put into sacks.) To make money easily and unexpectedly. *Hanno insaccato un mucchio di soldi alla morte dello zio.* "With their uncle's death they pocketed a lot of money."

INSALÀTA, *f.* (Lit., lettuce; salad.) **a)** *slang.* Money kept in one's pocket in a bundle. *Dalle tasche rigonfie estrasse una manciata di insalata.* "He pulled a handful of lettuce out of his pocket." **b)** *narc.* Mixture of tablets taken as a drug. *Si è fatta una stranissima insalata che a momenti la mandava al Creatore.* "She concocted a strange mixture of drugs that almost sent her to her Creator."

INSAPONÀRE, *vt.* (Lit., to soap.) To butter someone up. *È un maestro a insaponare sua zia per spillarle quattrini.* "He's a pro at buttering up his aunt for money."

INTAPPÀRSI, *vr., youth.* (Variation of > **tapparsi.**) To dress up. *Ti sei intappata per andare a fare la spesa?* "Did you dress up to go buy groceries?"

INTERDÉTTO, *adj., youth.* (Lit., declared incompetent.) Fool; silly. *Sembra un tipo profondo, invece è solo interdetto.* "He looks like he's thinking deep thoughts. On the contrary, he's brainless."

INTIGNÀRE, *vi., S.* To be dead set against something. *Non cercare di convincerla a parlargli. È una che intigna.* "Don't try to convince her to talk to him. She's the type who digs in her heels."

INTÌNGERE, *vi., C.* (Lit., to dip.) To possess sexually. **Andare a intingere.** To go around looking for sex. *Raccontano che vanno a intingere. Ci credi tu?* "They say they're going to get laid. Do you believe them?'"

INTORCINÀTO, *adj., C.* (Lit., tied in knots.) Confused; crooked. *Si è messa con lui, poi l'ha lasciato, l'ha ripreso, l'ha rimollato . . . Lui, poverino, è tutto intorcinato.* "She went out with him, then she left him; she went back to him, she left him again . . . the poor man is all tied in knots."

INTORTÀRE, *vt., N., youth.* (From "torta," cake.) To cajole; to coax. *L'ha intortata, l'ha fottuta e l'ha scaricata.* "He led her on, fucked her, and dumped her."

INTÓRTO, *m., N.* (From > **intortare.**) **Cacciar su un intorto a qualcuno/Fare intorto.** To work on persuading someone to do what one wants from him/her, including sex. *Per mesi aveva cacciato su un bell'intorto a Rachele, ma non riuscì mai a concludere.* "He worked on Rachele for months, but in the end he didn't get anywhere."

INTRALLAZZATÓRE, *m., youth.* (From "intrallazzo," shady deal.) Minister; secretary (considered inclined to shady deals by definition). *L'intrallazzatore è in debito con mio padre. Ti tiriamo fuori noi dai guai.* "The wheeler-dealer owes my father money. Don't worry, we'll get you out of trouble."

INTRIPPÀRSI, *vi. pronom.* **a)** *slang.* (From "trippa," tripe.) To stuff oneself. *Dio, mi sono intrippato per tre!* "Gee, I stuffed myself like a pig." **b)** *narc.* (From the English "trip.") To take drugs. *Tutti da Silvia, il sabato sera, a intripparsi ben bene.* "All at Silvia's house, Saturday night, for a nice trip together." **c)** *youth.* To get enthusiastic about something. *Sì, è un bel film, ma non è il caso di intripparsi.* "Yeah, it's a good movie. Not something to lose your mind over, though."

INTRIPPÀTO, *adj., narc., youth.* (From > **intripparsi**) **1.** Intoxicated with narcotics, especially LSD. *Intrippato? Per me è così di natura.* "Freaked out? No, I think he's like that by nature." **2.** A person who is in good shape, euphoric. *Siamo intrippate, eh, squinzie, perché alla festa viene quel figone!* "We're all psyched up, right, girls, because that famous hunk is coming to the party."

INTRONÀTO, *adj., N., youth.* (Lit., deafened by thunder.) Dazed; not too smart. *Mia zia se la prende da morire perché suo figlio è un po' intronato.* "My aunt gets all worked up because her son is a noodle."

INVERTÌTO, *m., rude.* (Lit., inverted.) A male homosexual. *Hai sentito che il parroco è un invertito?* "Did you hear that our priest is a homo?"

INZUCCÀRSI, *vr. recipr., N.* (From "zucca," pumpkin, meaning head.) To bump into someone or something. *Le uniche due macchine per chilometri e sono riuscite a inzuccarsi.* "The only two cars for miles, and they managed to crash."

INZUPPÀRE, *vt., rude.* **Inzuppare (il biscotto).** *See* **biscotto.**

INZUPPÀRSI. (Lit., to get soaked.) **a)** *vi. pronom., slang.* To get drunk. *Se continui a inzupparti con quell'intruglio finirai col cervello in poltiglia.* "If you keep on soaking up that concoction you'll end up with your brains fried." **b)** *vr., narc.* To take drugs. *Da quella sera che Claudio ci ha lasciato le penne, io non mi inzuppo più.* "I stopped doing drugs the night Claudio kicked the bucket."

INZUPPÀTA, *f., N.* (From > **inzupparsi, b.**) **a)** *narc.* **Farsi un'inzuppata.** To smoke hashish or marijuana with a group of people. *A me piace farmi le inzuppate, niente roba in solitudine.* "I like tea parties. I don't do drugs all alone." **b)** An act of sexual possession. *Non muoio se non scopo, però una bella inzuppata non fa male.* "I don't die if I don't do it, but a nice fuck is good for your health."

ÌTALO, *m., youth.* (Contraction of "italiano," Italian.) Professor of Italian. *L'italo è andato, ti parla solo più in latino.* "The Italian prof is out to lunch; he addresses everyone in Latin."

JACK, *Eng., m., youth.* **1.** Money. *Se non hai jack, come ci andiamo al cinema?* "If you don't have any dough, how can we go to the movies?" **2.** Tobacco. *Le sigarette se le fa lui, con del jack turco.* "He rolls his own cigarettes, using some Turkish tobacco." **3.** Penis. *Perché non le chiedi di aiutarti a inserire il jack? È una navigata.* "Why don't you ask her to help you put it in? She's a pro."

JOINT, *Eng., m.* **a)** *narc.* Marijuana joint. *Non s'è mai fatta un joint, ma dice che stasera vuole provare.* "She's never smoked a joint, but she wants to try tonight." **b)** *slang.* Low-level bar. *Era un posto figo, ma ormai è un joint. A me non interessa più.* "It used to be a great hangout, but it turned into a joint. I'm not interested in it any longer."

JOKER, *Eng., m.* Someone who takes other people in with a smile. *Quando sei un joker il bello è che le tue vittime non si incazzano neppure.* "The nice thing about being a joker is that your victims don't even hold it against you."

JOYSTICK, *Eng., m.* **a)** *narc.* **1.** Pipe for smoking opium or marijuana. *Dalla Cina si è portato a casa una collezione di joystick antichi.* "He brought back a collection of ancient joysticks from China." **2.** *See* **joint, a. b)** *slang.* Penis. *Ci sono tanti tipi di joystick. Questo serve a scopare.* "There are several kinds of joysticks. This one is for screwing."

JUNK, *Eng., m., narc.* Narcotics, especially heroin. *Io non* *ho più junk. Dobbiamo accontentarci di erba.* "I've run out of junk. We have to make do with grass."

JÙNKO, *m., narc.* (Italianization of "junk.") Drug addict. *Ha conosciuto quel junko al mare; adesso è incastrata anche lei.* "She met that junky at the sea resort. Now she's hooked too."

JUNKY, *Eng., m.* Pusher. *Se non trovi lavoro, puoi sempre fare il junky.* "If you can't find a job, you can always become a pusher."

K, *m., youth.* The letter "K" used euphemistically to mean **1.** > **cazzo. 2. Un K.** Nothing. *È inutile che tu faccia il muso lungo. Non ti dò un K.* "Pouting will get you nowhere. I'm not giving you zilch."

KAISER, *m.* (From German for "emperor.") **a)** *slang.* Euphemism for > **cazzo. b)** *youth.* **1.** School principal. *Non parlarmi del kaiser. M'ha espulso un'altra volta!* "Don't talk to me about our school principal. He expelled me again!" **2.** Nothing. *Io non ci capisco un kaiser di quello che sta dicendo.* "I understand zero of what she's saying."

KÀKKOLA, *f., youth.* See **caccola.**

KAPUT, *adj.* (From German "kaputt," out of order, broken.) Dead; destroyed; ruined. *Parlavo con lui solo ieri sera e oggi è kaput, finito.* "I was talking to him only last night, and today he's gone."

KARTONÀRE, *vt., youth.* See **cartonare.**

KARTÓNE, *m., youth.* See **cartone.**

KÀSSUS, *m., youth.* See **cazzo.**

KEEF, KEF, KIF, *m.* (English "kif, kiff.") **a)** *narc.* Marijuana. *Schifoso questo keef. Ti sei fatto fregare come al solito.* "This weed is horrible! You got screwed as usual." **b)** *youth.* **1.** Crappy thing. *Che keef quel programma TV.* "What crap that TV show is!" **2.** Unpleasant person. *Non voglio più vedere quel kif!* "I don't want to see that jerk ever again."

KIWI, *Eng. m., C., youth.* **Essere al/di kiwi.** (Lit., to be like a kiwi). To be depressed. *Lasciami perdere, sono davvero di kiwi.* "Leave me alone, I'm really down."

KOCÌSS, *m., youth.* (From the name of the Apache chief Cochise.) Hairdresser (because of practice adopted by some Native American tribes of removing their enemies' scalps). *Il tuo kociss si prende troppo sul serio. Sembri una recluta.* "Your hair stylist takes himself too seriously. You look like a rookie!"

LA, -LA, *f. pron.* (Lit., her; it.) Vagina. *La dà a tutti, perché t'incazzi?* "She gives it to just about everyone. Why do you lose your mind over it?"

LAGER, *German, m., youth.* (Lit., concentration camp.) School. *Almeno al liceo saremo nello stesso lager.* "At least in high school we'll be in the same concentration camp."

LÀMPADA, *f.* (Lit., lamp.) **a)** *slang.* Head. **Accendere la lampada.** (Lit., to turn on the lamp.) To try to come up with a brilliant idea; to pay attention. *Accendi la lampada, O.K.? Se no da questa montagna non scendiamo vivi.* "Think of something, OK? Otherwise we won't come down alive from this mountain." **b)** *youth.* **Farsi una lampada.** To get a tan (by using an ultraviolet lamp.) *Spende tutti i suoi soldi a farsi lampade.* "She spends all her money in tanning salons."

LÀMPADE, *f. pl., youth.* (Lit., lamps.) Eyes; look. *Se apri le lampade vedrai che il topo è kaput.* "If you open your eyes you'll see that the mouse is dead."

LAMPIÓNE, *m., N.* (Lit., street lamp.) Lanky person. *Sono una buffa coppia: lui un tappo, lei un lampione.* "They make a funny couple: he's knee-high; she's a pole."

LÀNA, *f.* (Lit., wool.) **1.** Very thick hair. *Ho detto al parrucchiere di sfoltirmi la lana: guarda come mi ha conciata!* "I asked the hairdresser to give me a trim: look what

163

he did to me!" **2.** Pubic hair. *Non aveva lana, forse si depilava anche il pube.* "She had no pubic hair, perhaps she shaved down there too."

LANTÈRNE, *f. pl., youth.* (Lit., lanterns.) **1.** *See* **lampade.** **2.** Car beams. *Come fanno gli altri guidatori a vederti se non accendi le lanterne?* "How can the other drivers see you if you don't turn on your beams?"

LÀRDO, *m.* (Lit., lard.) Money; riches. **Colare lardo.** (Lit., to drip lard.) To be very well-off. *Non farti scrupoli a chiedergli soldi: gli cola lardo da tutte le parti.* "Don't be shy about asking him for money; he's loaded."

LASÀGNA, *f., crim.* (Lit., a kind of pasta dish.) **1.** Wallet with several compartments. *Si vedeva dal gonfiore sul didietro che aveva una bella lasagna in tasca.* "You could see from the bulge in his trousers that he had a nice fat wallet in his pocket." **2.** Symbol of rank. *Tutti alti ufficiali alla parata, con le lasagne che luccicavano al sole.* "All the high brass were at the parade, with their insignia shining in the sun." **3.** Police officer. *Chiedi a quel lasagna; magari ti dà una mano.* "Ask that cop; maybe he'll give you a hand."

LASAGNÀRO, *m., crim.* (From > **lasagna.**) **1.** Pickpocket. *Sta' lontana da quel tipo, è un lasagnaro.* "Keep away from the guy; he's a pickpocket." **2.** Prison guard/Police officer. *See* **lasagna, 3.**

LATTÀIA, *f.* (Lit., milkmaid.) A woman endowed with a big bosom. *Passi a trovare la lattaia anche stasera?* "Are you stopping over to see Lady Milkjugs this evening too?"

LATTERÌA, *f.* (Lit., dairy.) Big female bosom. *Le piace mettere in mostra la sua latteria.* "She likes showing off her milkers."

LAVANDÌNO, *m., N.* (Lit., sink.) One who stuffs him/herself with a lot of food, indifferent to quality. *La bistecca puzza un po'? Dalla al lavandino, tanto lui ingoia tutto.* "The steak stinks a bit? Give it to that pig; he devours just about anything."

LAVORÀRE, *vi.* (Lit., to work.) **a)** *crim.* To engage in any dishonest activity so as to make a living. *Non si lavora più come una volta, a mano, adesso bisogna avere il computer.* "You can't live off manual tricks, like in the old days; now you need a computer." **b)** *youth.* To have sexual intercourse. **Lavorare di bocca.** (Lit., to work with one's mouth.) To practice oral sex. *Tina dice che non lo tradisce veramente, perché con Gianni lavora solo di bocca.* "Tina says she isn't really cheating on him, because she's only doing blow jobs with Gianni."

LAVÓRO, *m.* (Lit., job.) **a)** *crim.* Theft, or any other criminal activity that one does for a living. *Ha un lavoro tranquillo al porto, scarica sigarette di contrabbando.* "He's got an easy job at the docks, unloading smuggled cigarettes." **b)** *slang.* Sexual intercourse; erotic game. *Mi sembra il tipo che fa dei bei lavoretti di bocca.* "If you ask me, I'd say she's the type who does good mouth jobs."

LECCACÙLO, *m./f., rude.* (From "leccare," to lick, and "culo," ass.) Servile person. *Si capisce che fa carriera. Ha passato metà della sua vita a fare il leccaculo!* "He's moving up? What a surprise! He's been an ass-kisser all his life."

LECCÀTO/LECCATÌNO, *adj.* (Lit., overpolished.) Said of one who dresses and behaves in an over-sophisticated way. *Non pensavo ti piacessero gli uomini leccati.* "I didn't know you liked dandies."

LECCHÌNO/LECCÓNE, *m., rude. See* **leccaculo.**

LÉGGE DEL MÉNGA, *f., rude.* (Lit., the penis law.) Every man for himself. *Qui vige la legge del menga: nessuno ti aiuta, nessuno ti ripaga se ti fregano.* "The law of the prick rules here: no help if you're in need, no redress if someone screws you."

LÉGNA, *f., N.* (Lit., firewood.) **a)** *youth.* **1. Fare (della) legna.** (Lit., to make firewood.) To beat violently. *Perché gli avete fatto legna? Che v'ha fatto?* "Why did you thrash him? What did he do to you?" **2.** To have many love affairs. *Senti, uno così, abituato a far legna, non ti* *sarà mai fedele.* "Look, a guy like that will never be faithful to you. He's done too much hanky-panky all his life. **b)** *narc.* To take drugs. *Giuro che se fai ancora legna non mi vedi più.* "I swear that if you go on doing dope you'll never see me again."

LEGNÀRE, *vt., N.* (From > **legna.**) *See* **legna, a1.**

LÉNZA, *f., C./S.* (Lit., fishing line.) Cunning person not to be trusted. *Sembra una santerellina, invece è una bella lenza.* "She looks like butter wouldn't melt in her mouth. As a matter of fact, she's quite slick."

LEVÀRE, *vt.* (Lit., to take off.) **Levare le scarpe.** *See* **scarpa.**

LIÀNA, *f., youth.* (Lit., liana.) Public means of transportation. **Attaccarsi alla liana.** (Lit., to hang from a liana.) **1.** To take a bus/tram, etc. *O a fette, o attaccarsi alla liana. Scegli.* "We either catch a bus, or we walk. You choose." **2.** *See* **Attaccarsi al tram.**

LIBERÀRSI, *vr.* (Lit., to free oneself.) To have an abortion. *Si è liberata, ma adesso se n'è pentita.* "She got rid of the baby, but now she's sorry."

LIBÌDINE, *f., youth.* (Lit., lasciviousness.) Great pleasure, not necessarily sexual. *Una libidine la settimana bianca—una libidine mongola!* "We had an awesome ski vacation—you wouldn't believe it!"

LÌBO, *f., youth.* Contraction of > **libidine.**

LICENZIÀRE, *vt., youth.* (Lit., to dismiss, to fire.) To be flunked in school at the end of the year. *M'hanno licenziato anche quest'anno. A scuola non ci torno più.* "They held me back this year too. I'm dropping out of school."

LIFT, *Eng., m.* Euphoria induced by narcotics; cocaine. *Quando sei giù c'è solo il lift che fa qualcosa.* "When you're down, only the white lady can help."

LÌMA, *f., N.* (Lit., file.) **Fare la lima.** (Lit., to file.) To be stingy. *Fa la lima con le figlie. E pensare che è ricco sfondato.* "He's tight-fisted with his daughters. You wouldn't know he's filthy rich."

LIMÀRE, *vt., youth.* (Lit., to file.) To skip class. *Ma no, papà, non sto limando. C'è stato un allarme per una bomba a scuola.* "No, Dad, I'm not skipping class. There was a bomb scare at school."

LIMONÀRE/SLIMONÀRE, *vi.* (From > **limone,** lemon, because while petting, people "squeeze" one another as one does a lemon.) To pet. *Limonano un sacco, ma niente di più.* "They do some heavy necking, but nothing beyond that."

LIMONÀTA, *f.* **a)** *slang.* (From > **limone.**) Necking. *Perché vuoi andare in gita? Non è meglio una bella limonata?* "Why do you want to go hiking? Wouldn't you prefer a little necking?" **b)** *narc.* (From English "lemonade.") Low-quality heroin. *Non ho trovato nient'altro che 'sta limonata.* "I found nothing else but this lemonade."

LIMÓNE, *m.* (Lit., lemon.) **a)** *youth.* **Fare dei limoni.** (Lit., to do lemons.) *See* **limonare. b)** *narc.* **Farsi un limone.** To inject a dose of heroin. *Si va a far limoni in quel casolare, sei avvertita.* "We go to do smack in that farmhouse. You're forewarned." **c)** *crim.* **I limoni.** Members of the Italian Customs and Internal Revenue Police Corps (because of the color of their collar badges). *Oh, no, non i limoni di nuovo. Mi hanno appena spremuta una settimana fa.* "No, not the tax cops again! They squeezed me just a week ago!"

LÌNCE, *f., youth.* (Lit., lynx.) Stupid (by rhetorical inversion of shrewdness, the quality usually attributed to the lynx). *Che lince, Zeus, a fargli vedere dove tieni i soldi!* "What a genius, God, to show him where you keep the money!"

LÌPPA, *f., N.* (Lit., wood stick.) **Andare come una lippa.** (Lit., to move like a spinning stick.) To run like a shot. *Andava come una lippa, inseguito da due pulotti ansanti.* "He was running like a shot, followed by two cops out of breath."

LÌRA, *f.* (Lit., lira.) **a)** *slang.* Money. **1. Essere in lira.** To be well-off (at least for a time). *Andiamo a divertirci,* *visto che sono in lira.* "Let's go have some fun, since I'm flush with money." **2. Essere a corto di lira.** To be feeling the pinch. *Niente vacanze, quest'anno, siamo a corto di lira.* "No vacations, this year; we're short." **b)** *youth.* Worthless thing or person. *Potevi telefonare se non trovavi più le chiavi, no? Sei una lira.* "If you couldn't find your keys, you could have called, right? You're good for nothing."

LÌSCA, *f., crim.* (Lit., fish bone.) *See* **palo.**

LÌSCIO, *adj.* (Lit., smooth.) **a)** *slang.* **Andare liscio. 1.** To act without having to worry about possible complications. *Vai liscio, che ti copro io le spalle.* "Take it easy, I'll cover your back." **2.** To engage in sexual intercourse without any precaution. *Già, son sempre andati lisci. E quanti figli hanno?* "They always did it without any birth control. And how many children do they have?" **b)** *youth.* Mindless, unimaginative. *La prima volta che siete usciti insieme ti ha portato dove portava la sua ex? Che liscio!* "On your first date he took you where he used to go with his former girlfriend? What a square!"

LO, -LO, *m. pron.* (Lit., him; it.) Penis. *Lo vuole? L'hai dato a tutte, dallo anche a lei!* "She wants your thing, right? You gave it to all the others, give it to her too!"

LÒF(F)IO, *adj., N., youth.* (Lit., flabby.) Boring, ugly, insipid, worthless, shabby, etc. *C'è una sola parola per descriverlo: loffio.* "There's only one word for him: a nonentity."

LÓMBO, *m., C.* (Lit., loin.) One-thousand-lire note. *Vuoi cento lombi per quella felpa? È benedetta dal papa?* "You want a hundred thousand lire for that sweatshirt? Did you get it blessed by the pope?"

LÙCCIOLA, *f.* (Lit., firefly.) Prostitute (because both come out at night). *Noi siamo come le lucciole, brilliamo nelle tenebre . . .* (Song.) "We are like fireflies, we light up the darkness . . . "

LUCÌA, *f., N.* (Lit., Lucy.) Vagina. *See* **filiberta.**

LÙI, *m. pron.* (Lit., he/him.) **1.** Any person in a position of power and authority: God, one's father, one's school principal, etc. *"Chi ha detto che non si deve fare?" "Lui." "Lui chi?" "Dio."* "'Who says we shouldn't do it?' 'He did.' 'He who?' 'God.'" **2.** Penis. *Moravia ha scritto un romanzo in cui lui era il personaggio principale.* "Moravia wrote a novel in which the main character was his prick."

LUMÀBILE, *adj., youth.* (From > **lumare**.) Acceptable, bearable. *Da sballo certo non è, è lumabile.* "He's certainly not someone who turns you on. He's all right."

LUMACÓNE, *m., C.* (Lit., slug.) A persistent and "sticky" suitor. *Senti, fra cinque minuti vieni a dirmi che mi cercano, così mi libero del lumacone.* "I need you to come in five minutes saying that someone's looking for me, so I can get rid of this slug."

LUMÀRE, *vt., youth.* (From "lume," light.) To eye; to stare; to look at. *L'hai lumato bene? Eh, che ne dici?* "Did you get a good look at him? So what do you think?"

LÙMI/LUMÌNI, *m. pl., youth.* (Lit., lights.) Eyes. *A cosa ti servono i lumini se non lumi?* "What are your eyes good for, if you don't use them?"

LUMÌNO, *m., S.* (Lit., small light.) Passive male homosexual. *Mio figlio è uscito con Antonio, il lumino. Ora lo sa tutto il paese.* "My son went out with Antonio the fruitcake. Now the whole town knows about it."

LUNGAGNÓNE, *m., N.* (From "lungo," long.) **1.** Tall and lanky person. *Il suo destino era segnato: lungagnone com'era poteva giocare solo a pallacanestro.* "His fate was written. Such a lanky guy could only play basketball." **2.** A person who takes his/her sweet time. *È pronto il lungagnone o dobbiamo mandare i caramba a prenderlo?* "Is the snail ready or do we have to send the cops to pick him up?"

LÙNGO, *adj., youth.* (Lit., long.) **Andare lungo.** (Lit., to go flat.) To fall badly, especially from a motorbike. *Sono* *andato lungo, mi sono rotto due costole, ho fracassato la moto. Gran giorno.* "I took a bad fall; I broke two ribs; I smashed my motorcycle. One of those days."

LUÒGO DÓVE LA SCHIÈNA CÀMBIA NÓME, *idiom, m.* (Lit., the spot where the back changes name.) Buttocks. *Si è fatta male, sai, nel luogo dove la schiena cambia nome.* "She hurt herself down there, you know, in the gluteal region."

LÙPA, *f., youth.* (Lit., she-wolf.) Female Latin professor (alluding to the she-wolf who is the symbol of Rome). *La lupa ulula tutto il tempo, ma nessuno in classe l'ascolta.* "Our Latin teacher shouts all the time, but not a single one of the students listens to her."

LUPÀRA, *f., S., crim.* (Lit., sawed-off shotgun.) **Lupara bianca.** (Lit., white sawed-off gun.) Killing of a person followed by the disposal of the body. *Vittima di lupara bianca. Mai lo troveranno.* "He was the victim of a mafia killing. They'll never find him."

LUPÌNO, *adj., N., youth.* Great, big. *Ho una paura lupina.* "I'm scared out of my mind."

LÙSTRO, *adj., youth.* (Lit., bright.) **Stare lustro.** For someone not to have a chance. *Vuole altri soldi da me: sta lustro!* "He wants more money from me. He can forget about it!"

M, *f., slang, rude. See* **emme.**

MACCHERÓNI, *m. pl., racist.* (Lit., a kind of short pasta.) For a northern European, an Italian person. For a northern Italian, a person from southern Italy. *Dovevi vedere i maccheroni dare l'assalto al treno per andare in ferie in Sicilia.* "You should have seen those rednecks trying to get on the train that would take them to Sicily for vacation."

MACCHIÀRE, *vt., crim.* (Lit., to stain.) To behave against the interest of the mafia clan to which one belongs. *Ha macchiato con quelli di un altro clan; la pagherà cara.* "He was in cahoots with guys from another clan. He'll pay dearly for it."

MACCHIÀTO, *adj., crim.* (Lit., stained.) Repeat offender, so called because his/her record reports previous convictions and is therefore "stained." *Per quel colpo bisogna essere puri come angeli e Andrea è macchiato.* "For that robbery we need clean people. Andrea has a rap sheet."

MACÈLLO, *m., C.* (Lit., slaughter.) A lot. *A sentire Elton John c'era un macello di gente.* "There was a mob to hear Elton John."

MACÙBA, *m., narc.* (From the name of an aromatic tobacco produced until the 1930s in Macuba, Martinique.) Cocaine, or any drug taken by inhalation. *"Eleonora è tutta una zucchero!" "Sfido, vive a macuba."* "'Eleonora is peachy-creamy!' 'I'd be too if I lived on snow, like she does.'"

MACUBÌSTA, *m., narc.* (From > **macuba.**) Drug peddler. *Sono a secco; il mio macubista di fiducia ha deciso che era ora di emigrare.* "I'm out of dope; my trusty supplier moved to safer ground."

MADÀMA, *f.* (Lit., madam.) **a)** *slang.* The madam of a brothel. *La madama prese da parte il pivello, spiegandogli con pazienza cosa doveva fare.* "The madam took the beginner aside and patiently explained what he had to do." **b)** *crim.* The police. *In questo quartiere non c'è posto per noi e per la madama. Qualcuno se ne deve andare.* "In this area there isn't enough room for both us and the police. Someone has to go."

MADEMOISELLE, *f.* (Lit., Miss; taken from the French argot.) Passive male homosexual. *Accontentalo e fai la mademoiselle: è uno che ci può servire.* "He wants you to play the queen. Give him what he wants; he may be useful to us later."

MADÓNNA, *f., rude.* (Lit., the Virgin Mary.) **1. Della madonna**. Used as an intensifier. *Fa un freddo della madonna.* "It's cold as a witch." **2. Una madonna.** Nothing. *Vedi di pulire il finestrino, non ci vedo una madonna.* "Try to clean that window, OK? I can't see zilch."

MADONNÀRE, *vi., N.* (From > **madonna.**) To beat up. *Piantatela, l'avete madonnato abbastanza!* "Stop it! You've beat him up enough."

MADONNÀRO, *m., C.* (From > **madonna.**) **a)** *slang.* One who draws holy scenes on sidewalks using colored chalks. *Tu non ci crederai quanti soldi si becca facendo il madonnaro.* "You won't believe me if I tell you how much he makes drawing holy scenes on pavements." **b)** *youth.* A fan of the rock singer Madonna. *Che combini conciata da extragalattica? Sei diventata una madonnara?* "Why are you wearing that extraterrestrial outfit? Have you become a Madonna freak?"

MADÒNNE, *f. pl.* (From > **madonna.**) **1.** Curses. *Quando s'arrabbia tira certe madonne!* "When he gets angry he swears like a trooper." **2. Avere le madonne.** To be cross. *Davvero, non gli ho fatto niente. Lui ha sempre le madonne.* "I didn't do anything to him, I swear. He's such a crank."

MADÒSCA, *f. See* **madonna.**

MAGGIORÀTA, *f.* (Lit., increased.) A curvaceous woman. *Anita Ekberg è l'esempio classico della maggiorata fisica.* "Anita Ekberg is the classic example of an overly well-endowed woman."

MAGLIÓNE, *m., narc.* (Lit., sweater.) A dose of any kind of drug. *Siamo in cinque. Hai maglioni per tutti?* "There are five of us. Do you have enough dope?"

MAGNÀCCIA/MAGNÀCCIO, *m.* (From Roman dialect "magnare," to eat.) **a)** *C., slang.* Pimp. *Lui non la voleva pagare, lei ha chiamato il suo magnaccia . . .il resto lo sai.* "He didn't want to pay her. She called her pimp . . . the rest is history." **b)** *N., youth.* One who stands out as a student or a sportsman. *Vittorio è davvero un magnaccia del canottaggio!* "When it comes to rowing, Vittorio is a champ."

MÀGO, *m.* (Lit., wizard.) **a)** *slang.* Penis. *Sarai una strega, ma non hai ancora visto il mio mago!* "You may be a witch, but you haven't seen my wizard yet!" **b)** *youth.* Outstanding person, great lover. *Ti fa fare tutto quello che vuole, un vero mago.* "He makes you do whatever he wants. He's some wizard."

MÀGRA, *f.* (From the expression "una magra figura," lit., a poor figure.) **1.** A blunder. *Sono sicura che se la porto al vernissage mi fa fare qualche magra.* "I'm sure that if I take her to the art show opening, she'll make me feel sorry I did." **2.** Death. *Dice che ha visto la magra in faccia.* "He says he looked the grim reaper in the eye."

MÀLA, *f.* Contraction of "malavita," those who devote their lives to crime; crime. *Scrive solo più storie di mala.* "He writes exclusively underworld stories."

MALCAGÀTO, *m., N., rude.* (From "male," badly, and "cagato," defecated). Said of an ugly and poorly dressed person with whom no one wants to deal. *D'accordo, al matrimonio dobbiamo invitare tutto il paese, ma non quel malcagato di Augusto.* "OK, we have to invite the entire town to our wedding, but not that ugly slob Augusto."

MALÈFICO, *adj., youth.* (Lit., harmful.) Damned. *Che tu sia malefica! Non ti racconterò mai più niente delle mie cose.* "May you rot in hell! I'll never tell you anything again!"

MALLÒPPO, *m.* (Lit., bundle.) **a)** *youth.* Book. *Hai visto il mio malloppo? Devo ripassare la lezione di storia.* "Have you seen my book? I have to review my history lesson." **b)** *crim.* Loot. *Il malloppo è saltato fuori dopo vent'anni. Era sepolto in giardino.* "The loot popped up twenty years later. It had been buried in the garden."

MÀMMA, *f.* (Lit., mom.) **a)** *crim.* The police. *Se lo vai a raccontare alla mamma, con noi hai chiuso.* "If you tell the police, it's over with us." **b)** *narc.* Drug peddler; mother (because he/she helps out when the drug addict is in desperate need of a dose). *Ti prego, dimmi dov'è la mamma, che se non mi faccio muoio.* "Please, tell me where the candy man is. If I don't get a hit, I'll die."

MAMMÀNA, *f., S.* (From "mamma," mom.) **1.** The madam of a brothel. *Con lei come mammana le ragazze sono al sicuro, te lo dico io.* "With a madam like that around, the girls are safe, let me tell you." **2.** Midwife; backstreet abortionist. *È finita all'ospedale. C'è mancato poco che la mammana non l'ammazzasse.* "She ended up in the emergency room. That backstreet abortionist came close to killing her."

MAMMASANTÌSSIMA, *m., crim.* (Lit., Holy Virgin.) Big shot in a mafia clan (who is to be worshipped as if he were the Holy Virgin). *Il mammasantissima concedeva udienza una volta alla settimana.* "Once a week the big shot gave audience."

MÀMMOLA, *f.* (Lit., violet.) **1.** A girl who pretends to be innocent, timid, sexually inexperienced. *Faceva la mam-*

*mola, si tirava indietro, ma una volta a letto dovevi ve-
derla.* "She played coy, she feigned reluctance, but once I
got her into bed you should have seen her!" **2.** Prostitute.
Andiamo a coglier mammole stasera? "Shall we go pluck
some violets this evening?"

MANDOLÌNO, *m.* (Lit., mandolin.) Buttocks. *Ti tira, eh, il
suo mandolino!* "Her tush turns you on, doesn't it?"

MANDRAKE, *m., youth.* (From the comic strip character,
Mandrake the Magician.) Intelligent, shrewd, strong man,
almost unbeatable. *Vuoi sfidare a biliardo Ugo, che è un
mandrake?* "Are you sure you want to challenge the
unbeatable Ugo at the pool table?"

MANGANÈLLO, *m.* (Lit., club.) Penis. *Ha un manganello
poderoso, anche troppo.* "He's got a mighty stick, even
too mighty."

MÀNGIA, *m.* (From > **mangiare**) **a)** *slang* Pimp. *Ha
cambiato mangia: l'altro non ha fatto un cazzo quando
quei bastardi l'han menata.* "She changed pimps. The
other did fucking nothing when those thugs thrashed her."
b) *youth.* Corrupt public official, especially at high level.
*Il dott. Lupi, famoso mangia del Ministero della Sanità, è
finito in galera.* "Dr. Lupi, famous spoilsgrabber at the
Ministry of Health, has ended up in jail."

MANGIÀRE. (Lit., to eat.) **a)** *vi., slang.* To earn money
illegally by taking advantage of one's position. *Hanno
mangiato bene con gli appalti per i lavori pubblici.
Adesso vivono all'estero.* "They raked in a lot of money
with public works bids. Now they live abroad." **b)** *vt.,
crim.* **1.** To arrest. *L'han mangiato anche stavolta? Ma
perché non cambia lavoro?* "Did they nail him this time
too? Why doesn't he change his line of work?" **2.** To kill.
*Mangiando quei due hanno mandato un avvertimento a
tutti i macubisti del quartiere.* "They did them in. That
way they sent a message to all the pushers in the neighborhood."

MANGIASÙ, *m., N. See* **mangia.**

MANGIATÓIA, *f.* (Lit., manger.) Source of illegal gain.

Chi vuoi che controlli le commesse militari? Sono una mangiatoia! "There is no oversight of military expenditures, so they're an enormous feeding trough."

MÀNGO, *m., youth.* (Lit., mango.) **1.** Penis. *See* **banana. 2.** Skillful guy, deserving approval. *Fammi entrare nel tuo giro, è pieno di manghi.* "I want to hang out with you guys. You're a bunch of aces."

MÀNICO, *m.* (Lit., handle.) **a)** *slang, rude.* Penis. **Farsi un manico.** To masturbate (oneself). *Si svestiva apposta ogni sera davanti alla finestra aperta in modo che lui potesse farsi un manico?* "Did she undress every night before the lighted window on purpose, to help him jack off?" **b)** *youth.* **1.** A boy who follows the fashion and style of the > **paninari.** *Perché vuoi essere un manico? Non è neanche più di moda.* "Why do you want to be a preppie? It's not even in anymore." **2. Il manico del cuore.** The boy/man with whom one is in love. *Lo so anch'io che è pieno di difetti, ma è il mio manico del cuore.* "I know he's not perfect, but he's my lover boy." **3.** A gang/group leader. *Chiedi a Umberto Magno, è lui il manico.* "Ask Umberto the Great, he's the boss."

MANICÓMIO, *m., youth.* (Lit., lunatic asylum.) School. *Ancora due anni di manicomio, e poi c'è l'università. Ne uscirò pazzo.* "Two more years in that nuthouse and then there's college. When I get out, I'll be crazy."

MÀNO, *f.* (Lit., hand.) **a)** *N., slang.* **1. Una mano di botte.** (Lit., a handful of blows.) A beating. *Se ti vediamo ancora a girare qui intorno, vedrai che mano di botte!* "If we see you hanging around here again, you'll get a beating you won't easily forget!" **2.** Necking; sexual intercourse. *Se vuoi farti una mano con lei, posso metterci una buona parola.* "You want to have a ride with her, right? I'll see what I can do." **b)** *youth.* Five hundred thousand lire (five fingers, each finger (> **dito**) being worth one hundred thousand lire). *Una mano e due dita, tanto ti costerà la stampante.* "The printer will cost you seven hundred thousand lire."

MÀNO MÒRTA, *idiom, f.* (Lit., dead hand.) Furtive (mostly unwanted) fondling of women, usually in crowded places. *Non ci poteva credere: l'ambasciatore, approfittando della folla, le stava facendo la mano morta.* "She couldn't believe it. Taking advantage of the crowd, the ambassador was feeling her ass."

MANTRUGIÀRSI, *vr., youth.* To masturbate. *Sei ridotto a mantrugiarti?* "Are you so badly off that you have to flog your own meat?"

MANZÌRE, *vi., N., youth.* **1.** To be successful in one's erotic endeavors. *Non manzisce molto, però bisogna dire che ci prova.* "He doesn't get laid often, but he doesn't tire of trying." **2.** To be attractive, sexy. *Si è messa una mini che manzisce, anche troppo.* "She put on a miniskirt that turns you on, even too much."

MANZÌTA, *f., N., youth.* (From > **manzire, 1.**) Erotic conquest. *Quest'estate a manzite non sono andata male.* "This summer I've done pretty well in the erotic conquests department."

MARÀNZA, *m., youth, rude.* (Perhaps from the southern word "maranzana," eggplant, or by mixing "maranzana" and "Marocco," Morocco.) Tacky, uncouth, and provincial person; redneck. *Beh, sì, è un maranza, ma sai com'è, a letto . . .* "Well, he's an ape, true, but in bed . . ."

MARCANTÒNIO, *m.* (Probably from the name of the Roman triumvir Mark Anthony.) He-man. *S'è presa un bel marcantonio per marito; i soldi li porta a casa lei.* "She married quite a he-man; she's the one who brings home the bacon."

MARCÀRE, *youth.* (Lit., to mark, to score.) **1.** *vt.* To court a boy/girl insistently. (Taken from soccer jargon: to follow closely the player with the ball so as to prevent him from being effective in his game.) *L'ha marcata tutta la sera, ma lei non si è decisa.* "He came on to her all evening, but he didn't score." **2.** *vi.* To score (sexually). *"Hai marcato con Fiorella?" "Ebbene sì, ho marcato."* "'Did you score with Fiorella?' 'Sure did.'"

MARCHÉSE, *m.* (Lit., marquis.) Menstrual period. *Resto a casa, è venuto il marchese a farmi visita.* "I'm staying home, my period started."

MARCHÉTTA, *f.* (Lit., token.) **1. Fare le marchette.** To engage in prostitution. *Fa le marchette di tanto in tanto per integrare il lunario.* "She turns tricks every now and then to make ends meet." **2.** Male or female prostitute. (Called "marchetta" because in brothels prostitutes used to receive a token, rather than cash, for their work.) *Quell'elegantone là sarebbe una marchetta?* "That dandy, a hustler? Are you serious?"

MÀRCIA, *f.* (Lit., march; gear.) **Marcia indietro.** (Lit., reverse gear.) Coitus interruptus. *Ha fatto marcia indietro, ma ci sono rimasta lo stesso.* "He stopped short, but I got pregnant."

MARCIÀRCI, *vi., C.* (From "marciare," to march.) To take opportunistic advantage of a situation. *Racconta che è orfano, malato, senza lavoro e ci marcia.* "He tells people he's an orphan, sick, jobless—and he gets mileage out of it."

MARÌA, *f., crim.* (Lit., Mary.) (In paintings, each of the pious women present at Christ's crucifixion. Taken to mean feigned piety.) Deceiver, cheater. *Una maria, quel ragazzo, chissà cosa combinerà da grande.* "A slick customer, that kid, who knows what he'll be like when he grows up."

MARÌA/MARJA/MARY, *f., narc.* (From the Spanish "marijuana," spread from Mexico to the USA.) Drug made with cannabis. *Ma no, è solo maria, niente di pesante.* "Come on, it's only Mary Jane, nothing heavy."

MARÌA GIOVÀNNA, *f., narc.* See **maria.**

MARÌA MADDALÈNA, *f., crim.* (Lit., Mary Magdalene.) Police van. *Caricarono le battone sulla maria maddalena tra strilli e insulti.* "To the sound of cries and insults, they loaded all the hookers onto the milk van."

MARIÀNNA, *f.* (Lit., Mary Ann.) **a)** *crim.* Accomplice who tells a gambler the cards held by other players. *Mentre posava le birre sul tavolo da gioco, gli faceva da marianna.* "As he laid the beers on the poker table, he sent him signals about the other players' hands." **b)** *narc.* See **maria.**

MAROCCHÌNO, *m., N. racist.* (Lit., "Moroccan.") For northern Italians, a southern Italian. Now refers to all immigrants from North Africa. *Oh, no, un altro marocchino che vuole lavarmi il parabrezza!* "Oh, no, another wetback who wants to wash my windshield."

MÀRONS, *m. pl.* Pseudo Anglicism for > **marroni.**

MAR(R)ONÀRE, *vi.* (From > **marrone.**) To make a stupid mistake. *Non me lo dire, lo so che marrono a imprestargli di nuovo dei soldi.* "Don't say anything. I know I'm blowing it by lending him more money."

MAR(R)ONÀTA, *f.* (From > **marronare.**) Stupid mistake. *Marronata più, marronata meno, la mia vita non cambia.* "One fuck-up more, one less, my life will be the same."

MAR(R)ÓNE, *m. crim.* **1.** Stolen or smuggled goods seized by the police. *Hai visto? Il caramba si è intascato parte del marrone.* "Did you see that? The cop pocketed some of the goods." **2. Far marrone.** To fail in carrying out a criminal endeavor; to get caught red-handed. *Sono finiti dritti nella trappola della pula: hanno fatto un bel marrone.* "They fell right into the cops' trap: they got caught red-handed."

MARRÓNI, *m. pl., rude.* Testicles. **Rompere i marroni.** See **coglioni.**

MARTELLÀRE, *vt., S., youth.* (Lit., to hammer.) To strike one's fancy. *Non ti martella un bel viaggio in Marocco?* "Doesn't a nice trip to Morocco strike your fancy?"

MÀSO, *adj., m., f., youth.* (Contraction of "masochista," masochist.) *Sono due maso, ma dopo tutto sono adulti e consenzienti.* "They're both masochists, but what can you say? They're consenting adults."

MASSAGGIATRÌCE, *f.* (Lit., masseuse.) Female prostitute (who offers her services through the media under the pretense of doing massages). *L'annuncio diceva "massaggiatrice esperta." La realtà superò di gran lunga la fantasia.* "The ad promised an 'expert masseuse.' The reality went well beyond what he imagined."

MASSÀGGIO, *m.* (Lit., massage.) **1.** Blows. *Se non vuoi un bel massaggio, non cercare di spacciare droga vicino alla scuola!* "If you don't want a nice thrashing, don't try to peddle dope near the school." **2.** Sexual intercourse. *Dopo quello che ho saputo di te, io un massaggio non te lo faccio.* "After what I heard about you, you can forget about tumbling in the sack with me."

MÀSSIMO, *adj., youth.* (Lit., maximum.) **Il massimo.** The most. Intensifier with negative connotation: **Il massimo del niente.** (Lit., the maximum of nothing.) *"Avete combinato qualcosa ieri sera?" "Oh, sì, il massimo del niente."* "'So, what did you do last night?' 'All of nothing.'"

MÀTE, *f., youth.* (Contraction of "matematica," mathematics.) *Domani è una giornata folle: filo, due ore di latino, mate e inglese.* "Tomorrow is a crazy day: philosophy, two hours of Latin, math, and English."

MATERASSÀRE, *vt., youth.* (From "materasso," mattress.) To possess sexually. *Bacilli, slimonatine, O.K. Lasciarsi materessare? Niente.* "Pecks on the cheek, some necking, that's OK. Getting laid? No way."

MATTÀNZA, *f., crim.* (Lit., tuna killing.) Mass killings in a mafia war. *Ultime notizie!!! Mattanza a Palermo. Malinteso tra due capiclan?* "Latest news!!! Mafia massacre in Palermo. A misunderstanding between two bosses?"

MÀTTO, *adj., N., youth.* (Lit., mad.) **Da matti.** So much that one goes crazy for it. *"Ti piace l'heavy metal?" "Da matti."* "'Do you like heavy metal?' 'I'm crazy about it.'"

MATTÓNE, *m.* (Lit., brick.) **a)** *slang.* Boring, unbearable person or thing. *Che mattone 'sto oratore! Ce la filiamo?*

"What a bore this speaker is! Shall we slip away?" **b)** *youth.* Menstrual period. *Quando ha il mattone diventa insopportabile.* "When she's on the rag she's downright unbearable."

MATÙRA, *f., youth.* (Contraction of "maturità," a test all students have to take at the end of high school.) *Dò la matura a giugno.* "I take my high school finals in June."

MATÙSA, *m./f., youth.* (Contraction of "Matusalemme," Methuselah.) **1.** Any one with old-fashioned/traditional ideas. *Secondo quel matusa le donne nell'esercito non ci devono andare.* "According to that old-timer, women shouldn't go into the army." **2.** Parents. *Sei matta? Dire ai matusa che prendo la pillola!* "Are you crazy? I can't tell my old folks I'm on the pill!"

MÀZZA, *f.* (Lit., sledgehammer.) **1.** Penis. *See* **manganello. 2. Una mazza.** Nothing. *Non capisci proprio una mazza.* "You understand zilch."

MAZZÉTTA, *f., S.* (Lit., wad of banknotes.) **1.** Money extorted by organized crime from business people as "insurance" against accidents. *Un milione al mese di mazzetta volevano. Ho dovuto chiudere.* "They wanted one million lire a month for protection. I had to close down." **2.** Money paid by a prostitute to her pimp. *È un bastardo! Si prende la mazzetta e la spende con quella puttana.* "He's a scumbag! He takes my earnings and spends it on that whore!"

MÀZZO, *m., S., rude.* (Lit., bunch, cluster.) Buttocks, used in various expressions. **1.** Good luck. *See* **culo. 2. Farsi il mazzo/Farsi un mazzo così.** To bend over backwards. *Si è fatto un mazzo così per salvare la ditta, ma non ce l'ha fatta.* "He bent over backwards to save the firm, but to no avail." **3. Fare il mazzo a qualcuno.** To keep someone under pressure; to punish someone for not doing what he/she was supposed to do. *Mi ha fatto il mazzo perché, dice lei, i miei disegni erano tutti sbagliati.* "She gave me a real hard time because my drawings were all wrong—or so she says."

MAZZOLÀRE, *vt., youth.* (From "mazza," cudgel, club.) To treat someone harshly. *Ne ha combinata una delle sue, tu però non lo mazzolare troppo.* "He got into trouble again. Don't be too hard on him, OK?"

MÈGA, *youth.* (Greek "great.") **1.** *adj.* Great. *Sei riuscita a farti ridare i soldi? Sei mega.* "You managed to get our money back? You're awesome!" **2.** *prefix.* Used as an intensifier. *È una megafesta.* "It was a mega-party." *È stato un megasballo.* "We had a super high."

MEGAGALÀTTICO, *adj., youth.* (From "mega," great, and "galattico," at galaxy level.) Terrific. *Vieni a vedere* Titanic? *Megagalattico, dicono.* "Are you coming to see *Titanic?* They told me it's terrific."

MÉLA, *f., youth.* (Lit., apple.) Head. **Andare/Essere fuori di mela.** To fall head over heels in love with someone. *Uau, farsi a piedi venticinque chilometri per vederla. Questo si chiama essere fuori di mela.* "Wow, walking twenty-five kilometers just to see her. That's called falling head over heels."

MÉLE, *f. pl.* (Lit., apples.) **1.** Buttocks. *"Bianca ha delle belle mele, ti fanno venire l'acquolina in bocca.* "Bianca has such nice buns they make your mouth water." **2.** Cheeks. *Una volta, avere delle belle mele era considerato segno di salute e bellezza.* "Once upon a time, rosy cheeks were considered a sign of health and beauty."

MELÌNA, *f.* (From tactic in soccer of passing the ball aimlessly in an attempt to kill time.) **Fare (la) melina.** To waste time inconclusively; to try to delay what is coming. *Hanno fatto un po' di melina, però alla fine hanno accettato le nostre condizioni.* "They beat about the bush for a while, but they ended up accepting all our conditions."

MEL(L)ÓNE, *m.* (Lit., melon.) **1.** Head. *Cosa ti sei messa sul melone? Un vaso da notte?* "What did you put on your head? A chamber pot?" **2.** Buttocks. *See* **mele.**

MEL(L)ÓNI, *m. pl.* (Lit., melons.) Breasts. *È piccola pic-*

cola, con dei grandi meloni. "She's a tiny girl, with two huge boobs."

MENAGRÀMO, *m., N.* (From "menare," meaning to bring, and "gramo," a dialect term for bad, poor.) Jinx; dyed-in-the-wool pessimist. *Sei un menagramo. Perché dovrebbero fare sciopero proprio quando partiamo noi?* "You're a jinx. Why should they go on strike right when we're supposed to leave?"

MENÀRE, *vt., N./C., rude.* (From late Latin "minare," to push an animal ahead.) **1.** To beat up. *L'ha menata, eppure lei non vuole denunciarlo.* "He beat her up. Still, she doesn't want to turn him in." **2. Menare il cazzo.** (Lit., to push one's penis around.) To find something to be of little use. *Con le sue promesse verbali ti ci puoi anche menare il cazzo.* "He makes a lot of promises. They are all worth shit." **3. Menarla a qualcuno.** To harp on the same string for too long. *Me l'ha menata per una vita che suo marito la tradiva, il figlio si drogava. Insopportabile.* "She went on and on and on about how her husband cheated on her and how her son did drugs. Unbearable."

MENÀRSELO/MENÀRSI, *vi. pronom, rude.* (From > **menare**.) **Menarsi il cazzo/Menarselo.** (Lit., to push one's penis around.) To masturbate. *Tutte le sue donne sono sparite. Cosa vuoi che faccia? Se lo mena.* "All his women left him. What else can he do? He jacks off by himself."

MENÀTA, *f., N./C., rude.* (From > **menare**.) **1.** Nonsense, bullshit. *Racconta solo menate, ma, Dio solo sa perché, stanno tutti ad ascoltarlo.* "He bullshits all over the place, and yet, God knows why, everyone listens to him." **2.** Annoying thing or situation. *Dobbiamo andare a recuperarla perché la macchina l'ha lasciata a piedi. Che menata!* "We have to go pick her up because her car broke down. What a pain in the ass!"

MÉNGA, *m., youth, rude.* (From Latin "menchia, mentula," penis.) **1.** Penis. *See* **cazzo. 2. Del menga.** Worthless. *Ho* *comprato una radio del menga. È già rotta.* "I bought a radio that's worth shit. It's dead already."

MENÌNGI, *f. pl.* (From Greek "meninx," brain.) **a)** *slang.* Intelligence. **Spremersi le meningi.** (Lit., to rack one's brain.) *Mi sto spremendo le meningi, ma non riesco a ricordarmi come si chiama.* "I'm racking my brain, but I can't remember his name." **b)** *youth.* Very smart person. *Sarà anche meningi, ma lo fa cascare dall'alto.* "She may well be a rocket scientist, but she won't let you forget it."

MERCANZÌA, *f.* (Lit., merchandise.) **1.** Male sexual organs. *Se avessi visto la sua mercanzia, capiresti perché Barbara lo frequenta.* "If you had seen his equipment, you'd understand why Barbara dates him." **2.** Female sexual organs. *Quando si tratta di donne, dice che non vuole mercanzia usata . . . al giorno d'oggi.* "When it comes to women, he says he doesn't want used goods . . . in this day and age."

MÈRCE, *f.* (Lit., merchandise.) **a)** *crim.* Loot. *Quando l'hanno arrestato aveva già passato la merce al complice.* "When they arrested him he had already handed over the goods to his accomplice." **b)** *narc.* Any drug. *Tutti al porto stasera, c'è un carico di merce fresca in arrivo.* "Everyone at the docks tonight. There's a load of fresh stuff coming in."

MÈRDA, *f., rude.* (Lit., shit.) **a)** *slang.* **1.** Horrible thing or person. *Lasciarla sola con due bambini! Azione degna della merda che è!* "Leaving her alone with two little kids! That's worthy of a shit like him!" **2.** Trouble. **Essere nella merda.** To be in deep shit. *Nella merda ormai ci sei. Tappati il naso e procedi.* "At this point you're in deep shit. Hold your nose and keep going." **3. Di merda.** Miserable, worthless, unacceptable. *Un paese di merda, dove in galera ci finiscono solo gli onesti cittadini.* "A shitty country, where only honest citizens get sent to prison." **4. Restare di merda.** (Lit., to be like shit.) To be taken aback. *Sono arrivata alla festa con il suo rivale in affari. Ci è rimasto davvero di merda.* "I showed up at the party with his business rival. That made him feel like shit!" **5. Mangiare merda.** (Lit., to eat shit.) To be subjected to abuse with no possibility of redress. *Dopo aver mangiato merda sul lavoro per trent'anni, mi hanno licenziato di brutto.* "After eating shit on the job for thirty years, I got fired out of the blue." **6.** *Merda!* "Shit!" **b)** *narc.* **1.** Any drug. *Cosa viene a fare qui una signora come lei? A comprar merda?* "What is a lady like you doing here? Buying dope?" **2. Merda pesante.** Heroin. *Il mio cliente vuole solo merda pesante, O.K.?* "My client wants only heavy shit. OK?"

MERDÓSO, *m., youth, rude.* (From > **merda.**) Person whose behavior is beyond the pale. *Racconta in giro che gli ho attaccato l'AIDS, quel merdoso!* "He's spreading the rumor that he got AIDS from me, that piece of shit!"

MERLÙZZO, *m.* (Lit., cod.) Fool. *Se fai sapere a tutti che tieni tanti soldi in casa, sei proprio un merluzzo.* "If you tell the whole world you've got a lot of cash at home, you're what I call a sap."

MÈSCA, *f.,* **MESCÀL,** *m., narc.* Contraction of "mescalina," mescaline. *Ha scoperto la mesca durante quel viaggio in Messico. Adesso non ne può più fare a meno.* "He discovered mesc during that trip to Mexico. Now he's hooked."

MESTIÈRE, *m.* (Lit., trade.) Prostitution. **Fare il mestiere.** To be a prostitute. *Sai, a fare il mestiere se ne vedono di tutti i tipi.* "You know, when you're in the trade you meet all kinds of people."

MÉSTOLO, *m.* (Lit., ladle.) **1.** Power. **Avere il mestolo in mano.** (Lit., to hold the ladle in one's hand.) To lead the dance. *L'avvocato Pranzini ha novant'anni, ma in studio tiene lui il mestolo in mano.* "Mr. Pranzini is ninety years old, but he still leads the dance in his law firm." **2.** Penis. *Lei non si fa problemi. Quando vuole un mestolo, lo compra.* "She doesn't think twice. When she wants a stick to play with, she pays for it."

METAFÌSICO, *adj., youth.* (Lit., metaphysical.) Worthy of a genius, extraordinary. *Ma come fai a farti venire certi fumetti metafisici?* "How do you come up with such cool ideas?"

MÈTAL, *m./f.;* **METALLÀRO,** *m.;* **METALLÀRA,** *f., youth.* (From "metallo," as in "heavy metal kid.") A youth who dresses like a heavy metal musician, all in black, with studs and chains. *Oh, no, Mario in versione metal.* "Oh, no, Mario done up in metal."

MÈTRO, *m., N.* (Lit., meter; unit of measurement.) **a)** *slang.* **Dare dei metri.** (Lit., to give meters.) To leave in the dust. *Non per vantarmi, ma io a quello gli ho sempre dato dei metri.* "I don't want to brag, but I've always left him in the dust." **b)** *narc.* A gram of a drug. *Hai idea di quanta ero c'è in cinquanta metri?* "Do you have any idea how much H there is in fifty grams?" **c)** *youth.* **Fare dei metri.** (Lit., to do meters.) To run away. *Facciamo dei metri, ragazzi, c'è il kaiser in vista!* "Let's scram, guys, the principal is approaching!"

MÉTTERE, *vi., N.* (Lit., to put.) **1.** *rude.* **Andare a mettere.** To go around looking for sex. *È andato a mettere, non sa fare nient'altro.* "He's somewhere getting laid. That's all he does in life." **2. Vuoi mettere?** Said of things with which it is absurd to compare. *Vuoi mettere Des Moines con Los Angeles?* "I mean, what's the point of comparing Des Moines with Los Angeles?"

MÉTTERSI (Lit., to put oneself.) **1.** *vr.* **Mettersi con qualcuno.** To begin a sentimental relationship. *Si è messa con Alberto, ma non è convinta.* "She's going out with Alberto, but she's not convinced." **2.** *vi. pronom.* To pick a quarrel; to come to blows. *Ti metti coi più grandi, certo che te le danno.* "You pick a quarrel with bigger boys; of course they beat you up."

METTÌNCULO, *m., rude.* (From "mettere," to insert, and "culo," ass.) **1.** Active male homosexual. *Strettamente mettinculo, Eugenio.* "Eugenio is gay, but he only plays the macho role." **2.** Cheater; person who always gets his way. The opposite of > **prendiculo.** *Il mondo si divide in* *mettinculi e prendinculi.* "The world is divided into those who screw, and those who get screwed."

MEZZACALZÈTTA, *f., N.* (From "mezza," half, and "calzetta," sock.) Worthless person. *Cosa te ne importa di quello che pensa di te quella mezzacalzetta?* "Why do you care what he thinks of you? He's a zero."

MEZZASÈGA, *f., rude.* (From "mezza," half, and "sega," saw, meaning penis.) A man who is physically poorly endowed, and morally worthless. *Una mezzasega come lui può solo piantarti dei casini.* "A poor slob like him is going to make a mess of things for you, that's for sure."

MÌCCO, *m.* (Lit., young monkey.) **1.** A sucker, chosen as the victim of a theft. *Ecco il nostro micco che si accinge ad attraversare la strada.* "There's our sucker about to cross the street." **2. Fare micco.** To play a trick on someone. *Se ti metti con me, lo facciamo micco.* "If you team up with me, we'll con him."

MICRÀGNA, *f., S.* (From Latin "hemicrania," migraine.) Poverty; economic hardship. *Io, che vengo da una grande famiglia, finire in questa micragna!* "That I, who come from a great family, should wind up here in the gutter!"

MICRAGNÓSO, *adj., S.* (From > **micragna.**) Poor; mean; stingy. *Pensa quanto è micragnoso: neanche il caffè le offre!* "You won't believe how stingy he is: he doesn't even pay for her coffee."

MIGNÒTTA, *f., C., rude.* Prostitute. *Si comporta da mignotta; almeno si facesse pagare.* "She acts like a whore. At least she should make some money out of it." **Figlio di mignotta!** *See* **figlio.**

MÌNCHIA, *m., S., rude.* (From Latin "mentula," penis.) **1.** Penis. *See* **mestolo. 2. Minchia!** Wow! Hell! *Minchia, che sberla di ragazza!* "Wow, what a big girl!"

MINCHIÀTA, *f., S., rude.* (From > **minchia, 1.**) **1.** Nonsense; stupid thing or action. *Sai dove trovi Vincenzo: seduto al bar a dire minchiate.* "You know where to find Vincenzo: in that bar, busy telling crap." **2.** Poorly done thing. *Una minchiata degna di te, questo lavoro di muratura.* "This shitty brickwork is completely worthy of you."

MINCHIÓNE, *m., S., rude.* (From > **minchia, 1.**) Sucker. *Povero minchione, cornificato dalla moglie e dall'amante.* "Poor jerk, cheated on by both wife and lover."

MISTER, *Eng., m., narc.* Drug peddler. *Non decido io se ti diamo roba a credito. Chiedi al mister.* "I'm not the one who decides if we give you dope on credit. Ask the boss."

MÌTICO, *adj., youth.* (From > **mito.**) Mythical, meaning impressive. *Mitica festa, da iscrivere negli annali.* "Awesome party, to go down in history."

MÌTO, *m., youth.* (Lit., myth.) Said of a fascinating, amazing person. *Hai mai visto sua sorella? Un mito.* "Have you ever seen his sister? A goddess."

MODAIÒLO, *m.* (From "moda," fashion.) A person who follows the dictates of fashion obsessively. *Non è veramente elegante, troppo modaiola.* "She's not really stylish; she's too fashion-conscious."

MÒFFO, *adj., N., youth.* Tired; disheartened. *Non essere così moffo, la vita non è mica finita.* "Don't be so blue. Life's not over."

MOLLÀRE, *S.* **1.** *vt.* To give up; to leave, especially in a love affair. *Perché Elio m'ha mollata, perché?* "Why did Elio dump me? Why?" **2.** *vt.* To give; to inflict. *Sai, in partita molli sempre qualche calcio.* "You see, during a soccer game you always give some kicks." **3.** *vi.* To stop; to quit. *E molla, che ci hai stancato con le tue pive!* "Lay off! You've worn us out with your wailing." **4.** *idiom, rude.* **Boia chi molla!** Slogan of right-wing activists (from a fascist slogan). Whoever gives up the struggle is a traitor. *Avanti, diamo una lezione a quei comunisti, e boia chi molla!* "Come on, let's teach those reds a lesson! And damn anyone who lets up!"

MOMÉNTO, *m.* (Lit., moment.) **a)** *narc.* Time when the effect of a drug is at its peak. *Vive per il momento, per* *questo si pera.* "He lives to get off, that's why he shoots up." **b)** *youth.* Emotional and physical state of intense well-being. *Carlo mi dà dei momenti, dei momenti . . . metafisici.* "Carlo gives me some kicks . . . metaphysical kicks."

MÓNA, *N.* (From Venetian term for vagina.) **1.** *f.* Vagina. *Non era giusto, diceva, che tutti si godessero una mona tranne lui.* "It wasn't fair, he kept on saying, that every man had a pussy to enjoy except him." **2.** *m.* Sucker. *Mona d'un mona, perché hai firmato quel contratto?* "Shit-for-brains! Why did you sign that contract?"

MONÀTA, *f., N.* (From > **mona.**) *See* **minchiata.**

MÓNGOLO/MONGOLÒIDE, *adj., m., youth.* (Lit., mongoloid.) Not very bright; slow; daft. *Non ho capito come abbia fatto ad arrivare alla laurea, mongolo com'è.* "I don't understand how he got a college degree. He's really thick."

MONTÀTO, *adj., youth.* (Lit., assembled.) *See* **cissato.**

MÒRDERE, *vt.* (Lit., to bite.) **a)** *crim.* To arrest. *S'è fermato dalla sua bella, così s'è fatto mordere.* "He stopped over at his girl's place, where they nabbed him." **b)** *youth.* To concern, to worry. *Che cos'è che ti morde?* "What's eating you?"

MÒRFA, *f., narc.* (Contraction of "morfina," morphine.) *Ruba la morfina a sua zia, che è medico.* "He lifts morph from his aunt, who's a doctor."

MORTÀCCI, *m. pl., C., rude.* (From "morti," the dead.) **Li mortacci!** (Lit., may your [his/theirs] dead be damned!) To send someone to hell. *Per colpa tua mio figlio è in galera, li mortacci tuoi!* "It's your fault my son is in jail. May you go to hell!"

MÒRTE, *f., narc.* (Lit., death.) Drug. *La droga viene anche chiamata "morte," e lei ne è morta.* "Dope is also called 'death,' and she died of it."

MÒRTO. (Lit., dead.) **a)** *m., crim.* Loot. *Hai nascosto bene il morto? C'è la pula in giro.* "Did you hide the goods well? The police are around." **b)** *idiom, slang.* **Morto di fame.** (Lit., dead from hunger.) Good-for-nothing. *Nessun lavoro va bene per quel morto di fame.* "No job is good enough for that good-for-nothing." **c)** *adj., youth.* Listless person. *'Sto posto sembra un cimitero, tanto siete tutti morti.* "You're all such zombies. This place might as well be a cemetery."

MÒSSA, *f., C.* (Lit., move.) **Darsi una (s)mossa.** To get moving; to change strategy. *Datti una mossa, che se no ci inchiappettano per il resto della vita.* "Do something, otherwise they'll screw us for the rest of our lives."

MÒSTRO/MÙSTRU, *m., N., youth.* (Lit., monster.) Term of endearment among friends and schoolmates. *Mostro mio, come mi sei mancato.* "Beloved monster, how I missed you!"

MOSTRUÒSO, *adj., youth.* (Lit., monstrous.) Beautiful, exceptional. *Un'idea mostruosa, anche se di difficile realizzazione.* "An awesome idea, even though hard to realize."

MOVIMÉNTO, *m.* (Lit., movement.) **a)** *slang.* Circle of acquaintances who are actual or potential sexual partners. *Cambiamo posto, qui non c'è movimento.* "Let's go someplace else. There's no action here." **b)** *crim.* Positive environment for illegal traffic (of any kind, including narcotics). *Bisogna rinnovare la nostra strategia: non c'è più movimento tra gli studenti delle superiori.* "We have to change strategy. Business is at a standstill with high-school students."

MOZZARÈLLA, *f., C.* (A kind of cheese.) A spineless man. *Già sua madre gli diceva, disperata: "Sarai sempre una mozzarella."* "His mother used to tell him, in despair: 'You'll always be a wimp.'"

MÙFFA, *f., crim.* (Lit., moss.) The police. *Corre voce che la muffa stia preparando una retata.* "I heard through the grapevine that the police are preparing a roundup."

MÙFFO, *m., crim.* Spy; police informer. *Me l'ha detto quel* *muffo che è meglio cambiare aria.* "That tipster told me I'd better get a change of scenery."

MÙNGERE, *vt.* (Lit., to milk.) **1.** To practice oral sex. *Le sussurrò, una mano sul ginocchio: "Ci sono dei vantaggi a mungerlo."* "'He whispered, his hand on her knee: 'There are rewards for sucking it.'" **2.** To worm money out of someone through cunning or fraud. *Ha sposato quel bellimbusto che l'ha munta ben bene e poi è sparito.* "She married that dude who squeezed her dry and then disappeared."

MÙSTA, *f., N., youth.* Face, grimace. *Non farmi quella musta, non è colpa mia se abbiamo perso il treno.* "Don't look at me that way. It's not my fault if we missed the train."

MÙTUA, *f.* (Lit., health insurance plan.) **Della mutua.** Malfunctioning; worthless. *Mi hanno venduto una lavastoviglie della mutua!* "They sold me a lemon, not a dishwasher!"

N

NA(AA)!, *adv., youth.* No! "*Le hai poi chiesto se voleva venire con te in campeggio?*" "*Naaa! Non tirava l'aria giusta.*" "'Did you finally ask her to come camping with you?' 'No, it wasn't the right moment.'"

NÀCCHERE, *f. pl.* (Lit., castanets.) **1.** Testicles. *Sai com'è, la gente dice nacchere per non dire coglioni.* "You know how it is, people say 'castanets' so as not to say 'balls.'" **2.** Big bosom. *Ha due nacchere, non due tette!* "She's got two buckets, not two tits."

NÀFTA, *f., narc.* (Contraction of "naftalina," mothballs.) Cocaine. *Ha la casa piena di nafta, mica se ne accorge se gliene prendi un po'.* "He has joy powder all over the place, so he won't even notice if you take some."

NÀIA/NÀJA, *f., N.* (From military jargon for "people, race," perhaps from Latin "natalia," progeny, or "canaja," canaille, rabble.) (Compulsory) military service. **Essere sotto la naia.** To serve in the military (having been drafted). *Era sotto la naia da sei mesi quando ha tentato il suicidio.* "He had been in the army for six months when he tried to commit suicide."

NÀPOLI, *m./f., N., racist.* (Lit., Naples.) For northern Italians, a person born in any part of southern Italy. *Hei, Napoli, nostalgia delle mozzarelle di casa?* "Hey, Naples, feeling homesick for homemade mozzarella?"

NASÀRE, *vt., N.* (From "naso," nose.) To become aware of;

to get wise. *L'affare è andato a monte, perché lui ha nasato che c'era qualcosa di poco pulito.* "The deal went belly up, because he smelled something fishy."

NASÀTA, *f., N., youth.* (Lit., hitting something with one's nose.) Letdown; an (unjustifiable) defeat. *Una nasata, prenderle a pallacanestro da quei pivelli!* "You got creamed playing basketball against those peewees!"

NÀSO, *m., C.* (Lit., nose.) **Da naso. 1.** Person or thing not to be trusted. *Fare il prestanome per quel pescecane? Secondo me, ti ha fatto una proposta da naso.* "To play the front man for that shark? That's a fishy proposition, if you ask me." **2.** *rude.* Homosexual. *Con quello lì lei non corre sicuramente nessun rischio: è da naso.* "She's certainly safe with him. He's a man's man."

NÀSSA, *f., N., youth.* (Lit., type of fishing net.) Vagina. *Se entri nella sua nassa, non ne uscirai mai più. È una strega quella lì!* "If you get caught in her trap, you'll never get out again. She's a witch!"

NÉBBIA!, *interj.* (Lit., fog.) Ignorance; stupidity. *Gliel'ho spiattellato in faccia quello che penso di lui, ma lui . . . nebbia!* "I told him to his face what I think of him, but he just stood there and smiled."

NEGATÌVO, *adj., youth.* (Lit., negative.) Not approvable; displeasing. *Se fossi in te, non mi farei vedere troppo con Gianna: la trovano tutti negativa.* "I wouldn't be seen with Gianna too much if I were you. No one likes her."

NÉMBO, *m., youth.* (From "Nembo Kid," Italian name for Superman.) **Andare da nembo.** To be with it; to be outstanding. *Sembra che non studi mai, eppure a scuola va da nembo.* "He looks like he never does his homework, yet he's tops at school."

NÉRA, *f., crim.* (Lit., black.) The police, because of the color of their old uniforms. *La nera è alla caccia di quelli che hanno ammazzato due dei loro. Stattene tranquillo per un po'.* "The police are chasing those guys who killed two cops. Keep a low profile for a while."

NÉRO, *m.* (Lit., black.) **a)** *slang.* Priest, because of the color of his frock. *S'è travestito da nero e s'è fatto raccontare tutti i peccatucci della signora. Che elemento!* "Disguised as a priest, he got that lady, you know who, to tell him all her sins. He's something else!" **b)** *crim.* Previous offender/Convicted felon. *Più nero di lui non ne trovi nessuno; ne ha fatte di tutti i colori.* "You can't find anyone with a longer rap sheet. He's committed all sorts of crimes." **c)** *narc.* Hashish (of good quality). "*Hai del nero?*" "*No, solo della bianca stavolta.*" "'Got any black hash?' 'No, only some lady snow, today.'"

NEUTRÀLE, *adj., youth.* (Lit., neutral; neuter.) One who shows neither heterosexual nor homosexual tendencies. *Beh, senti, ci sono anche i neutrali a questo mondo, cui il sesso non interessa davvero.* "Well, some people *are* neuter; sex doesn't interest them, period."

NÈVE, *f., narc.* (Lit., snow.) Cocaine. *Dalle bustine rotte la neve cadeva abbondante, coprendo tutto il tappeto.* "Snow was falling copiously from the torn bags, covering the entire rug."

NÌBBA/NÌSBA, *indef. pron., N.* Nothing. "*Hai saputo qualcosa dal pulotto?*" "*Nisba.*" "'Did you get anything out of that cop?' 'Nada.'"

NIX, *indef. pron.* (From German "nichts," nothing.) *See* **nibba.**

NÓCI, *m. pl.* (Lit., walnuts.) Blows, especially to the head. *Gli hanno dato una tale dose di noci che non lo riconoscevo più.* "They gave him such a thrashing that I didn't recognize him."

NON CI PIÒVE, *idiom.* (Lit., it's not raining on that.) It's absolutely certain. *I soldi li tirerà fuori: non ci piove.* "He'll fork over the money. I bet my life on it."

NON ESÌSTE, *idiom, youth.* (Lit., it does not exist.) **1.** Not up to it; a nonentity. *Chiedere aiuto a Sara? Ma se è una che non esiste!* "Ask Sara for help? She's a nonentity!" **2.** It can't be. *In vacanza coi miei? Non esiste.* "Go on vacation with my folks? No way!" **3.** Listless; dull. *Quest'anno la ganga della spiaggia non esiste proprio.* "This year the beach crowd is so boring you could shoot yourself in the head." **4.** Exceptional, beyond belief. *Dove hai comprato quel piumino? Non esiste!* "Where did you get that down jacket? It's out of this world!"

NÒNNO, *m., N.* (Lit., grandfather.) **a)** *slang.* Drafted soldier close to discharge (and therefore "old," and experienced). *Guarda che i nonni sono cattivi: stagli alla larga.* "All oldtimers are nasty. Stay away from him." **b)** *youth.* An old person, or considered so by young people. *Ehi, nonnetto, che ci fai su quella Suzuki?* "Hey, gramps, what are you doing with that Suzuki?"

NÒTTOLA, *f., C.* (Lit., nocturnal bird.) Night watchman (because he/she moves from door to door, like a bat.) *La nottola fa il giro ogni ora: abbiamo tutto il tempo per aprire la serranda.* "The night guard does his rounds once an hour. We've got all the time we need to pry the gate open."

NÙ(F)FIA, *m., N., narc.* (From the Piedmontese "nüffier," to sniff.) Cocaine. *Nufia ce n'è un casino, ma nessuno compra.* "There's a lot of nose candy around, but no buyers."

NUF(F)IÀRE, *vt.* (From > **nuf(f)ia.**) To sniff. *See* **annusare.**

NÙMERO, *m.* (Lit., gag, show piece.) **1.** Absurd behavior. *La commessa l'ha beccata che spostava i vestiti da uno scaffale all'altro: s'è fatta un numero!* "She was caught red-handed by the shopkeeper, as she moved clothing around in the store." **2.** Comic blunder. *Ha urtato un banchetto al supermercato e si è tirato addosso una pila di scatolette: un numero!* "He did a number at the store, hitting a stand and burying himself under a pile of cans." **3.** Comical and peculiar person. *Porta quel tuo amico di Milano alla festa: è proprio un numero!* "Bring that friend of yours from Milan to the party: he's quite a number."

ÒCA, *f., N.* (Lit., goose.) **1.** *Porca l'oca!* (Lit., damn the goose!) Damn! *Porca l'oca, ho fatto tardi anche sta-mattina!* "I'm late this morning too. Damn!" **2. Andare in oca.** To forget something; to be absent-minded. *Vedrai, si saranno dimenticati l'appuntamento. Quei due vanno sempre in oca.* "They must have forgotten our appointment. Those two are always in outer space."

ÒCCHIO, *m., youth.* (Lit., eye.) **Stare in occhio.** To be on the lookout. *Sta in occhio, che io cerco di fregare il testo del prossimo compito di latino.* "Watch out for me, I'm trying to snatch the text of our next Latin test."

OKÀPPA, *interj.* Italian reading of the English "OK." *"In biblio alle tre?" "Okappa."* "'In the library at three?' 'OK.'"

ÒLIO, *m., S.* (Lit., oil.) **a)** *crim.* **Olio per la lampada.** (Lit., lamp oil.) Money to be paid to organized crime for protection. *Io olio per la lampada non ve ne dò più. Fate quello che volete.* "I'm not giving you any more protection money. Do as you please." **b)** *narc.* Resin that drips from hashish when it gets pressed. **Fumare olio.** (Lit., to smoke oil.) To smoke tobacco imbued with this oil. *Non ho abbastanza lira, devo accontentarmi di fumare olio.* "I don't have enough money. I'll have to make do with smoking scented tobacco."

OMOSÈX, *adj.* (From "omosessuale," homosexual.) *Mia*

sorella è omosex: l'ha annunciato ufficialmente. "My sister announced she's gay. She's come out of the closet."

ÒRBITA, *f., narc.* (Lit., orbit.) **Essere in orbita.** (Lit., to be in orbit.) To be under the influence of narcotics. *È una con cui puoi parlare solo quando è in orbita.* "You can only talk to her when she's high."

ORCHÈSTRA, *f., crim.* (Lit., orchestra.) Gang of thieves. *È un'orchestra molto affiatata: te la raccomando per i colpi difficili.* "As an orchestra they play well together. I recommend them highly for complex heists."

ORECCHIÓNE, *m., C., rude.* Passive male homosexual. *Fammi posto che arriva l'orecchione, mica lo voglio vicino.* "Look who's coming: that queer. Make room for me, I don't want to sit next to him."

ORGANÉTTO, *m., crim.* (Lit., barrel organ.) Wallet (because its shape is similar to that of organ bellows). *See* **fisarmonica.**

ORGÀSMO, *m., youth.* (Lit., orgasm.) Any excited state, mental and physical. *Pensa che, una volta, era persino riuscita a toccare Lady Diana! Che orgasmo!* "Once she even managed to touch Lady Diana. What a kick!"

ORIZZONTÀLE, *f., rude.* (Lit., horizontal.) Prostitute (because of the position in which she mostly practices her trade). *Con quella nebbia persino le orizzontali erano sparite.* "There was so much fog that even the street-walkers were nowhere to be seen."

OSCÈNO, *adj., youth.* (Lit., obscene.) Anything that awakens amazement and surprise. *Ha vinto sempre lui a poker ieri sera: una cosa oscena!* "He won every poker game last night. Outrageous!"

OSTERÌA, *f., youth.* (Lit., tavern.) The first word of each strophe of well-known student songs, which are all obscene. *Osteria numero venti,/ se la fica avesse i denti,/ quanti cazzi in ospedale,/quante fiche in tribunale!* "This is inn number twenty,/ If cunts had teeth,/ then how many pricks in the emergency room,/and how many cunts in court!"

ÒSTIA, *f.* (Lit., wafer.) **1.** *f.* Nothing. *Qui non si vede un'ostia.* "You can't see zilch here." **2.** *interj., rude. Ostia!* "Christ!"

ÒSTREGA, *See* **ostia,** 2.

OTTANTACINQUÌNO, *m.*/**OTTANTACINQUÌNA,** *f., youth.* (From "ottantacinque," eighty-five.) Any student who took part in the protest movement beginning in 1985, which demanded concrete educational reforms, and which refused any ideological identification. (As opposed to a "sessantottino," a member of the 1968 student movement, where ideology was of primary importance.) *Non parlarle di -ismi, lei è un'ottantacinquina.* "Don't talk to her about '-isms,' she's an eighty-fiver."

OUT, *Eng., adv., youth/narc.* **1. Essere out.** (Lit., to be out.) To be drugged; to be lost. *Il poliziotto si grattò la testa, stupito: erano tanti, erano tutti out.* "The cop scratched his head in amazement. There were so many of them, all of them freaked out." **2.** Out of the ordinary; original. *Finalmente uno un po' out. In quella scuola sembrano fatti tutti con lo stampino.* "Finally, someone who stands out. In that school they all look mass-produced."

OVERDOSE, *Eng., f.* **a)** *narc.* Overdose. *"Morto?" "Morto. Era la terza overdose in una settimana."* "'Dead?' 'Dead. It was his third overdose in a week.'" **b)** *youth.* **1.** Excessive amount of something unpleasant. *Mi ha interrogato per due ore. Una roba da overdose.* "She called on me in class; two hours of questioning. A killer!" **2.** Negative experience. *Il colloquio per quel posto di lavoro? Un'altra overdose.* "My job interview? Another nonstarter."

P, *f., rude.* The letter "p" used euphemistically to mean >
puttana.

PACCÀRE, *N., youth.* (From "pacco," package.) **1.** *vt.* To
touch. *Ehi, che modi! E chi t'ha paccato?* "Cool it, no
one touched you!" **2.** *vi.* To neck. *Pensi che ce ne sia
qualcuna disponibile a paccare qui?* "Do you think any
of them are available for some necking?"

PÀCCO, *m.* (Lit., package.) **a)** *crim.* **1.** Stolen goods; loot.
*Hai un camion, vero? Allora ti interessa venire a caricare
un pacco?* "You have a truck, right? They left some goods
to be shipped. Interested?" **2.** Buttocks. *Sposta quel
pacco, che ci devo stare anch'io.* "Move your ass, I need
a place to sit too." **b)** *N., youth/narc.* **1. Disfare un pacco.**
(Lit., to open a package.) To seduce a woman. *Un bel
pacco da disfare, la Maria.* "I like the idea of taking the wrapping off Maria." **2. Fare (su) il pacco/
Tirare un pacco.** (Lit., to wrap a package.) To play a
trick on someone. To steal someone else's drug. *Se lasci
l'erba in giro, certo che qualcuno ti fa su il pacco.* "If you
leave your grass sitting around, you can be sure someone
will lift it." **3.** To stand someone up on a date. *Ti sei
pentita di aver detto di sì, ma non vuoi tirargli un pacco.
È un problemino.* "You regret having said yes, but you
don't want to stand him up. You've got a problem." **4.**
Boring person or situation. *Che pacco, suo cugino, con le
sue storie di pesca!* "His cousin is always telling fishing

stories. What a bore!" **5.** A lot. *Suo fratello è un pacco figo.* "Her brother is real cool."

PACCÓNE, *m., narc.* (From > **pacco, b.**)) **1.** Flash, high when taking drugs. *Ti è piaciuto quel paccone, eh?* "You enjoyed that flash, didn't you?" **2.** Good vibes. *Emana dei pacconi megagalattici: quasi quasi mi butto.* "He gives off good vibes; I'm tempted to have a go at it."

PACCÓSO, *adj., N., youth.* (From > **pacco, b4.**) **1.** Boring, unpleasant. *"Vieni già via?" "Tutti paccosi, là dentro, è un'arterio."* "'Are you leaving?' 'Everyone's boring in there, it's like a nursing home.'" **2.** Exciting, lovable. *Paccosa la Samanta? Sì, quando ne ha voglia.* "You say Samanta is appetizing? Well, when she's in the mood."

PACIUGÀRE, *vi., N.* (Lit., to stir together liquid or semi-liquid substances.) To rummage; to make a mess. *Hai paciugato abbastanza nei miei cassetti o vuoi farti anche l'armadio?* "Have you rummaged in my drawers enough, or would you like to try the closet too?"

PACIÙGO, *m., N.* **1.** Mixture. *Mangi quel paciugo?* "Are you eating that stuff?" **2.** Mess, confusion. *Hanno buttato tutto all'aria per cercare le chiavi della barca. Dovevi vedere che paciugo!* "They turned the boat inside out looking for the keys. You should have seen the mess!"

PADÈLLA, *f., N.* (Lit., frying pan.) **a)** *slang.* Oily stain on clothes. *Te le pagano a cottimo, che sei sempre pieno di padelle?* "Are you paid by the piece? You're always full of stains." **b)** *narc.* A spoon used to melt heroin. *Hai visto la mia padella? Dio, come faccio senza?* "Have you seen my spoon? God, what am I going to do without it?"

PADELLÓNE, *m.,* **PADELLÓNA,** *f., N.* (From > **padella, a.**) **a)** *slang.* One who stains his/her clothes often. *Arriva Miss Padellona, l'artista della macchia.* "Here comes Miss Spot, the great staining artist." **b)** *youth.* LP record. *Ti ricordi i bei tempi, quando si andavano a comprare i padelloni?* "Do you remember the good old days, when we used to buy LPs?"

PÀGA, *f., N.* (Lit., wage.) **1. Dare la paga a qualcuno.** (Lit., to pay someone's wages.) To get the better of someone; to beat someone. *Da me non se lo aspettava, quel bauscia, e invece gli ha dato la paga.* "That braggart didn't expect me to get the better of him, but I did!" **2. Prendere la paga.** (Lit., to get one's wages.) To get the worst of it; to be beaten. *Avete preso la paga? Beh, non si può sempre vincere.* "You got beaten? Well, you can't win every time."

PÀGLIA, *f.* (Lit., straw.) **a)** *slang.* **1.** Cigarette. *Tirava fuori le paglie dai posti più impensati, come un mago.* "He pulled cigarettes out of the strangest places, like a magician." **2.** A nonentity. *Un po' di paglia: quello era il personale a disposizione per fare il colpo.* "A bunch of weenies: that was the personnel he had available for doing the robbery." **b)** *narc.* Joint. *No, niente paglia, sono a dieta.* "No grass for me. I'm off it these days."

PAGLIÓNE, *m.* (Lit., pallet.) **Bruciare il paglione. 1.** Not to pay a prostitute for her services. *"Chi l'ha conciato così?" "Il magnaccia della Giusi, perché Tommaso aveva bruciato il paglione."* "'Who beat him black and blue?' 'Giusi's pimp, because Tommaso stiffed her.'" **2.** Not to honor one's word. *Nessuno fa più affari con lui, perché lo sanno tutti che brucia il paglione.* "No one does business with him anymore, because it's well known that he doesn't keep his word."

PALCHÉTTO, *m., crim.* (Lit., theater box.) An apartment that can be broken into through the balcony. *Se vuoi, possiamo farci il palchetto del quinto piano, che è vuoto.* "If you're interested we could go in through the balcony, and do the fifth-floor apartment, which is empty."

PÀLLA, *f., youth.* (Lit., ball [full of air and therefore empty].) **1.** Lie. *Che palla vai raccontando che io me la faccio con Michele?* "What is this crap you're spreading around that I'm in cahoots with Michele?" **2. Nuovo di palla.** Brand new. *Guduriose quelle fanghe. Nuove di palla?* "I'd die for those shoes. Are they brand new?" **3.**

A palla. With the speed of lightning; at the maximum level. **Scappare a palla.** (Lit., to flee like a ball.) *Hanno messo lo zucchero nel serbatoio della sua macchina e poi, via, sono scappati a palla.* "After putting sugar in his gas tank, they took off like bats out of hell." **4. Essere in palla.** (Lit., to be on the ball.) To be in great shape. *"Ti vedo vispo." "Sono in palla, caro, in palla."* "'You're looking good.' 'I'm doing great, my friend, just great.'" To be confused, dazed, and therefore slow on the uptake. *"Attento, è rosso!" "Oddio, sono veramente in palla."* "'Watch out, you've got a red light!' 'Gee, I'm screwing up real bad.'"

PÀLLE, *f. pl., rude.* (Lit., balls.) Testicles. **Avere le palle piene di qualcosa/qualcuno.** (Lit., to have one's ball full of something/someone.) Not to be able to take it any longer. *Lo so che non ne ha colpa se sta male, ma io di lei ne ho proprio piene le palle.* "I understand she can't help it if she's sick, but I've had enough of her." **Avere le palle quadre/sfaccettate.** (Lit., to have square balls/ faceted balls, that is, as hard as crystal.) To be tough; to be very good at whatever one does. *Non farti scrupoli con lui: ha le palle quadre.* "Don't be afraid of coming down hard on him. He's got balls." **Farsi due palle così.** (Lit., to make one's balls this big.) To work hard; to bend over backwards. *Mi sono fatto due palle così per tirarlo fuori dal carcere e lui si è fatto riprendere.* "I busted my balls to get him out of prison and he got himself arrested again." **Levarsi/Togliersi/Andarsene fuori dalle palle.** (Lit., to get off someone's balls.) To rid someone of one's annoying presence. *Dille che le stanno rubando la macchina, così se ne va fuori dalle palle.* "Tell her they're stealing her car, so she'll leave us alone." **Rompere le palle.** To break someone's balls, i.e., to annoy someone immensely. *Mio figlio mi ha rotto talmente le palle che alla fine gli ho comprato il motorino.* "My son busted my balls so much that I gave in and bought him a moped."

PALLONÀRO, *m., C., rude.* (From > **palla, 1.**) Liar; braggart. *Il venticinque per cento di profitto ti ha promesso?*

Come pallonaro è notevole. "He promised you a twenty-five percent profit? As a bullshitter he's outstanding."

PALLONCÌNO, *m., youth.* (Lit., balloon.) Condom. *Ricordati i palloncini, se no, niente su e giù!* "Remember to bring rubbers, otherwise, no hanky-panky."

PALLÓNE, *m., youth.* (Lit., ball.) **1.** Head. **Essere/Andare nel pallone.** (Lit., to be in a balloon.) To get confused. *Va nel pallone per niente. Non deve assolutamente fare lui la presentazione al cliente.* "He clams up just like that. He must not make the presentation to our client." **Fare un pallone così.** (Lit., to make someone's head this big.) To drive someone crazy. *Figurati che suo marito le ha fatto un pallone così perché ha speso troppo per le scarpe.* "Listen to this one. Her husband drove her nuts complaining that she paid too much for her new shoes." **2.** Buttocks. *Con un pallone così può star comodo anche seduto su un letto da fachiro.* "With that lardass of his he'd be comfortable seated on an iron bed." **3. Pallone (gonfiato).** Stuffed shirt. *Come tutti i palloni gonfiati si offende per un nonnulla.* "Like all stuffed shirts he's thin-skinned."

PALLÓSO, *adj., youth.* Boring, unbearable. *Saranno sofisticati, ma i film francesi io li trovo pallosi.* "French films may be sophisticated, but I find them boring."

PÀLO, *m.* (Lit., pole.) **a)** *slang.* **1.** Accomplice on the lookout. *La vedi quella all'angolo, che fa finta di cercare clienti? È lei il palo.* "You see that woman on the corner, pretending to be a hooker? She's the lookout." **2.** Penis. *Pensa te, quando ha visto il mio palo si è spaventata e si è messa a strillare.* "Would you believe it? When she saw my stick she freaked out and started to scream." **b)** *N., youth.* **1.** One million lire. **Alzare un palo.** (Lit., to raise a pole.) To earn one million lire. *Un palo al mese riesco ad alzare con quel lavoro. Un bello schifo.* "That job pays only one million lire a month. Nothing." **2.** Date. *Perché non provi a chiederle un palo?* "Why don't you ask her out?"

PANÀTO, *adj., N.* (Lit., breaded and ready to be fried.) Taken in; involved in a disastrous situation from which there is no escape. *Se quelli tirano fuori le pistole siamo panati.* "If those guys take out their guns, we're cooked."

PÀNE, *m., C.* (Lit., bread.) **Mangiare pane e volpe.** (Lit., to eat bread and fox.) To be/To believe oneself to be very cunning. *La sua parola d'ordine per il computer è la sua data di nascita. Ha mangiato pane e volpe!* "His computer password is his birthdate. He's such a fox!"

PANÈLLA, *f., youth.* A young girl who follows the fashion and behavior of > **paninari.** *Fa la panella, ma si vede che non fa per lei.* "She thinks she's with it, but you can see it's not her style."

PANÉTTO, *m., C.* Passive male homosexual. *Si vuol fare quel ragazzo, ma per me quello non è un panetto.* "He'd like to pick up that boy, but I'd say he's not queer."

PANIÈRE, *m.* (Lit., basket.) **1.** Buttocks. *Il paniere è un po' sul pesante, comunque è una bellona.* "Her ass is somewhat big, but altogether she's quite sexy." **2.** Vagina. *Il suo paniere di qua, il suo paniere di là . . . era ossessionato.* "Her piece, he talked only about her piece . . . he was obsessed."

PANINÀRO, *m., N., youth.* (From the name of the bar "Panino," in Milan, the gathering place for young people who then became known as "paninari.") Upper-middle-class, big-city boy or girl who aims at being always fashionable. *Le Timba sono giù coi paninari. Adesso il massimo sono le Superga alla caviglia.* "Timberland shoes are out with the with-it crowd. Now the big hit is ankle-high Superga shoes."

PÀNNA, *f., youth.* (Lit., cream.) **1.** Sperm. *Non ti piace la panna? Che delusione!* "You don't like cream sauce? Too bad!" **2.** Soft, sweet, and attractive girl. *Mi sono trovato una sbarbina che è una panna.* "I found a young chick who's a peach."

PANÒZZO, *m., youth. See* **paninaro.**

PANTÈRA, *f.* (Lit., panther.) Fast and powerful police car. *Quattro pantere per arrestare quel pirla. Che esagerati!* "Four cars to arrest that jerk. What a waste of taxpayers' money!"

PANTÒFOLA, *f.* (Lit., slipper.) **a)** *crim.* Wallet (so called because it becomes floppy, as slippers do.) *Più che altro io alzo pantofole, niente di violento.* "I mostly do wallets, nothing violent." **b)** *N., slang.* Hand. *Si sentì afferrare dalle sue pantofole e sollevare di peso, come se fosse stata una piuma.* "She felt his paws grabbing her and lifting her up, as if she were as light as a feather."

PAPÀVERO, *m., N.* (Lit., poppy.) **1.** Bigwig. *Dovrò far intervenire un alto papavero per evitare l'estradizione.* "I'll have to ask a bigwig for help to avoid extradition." **2.** Blow. **Dare un papavero.** To smack (because the cheek that has received the blow turns red). *Mio padre ha sempre detto che se dai qualche papavero ai bambini crescono meglio.* "My father has always contended that children grow up better if you smack them every now and then."

PAPÌRO, *m., youth.* (Lit., papyrus.) **1.** Letter; document. *Avrò avuto cinquanta papiri con me, ma ovviamente mi mancava quello giusto.* "I must have had fifty documents with me, but of course the right one was missing." **2.** Diploma. *Ha preso il papiro, poi un secondo papiro, ma non è andato da nessuna parte.* "He took one degree, then another, but he went nowhere."

PÀPPA. (Lit., baby food.) **a)** *f., slang.* **1.** Food. **Fare la pappa.** To eat. *Non piangere, adesso facciamo la pappa.* "Don't cry, you're going to have your meal soon." **2. Avere la pappa fatta.** To be spoon-fed. *Ha sempre avuto la pappa fatta, per questo non sa far niente.* "He's always been spoon-fed, that's why he doesn't know how to do anything." **3. Pappa e ciccia.** See **culo e camicia. b)** *crim.* **1.** *f.* **Farsi la pappa.** (To make oneself dinner.) To steal the loot from one's accomplices. *Si è fatto la pappa e poi si è nascosto su una remota isola dei Caraibi. E chi* *lo trova più?* "After cheating his accomplices, he went in hiding on a remote Caribbean island. Who's going to find him there?" **2.** *m.* Pimp (also in the form **pappóne**). *Con lei quel pappa vive anche troppo bene.* "Thanks to her that pimp lives way too well."

PAPPÀRE, *vt.* (From > **pappa.**) **1.** To eat voraciously. *S'è pappato mezzo chilo di spaghetti al pomodoro!* "He gobbled down half a kilo of spaghetti with tomato sauce!" **2.** To steal money; to appropriate other people's money with which one has been entrusted. *Le ha raccontato la triste storia della malattia di sua madre e le ha pappato i soldi dell'eredità.* "He told her the sad story of his sick mother and made off with her inheritance."

PAPPÓNE, *m., C.* (From > **pappare.**) **1.** Voracious eater. *Appartiene almeno a quattro circoli della buona cucina: è un gran pappone.* "He belongs to at least four gourmet clubs. He's a great eater." **2.** One who appropriates public money. *L'ha detto esplicitamente all'inizio della sua carriera: "Mi metto in politica per fare il pappone."* "He said it openly at the beginning of his career: 'I'm going into politics to get rich with other people's money.'" **3.** Pimp. *See* **pappa.**

PÀRA, *f., narc./youth. See* **paranoia.**

PARACADÙTE, *m., N.* (Lit., parachute.) Condom. *Ogni sport ha i suoi attrezzi: quando scopi è meglio usare il paracadute.* "Each sport has its own tools. When you screw it's best to use the parachute."

PARACULÀGGINE, *f., rude.* Being a/Acting as, a > **paraculo.**

PARACÙLO, *m., C., rude.* (From "para," to shield, and "culo," ass.) **1.** One with the nerve to do whatever it takes to attain a goal. *Tu sarai anche un duro, ma quello è un paraculo.* "You may be a tough guy, but he's got what it takes to get the thing done." **2.** Passive male homosexual. *Senti, se essere circondati da paraculi ti mette in ansia, ce ne andiamo.* "Look, if having all these faggots around makes you feel anxious, we can go."

PARÀNCIA, *f., S., narc.* **Essere in parancia.** To be in a state of great anxiety because the effect of drugs is waning. *Eri in parancia, per quello volevi abortire. Cosa ne pensi adesso?* "You were crashing, that's why you wanted to have an abortion. How are you feeling about it now?"

PARANÒIA, *f., youth/narc.* (Lit., paranoia.) **1.** Breakdown caused by an ineffective injection of drugs. *Con quel pusher ho chiuso. La sua roba mi lascia sempre in paranoia.* "I'm through with that pusher. I always freak out on his dope." **2. Andare in paranoia.** To go crazy for someone or something. *Angela va in paranoia per delle cretinate.* "Angela loses it for the silliest of reasons." **3. Essere in paranoia.** To be angry, scared, depressed. *Io in paranoia per un po' di ultrà sugli spalti? Ma va!* "Me, freaking out because of a few hooligans in the stadium? Of course not!"

PARÀNZA, *f., S., crim.* A group of thieves who work together. *Gira al largo da quella paranza, se na finisci in galera con loro.* "Keep away from that bunch of thieves; otherwise you'll end up in the cooler with them."

PARCHEGGIÀRE, *vi., youth.* (Lit., to park.) To stop; to spend some time in a place. *Parcheggia ogni sera al biliardo fino a mezzanotte.* "You can find him every night until midnight at the pool bar."

PARCHEGGIÀTO, *adj., N., youth.* (Lit., parked.) **Stare parcheggiato.** (Lit., to be parked.) To keep one's cool; to keep quiet. *E state un po' parcheggiati, che il ferro lo si ritrova!* "Chill out, now. We'll find the motorcycle."

PARÈNTE, *m., narc.* (Lit., relative.) Drug peddler. *Non vuole più essere mio parente perché la narcotici mi tiene d'occhio, dice lui.* "He doesn't want to be my connection anymore because he says that the vice squad is keeping an eye on me."

PARTÈNZA, *f., narc.* (Lit., departure.) The moment a narcotic takes effect. *Ha fatto una falsa partenza, ma non ha più roba per ricominciare.* "He didn't have a good trip, but he has no dope left."

PARTÌRE, *vi.* (Lit., to leave.) **1.** To die. *Sono partiti troppo presto! La vita è una schifezza.* "They left way too early! Life is a bitch." **2.** To lose one's cool. *Gli basta poco per partire.* "It doesn't take much to make him fly off the handle."

PARTÌTO, *adj.* (From > **partire.**) **a)** *slang.* Said of someone who has lost contact with reality. *Poveretta, è proprio partita! Credi che ci riconosca?* "Poor thing, she's really gone! Do you think she recognizes us?" **b)** *narc.* Said of a person who begins to feel the effects of drugs. *Sono partito! Auguratemi buon viaggio!* "I'm off! Wish me a good trip!"

PASSÀGGIO, *m., S.* (Lit., passage.) **Prendersi un passaggio.** (Lit., to avail oneself of a ride.) To take the liberty of fondling a woman. *Quello si prendeva passaggi con le segretarie, fino a quando non ha trovato quella che gli ha fatto causa.* "He used to fondle his secretaries, until he found one who sued him."

PASSÀRE, *vt., C.* (Lit., to pass.) To sleep with someone. *Li ha passati tutti.* "She has slept with just about everyone."

PASSE-PARTOUT, *French, m., N.* (Lit., master key.) Penis. *Lui ha veramente un passe-partout: non ce n'è una che gli dica di no.* "His dick must have magic powers. No woman has ever told him no."

PÀSSERA/PASSERÌNA, *f., N./C.* (Lit., hen sparrow.) Vagina. *Sua madre parlava con le altre donne della sua "passerina." Lei era completamente confusa.* "Her mother was chatting with the other women about her 'little birdie.' She was totally confused."

PÀSSERO, *m.* (Lit., sparrow.) Penis. *Povero passero solitario, senza una bella passerina a tenergli compagnia.* "Poor bird, so lonely, without a nice birdie to keep him company."

PASTÌCCA, *f., narc.* (Lit., tablet.) Narcotic. *Mangia pasticche, parla di pasticche, sogna pasticche . . . è un pasticcato.* "He talks about pills, eats them, dreams about them . . . he's a pillhead."

PASTICCÀRSI, *vi. pronom., narc.* (From > **pasticca.**) *See* **impasticcarsi.**

PASTRUGNÀRE, *vt., N.* **1.** To mix together. *See* **paciugare. 2.** To fondle. *Perché si lasciasse pastrugnare da lui, lei non sapeva spiegarselo.* "Why she let him fondle her, she didn't understand herself."

PASTURÀRE, *vi., N.* (Lit., to pasture.) To wander about, looking for erotic encounters. *Si era ormai abituato a pasturare senza concludere niente.* "He got used to wandering about looking for sex without ever getting any."

PATÀCCA, *f., N.* (Lit., big but worthless coin.) **1.** Lie. *Corre voce che sia stato nominato cavaliere? Una patacca che ha messo in circolazione lui.* "Rumor has it he's been knighted. What a tall tale he's spreading around." **2.** False antique. **Rifilare la patacca.** (Lit., to palm off a false coin.) To trick someone. *A chi è facile rifilare la patacca? Ai vanesi, agli arroganti, ai babbei, insomma.* "Who are the targets of people who palm off phony stuff? The vain, the arrogant, and the dumb."

PATACCÀRO, *m., C.* (From > **patacca, 2.**) Grifter. *Insomma, sei venuto dal pataccaro perché vuoi che freghi la vecchietta al posto tuo.* "So, you came to the grifter because you want him to swindle the old lady for you."

PATATÌNA, *f., N.* (Lit., small potato; chips.) **1.** Vagina. *Sì, tutte le bambine hanno la patatina.* "Yes, every girl has a little pussy." **2.** Girl. *Guardava sua figlia, una patatina piccola e simpatica, certo non bella.* "He was looking at his daughter, a lovable little girl, not a beauty by a long shot."

PATÓNZA/PATÓNZOLA, *f., N. See* **patatina.**

PÀTTE, *f. pl., N.* **1.** Hands. *Ha delle patte grassocce, ma dovresti vedere come sono agili.* "He's got fat paws, but you should see how quick they are." **2.** Feet. *Come puzzano le tue patte! Rimettiti subito le scarpe.* "Your feet do stink! Put your shoes back on right away."

PAURÓSO, *adj., C., youth.* (Lit., fearful; dreadful.)

Extraordinary, incredible, both positively and negatively. *Ha avuto un culo pauroso a riportare la macchina subito prima che il grigio rientrasse.* "He had terrific luck. He brought back his old man's car right before he came home."

PAZZÈSCO, *adj., N., youth.* (Lit., maddening.) Awesome; incredible. *Ha rovesciato le lasagne in grembo all'ospite d'onore: una figura pazzesca.* "She dropped the lasagne right into the lap of her guest of honor: an amazing blunder."

PÈCORA, *f., crim.* (Lit., sheep.) Prostitute. **Portare/Tenere le pecore in pastura.** (Lit., to take the sheep to pasture.) To live off a group of prostitutes. *Ma che agenzia di modelle! Tiene le pecore in pastura, quello fa.* "Forget the modeling agency! He lives off hookers, that's what he does."

PECÙNIA, *f., youth.* (Latin "pecunia," money.) Money. *Non tengo pecunia, capito?* "I've got no money, dig?"

PEDÀGNA, *m., C.* (Lit., foot.) **A pedagna.** On foot. *C'è chi va a benza e chi a pedagna: io appartengo alla seconda categoria.* "There are the gas-propelled and the foot-propelled: I belong to the latter category."

PEDALÀRE, *vi., N.* (Lit., to pedal.) To run away; to make oneself scarce. *Se vi trovo ancora una volta a spiarla dalla finestra, siete finiti. Adesso, pedalate!* "If I find you peeping at her through the window one more time, you're cooked. Get moving!"

PEDÀLI, *m. pl.* (Lit., pedals.) **Andare a pedali.** To walk. *No, dico, per andare a questa velocità tanto vale andare a pedali.* "I'm only saying, if we keep on crawling at this speed, we might as well walk."

PEDALÌNO, *m., C.* (Lit., sock.) Shallow and uninteresting person. *Ma no, sai, non è repellente, è un . . . un pedalino, ecco.* "No, he isn't repulsive, you know, he's . . . a nonentity, that's what he is."

PÈDE/PEDÈ, *m., N.* (French "pédé," pederast.) Homosexual. *Lo chiamano pedé, alla francese, perché è un tipo tanto raffinato. Resta però un finocchio.* "They call him *pédé*, French style, because he is so sophisticated. That doesn't change the fact that he's a fag."

PÈD(R)O, *m., N.* Deformation of "pederasta," passive male homosexual.

PELÀRE, *vt.* (Lit., to shave.) To fleece. *A quel tavolo da poker non mi vedono più: m'han pelato tre sere di fila.* "They won't see me ever again at that poker table. They fleeced me three nights in a row."

PÈLLE, *f.* (Lit., skin, hide.) **Farsi una pelle. 1.** *C.* To possess sexually. *Lo sai di cosa parlano gli uomini nello spogliatoio: qual è il modo migliore per farsi una pelle.* "You know what men talk about in the locker room; the best way to get pussy." **2.** *N.* To eat voraciously. *Non fatevi una pelle, ragazzi, ce n'è per tutti.* "Don't choke on the food, boys, there's enough for everyone."

PELLEGRÌNO, *m.* (Lit., pilgrim.) **1.** Penis. *Adesso capiva che il pene veniva detto "pellegrino" perché era sempre alla ricerca di una dimora accogliente.* "He understood now why the penis was called 'the pilgrim,' because it wandered around looking for a welcoming abode." **2.** Inexperienced and ignorant person. *Mario, che è un pellegrino, si è messo a gestire la società di investimenti da solo. Ti puoi immaginare il risultato.* "Mario, who is a doodle, decided to manage the investment firm himself. You can guess the outcome."

PÉLO, *m., N.* (Lit., one hair; fur.) **a)** *slang.* **1.** Pubic hair. *Si vedeva dal pelo che era una bionda tinta.* "One knew from the color of her pubic hair she was a fake blonde." **2. Con tanto di pelo.** Merciless; without scruples; tough. *Gianni è uno con tanto di pelo, per quello fa i soldi.* Gianni has few moral scruples; that's why he's so good at making money. **b)** *youth.* **1.** Hair; hairdo. **Farsi il pelo nuovo.** To have one's hair cut. *Vedo che ti sei fatta il pelo nuovo, mezzo viola e messo pistacchio.* "I see you got a new hairdo, half mauve and half pistacchio."

PELOTAS, *Spanish, m. pl.* (Lit., balls.) Testicles. *See* **palle.**

PENDÀGLI, *m. pl., C.* (Lit., pendants.) Testicles. *See* **palle.**

PÈNDERE (DA QUÈLLA PÀRTE), *vi.* (Lit., to lean [on that side].) Euphemism for "being homosexual." *Non lo sapevi che pende da quella parte?* "Didn't you know he's gay?"

PENETRÌL, *m.* (Brand name of an imaginary medicine supposed to cure sexual ailments. From the verb "penetrare," to penetrate.) Penis. *Il Penetril è un rimedio eccellente contro depressioni e stati ansiosi di origine onanistica e/o dovute a fallopenia.* "Penetril is excellent in curing depression and anxious conditions due to onanistic practices and insufficient access to the penis."

PÉNNA, *f.* (Lit., pen; feather.) **a)** *slang.* Penis. **Alzare la penna.** (Lit., to lift the feather.) To have an erection. *Alza la penna con grande difficoltà.* "It's very hard for his pole to stay up straight." **b)** *C./N., crim.* Lockpick. *La penna nuova aprì la porta in un batter d'occhio.* "The new lockpick opened the door in no time." **c)** *youth.* Girl; woman. *Penne nuove in giro o le solite racchie?* "Any fresh chicks around, or are we stuck with the same old hens?"

PENNÈLLO, *m., N.* (Lit., paintbrush.) *See* **penna, a)** and **b).**

PÈNNICA/PENNICHÈLLA, *f., C.* After-meal nap. *La pennichella giornaliera non gliela toglieva nessuno, cascasse il mondo.* "No one, no matter who, could deprive him of his daily nap."

PEÒCIO, *m., N., rude.* (From Venetian for "pidocchio," louse.) Ugly and clumsy girl. *Se la porta a letto, ma si vergogna a farsi vedere in giro con quel peocio.* "He sleeps with her, but he's ashamed to be seen with that ugly girl."

PÈPPIA, *f., N.* **1.** Gossip, mistress. *Che peppia la tua vicina, mi avrebbe già fatto cambiar casa!* "If that gossip were my neighbor, I would have already moved someplace else." **2.** Passive male homosexual. *Poveretto, lo* *trattano tutti male perché è una peppia.* "Poor guy, they all treat him badly because he's queer."

PÉRA, *f.* (Lit., pear.) **a)** *slang.* Head. **1. A pera.** (Pear-like.) With neither rhyme nor reason. *Ho smesso di ascoltare quello che dice, perché il più delle volte parla a pera.* "I stopped listening to him, because most of the time he talks crap." **2.** *Fatti una pera!* "Go to hell!" **b)** *narc.* Syringe; drug injection. **Farsi una pera.** To inject drugs. *Si è fatto una pera, per quello è così vispo.* "He shot up, that's why he's so lively."

PERÀRSI, *vi. pronom.,* N., *narc.* (From > **pera, b).**) To inject drugs. *All'Hotel Ero ci si pera da mane a sera.* "At the Hotel Henry you can shoot up any time."

PERÉTTA, *f., narc.* (Lit., pear switch.) *See* **pera, b).**

PÈRSO, *adj., youth/narc.* (Lit., lost.) **1.** Confused; dazed. *"Hei, c'è nessuno qui?" "Niente, è persa."* "'Hello, anyone home?' 'Forget it, she's gone.'" **2.** Used as an intensifier. *È fumato perso.* "He's completely smoked."

PÉSCE, *m.,* C./S. (Lit., fish.) **a)** *slang.* Penis. *All'inizio del matrimonio, diceva, il pesce non le piaceva molto, poi però aveva cambiato idea.* "When they were first married, she said, she didn't like his cock much, but then she changed her mind." **b)** *youth.* **1.** Thug, especially in the locution **brutto pesce** (lit., ugly fish). *Che brutto pesce ha pescato Bruna in quella bettola.* "What a thug Bruna picked up in that joint." **2.** Fool; sucker. *Io ti prendo il pesce, tu lo pulisci, O.K.?* "I'll find you a sucker, and you take him to the cleaners, OK?"

PÉSO, N., *youth.* (Lit., weight; heavy.) **1.** *m.* Boring; heavy. *Quella è un bel peso!* "She's a pain!" **2.** *adv.* Determined, fearless. *Se vuoi fargli capire che fai sul serio devi andar giù peso.* "If you want to make it clear to him you're serious, you've got to come down heavy." **3.** *adj.* **Pesissimo!** Excellent! *"Pizza, birra e una fumatina, eh?" "Pesissimo!"* "'Pizza, beer, and a little smoke, OK?' 'Perfect!'"

PESTÀRE, *N.* (Lit., to pound.) **a)** *slang.* **1.** *vi.* To play a keyboard instrument/To type loudly and badly. *Piantala di pestare su quel piano. È spaventoso!* "Stop banging that piano. It's horrible!" **2.** *vt.* To beat. *Non lasciatevi pestare da quei pivelli, O.K.?* "Don't let those rookies give you a beating, OK?" **3.** *vi.* To have sexual intercourse. *Cosa vuoi pestare con quella? Come ti avvicini, ulula.* "It's impossible to get it on with her. If you as much as move an inch toward her, she starts screaming." **b)** *vi., youth.* **1. Pestare (dùro).** To dance frantically. *Ho pestato così duro sabato sera che ho perso tre chili.* "I pounded the dance floor so hard on Saturday night I lost three kilos." **2.** To get what one wants/To get oneself respected. *Lui pesta duro con tutti, ma un giorno di questi ne troverà uno che pesta più di lui.* "He's macho, but one of these days he'll find someone who's even more so."

PESTÈLLO, m. (Lit., pestle.) Penis. *See* **penna.**

PESTÓNE, *m., N., youth.* (From > **pestare, b2.**) A person who gets what he wants. *Un pestone, certamente, non molto raffinato però.* "He's macho, no doubt about that; not the greatest of gentlemen either."

PETRÒLIO, *f., N.* (Lit., oil.) **a)** *slang.* Alcoholic beverage. *Beve petrolio dalla mattina alla sera, ma non l'ho mai visto ciucco.* "He drinks booze from morning to night, but I've never seen him drunk." **b)** *youth.* Gasoline. *Certo che la spider della BMW ciuccia un casino di petrolio. Che cosa ti aspettavi?* "Your new BMW Spider guzzles a lot of gas? Well, what did you expect?"

PÈZZA, *f.* (Lit., patch.) **a)** *slang.* Person. *Non è una cattiva pezza, solo non ha tanta iniziativa.* "He isn't a bad guy. He doesn't have much entrepreneurial spirit, that's all." **b)** *youth.* **1. Non filare uno di pezza.** To pay no attention to someone. *Se non lo filiamo di pezza magari ci lascia in pace.* "If we pretend he's not there, maybe he'll leave us alone." **2. Prendersi una pezza per qualcuno.** To have a crush on someone. *Era tanto che Cristina non si* *prendeva una pezza così.* "Cristina hadn't had such a crush on someone for quite a while."

PÈZZE, *f. pl.* (Lit., patches.) **Avere le pezze al culo.** (Lit., to wear patches on one's ass.) To be penniless. *Ebbene sì, ho le pezze al culo, e allora? Non ho mica ammazzato nessuno!* "True, I'm down and out. So? At least I didn't kill anyone!"

PÈZZO, *m.* (Lit., piece.) **a)** *crim.* **1.** Gun. *Quanti pezzi ti sei portato dietro, credi che dobbiamo attaccare Guadalcanal?* "How many pieces did you bring along? Do you think we're about to attack Guadalcanal?" **2. Pezzo da novanta.** (A piece worth ninety. In some lotteries, ninety is the highest number.) Big shot. *Chiudi la bocca, che se ci sente il pezzo da novanta siamo fottuti!* "Shut up! If the big shot hears us, we'll be dead meat in no time." **b)** *youth.* **1.** Motorcycle. *Dodici gambe per quel pezzo è il mio ultimo prezzo.* "One million two hundred thousand lire for that motorcycle is my final offer." **2. Fare un pezzo a qualcuno.** To tell someone off. *Quando l'ha vista con Silvio le ha fatto un pezzo in pubblico!* "When he saw her with Silvio, he told her off right then and there." **3. Battere il pezzo.** To court someone. *Lui con Cinzia batte il pezzo con determinazione, con che risultati non so.* "He's been working hard on getting Cinzia. Don't ask me the results."

PIÀGA, *f., N.* (Lit., plague.) A bore; a whiner. *La pagano per fare la piaga, eh?* "They pay her for playing the whiner, don't they?"

PIALLÀRE, *vt., youth.* (Lit., to plane.) To knock down/flatten someone in a fight. *Via, andiamo via, che l'ultima volta quei brutti ceffi m'han piallato!* "Let's scram! The last time I was here those three mugs flattened me."

PIANÒLA, *f., crim.* (Lit., pianola.) Police informer (perhaps because he/she "sings" like a pianola). *"Una pianola come quella la si trova raramente," pensò l'ispettore di polizia.* "'Not so easy to find another canary like this one,' 'the police inspector thought.'"

PIÀNTA, *f., N., crim.* (Lit., plant.) **1.** Policeman, prison guard. *Cercavano di far muovere la pianta dal suo posto, ma non c'era niente da fare.* "They were trying unsuccessfully to make the prison guard move from his post." **2.** Person on the lookout. *See* **palo. 3. In pianta.** Said of stolen goods that are well hidden. *E molla di rompere! Te l'ho detto dieci volte: il malloppo è in pianta.* "Stop being a pain in the neck! I told you ten times: the goods are safe."

PIANTÀRE, *vt.* (Lit., to plant.) **1.** To leave (one's beloved). *Ma cosa gli ho fatto per farmi piantare?* "What did I do to make him dump me?" **2. Piantarla.** To cut it out. *E piantala di borbottare, sei insopportabile.* "Still grumbling? You're impossible, cut it out!" **3. Piantare casino.** *See* **casino. 4. Piantarlo.** (Lit., to plant it, i.e., one's penis.) To possess sexually. *Non lo piantava più da molto tempo. Ci sarebbe ancora riuscito?* "He hadn't screwed a woman in a long time. Would he still be able to do it?"

PICCIONCÌNI, *m. pl., C.* (Lit., young pigeons.) **1.** Lovebirds. *Fai una fotografia a quei due piccioncini seduti sulla panchina. Sono tanto teneri.* "Take a picture of those two lovebirds on the bench. They're so sweet." **2.** Small breasts. *A tredici anni non aveva ancora le tette, solo due piccioncini.* "At thirteen she didn't have boobs yet, just two little titties."

PICCIÒTTO, *m., S., crim.* (Lit., youngster.) Young member of a mafia clan. *Ehi, picciotto, tu fai quello che ti si dice; oppure . . . Ci siamo capiti?* "Hey, kid, you do what you're told to; otherwise . . . capeesh?"

PÌCCO, *m., N., crim.* (Lit., peak.) **Andare a picco.** (Lit., to sink.) To be wanted by the police. *Non fermarti a parlare con lui, è andato a picco.* "Don't stop and talk to him. He's wanted."

PÌCCOLA, *f., N./C., narc.* (Lit., small.) **1.** A dose of heroin. **Farsi/Prendersi una piccola.** To do a dose of heroin. *Tre piccole tutte insieme? Non vorrei morire!* "You want to do three hits together? Do you want to die?" **2. Piccola**

droga. Cigarette. *In mancanza di meglio, facciamoci 'sta piccola droga.* "Let's have this stick, since we can't do any better."

PICCÓNE, *m.* (Lit., pick.) **1.** Penis. *Anselmo crede che basti saper menare il piccone per avere successo con le donne.* "Anselmo thinks that success with women depends solely on how well you use your tool." **2.** Said of a hard and not-too-subtle way of doing things. *Il Ministro del Tesoro vorrebbe adottare la politica del piccone con il debito pubblico.* "The Minister of the Treasury would like to go after the public debt with an ax."

PÌCIA, *f., N., rude.* (Feminine of > **picio**.) Whore; harlot. *Sei una picia, ecco cosa sei, a strusciarti con tutti al bar!* "You're a whore, that's what you are, rubbing against everyone at the bar!"

PÌCIO, *m., N., rude.* (Perhaps from a dialect word for "piccolo," small.) Penis; jerk. *Un picio pensa solo a come mettere a bagno il picio, è inevitabile.* "It's not surprising that a prickhead is always thinking of how to dunk his prick."

PIDOCCHIÉTTO, *m., C.* (Lit., little louse.) **1.** A low-level, badly frequented hotel. *L'aveva portata in un pidocchietto mostruoso, così finirono per non farne niente.* "He took her to a sleazy joint, so they ended up doing nothing." **2.** Dirty cinema in lower-class neighborhoods. *Hanno chiuso l'ultimo pidocchietto della città. Adesso vedrai quanto scuci per vedere* Titanic. "They closed down the last cheap movie theater in town. Wait and see how much you'll cough up to see *Titanic*."

PIÈDI, *m. pl., C., youth.* (Lit., feet.) **Essere/Stare a piedi.** (Lit., to be on foot.) **1.** To be without a romantic/sexual partner. *Stai a piedi anche tu? Andiamo a consolarci al bar.* "You're single too? Let's go to that bar and cheer ourselves up." **2.** To be badly off. *Cosa vorresti dire quando mi dici "sto a piedi." Vuoi soldi?* "What do you mean when you tell me 'I'm stranded?' You want money?"

PIEDIPIÀTTI, *m.* (Translation of English "flatfoot.") Cop. *Faceva il piedipiatti di giorno, e di notte il portiere in un motel sull'autostrada.* "He was a cop during the day, and at night he sat behind the reception counter in a small motel on the expressway."

PIÈNO, *m.* (Lit., full.) **Fare il pieno.** (Lit., to fill up the tank.) **a)** *slang.* **1.** To stuff oneself with food and/or alcohol. *Aveva fatto il pieno ed ora dormiva stravaccato sul divano.* "After tanking up, he fell asleep all dressed on the sofa." **2.** To get pregnant. *"Ha fatto il pieno?" "Sì, per la quinta volta, e sono tutti e due praticanti."* "'Did she get knocked up?' 'Yes, for the fifth time, and they're both religious people.'" **b)** *youth.* To have had enough. *Ho fatto il pieno del lager, del kaiser, di tutto!* "I've had enough of school, of the principal, of the whole damned thing!"

PÌFFERO, *m., N./C.* (Lit., pipe.) **1.** Long and imposing nose. *Chissà come faceva a vederci con quel piffero tra gli occhi!* "Who knows how he could see anything with that long beak between his eyes!" **2.** Penis. *See* **flauto. 3. Col piffero!** Euphemism for **col > cazzo!**

PIGLIANCÙLO, *m., rude.* (From "pigliare," to catch, and "culo," ass.) **1.** Passive male homosexual. *Tu sei orripilato, ma a lui piace fare il piglianculo.* "You may be horrified, but he likes being a faggot." **2.** A despicable, spineless person. *Al mondo ci vogliono anche i piaglianculo; se no tu come faresti a campare?* "You need wimps and suckers in the world; otherwise how could you make a living?"

PÌL(L)A, *f., N., youth.* (Probably from the expression "una pila di soldi," a pile of money.) Money. *"Quanti soldi ha?" "Non lo vuoi sapere. Una pila, comunque."* "'How much money does he have?' 'You don't really want to know. A pile, anyway.'"

PILLÓLA, *f.* (Lit., pill.) Bullet. *Mise solo due pillole nel tamburo: una per lei e una per sé.* "He put only two bullets into his revolver: one for her, the other for himself."

PÌNCO PALLÌNO, *m., idiom.* **1.** John Doe. *"Con chi hai parlato al Ministero?" "Ma, non so, un Pinco Pallino qualunque."* "'Who did you talk to at the Ministry?' 'I don't know, some John Doe.'" **2.** A nobody. *È un pinco pallino qualsiasi e si presenta qui con tante pretese!* "He's nobody, but he shows up with all these demands!"

PINCÓNE/PINGÓNE, *m., N., youth.* (Possible mix of "pinguino," penguin, and "coglione," testicle.) Stupid and uncouth person. *"Non ti fa un po' pena?" "No, è troppo un pingone."* "'Don't you feel sorry for him, at least a bit?' 'No, he's a real moron.'"

PINGUÌNO, *m., C.* (Lit., penguin.) **a)** *slang/crim.* **1.** One whose bearing is ridiculously stiff (e.g., military people in uniform). *Guarda i pinguini in parata! Sono patetici.* "Look at those penguins parading down the street! They do look pathetic." **2.** One who keeps watch. *È Ugo il pinguino per quel colpo? Li beccheranno di sicuro.* "Ugo is the lookout for that heist? They'll get caught for sure." **b)** *youth.* Priest. *Se non hai detto al pinguino che prendi la pillola, l'assoluzione non vale.* "If you didn't tell your priest you take the pill, the absolution isn't valid."

PÌNNE, *f. pl., C., youth.* (Lit., fins.) **1.** Feet. *See* **fette. 2. Fare le pinne.** To make one's motorcycle rear up as if it were a horse. *Fa le pinne per fare colpo sulle squinzie.* "He rides around doing wheelies to impress the chicks."

PIÒGGE, *f. pl.* (Lit., rains.) Menstrual period. *Ha le piogge, per quello è nevrastenica.* "She's got her period; that's why she's a nervous wreck."

PIÒLA, *f., N.* (From the French "piaule," tavern.) Lower-class drinking and card-playing place. *Fino a poco tempo fa in piola ci trovavi solo uomini in pensione, dediti alle carte.* "Until a few years ago all you found in local joints were retired men devoted to playing cards."

PIÓMBA, *m., N.* (Probably feminine of "piombo," lead.) Drunkenness; exhaustion. *Con la piomba che si ritrova-*

va addosso voleva solo un letto. "With all the booze he had in him, he wanted nothing but a bed."

PIÒ(T)TA, *f., N.* (Probably from Latin "plautus," flat.) **1.** One-hundred lire coin. *E cosa ci fai con una piota al giorno d'oggi? Nulla, assolutamente nulla.* "What do you do nowadays with a hundred lire? Nothing, zilch." **2.** Foot. **Andare a piotte.** To walk. *See* **fette. 3. Stare in piota.** To take good care of oneself. *Sta in piota, che il peggio è passato.* "Take heart, the worst is over."

PIOTTÀRO, *m., C., youth.* (From > **piotta, 1.**) One who carries very little cash. *Lui fa il piottaro, così non ha mai soldi per pagare. Comodo, eh?* "He's always short of money, so he can't pitch in with the others. Handy, eh?"

PIÒVERE, *v. impers.* (Lit., to rain.) **a)** *crim.* **1.** *Piove!* (Lit., it's raining.) Watch out! The police! **2. Piove e non piove.** (Lit., maybe it's raining, maybe not.) Uncertain "business" opportunity. *Gli ho parlato di nuovo di quell'affare, ma piove e non piove.* "I talked to him again about that deal, but it's very iffy." **b)** *youth.* **Come se piovesse.** (Lit., as if it were pouring.) In great quantity. *"Hai visto quanti galli al parco?" "Come se piovesse."* "'Did you see how many lover-boys there are at the park?' 'Like leaves on trees.'"

PIÒVRA, *f.* (Lit., octopus.) **1.** The Italian mafia. *La piovra ha messo le mani sulla città.* "The Mob has taken over the town." **2.** Any organization that controls drugs/arms traffic. *Ogni ondata di immigranti vuol dire una nuova piovra, questo si sa.* "Each wave of immigrants means a new mafia, that's well known."

PIPÌ, *f.* (From the French "pipi," through reiteration of the first syllable of the verb "pisser," to piss.) **1.** Child's penis. *Le bambine si erano nascoste dietro al cespuglio per spiare il suo pipì.* "The little girls had hidden behind the bush to peep at his weenie." **2.** Urine. *Hai fatto pipì, che è ora di andare a nanna?* "Did you do pee-pee? It's time to go to bed."

PIPÌNO IL BRÈVE, *idiom, m.* (From the name of the

Frankish king, Pippin the Short.) Small penis. *Col suo pipino il breve non è che possa avere un grande impero.* "With that tiny prick, he can't have a very large empire."

PÌP(P)A, *f., C./N.* **a)** *slang.* **1.** Male masturbation. **Fare una pipa.** To masturbate a man. *Si era specializzata a far pipe.* "She specialized in hand jobs." **Farsi una pipa.** To masturbate oneself. *Deluso dall'amore, passa il tempo a farsi pipe.* "Disappointed by love, he spends his time doing himself." **Farsi pipe.** To waste one's time on inconclusive activities. *Dato che non ha problemi di soldi, può permettersi di passare il suo tempo a farsi pipe.* "Since he doesn't have to worry about money, he can spend his time diddling around." **2. Fare pipa.** To keep one's mouth shut. *Fa' pipa, che l'altra volta hai piantato un bel casotto.* "Keep your mouth shut. Last time you messed things up real nice." **b)** *narc.* Smoking dope with others. *Con quell'erbetta che ci ha procurato Max ci facciamo una bella pipa della pace.* "We can have a nice tea party with that grass Max brought." **c)** *youth.* **1.** Boring thing or person. *Le tieni compagnia tu, io di quella pipa non ne posso più.* "Why don't you keep her company? I've had enough of that bore." **2.** Unusual, amusing thing or person. *Mai sentito uno che mescola tedesco e russo! È una pipa.* "Never heard of anyone who mixes German and Russian together. He's quite a character."

PIP(P)ÀRE, *vi.* (From > **pi(p)pa, b.**) **a)** *slang.* To smoke/sniff tobacco. *Dice che va di moda pippare e lei segue sempre le mode.* "She says sniffing tobacco is in fashion, and she *always* follows fashion." **b)** *narc.* To smoke dope; to inhale cocaine. *Pippiam, pippiam, pippiamo . . . pippiam, pippiam mio bene . . .* "Let's sniff, let's sniff my dear . . . let's sniff, let's sniff together . . . "

PÌPPO, *m.* (Nickname for "Giuseppe," John.) Menstrual period. *See* **gigi.**

PIRÌLLO, *m.* Child's penis. *I maschietti hanno tutti il pirillino, Luca.* "Every boy has a weenie, Luca."

PÌRLA, *m., N., rude.* (Probably from an old word for "spinning top.") **1.** Penis. *See* **picio. 2.** Blockhead. *See* **picio. 3. Faccia da pirla.** *See* **faccia.**

PIRLÀTA, *f., rude.* (From > **pirla.**) *See* **cagata.**

PISCHÈLLO/PISCHÈRLO, *m., youth.* (Probably from English "pipsqueak.") Greenhorn; inexperienced youth. *Perché ti sei fidato di quella pischerla?* "Why did you trust that pipsqueak?"

PISCIÀRE, *vi., rude.* **1.** To pee. **Pisciarsi addosso.** (Lit., to wet one's pants.) *See* **cacare. 2. Pisciare sopra a qualcosa.** (Lit., to pee onto something.) To despise something; not to give a damn. *Preferisce farsi fregare da quel lestofante che mettersi in affari con me? Ci piscio sopra, io!* "He prefers getting screwed by that knave to doing business with me? I don't give a damn!" **3. Far pisciare.** (Lit., something to make you piss.) Ludicrous. *Giulio avrebbe scoperto una cura per l'epatite C? Ma non farmi pisciare.* "Giulio is supposed to have discovered a cure for hepatitis C? Don't make me laugh!" **4.** To give; to cough up. *Sono mesi che piscio soldi senza vedere niente di concreto.* "I've been pouring money for months with no results worth mentioning."

PISCIÀTA, *f., rude.* (From > **pisciare.**) Repetitious and boring speech or written work. *Con belle parole, ma praticamente mi han detto che il mio romanzo è una pisciata.* "They put it nicely, but they told me that my novel is a bloody bore."

PISELLÌNO, *m.,* Diminutive of > **pisello.**

PISÈLLO, *m.* (Lit., pea.) Penis. *"Vuoi vedere il mio pisello?" le domandò il ragazzo tra lo sfrontato e l'imbarazzato.* "'Do you want to see my thing?' 'the boy asked, half bragging and half pleading.'"

PISQUÀNO, *m./*PISQUÀNA, *f., N., rude.* (Probably from English "pipsqueak.") Blockhead; jerk. *La Olga è una pisquana a raccontarti che allo stupratore ricercato interessano esattamente le donne come te.* "Olga is a real jerk for telling you that the rapist wanted by the police is interested precisely in women like you."

PISTÒLA/PISTOLÓNE, *m., youth.* (Lit., pistol.) **1.** Penis. See **aggeggio. 2.** Sucker. *Nanni si conferma il re dei pistola a vantarsi con tutti del suo affare con la moglie dell'avvocato.* "Nanni confirms his reputation as the king of fools by bragging about his affair with that lawyer's wife."

PISTONÀRE, *vi., N., youth.* To drive somewhere; to drive fast. *Ehi, calma, non pistolare così.* "Slow down, don't drive that fast!"

PITTÀRE, *vt.* (From "pitta," focaccia.) **a)** *slang.* **1.** To swindle/to steal. See **cuccare, a). 2.** To eat. *Pittato bene dalla Betti?* "Did you eat well at Betti's?" **b)** *youth.* To be successful in one's erotic endeavors. See **cuccare, b8.**

PIUMÌNA, *f., N., youth.* (From "piumino," down jacket, which is filled with "piume," feathers, down.) A young girl who follows the fashion and behavior of > **paninari.** *Faceva la piumina—solo roba firmata e capello impeccabile. Adesso è passata al genere punk.* "She used to be with-it—only designer clothes and impeccable hairdos. Now she's moved on to the punk style."

PIVÈLLO, *m./***PIVÈLLA,** *f., youth.* Inexperienced boy or girl. *Negli affari di sesso la Patrizia non è mica tanto pivella, sai?* "You know, Patrizia isn't such a rookie in the sex department."

PÌZZA, *f.* **a)** *slang.* **1.** Reel of film. *Le pizze del film sono bruciate con il resto della casa: unica copia!* "The reels of the movie burned with the rest of the house: The only copy!" **2.** A bore. *Na pizza quel prete, io alle sue prediche non ci vado più.* "That priest is a real bore. This is the last time I listen to his sermons." **b)** *youth.* (Probably from "pizza," insect bite mark.) Acne; pimples. *"Cecilia dov'è?" "In ibernazione: ha una pizza pazzesca."* "'Where is Cecilia?' 'In hiding. You should see her pimples.'"

PIZZICÀRE, *vt.* (Lit., to pinch.) **1.** To catch in the act; to arrest. *Hanno pizzicato tutta la banda mentre si sparti-vano il bottino.* "They nabbed the whole gang while they were divvying up the loot." **2. Se vi pizzica.** If you like to. *Se vi pizzica, si può anche fare un po' di sci nautico oggi.* "If it gives you a kick, we could go water skiing today."

PÌZZICO, *m., narc.* (Lit., a pinch [of tobacco].) A pinch of cocaine. *E dai, provala, un pizzico di cocaina non ha mai ucciso nessuno!* "Come on, try it, a pinch of coke never killed anyone!"

PÌZZO, *m.* (Lit., goatee.) **a)** *crim.* Money extorted in exchange for "protection." *See* **mazzetta. b)** *slang, C./S.* **Mettere a pizzo.** To save (money). *La donne del quartiere mettono a pizzo un tanto al mese e lo investono insieme.* "The neighborhood women salt away a little bit every month and invest it together."

PLAYÀRE, *vt., youth.* (Italianization of English verb "to play.") To play; to broadcast. *Che playamo alla festa?* "What shall we play at the party?"

PLIZZÀTO, *youth.* **1.** *m.* Fruitshake. *S'è fatta tre plizzati alla fragola in mezz'ora!* "She gobbled down three straw-berry fruitshakes in half an hour!" **2.** *m.* Oral sex. *See* **frullato. 3.** *adj.* Very lively; exciting. *Sono tipi troppo plizzati!* "Those guys are so unbelievably cool!"

PÒCCE, *f. pl., N., youth.* Breasts. *"Ma dove ha preso quelle pocce?" "Se l'è fatte fare al silicone."* "'Where did she get those boobs?' 'She had them done up with silicone.'"

POLLÀIO, *m., youth.* (Lit., chicken coop.) Mess; confu-sion; racket. *Metti cinque pivelle insieme e la casa diven-ta un pollaio.* "Put five chicks together and your home will turn into a mess."

POLLÀRE, *vi., N., youth.* (From "pollo," chicken.) To sleep all together, like chickens. *"Polli con noi venerdì sera?" "No, ho un combino."* "'Will you come to our sleepover on Friday night?' 'No, I've got a date.'"

POLLÀSTRA, *m.* (Lit., pullet.) Attractive girl, chick (ready to be "plucked"). *Si è allevato quella pollastra piano piano, ma dice che ne valeva la pena.* "It took him a long time to get that chick ready, but he says it was worth it."

POLLÀSTRO, *m.* (Lit., chicken.) *See* **pollo.**

POL(L)EGGIÀRSI, *vi. pronom., youth.* (From "pollo," chicken, which is roosting.) To choose as one's dwelling (and to sleep in it). *Potrei polleggiarmi nella villa dei miei, ma il quartiere è una pizza mostruosa.* "I could roost in my folks' villa, but the neighborhood is such a bore!"

PÒLLO, *m.* (Lit., chicken.) **a)** *crim.* **1.** The designated victim for a "plucking." *Il pollo che stiamo cercando è un tipo azzimato, perbene, che vive con la mamma vedova . . .* "The chicken we're looking for wears Brooks Brothers, is an earnest type, lives with his widowed mother . . ." **2. Fare un pollo.** To rob, to con someone. *Si piazza al Grand Hotel e fa polli alle signore sole.* "He plunks down at the Grand Hotel and stiffs lonely ladies." **b)** *narc.* Small drug peddler. *Ho perso il pollo! Me l'hanno messo in galera.* "I lost my local contact! They put him in jail!"

POLSÌNI, *m. pl., N., crim.* (Lit., cuffs.) Handcuffs. *Era tutto elegante, tranne che per i polsini che i due caramba gli stavano mettendo.* "He was very elegant, except for the handcuffs the two cops were snapping on his wrists."

PÓLVERE, *f., N.* (Lit., dust.) **a)** *narc.* Cocaine (also called **polverina, polvere bianca, polvere d'oro, polvere folle**). *In casa loro c'è molta polvere.* "There's a lot of powder in their home." **b)** *youth.* Haughtiness; conceit. *Mette giù un sacco di polvere perché l'han chiamata per il provino alla TV.* "She's been called for a TV audition and, boy, she won't let you forget it!"

PÓMI, *m. pl.* (Lit., apples.) Breasts. *See* **pocce.**

POMICIÀRE, *vi., C.* (In Roman dialect, "sfregarsi," to rub one against the other.) To neck. *Altro che ballare! Quello io lo chiamo pomiciare.* "You call that dancing? I call it necking."

POMICIÀTA, *f., C.* (From > **pomiciare.**) **a)** *slang.* Necking. *Primo, meglio una pomiciata che niente. Secondo, non sai mai a cosa può portare . . .* "First, a little necking is better than nothing. Second, you never know where it may lead . . ." **b)** *crim.* Frisking. *Una lunga pomiciata m'hanno fatto, ma non hanno trovato nulla.* "They frisked me for a long time, but found nothing."

POMICIÓNE, *m., C.* (From > **pomiciare.**) A man who seeks any chance of being in close physical contact— desired or not—with a woman. *Oddio, c'è il pomicione! Stasera te lo becchi tu, è il tuo turno.* "Oh, no, there's the lech! Tonight he's all yours: it's your turn."

POMPÀRE, *vt., N.* (Lit., to pump.) **1.** To confirm someone's exaggerated opinion of him/herself in order to get some gain. *Ti deve aver pompato ben bene per farsi scrivere il saggio di filosofia.* "You wrote his philosophy essay for him. He must have massaged your ego quite well." **2.** *rude.* To possess sexually. *See* **ciulare. 3.** *rude.* To give someone a blow job. *Dice che se non glielo pompa se ne cerca un'altra.* "He says that if she doesn't suck his cock he'll dump her for another woman."

POMPINÀRO, *m.*/**POMPINÀRA,** *f., C., rude.* (From > **pompino.**) A person who gives blow jobs. *Fa la pompinara per i vecchietti. Per quello sta bene a soldi.* "She sucks off old duffers. That's why she's well-off."

POMPÌNO, *m., rude.* Blow job. *Niente pompini? Ma cosa lo paghi a fare?* "No blow jobs? What are you paying him for?"

PONGÀRE, *vi., N., youth.* To neck. *See* **pomiciare.**

POPÒ, *m.* Excrements. (Term used especially with children.) *Hai fatto la popò oggi?* "Did you do poo-poo today?"

POPPÀNTE, *m., f.* (From "poppare," to suck.) Greenhorn; baby. *Sarebbe grandioso scoparsi la madre di Pinuccia,* *vero, ma tu sei un poppante, scordatela.* "Pinuccia's mother would surely be a great lay, but you're a baby. Forget it."

PÓPPE, *f. pl.* Bosom. *Aveva delle grandi poppe, come quelle che si vedono nei quadri rinascimentali.* "She had large tits, like the ones you can see in Renaissance paintings."

PORCÀTA, *f., rude.* (From > **porco.**) **1.** Evil deed. *M'ha fatto una porcata di quelle! Ha fatto leggere ai suoi amici le nostre lettere d'amore.* "He really went beyond the pale! He showed our love letters to his friends." **2.** Badly done thing (which turns out to be a cheat for the customer). *Lascia perdere quella porcata. Ti porto io dove si compra meglio.* "Leave that crap alone. I'll take you where you can buy something much better."

PORCELLONÀTA, *f.* (From > **porcellone.**) Naughty deed. *Niente sado-maso con lui, solo qualche porcellonata.* "No S&M with him, only fun and games."

PORCELLÓNE, *m.* (From "porcello," little pig.) One who is available for any kind of sexual endeavor. *Lo hanno invitato a una serata con scambio delle partner e lui ha detto, "Perché no?" Un bel porcellone.* "They invited him to a partner-swapping evening. He answered, 'Why not?' Quite a pig."

PORCHERÌA, *f.* (Lit., vile deed.) Euphemism for sexual acts. *Alla vostra età non dovreste neanche parlare di certe porcherie.* "At your age you shouldn't even talk about those dirty things."

PORCHIZZÀRE, *vt., youth, rude.* (From > **porco, 1.**) To possess sexually. *Mimma ti sta guardando in un certo modo. Secondo me, la puoi porchizzare.* "Mimma is looking at you in a way . . . I think you can have her, if you want her."

PÒRCO, *m., rude.* (Lit., pig.) **1.** A sexual pervert. *Devi vedere casa sua: catene e fruste dappertutto. Dev'essere un vero porco.* "You should see his place: chains and whips everywhere. He must be a real pig." **2. Cani e porci:** *See* **cani.**

PORTÀRE, *vt.*, (Lit., to take/to bring.) **Portare via le suole/i tacchi:** *See* **suole.**

POSÀRE, *vt.*, *crim.* (Lit., to lay down.) To expel someone from a mafia clan. *Dopo che ti han posato non hai molto da vivere.* "Once they've expelled you from the clan you're not long for this world."

POSITÌVO, *youth.* (Lit., positive.) **1.** *adj.* Interesting; captivating; skillful. *Un ganzo positivo, dicono, che socializza le sue cose tra quelli della ghenga.* "An OK guy, they say, who shares his stuff among his gang." **2.** *interj.* Certainly! *"Si fanno con la neve, secondo te?" "Positivo!"* "'Do they do snow, you think?' 'Hell, yes!'"

POSTERIÓRE, *m.* (Lit., rear, back.) Buttocks. *Non poteva fare a meno di sentire lo sguardo dell'uomo fisso sul suo posteriore.* "She couldn't help being aware of the man's eyes staring at her behind."

POSTÌNO, *m.* (Lit., mail carrier.) **a)** *narc.* Drug courier. *Fa finta di fare l'uomo d'affari, in realtà fa il postino dalla Colombia.* "He pretends he's a businessman. In fact, he's the Colombia connection." **b)** *youth.* **Fare il postino.** (Lit., to be a mail carrier.) Never to stay still in the same place. *Potrebbe essere in dieci posti diversi. Sai che lui fa il postino.* "He could be in any of ten different places. You know he's always on the move."

POTÀBILE, *adj.* (Lit., drinkable.) Acceptable. *"Com'era la cena?" "Potabile."* "'How was dinner?' 'OK, I guess.'"

PÓZZO, *m.*, *youth.* (Lit., well.) **Un pozzo.** A lot. *Hanno sbevazzato un pozzo ieri sera.* "They lapped up a lot of stuff last night."

PRECÌSO, *adj.*, *youth.* (Lit., precise.) Person or thing conforming to group norms or rules; appropriate; tasteful. *Precisa quella tosatura, chi te l'ha fatta?* "Smart hairdo. Who did it?"

PRÈNDERE, *vt.* (Lit., to take.) **a)** *N.*, *slang.* **1.** To charge a certain amount for a good or a service. *M'han preso solo due gambe per quel videoregistratore. Mah!* "They charged me only two hundred thousand lire for that VCR. Strange!" **2.** *rude.* **Prendere qualcuno per il culo/ Prenderla/Prenderlo nel culo:** See **culo. b)** *narc.* For a drug to take effect. *È la terza volta che quell'ero mi prende male. Quel parente m'ha fregato di nuovo.* "It's the third time that H made me freak out. That pusher sold me crap again." **c)** *youth.* To attract; to take emotionally. *È così presa da quella storia che non sa più dove vive.* "She's so taken by that story she no longer knows where she is."

PRÈNDERLA/PRÈNDERLO IN QUEL PÓSTO, *idiom, rude.* See **prenderlo/la nel > culo, a2.**

PRENDÌNCULO, *m., N., rude.* (Lit., someone who takes it in the ass.) See **piglianculo.**

PREPPIE/PREPPY, *Eng., adj., youth. Legge solo riviste preppy.* "He reads only preppie magazines."

PREPPÌNA, *f., youth.* (From English "preppie.") Preppie girl. *Camicette inamidate e gonne a pieghe: devi vederla in versione da preppina!* "Starched shirts and pleated skirts: you should see her in her preppie version."

PRÉSA, *f.* (Lit., taking.) **a)** *narc.* A drug dose (especially cocaine). *Sta flippando al solo pensiero che ha solo più tre prese.* "She's freaking out at the thought she only has three hits left." **b)** *slang, rude.* **Presa per il culo:** See **culo, a2.**

PROBLÈMA, *m., C.* (Lit., problem.) **Non c'è problema.** No problem; it's all right. *"Mi tengo il ferro fino a domenica, Okappa?" "Non c'è problema."* "'I'll keep the motorcycle till Sunday, OK?' 'No problem.'"

PROF, *m./f./***PRÒFIO,** *m./***PRÒFIA,** *f., youth.* High school teacher. *I prof sono tutti uguali: il principio di realtà è andato.* "Teachers are all the same; they've lost the reality principle."

PROVÀRCI, *vi., C.* (Lit., to give it a try.) To come on to someone. *Voleva provarci di nuovo con Isabella, ma quella è una che non perdona.* "He wanted to give it a second try with Isabella, but she's the unforgiving type."

PROVOLÓNE, *m., C., youth.* (Lit., a kind of cheese.) A boy who comes on to girls in an annoying way. *Tutto quello che offre il mercato stasera sono provoloni e mozzarelle.* "All the market has to offer tonight is slugs and wimps."

PRÙDERE, *vi., rude.* (Lit., to itch.) **Prudere il cazzo a qualcuno.** (Lit., for one's penis to itch.) To be horny. *"Ma a lui il cazzo gli prude sempre?" "Evidentemente non conclude mai."* "'Is he horny all the time?' 'Apparently he never scores.'"

PRÙGNA, *f.* (Lit., plum.) Vagina. *See* **albicocca.**

PSICHEDÈLICO, *adj.* (Lit., psychedelic.) **a)** *narc.* Stimulating; extremely pleasant. *Una fumata collettiva psichedelica, irripetibile.* "A group smoke that psyched us all up. Can't repeat that." **b)** *youth.* Mad; off the wall. *Bea, detta la psichedelica, si è ficcata con Momo, psichedelico pure lui: possono aprire un manicomio.* "Bea, aka the Loony, paired up with Momo, who's loony too. They could open a lunatic asylum."

PUC(C)IÀRE, *vt., N., rude.* (From Piedmontese "pocé," to dip.) To possess sexually. *See* **intingere.**

PÙFFI, *m. pl., youth.* (From "puff," onomatopoeic term indicating the deflating of a thing full of air or gas.) **1.** Debts. *Deve vendersi la collezione dei dischi dei Pink Floyd perché è pieno di puffi.* "He's forced to sell his Pink Floyd collection because he's got megadebts." **2. Fare puffi:** *See* **fare > fughino.**

PÙFFO, *m., youth.* (From the name of a puppet.) *See* **pivello.**

PUGNÉTTA, *f., N.* (From "pugno," fist.) **1.** Male masturbation. *Pensa che a quindici anni non sapeva neanche farsi una pugnetta.* "He was fifteen and didn't even know how to whack off. Can you believe it?" **2. Mandare qualcuno a far delle pugnette.** To send someone packing. *Non sono stata io a malmenare il tuo gatto. Va' a far delle pugnette!* "I didn't harass your cat. Go to hell!" **3. Una pugnetta.** Nothing. *Se continui così resterai con una pugnetta!* "If you go on this way, you'll end up with nothing."

PUGNETTÀRO, *m., C.* (From > **pugnetta, 1.**) A person who devotes himself to masturbation. *A forza di fare il pugnettaro, gli è venuta una mano più grossa dell'altra.* "He's been jerking off for so long one of his hands has grown larger than the other."

PULÉ, *m., N., crim.* (From > **pula.**) Policeman. *Hei, pulé, vi divertite a tenere d'occhio i pericolosi scioperanti sotto il solleone?* "Hey, officers, how do you like keeping an eye on those dangerous strikers with this heat?"

PULÌTO, *adj.* (Lit., clean.) **a)** *slang.* Penniless. *Ma cosa vuoi rubarmi? Non vedi che sono pulito?* "What do you want to take from me? Can't you see I'm broke?" **b)** *narc.* **Essere pulito.** To carry neither drugs nor weapons. *Una pistola, dell'erba . . . Ma sei impazzito? A far il colpo ci andiamo puliti.* "A gun, some grass . . . Have you lost your mind? We want to be squeaky clean when we do that heist."

PÙL(L)A, *m., N.* Contraction of "polizia," the police. *Senti, tra la pula e i caramba, alle manifestazioni è meglio avere la pula.* "Look, if at a demonstration you have to choose between regular police and special forces, it's better to have the cops."

PULÒTTO, *m., youth.* (From > **pula.**) Policeman. *See* **pulé.**

PÙNGERSI, *vr., narc.* (Lit., to prick.) To shoot narcotics. *Sa, l'adolescenza è una gran cagata, a un certo punto uno prova anche a pungersi.* "You see, adolescence really stinks, so the moment comes when you try to shoot up."

PUNKETTÀRO, *m.*/**PUNKETTÀRA,** *f., youth.* (From English "punk.") One who adopts the punk style. *Un giovane Madonnaro/trovando il CD troppo caro/si trasformò in punkettaro/e degli alternativi divenne il* *faro.* "A young Madonna-follower,/who found her CDs too dear,/became a punk-follower/and the nonconformist leader."

PÙNTA, *f., N., crim.* (Lit., point, tip.) **1.** Knife. *Cosa ci faccio con 'sta punta? Non buca neanche la mozzarella.* "What good is this knife? It doesn't even slice mozzarella." **2. Stare alla punta.** To prostitute oneself. *No, non è che sia senza una lira, sta sulla punta per fare un'altra esperienza di vita, dice.* "She's not down and out. She's in the trade to rake up more life experiences, she says."

PUNTÀRE, *vt.* (Lit., to stalk prey.) To stare intensely at someone to whom one feels sexually attracted. *La bionda all'altro estremo del bancone ti punta, te n'eri accorto?* "That blonde at the other end of the counter is stalking you, did you know that?"

PUNTÀTA, *f., C.* (Lit., short visit.) Date. *Non rinuncerebbe alla puntata con Irene per tutto l'oro del mondo.* "He wouldn't give up his date with Irene for all the gold in Fort Knox."

PUNZECCHIÀRSI, *vr., narc.* (Lit., to prick.) To shoot narcotics. *See* **pungersi.**

PÙRA, *f., narc.* (Lit., pure.) Drug in pure form; uncut. *Se ti pungi con questa pura vai al Creatore. Ci siamo capiti?* "If you shoot up with this pure stuff, you'll go straight to your Creator. Got it?"

PÙSCER/PUSHER, *m.* (From English "pusher.") **a)** *narc.* Big drug peddler. *Il pusher vive in un villone con piscina? Non mi dire!* "That pusher lives in a villa with a swimming pool? Don't tell me!" **b)** *youth.* Despicable person, who gets what he wants through cunning and deceit. *Parlando di puscer, Alex mi ha minacciato di denunciarmi se non entro nel suo giro di prostitute.* "Speaking of snakes, Alex threatened to turn me in if I don't become one of his girls."

PUTTÀNA, *f., rude.* (From "puta," girl.) **1.** Whore. **Andare a puttane. 1.a.** To look for sex for hire. *Sai chi va a puttane quasi tutte le sere? Il parroco!* "You know who goes whoring almost every night? Our priest!" **1.b.** For something to go sour. *Abbiamo messo tutti i nostri risparmi nella società di importazioni, ma è andato tutto a puttane.* "We invested all our savings in the import firm. Now it's all gone belly up." **2.** Any woman who gives her partner sexual and sentimental aggravation. *Una puttana sei, a non lasciarmi vedere mio figlio!* "You're a bitch not to allow me to see my son!" **3.** One who behaves immorally to get what he/she wants. *Quella puttana di Roberto è scappato in Argentina. Adesso me la vedo io con i creditori.* "That sonofabitch Roberto left me here to face our creditors and fled to Argentina." **4. Figlio di puttana:** *See* **figlio.**

PUTTANÀIO, *m., rude.* (From > **puttana, 1.**) **1.** Whorehouse. *Una volta i puttanai erano controllati dallo stato; per me era meglio.* "Brothels used to be controlled by the state. I think that the situation was much better." **2.** Mess, chaos; trouble. *È saltato fuori che lui ha avuto un figlio con un'altra tanti anni fa. Che puttanaio!* "It turns out he had a child with another woman many years ago. What a mess!" **3.** A lot. *Come fai a raccapezzarti con quel puttanaio di carte sulla scrivania?* "How can you figure anything out with that messy pile of papers you have on your desk?"

PUTTANÀTA, *f., rude.* (From > **puttana, 1.**) Stupid and badly done action or thing. *See* **cazzata, 2.**

PUTTANÈLLA, *f., rude.* (Diminutive of > **puttana, 1.**) A girl who is sexually "easy." *Lei ti tirava e ti ci sei messo, pur sapendo che era una puttanella. Cazzi tuoi.* "She turned you on and the two of you started dating. But you knew then she was a bit of a slut. That's your problem."

PUTTANIÈRE, *m., rude.* (From > **puttana, 1.**) Philanderer. *Non capisco come abbia fatto Elisabetta a sopportare quel puttaniere tutti questi anni.* "I don't understand why Elisabetta put up with that whoremonger all these years."

PÙZZA, *f., C.* (Lit., stink.) **1. Avere la puzza al naso.** To be a snob. *Io sono troppo terra terra per te? Da quando in* *qua hai tutta quella puzza al naso?* "I'm too much of a man of the people for you? Since when are you such a snob?" **2. Andare in puzza.** To get angry. *Va in puzza con la stessa rapidità con cui gli altri dicono "ba."* "He flies off the handle as quickly as others say 'bah.'"

PUZZÀRE, *vi., C.* (Lit., to stink.) **1.** Not to appreciate something. *Ti puzza la vita?* "Are you tired of living?" **2. Mi/Ti/etc. puzza.** For someone to have well-founded suspicions. *Le puzza che suo marito abbia un'altra.* "She smells a rat; she thinks her husband is seeing another woman."

PUZZÓNE, *m./***PUZZÓNA,** *f., C., rude.* (From > **puzza.**) A skunk. *L'avrei detto un tipo strano, ma non un puzzone.* "I would have said he was a bit of a weirdo, but not a skunk."

QUÀGLIA, *f., N.* (Lit., quail.) **a)** *slang.* **1.** Prostitute/Sexy girl. *Bella quaglia all'angolo della strada. Dici che batte?* "Nice chick at that street corner. Do you think she's for hire?" **2.** Sucker. *Hanno beccato una quaglia che ha creduto alle loro belle parole.* "They found a nice sucker who took their promises at face value." **b)** *crim.* Wallet. **Arrostire la quaglia.** (Lit., to roast the quail.) To pick someone's wallet. *Tutto quello che han trovato, arrostendogli la quaglia, è stato un mucchio di soldi falsi!* "When they picked his wallet all they found was a lot of phony money."

QUAGLIÀRE, *vi., N./C.* (Lit., to curdle.) **a)** *slang.* For something to come to a positive conclusion. *Sulla carta i suoi progetti sono sempre meravigliosi, ma non quagliano mai.* "His projects are wonderful on paper, but they never work in reality." **b)** *youth.* To be pleasing to someone; to be convincing. *Quella cappella con quella giacca? Non quagliano.* "That hat with that coat? They don't match."

QUÀNTO GÌRI? *Idiom, youth.* (Lit., How much have you revolved?) What time is it? *Ho dimenticato l'orologio. Quanto giri?* "I forgot my watch. Do you have the time?"

QUARANTACÌNQUE, *m., crim.* (Lit., forty-five.) Irrelevant person (because forty-five is half ninety, as used in the expression > **pezzo da novanta.**) *È solo un quarantacinque, ma i suoi confetti ti fanno fuori lo stes-*

so. "He's small fry, but his bullets will kill you just as well."

QUATTRÒCCHI/QUATTR'ÒCCHI, *m. pl.* (Lit., four eyes.) **1.** Glasses. *"Hai visto i miei quattr'occhi?" "Li hai sul naso!"* "'Have you seen my glasses?' 'Yes. They're on your nose!'" **2.** A person who wears glasses. *Stai parlando del quattrocchi là nell'angolo, pelato e vestito stile anni sessanta?* "Are we talking about that four-eyes standing over in that corner, bald and dressed sixties-style?"

QUÉLLA CÒSA, *f., idiom.* (Lit., that thing.) Sexual intercourse. *Stanno insieme, ma non so se abbiano fatto quella cosa.* "They're dating, but I don't know if they've done it."

QUÉLLO, *demonstr. pron., m.* (Lit., that.) *See* **quella cosa.**

QUÉL PAÉSE, *idiom., m.* (Lit., that town.) **Mandare a quel paese.** (Lit., to send someone to another country.) To send someone packing. *Va' a quel paese, che di gente come te qui intorno non ne vogliamo!* "Get lost! We don't want people like you around here."

QUÉL PÓSTO, *idiom. m.* (Lit., that place.) **Prenderla in quel posto.** *See* **culo, a2.**

QUÌBUS, *Lat., m.* (Lit. to whom/to which.) *See* **conquibus.**

RABÀRBARO, *m., youth.* (Lit., rhubarb.) A surly, asocial person. *Stai cercando di risocializzare quel rabarbaro, che sei sempre lì a parlare con lui?* "You're always talking to that crank. Are you trying to reeducate him?"

RÀCCHIO, *m.*/**RÀCCHIA,** *f.* /**RACCHIÓNA,** *f., S, rude.* A very ugly person, especially female. *Lei è una racchiona, ma sapessi quanti soldi ha!* "She's a scarecrow, but if you only knew how much money she has!"

RACCHIÙME, *m., youth, rude.* (From > **racchio.**) A group of ugly girls. *"Solo racchiume in giro." "Perché, voi vi credete un gruppo di Adoni?"* "'We're in monsterland here.' 'Whereas you, on the contrary, consider yourselves gods?'"

RÀDIO SÈRVA, *idiom, f., youth.* (Lit., gossip radio.) A gossip; a slanderer. *Queste sono le informazioni che ho io. Se vuoi saperne di più, domanda a radio serva.* "This is the information I have. If you want to know more, ask that gossip."

RAFFREDDÓRE, *m., N., crim.* (Lit., cold.) **Prendere un raffreddore.** (Lit., to catch a cold.) To get arrested. *"Non ho più visto il Gianni ultimamente." "Eh, ha preso un raffreddore! Ne avrà per un po."* "'I haven't seen Gianni lately.' 'He got nabbed. He'll be away for a while.'"

RÀGANA, *f., N./C., youth, rude.* (Lit., green lizard.) A very ugly girl. *See* **racchia.**

RÀGNA, *f., N., youth.* (Feminine of > **ragno.**) Vagina. *Una bella ragna può tesserti una di quelle ragnatele che non ne esci più.* "A pussy can become so comfortable that you'll never want to leave it."

RÀGNO, *m.* (Lit., spider.) Penis. *Un ragnetto ha, che quasi non lo vedi.* "He has a small thing, so small you almost miss it."

RAM, *adj., youth.* **1.** Acronym for "ridotte attitudine militari," partially fit for military service. *Quanto vuoi per dirmi come hai fatto a farti fare ram alla visita di leva?* "How much do you want for telling me how you got rejected at the induction physical?" **2.** Acronym for "random access memory." Someone/Something to be forgotten as soon as possible. *Dario? Uno ram, non voglio neanche parlarne.* "Dario? I don't even want to talk about him."

RAMÀZZA, *f., N., youth.* (From Piedmontese "ramassa," broom.) **Essere di ramazza.** (In the army, to be assigned to sweeping the floor.) To be assigned a lowly and unpleasant chore. *Sono sempre io di ramazza, solo perché sono il più giovane!* "I get all the worst chores because I'm the youngest!"

RAMAZZÀRE, *vt., N.* (From > **ramazza.**) To pick up; to collect. *Abbiamo ramazzato un bel po' di lira al casinò.* "We swept up quite a lot of money at the casino."

RÀMBO, *m./***RÀMBA,** *f., youth.* (From Rambo, the movie character.) Physically strong, aggressive, and uncouth boy or girl. *Lo sapevo che gli piacevano le donne forti, ma una ramba così!* "I knew he liked strong women, but she's a tank!"

RAMÉNGO, *m., N.* (Lit., stick.) **1. Andare a ramengo.** To go to rack and ruin. *Piero si è rotto la schiena, Giovanni ha deciso di andare in America. Il nostro progetto è andato a ramengo.* "Piero broke his back. Giovanni decided to go to the States. Our project went down the drain." **2. Mandare qualcuno a ramengo.** To send someone to the devil. *Tu l'hai mandato a ramengo e avevi* *ragione. Però quello là è un mafioso.* "You were right to send him packing. However, he's a mafioso."

RAMPÀNTE, *m./f., N.* (Lit., rampant.) A yuppie. *Qualche anno fa, il simbolo dei rampanti era la Volvo giardinetta; adesso è il telefonino.* "A few years ago, the symbol of the yuppies was the Volvo station wagon; now it's the cellular phone."

RÀNDA, a) *f., N., crim.* (Contraction of "randagio," stray animal.) Homeless person. *Frequenta i randa un casino: dice che hanno delle storie di vita da sballo.* "He hangs around the homeless a lot. He says their life stories are something else." **b)** (Lit., spanker.) **A tutta randa.** (Lit., full sail.) *Idiom, youth.* At full speed. *Andava a tutta randa. Sai, aveva due pulotti alle calcagna.* "With two cops on his heels, he was going full speed ahead."

RANDOM, *Eng., adj., youth.* **A random.** Random, casual. *Non sapendo quale prendere ho scelto a random.* "I didn't know which one to take, so I chose at random."

RÀPA, *f.* **a)** *slang.* (Lit., turnip.) **Testa di rapa.** (Lit., turnip head.) Blockhead; slow on the take. *Pianta ancora pasticci con il fax, è una testa di rapa!* "He keeps on messing up the fax machine. He's so slow!" **b)** *crim.* Contraction of "rapina," robbery. **Rapa dura.** (Lit., hard robbery.) Dangerous robbery. *Il commissariato di polizia è troppo vicino alla banca. Quella è una rapa dura.* "The police station is too close to the bank. That's a tough heist." **Rapa bianca.** (Lit., white robbery.) Unsuccessful robbery. *I colpi che ho fatto con te sono stati tutti rape bianche. Porti male?* "All the robberies I did with you have gone badly. Are you jinxed?"

RAPINÀRE, *vt., N./C.* (Lit., to rob.) To make someone pay an absurdly high price. *Non andare in quel negozio che ti rapinano.* "Don't go to that store. They rip you off."

RÀVA, *f., N.* (Dialect for "rapa," turnip.) **La rava e la fava.** (Lit., the turnip and the fava bean.) The (gossipy) details of a person or story. *Alla festa ci siamo sedute in un angolo e mi ha raccontato le rava e la fava.* "At the party we sat in a corner and she told me the whole story."

RAVANÀRE, *vt., N.* (From "rafano," radish.) **a)** *slang.* To scheme. *Non mi piace quando Pietro e Luciano parlottano in quel modo: stanno ravanando qualcosa.* "I don't like to see Pietro and Luciano whispering to each other. They're certainly scheming." **b)** *youth.* To look for an occasional sexual partner. *Visto che non sembra fatto per le grandi storie d'amore, si accontenta di ravanarne qualcuna.* "Since he seems not to be made for great love dramas, he makes do with occasional sex."

RECCHIÓNE, *m., S., rude.* Passive male homosexual. *See* **orecchione.**

REGGITÉTTE, *m., youth.* (From "reggere," to hold up, and "tette," tits.) Bra. *Quello sarebbe un reggitette? Ma se non si vede nemmeno.* "That thing is a bra? It's so small I can't even see it."

REGINÉTTA, *f., narc.* (Lit., young queen.) Pure cocaine of high quality. (Probably from "reginetta delle nevi," snow queen.) *Sarà anche reginetta delle nevi, ma io non ho quella pecunia lì.* "I'm sure it's the queen of snow, but I don't have that kind of money."

REGOLÀRE, *youth.* (Lit., regular; ordinary.) **1.** *adj.* In conformity with the dictates of fashion. *"Trovi che queste fanghe stile militare sono regolari?" "Regolarissime."* "'Do you think those military boots are with it?' 'Totally cool.'" **2.** *m./f.* Boy or girl who is liked by the other members of the group. *Sono due regolari; vengono invitati a tutte le feste.* "They're two cool people; they get invited to every party."

REGOLÀTA, *f.* (From "regolare," to regulate.) **Darsi una regolata.** To calm down. *Quando ha visto che l'altro automobilista tirava fuori il crick si è dato una regolata.* "As soon as he saw the other driver pulling out the jack, he cooled down at once."

RELÌTTI, *m. pl., youth.* (Lit., wrecks.) Parents, because they are considered old and thus in poor shape. *I suoi relitti sono andati a scalare il Cervino e a momenti ci* *rimanevano.* "His old folks went climbing the Matterhorn. They came close to joining the angels."

REMÀRE, *vi.* (Lit., to row.) Not to be up to the task; to be in trouble. *Ce la mette tutta a scuola, ma rema come una pazza.* "Even though she works really hard in school, she's going nowhere."

RETROMÀRCIA, *f.* (Lit., reverse gear.) *See* **marcia indietro.**

RICARBURÀRSI, *vr., youth.* (Lit., to carburet again.) To recharge physically and emotionally. *Prima della partita di calcio bisogna ricarburarsi.* "We'd better pump ourselves up before the soccer game."

RÈTRO, *adj., m., youth.* (Contraction of "retrogrado," backward.) Old-timer. *Hai chiesto consiglio a tutti, chiedilo anche al retro, magari ti dà quello giusto.* "You've asked everyone for advice. Ask the old-timer too; he may give you the right idea."

RICCHIÓNE, *m., C., rude. See* **orecchione.**

RÌCCIO, *m., C.* (Lit., hedgehog.) **Scopare come un riccio.** (Lit., to go at it like a hedgehog.) To be sexually indefatigable. *Non hanno niente in comune, dici? Ah, ma scopano come dei ricci.* "They have nothing in common, you think? Perhaps, but they fuck like minks."

RICOTTÀRO, *m., C.* (From "ricotta," a kind of cheese.) **a)** *slang.* Pimp. *Vittoria ha cambiato vita: s'è trovata un ricottaro e batte il marciapiede.* "Vittoria has indeed changed her life. She found herself a pimp and now she pounds the pavement." **b)** *crim.* Promising young member of a criminal group. *Il ricottaro ne ha già ammazzati tre: di lui ci si può fidare.* "Our rookie has already killed three people. We can trust him."

RIÉNTRO, *m., narc.* (Lit., reentry.) The moment when sensations return to normal, because the effect of a drug is waning. *Ah, il rientro, veramente triste.* "Coming down from dope is grim, really grim."

RÌGA, *f., youth.* (Lit., line.) **1.** Vagina (by modification of the initial letter in the word "figa," cunt). **2.** Attractive girl or woman. *See* **fica, 1, 2.**

RÌGHE, *f. pl., youth.* (Lit., lines.) **Due righe. 1.** A lot. *"Ti piacerebbe vederla come mamma l'ha fatta?" "Due righe!"* "'Would you like see her in her birthday suit?' 'Yes, yes!'" **2.** No; not at all. *"Che dici, ci facciamo una scopatina?" "Due righe!"* "'How about a nookie?' 'Forget it!'"

RÌMBA. a) *f., narc.* Narcotics. *A lei basta che ci sia della rimba, non importa di che genere.* "All she wants is dope, any kind." **b)** *m./f., youth.* (Perhaps contraction of "rimbambito," in one's dotage.) Imbecile. *Il rimba non ha neanche capito che gli facevano fare da prestanome.* "The imbecile didn't even understand that they were using him as their front man."

RIMBALZÀRE, *vi., C., youth.* (Lit., to bounce off.) To be of interest, to matter; to be known to someone. *A me quel ferro lì non rimbalza, se rimbalza a te . . .* "That motorcycle doesn't interest me, if it interests you . . ."

RIMEDIÀRE, *vt., N./C., youth.* (Lit., to scrape together.) *See* > **rimorchiare.**

RIMORCHIÀRE, *vt., youth.* (Lit., to tow.) To pick up a boy/girl with the aim of having sex with him/her. *Dato che vuole rimorchiare molto non può andare tanto per il sottile.* "He wants to pick up a lot of girls, so he can't be too picky."

RIMÒRCHIO, *m., C., youth.* (Lit., towing; trailer.) **1.** Successful approach aimed at finding a sexual partner. *No, nessun rimorchio in spiaggia, meglio andare al parco dei divertimenti.* "No, no cruising at the beach. We'd better go to the amusement park." **2.** A boy/girl who has been picked up. *Abbiamo fatto un rimorchio doppio, però non si capiva qual era il mio e quale il suo.* "We did a double pick up, but it wasn't clear who would go with whom."

RÌNCO/RINCOGLIONÌTO, *adj., rude.* (Lit., turned into a testicle.) Feeble-minded; exhausted. *Sono così* *rincoglionito che non riesco neanche a legarmi i lacci delle scarpe.* "I'm so burned out I can't even tie my own shoelaces."

RINCOGLIONÌRSI, *vi. pronom., rude.* (Lit., to get turned into a testicle.) To become stupid; to get exhausted. *Ragazzi, piantatela di guardare la TV, se no vi rincoglionite completamente!* "Kids, why don't you stop watching TV, so you won't turn into complete idiots?"

RIPASSÀTA, *f.* (Lit., revision.) **1. Dare una ripassata.** To give someone a dressing down. *Il preside l'ha beccata che scarabocchiava i libri della biblioteca e le ha dato una bella ripassata.* "The principal found her scribbling on the library books, and gave her quite a dressing-down. **2.** *rude.* **Dare una ripassata a una donna.** To possess sexually. *Visto che fa la puttana con tutti, stasera le dò io una ripassata.* "She enjoys being everyone's whore, right? Fine, tonight it's my turn."

RISPÈTTO, *m., S.* (Lit., respect.) **Uomo di rispetto.** (Lit., a man deserving respect.) Euphemism for "mafioso." *Non date fastidio a don Salvatore, che è uomo di rispetto.* "Don't bother Don Salvatore; he's an important man."

RISULTÀRE, *vi., C., youth.* (Lit., to ensue.) To be congenial, to be pleasing to someone. *Anche tu col computer? Pensavo che non ti risultasse.* "You've got a computer too? I thought you weren't into that stuff."

RITÓRNO, *m., narc.* (Lit., return.) Final moments of a narcotic trip. *Gestisce male il ritorno; dovrebbe piantarla di farsi.* "She handles the crash badly; she should quit getting high."

RIVOLTÀTO, *adj., rude.* (Lit., turned inside out.) Male homosexual. *See* **invertito.**

RÒBA, *f.* (Lit., stuff.) **a)** *slang.* **1.** Penis. *See* **coso. 2.** Vagina. *See* **cosa. b)** *crim.* Stolen goods. *Guarda, ho ancora qui la roba dell'ultimo colpo: portala a un altro.* "Look, the goods from the last robbery are still here. Take them to someone else." **c)** *narc.* Drug. **Roba scrausa.** Cut or low-quality drug. *Si capisce che ti danno roba scrausa a quel* *prezzo lì.* "At that price, of course they'll only give you lemonade."

ROBÀRSI, *vr., N., narc.* (From > **roba, c.**) To take drugs. *Si roba con qualunque sostanza stupefacente, inclusa la colla.* "He gets high on anything, he doesn't care what. Even glue."

ROCCHETTÀRO, *m./***ROCCHETTÀRA,** *f., youth.* (From English "rock" as in "rock and roll.") A somewhat uncouth youth; a big fan of rock music. *Fa il rocchettaro di professione: lo pagano perché faccia casino ai concerti.* "He plays the professional rock fan. They pay him to make a racket at rock concerts."

RÓDERE (IL CÙLO), *vi., rude.* (Lit., for one's ass to be eaten up.) For something to be so annoying as to be unbearable. *Mi rode che lei gli abbia raccontato che lui mi piace ancora, se mi rode!* "If I think she told him I'm still interested in him, I get really pissed off!"

RÓGNA, *f.* (Lit., scabies.) **Cercar rogne.** To look for trouble. *T'ho visto, sai, sempre lì a girare intorno alla villa. Cerchi rogne?* "I saw you hanging around the villa. Looking for trouble?"

ROKKETTÀRO: *See* **rocchettaro.**

ROLLÀRE. (Italianization of English "to roll.") **a)** *slang.* **1.** *vt.* To roll a cigarette. *Dovresti vedere come si rolla le sigarette a dodici anni.* "You should see how well he rolls cigarettes at twelve." **2.** *vi.* To practice prostitution. *Lei dice di no, ma io sono sicuro che rolla.* "She says it's not true, but I'm sure she turns tricks." **b)** *vt., narc.* To make a joint by mixing tobacco and hashish/marijuana. *Non c'è molto fieno; possiamo rollarlo un po'.* "There isn't much weed; we can mix it up a bit." **c)** *vi., youth.* **1.** To neck. *Ti ricordi le feste da ragazzini: lenti, luci spente e avanti che si rollava.* "You remember teenage parties: slow dances, dimmed lights, and then the necking started."

ROLLÀTA, *f.* **a)** *narc.* (From > **rollare, b.**) To smoke a joint with a group of people. *C'è gente con cui non vorresti mai fare una rollata.* "There are some people you'd never want to have a tea party with." **b)** *youth.* (From > **rollare, c.**) Necking. *Una rollatina dopo cena è una cosa simpatica, ma non ti concilia il sonno.* "A little necking after dinner is nice, but it doesn't help you fall asleep."

ROMMEL, *m., youth.* (From the name of the World War II German general Rommel, nicknamed "Desert Fox" for his cunning.) Someone who has the illusion of being very astute. *Ecco il rommel che si avvicina di soppiatto, convinto che nessuno l'abbia visto.* "Here's our friend the fox approaching stealthily, convinced no one has noticed him."

RÓMPERE, *vt., rude.* (Lit., to break.) **a)** *slang.* To deflower a woman. *L'ha rotta a tredici anni, quello stronzo!* "He picked her cherry when she was thirteen, that jerk!" **b)** *youth.* **Rompere (i coglioni, le palle, le scatole).** To be a pain in the ass. *Rompe, la vecchia, rompe, ma se non le pulisco la cantina niente grana.* "My mother is a real pain, but if I don't clean the basement I get no money." *See* also **coglioni, 1.**

RÓMPERSI, *vi. pronom., youth, rude.* (Lit., for someone to be broken.) To get pissed off. *Loredana gli ha piantato l'ennesima scenata e lui si è rotto definitivamente.* "Loredana made a fuss one more time and he decided he had had enough."

ROMPIBÀLLE/ROMPICÀZZO/ROMPICOGLIÓNI/ ROMPIPÀLLE/ROMPISCÀTOLE, *m./f., rude.* (From "rompere," to break and > **balle, cazzo, coglioni, palle, scatole.**) A bore; an annoying person. *Tu dirai che sono un rompiballe, ma se continui a trapanare il muro ti ritrovi nell'appartamento di fianco.* "You may say I'm a pain in the neck, but if you go on drilling that wall you'll end up in the adjoining apartment."

ROMPIMÉNTO, *m., rude.* (From > **rompere, b.**) An annoying, unbearable situation. *Un rompimento il Natale in famiglia!* "Christmas with the family. What a pain!"

ROSÀRIO, *m.* (Lit., rosary.) **Sgranare il rosario.** (Lit., to say the rosary.) **a)** *slang.* To curse repeatedly. *Quando ha*

*visto che gli avevano rubato la macchina si è messo a
sgranare uno di quei rosari!* "When he saw his car had
been stolen, he started swearing like a trooper." **b)** *crim.*
To shoot several shots. *Sgranarono il rosario per essere
ben certi di farlo fuori.* "They emptied their chambers to
make sure they had killed him."

RÒTA, *f.* **In rota. a)** *narc.* Withdrawal crisis. *Dai, dammela
a credito, che sono in rota!* "Come on, give me some
dope on credit; I'm going cold turkey!" **b)** *youth.* Without
a sexual partner. *Dopo un po' che sei in rota, finisce che
ti abitui.* "After you've practiced abstinence for a while,
you get used to it."

ROTTINCÙLO/RÓTTO IN CÙLO, *m., C., rude.* (Lit.,
broken in the ass.) **1.** Passive male homosexual. *See*
piglianculo, 1. Extremely lucky individual. *La nebbia è
sparita proprio quando lui ha incominciato la discesa
dello slalom: che rotto in culo!* "The fog lifted just as he
started his slalom descent. He's so fucking lucky!"

RÓTTO, *adj.* (Lit., broken.) **a)** *narc.* A person whose arms
are marked by needle marks; more generally, a drug
addict in bad shape. *Non la vedi com'è rotta? Se continua così, presto andremo al suo funerale.* "Don't you
see she looks like a sieve? If she goes on this way, we'll
be going to her funeral soon." **b)** *youth, rude.* **Averlo
rotto.** (Lit., to have a broken [ass].) To be unbelievably
lucky. *Ce l'ha rotto al punto che nessuno vuole più giocare a poker con lui.* "He's so lucky no one wants to play
poker with him anymore."

ROTTÙRA, *f., youth.* (Lit., break, from **> rompere, b.**) Big
nuisance; boring situation. *Il documentario sulla pesca
era una rottura, ma siamo sopravvissuti.* "The documen-
tary about the fishing industry was a bore, but we sur-
vived it."

RÓZZI, *m. pl.* (Lit., the uncouth ones.) Policemen. *T'hanno
malmenato per farti parlare? E cosa ti aspettavi dai
rozzi?* "They beat you up to make you talk? What did you
expect from those cops?"

RUGÀRE, *vi., N.* (From Latin "rogare," to ask.) To annoy; to bore. *Mi ruga che Maria abbia preso il mio posto sul lavoro.* "It pisses me off that Maria has taken my place at work."

RÙLLO, *m.* (Lit., roll.) **a)** *slang.* Penis. *Secondo me la mena troppo con le prodezze del suo rullo.* "I think he's carrying on too much about the achievements of his prick." **b)** *youth.* **Un rullo.** A lot. *Vuoi un rullo di lira? Seguimi e fa' quello che ti dico.* "Do you want to make a lot of money? Follow me and do as I say."

RUÒTE, *f. pl., N., crim.* (Lit., wheels.) Shoes. **Menare le ruote.** (Lit., to push the wheels.) To flee. *Pula a sinistra, kaiser a destra: compagni, meniamo le ruote!* "Cops on the left, principal on the right: comrades, let's get out of here!"

RUSCÀRE, *vi., N.* (From Piedmontese "rusché," to hoe the ground.) **a)** *crim.* To steal. *Un esperto a ruscare, era il terrore dei gioiellieri.* "An expert thief, he was the terror of the city's jewelers." **b)** *youth.* **1.** To work, to study hard. *Ho ruscato per tre giorni, ma mi sono beccato un quattro lo stesso.* "I went all out for three days, but I got an F all the same." **2.** To neck. *See* **pomiciare.**

RÙSCO, *m.* (From > **ruscare.**) **a)** *crim.* Theft. *Un bel rusco alla posta e poi sarebbe andato in pensione.* "One more robbery at the post office and then he would retire." **b)** *youth.* Hard work. *Un rusco! Non so come faccio a stare ancora in piedi.* "What a killer job! I don't know how I'm still standing."

SÀCCA, *f., S., youth.* (Lit., bag.) Pocket. *Perché non vuoi farmi vedere che cos'hai messo in sacca?* "Why don't you want to show me what you put in your pocket?"

SACCAGNÀRE, *vt., N.* (From "saccagno," knife.) To wound; to beat up. *Con mia moglie non ci riprova più: l'ho saccagnato ben bene!* "He won't harass my wife again. I beat him black and blue."

SACCAGNÀTO, *adj., N.* (From > **saccagnare.**) Feeling broken (after strenuous physical exercise). *Bella scalata, ma adesso sono tutto saccagnato.* "Nice climb, but now I feel like a wreck."

SÀCCO, *m.* (Lit., sack, bag.) **a)** *slang.* **1.** Stomach. *Quel signore è al terzo secondo! Deve avere un sacco che non finisce più!* "That gentleman over there is on his third main course. He must have a bottomless pit." **2.** *rude.* Buttocks. **Rimanere con le pive nel sacco.** (Lit., to be left with a penis up one's ass.) To be handed a humiliating defeat; to be swindled. *Secondo loro, fare affari in Russia sarebbe stata una vacanza, invece sono rimasti con le pive nel sacco!* "They bragged that doing business in Russia would be a breeze. Instead they got screwed real bad." **b)** *youth.* **1.** One-thousand-lire banknote. *Ho un sacco di sacchi, il che vuol dire che sono praticamente al verde.* "I've got a lot of small bills, which means that I'm more or less clean." **2.** Folding someone's sheets so that one cannot get into bed. (Trick played in army barracks or boarding schools where the victim is going to be caught and punished by inspecting teams.) *Gli hanno fatto il sacco il terzo giorno che era militare.* "They short-sheeted his bed the third day he was in the army." **3. Un sacco.** A lot. *La nuova BMW mi piace un sacco.* "Do I like the new BMW? Oh, yeah!"

SACCÒCCIA, *f., C.* (Lit., pocket.) **Prenderla/Prenderlo in/nella saccoccia.** (Lit., to take it up one's ass.) To be defeated without having any capacity to react. *Ma che uomo sei, che te la prendi sempre nella saccoccia?* "Only a wimp like you would let them do what they did to you."

SACRAMENTÀRE, *vi.* (Lit., sacrament.) To curse. *"Ma che ha da sacramentare così?" "Gli hanno tagliato i copertoni."* "'Why is he swearing like a trooper?' 'He found his tires slashed.'"

SÀDO-MÀSO, *adj., youth.* Contraction of "sadomaso-chista," sadomasochist. *Sado-maso proprio non è, però le piacciono i giochetti strani.* "She isn't quite S&M, but she does like kinky games."

SALÀME, *m.* (Lit., salami.) **1.** Penis. *Mi ha offerto gentilmente del salame, mai più pensavo si riferisse a . . . quello.* "He kindly offered me some salami. I was miles away from thinking he was talking about . . . that thing." **2.** Silly and naive person. *Che salame, a piangere perché non ti hanno invitato alla festicciola.* "Only a silly goose would cry like that because she wasn't invited to their little party."

SALASSÀRE, *vt.* (Lit., to bleed.) **a)** *slang.* To overcharge someone for goods or services. *Il negozio all'angolo ha chiuso. Finalmente! Ha salassato la gente per anni.* "The corner store closed down for good. Finally! They've been ripping people off for years." **b)** *crim.* To rob someone using force. *Adesso non vi accontentate più di rubacchiare, salassate pure!* "Lifting stuff here and there is no longer good enough for you. Now you do armed robberies!"

SALÀSSO, *m.* (Lit., blood-letting.) Absurdly high expense.

Rifare il bagno è stato un bel salasso. "They charged us a lot for redoing our bathroom. It was a rip-off!"

SÀLMA, *f., youth.* (Lit., corpse.) Old person. **Le care salme.** (Lit., the dear corpses.) Parents. *Le care salme mi lasciano andare in vacanza col mio manico del cuore. Incredibile!* "My old folks are letting me go on vacation with my boyfriend. Unbelievable!"

SALMÓNE, *m.* (Lit., salmon.) **a)** *slang.* Penis. *See* **cefalo. b)** *crim.* Cocaine (because both are expensive.) *Hai solo venti sacchi per il salmone? Ma non farmi ridere!* "You want to buy coke with just twenty thousand lire? Forget it!"

SÀLSA, *f., youth.* (Lit., tomato sauce.) Blood (because of similar color). *Io non posso sopportare la vista della salsa.* "I can't even stand the sight of blood."

SÀNO, *adj., youth.* (Lit., healthy.) **1.** Amusing, attractive. *Sani i fratelli Lanza, portano sempre dei CD mega.* "The two Lanza brothers are OK; they always bring some mega-CDs." **2. Cresce sano/sana.** He/She is all right. *"Come va tua sorella dopo l'operazione?" "Cresce sana."* "'How is your sister doing after surgery?' 'She's doing all right.'"

SÀNTA, *f., crim.* (Lit., saint.) Handbag. *Porta la santa stile Regina Elisabetta: basta tagliare il manico ed è fatta.* "She carries her bag like Queen Elizabeth. All you have to do is to cut the handle."

SANTANTÒNIO, *m., crim.* (From "Sant'Antonio," Saint Anthony, well known for his self-punishing practices.) Thrashing, especially in prison. *Dopo che le guardie gli han fatto il santantonio, avresti dovuto vedere come pregava!* "After the prison guards taught him a lesson, you should see how fast he learned!"

SANTÌNO, *m., crim.* (Lit., holy picture.) Police mugshot. *La polizia m'ha fatto vedere il tuo santino, sai, ma io non ho cantato.* "The police showed me your picture, you know, but I kept my mouth shut."

SANTÌSSIMI, *m. pl., N.* (Lit., most holy ones.) Testicles.

Non farmi girare i santissimi con le tue faccende di avvo-cati! "Stop being a pain in the balls with your endless business with lawyers!"

SÀPIENS, *Lat., m./f., youth.* (From "*Homo sapiens.*") Parent; father; mother; elderly person; professor. *Il sapiens e la sapiens non vogliono saperne di mollarmi la carretta per Capodanno.* "No car for New Year's Eve. My folks don't even want to hear about it."

SAPÓNE, *m.* (Lit., soap.) **Dare del sapone a qualcuno.** (Lit., to soap up someone.) *See* **insaponare.**

SARÀFFO, *m., N.* (Probably from the old "saraffa," trick.) **a)** *slang.* Cunning and strong person. *Quel saraffo ha cercato di fregare l'assicurazione, ma stavolta è finito dentro.* "That crook tried to cheat the insurance company, but this time he got locked up." **b)** *youth.* Womanizer. *See* **cucador.**

SBAFÀRE, *vt., C.* (From > **sbafo.**) To eat voraciously. *Mi sono sbafata quattro fette di torta al cioccolato.* "I gobbled four slices of chocolate cake."

SBÀFO, *m., C., youth.* **A sbafo.** A meal one manages to have without paying. *Con due smancerie Oreste si infila in tutte le feste, così mangia a sbafo.* "Oreste just kisses the hostess's hand, pays the host a compliment, and gets in to every party and eats for free."

SBALLÀRE. (Lit., for a motor not to work properly, or at all.) **a)** *vt., crim.* **1.** To kill. *Ha sballato un pulotto, adesso sono sorci verdi per lui.* "He offed a cop. Now he's in deep shit." **2.** To deal in stolen goods. *Hai sballato quella roba? No? Ma te l'avevo detto che scottava!* "Did you get rid of those goods? No?! I told you they were hot!" **b)** *vi., narc.* To get high by taking drugs (of any kind). *Non ti fa sballare neanche più la morfa? Sei nei guai.* "You don't even get high on morph anymore?! You're in trouble." **c)** *vt., youth.* To flunk a test in school. *Non ha mai sballato un compito di mate in vita sua: un einstein.* "She hasn't flunked a single math test in her entire life. She's a genius."

SBALLÀTO, *adj.* (From > **sballare.**) **a)** *narc.* Intoxicated with narcotics; high. *Zitti, ci sono i grigi! Cercate di non far vedere che siete sballati!* "Quiet, my folks are in! Don't let them see you're stoned." **b)** *youth.* **1.** Wrong. *I tuoi conti per quanto ci costa il viaggio in Messico? Tutti sballati.* "Your calculations about the price of our trip to Mexico? All way off the mark." **2.** Dazed; out of sorts. *Non mi parlare di cose difficili, oggi sono sballata.* "Don't tell me anything complicated. Today I'm out of sorts." **3.** Sloppily and shabbily dressed. *Da quando in qua si va in giro così sballata, signorina bella?* "What's this new habit of going out looking like a bag lady, my little dear?"

SBÀLLO, *m.* **a)** *narc.* Being high under the influence of drugs. *È l'unico che conosco che quando è in sballo diventa cattivo.* "He's the only one I know who turns nasty when he's high." **b)** *youth.* An exciting, outstanding, marvelous person, situation, or thing. *Ho provato la mia macchina sulla pista da corsa. Uno sballo!* "I tried my car at the racetrack. What a flash!"

SBALLÓSO, *adj., youth.* (From > **sballo, b.**) Awesome, exciting, marvelous. *Non avrei mai creduto che il paracadutismo fosse così sballoso.* "I didn't expect parachuting would be such a turn-on."

SBÀRBA, *m., crim.* (Lit., without a beard.) Young male homosexual who practices prostitution. *Prima lo faceva per divertirsi, adesso è uno sbarba professionista, però.* "He started doing it for fun, but now he's a gay hustler by trade."

SBARBÀTO/SBARBATÈLLO/SBARBÌNO, *m., youth.* (From > **sbarba.**) Greenhorn; young person. *La signora Carducci, sai la bellona quarantenne, s'è presa uno sbarbatello.* "Mrs. Carducci, you know, that foxy forty-something, got herself a young stud."

SBARBÌNA, *f., N., youth.* A young girl who plays the *femme fatale.* *Ah, anche oggi Cinzia fa la sbarbina, occhioni truccati e gonna fasciante.* "Cinzia is in her Lolita mode today, heavy make-up and tight skirt."

SBARELLÀRE, *vi., N.* **1.** To sway; to totter. *Ma perché sbarella così? È bevuto?* "Why is he swaying like that? Did he drink too much?" **2.** Not to connect; not to think straight. *Non badare a quello che ho detto ieri sera. Sbarellavo totale.* "Don't mind what I said last night. I wasn't thinking straight."

SBÀTTERE, *vt., rude.* (Lit., to slam.) To possess sexually. *L'hanno sbattuta in tanti, puoi aggiungerti anche tu alla lista.* "A lot of men have had a go at her; you can add yourself to the list."

SBÀTTERSENE, *vi. pronom., rude.* (From > **sbattersi, c2.**) *See* **fregarsene.**

SBÀTTERSI. (From > **sbattere.**) **a)** *vi. pronom., slang.* To bend over backwards to get something done. *Ci siamo sbattuti come dei pazzi per finire il tetto prima dell'inverno.* "We bent over backwards to be able to get the roof finished before winter." **b)** *narc.* **1.** *vi. pronom.* To use any means to get money for buying drugs. *Mi sono sbattuta per tutta la città per raccogliere la grana e questa è tutta la merda che mi dai?* "I hustled all over town to find the money and this is all the shit you're giving me?" **2.** *vt. pronom.* To get rid of; to eliminate. *Non esce stasera: si sta sbattendo la sbornia di ieri.* "He isn't going out tonight. He's getting rid of last night's drinking spree." **c)** *vr., youth.* **1.** To dance. *Andiamo a sbatterci allo Studio X? Mi dicono che è un posto cosmico.* "Do you want to go boogie at Studio X? They tell me it's out of this world." **2.** *vi. pronom., rude.* To have sex. *Non si sbattono più da mesi.* "They haven't tumbled in the sack for months."

SBATTIMÉNTO, *m.* **a)** *youth.* (From > **sbattere.**) **1.** Sexual intercourse. *Un po' di sbattimento ce l'ho con Tina, ma non so mai quando.* "I do a little screwing with Tina, although I never know when." **2.** Boring situation or thing. *Ci mancava il suo comizio. Che sbattimento!* "The last thing I needed at that rally was his speech. What a pain!" **b)** *slang.* (From > **sbattersene.**) Culpable indifference. *Dal comune non ottieni mai niente, c'è uno sbattimento generale.* "You never get anything from city hall. The people who work there don't give a damn." **c)** *narc.* (From > **sbattersi, b1.**) The things one does so as to get drugs. *Mi sono fatta uno sbattimento pazzesco e poi lui non aveva ricevuto la merce.* "After hustling like crazy I found out he hadn't got the stuff."

SBAVÀRE, *vi.* (Lit., to drool.) **Sbavare dietro a qualcuno/qualcosa.** (Lit., to be drooling over someone/something.) To show a strong desire for someone/something. *Sbava per me, lo so, ma per adesso lo lascio lì a soffrire.* "He's drooling over me, I know. He can do that for a while, then we'll see."

SBÈRLA, *f.* (Lit., slap.) Imposing person or part of the human body. *Che sberla di ragazza!* "What a big girl!"

SBIELLÀRE, *vi., C.* (Lit., what happens when pistons go out of phase.) **1.** To lose one's balance; to stagger. **2.** Not to think straight. *See* **sballare.**

SBIELLÀTO, *adj., youth.* (From > **sbiellare.**) **1.** Loony. *Mi ha raccontato storie di fantasmi tutta la sera. È di uno sbiellato!* "He told me ghost stories all evening. He's a real wacko." **2.** Desperately in love. *La Tina sbiellata? Questa è una novità.* "Tina head over heels? This is news."

SBÌRRO, *m.* (Probably from the Latin "birrum," hooded cloak.) Policeman. *Cosa volevano da te gli sbirri?* "What did the cops want from you?"

SBÒBBA, *f.* **a)** *slang.* Slop. *Per definizione, la sbobba è quella roba che passa per minestra in caserma.* "By definition, slop is what they call soup in the army." **b)** *youth.* Sperm. *Fa la sbobba da solo, cos'altro vuoi che faccia?* "He makes his own milk. What else can he do?"

SBOLOGNÀRE, *vt.* (From the expression "vendere oro di Bologna," to sell gold from Bologna, i.e., something worthless.) **a)** *slang.* To get rid of someone/something unpleasant; to pass the buck. *Sono riuscito a sbolognargli il mio vecchio computer; in teoria funziona ancora.* "I managed to palm off my old PC on him. It still works, in theory." **b)** *narc.* For one's body to get rid of the effects of drugs. *Adesso che hai sbolognato la scimmia, possiamo parlare seriamente?* "Did you sleep off your monkey? So, can we have a serious talk?"

SBOMBÀTO, *adj., youth.* (From "bomba," bomb, plus "s.") Mentally and/or physically exhausted. *Non mi chiedere di fare niente di complicato: sono sbombato.* "Don't ask me to do anything complicated. I'm beat."

SBÒRNIA, *f.* Drunkenness. *Ha la sbornia allegra, beata lei.* "She's the happy-drunk type, lucky her."

SBÒR(R)A, *f., N.* Sperm. *Ti dà una mano a produrre sborra o no?* "Does she help you produce whipped cream or not?"

SBOR(R)ÀRE, *vi., N.* (From > **sbor(r)a.**) To ejaculate. *Lo ama, certo, ma dice che sborra troppo presto.* "She loves him dearly, but she says he shoots off too soon."

SBRACÀRSI/SBRAGÀRSI, *vi. pronom.* (Lit., to take one's pants off.) **1.** To let oneself go. *Resta in pigiama per tutto il fine settimana: si sbraca un filo troppo, secondo me.* "He spends the weekend in his pajamas. He lets himself go a bit too much, if you ask me." **2.** To behave in an undignified way in the pursuit of one's aim. *Senatore di qua; senatore di là . . . —Si sbraca, ma non farà carriera lo stesso.* "Senator, may I help you; senator, you're so important . . .—He's become an asslicker, but he won't go far." **3.** To get worse; to go down the tube. *Tutto il paese si è sbracato ormai, Dio solo sa chi ce ne tira fuori.* "The whole country is going down the drain. God only knows who's going to get us out."

SBRACÀTO/SBRAGÀTO, *adj.* Sloppy; tacky; loud. *Troppo sbracati quei pantaloni, sembri un clown.* "Those pants are too baggy. They make you look like a clown."

SBRÀGO, *m.* **a)** *slang.* Collective loss of style and composure. *Troppo sbrago per la tua preppina, vero?* "Too much wild stuff for your preppie girl, right?" **b)** *youth.*

Che sbrago! What a great thing! *Il tema della festa di Carnevale era il bordello. Che sbrago!* "The costume theme for the Mardi Gras party was brothels. That was funky!"

SBRASÀTA, *f., C.* A braggart's action or speech. *Se ascolti lui, inviti a Montecarlo, strette di mano con Blair, Clinton che lo consulta . . . una sbrasata.* "If you listen to that braggart he gets invited to Montecarlo, he shakes hands with Blair, Clinton asks for his advice . . . yeah right."

SBRASÓNE, *m., C.* Braggart. *Credevamo tutti che fosse uno sbrasone, invece Yeltsin l'ha ricevuto per davvero.* "We all thought he was a braggart. It turns out he really was received by Yeltsin."

SBRÉGO, *m., N.* **1.** Tear. *Se trovo chi mi ha fatto 'sto sbrego nel giaccone di pelle, lo ammazzo!* "If I find out who slashed my leather jacket, I'll kill him!" **2.** Vagina. *See* **asola.**

SBRILLENTÀTO, *adj., C.* (Probably a mixture of "sbrindellato," ragged, and "allentanto," slackened.) A piece of clothing that has lost all form and shape. *Lei dice che si mette cose casual, ma io le chiamerei sbrillentate.* "She says she dresses casual. I'd call it rags."

SBRINCIÀRE, *N.* **1.** *vt.* To sprinkle. *Bambini, piantatela di sbrinciare la signora con la pistola ad acqua, se no niente giro sull'ottovolante.* "Kids, stop spraying that lady with the water pistol, otherwise no roller-coaster ride." **2.** *vi.* To ejaculate. *Ha sbrinciato sul divano di velluto di mammà, quell'idiota!* "He shot off on my mom's velour sofa, that idiot!"

SBRODÀRE/SBRODOLÀRE, *vi., rude.* (Lit., to drool.) To ejaculate. *See* **sbor(r)are.**

SBRODOLÀTA, *f.* (From "sbrodolare," to drool.) A long and boring speech. *Una sbrodolata, il discorso inaugurale dell'anno accademico. Ci siamo abbioccati tutti.* "The inaugural speech for the new academic year was endless. We all dozed off."

SBUCCIÀRE, *vt., youth.* (Lit., to peel.) To undress a

woman. *Dava lezioni di seduzione, dicendo che, primo, le donne bisogna sbucciarle piano piano.* "He gave lessons in seduction technique, saying that, first, you must peel off a woman's clothes slowly."

SCACIÀTO, *adj., C.* Sloppy; in bad shape; cheap. *Non crederai di venire alla Cresima di tua cugina così scaciato?* "You're not thinking of coming to your cousin's confirmation dressed in rags like that, are you?"

SCAFÀTO, *adj., C.* (Lit., out of one's shell.) Shrewd; experienced. *"Prendere Renato come socio? Troppo giovane." "Sì, ma è già molto scafato."* "'You're thinking of taking Renato as a partner?' 'He's way too young.' 'Yes, but he's a whiz kid.'"

SCÀFO, *m.* (Lit., hull.) Female body. *See* **carrozzeria.**

SCÀGLIA, *f., N./C., rude.* (Lit., fish scale.) Low-level prostitute. *S'accontenta di quella scaglia perché gli costa quasi niente.* "She's a cheap whore, but she's all he can afford."

SCANNÀRSI, *N.* **1.** *vr.* To bend over backwards. *Dopo essersi scannato tutta la vita, è morto di infarto a cinquantacinque anni.* "After working like mad all his life, he died at fifty-five from a heart attack." **2.** *vr. recipr.* To be forced into fierce competition. *Io ti avviso, in America si scannano come dei pazzi. Non credo ti piacerà.* "I'm warning you. In America they're always at each other's throats. You won't like it."

SCANNÀTO, *adj.* (From > **scannarsi.**) **a)** *slang.* Penniless. *"Com'è che sei così nero?" "Sto scannato di nuovo."* "'Why are you in such a bad mood?' 'I'm down and out again.'" **b)** *youth.* Experienced; uninhibited. *Se Elio fosse qui, andrebbe subito a chiedere a quella signora se ci sta: è uno scannato.* "If Elio were around, he would ask that lady out at once. He's a pro."

SCANNATÓIO, *m., N.* (From > **scannarsi.**) **1.** Joint frequented by unsavory characters. *Ci sono stata, una volta, in quello scannatoio. Che tipi là dentro!* "I was in that joint once. It's full of thugs." **2.** Small apartment or room

257

used only for sexual encounters. *Cosa me ne facevo dello scannatoio? Sono single da un anno.* "Why should I keep that love nest? I've had no sex for a year."

SCAPOLÀRE, *vi.* To avoid; to escape. *Hanno scapolato al momento giusto, prima che chiedessero dei contributi pecuniari.* "They sneaked away at the right moment, before the hat was passed."

SCAPPUCCIÀTO, *adj.* (Lit., without cap.) Circumcised. "*Perché è scappucciato?*" "*È nato negli Stati Uniti, dove lo facevano a tutti.*" "'Why is he circumcised?' 'He was born in the U.S., where it was done to every male.'"

SCARAFÓNE, *m., S.* (In southern dialects, "scarafaggio," cockroach.) **a)** *slang.* **Uno scarafone.** A liter of wine. *Ehi, vacci piano, è il secondo scarafone che attacchi.* "Slow down, that's your second liter." **b)** *crim.* **Fare lo scarafone.** To escape (like a cockroach that squeezes through any opening). *Quando il briga si è abbioccato, lui ha fatto lo scarafone e chi s'è visto s'è visto.* "As the cop dozed off, he sneaked out and made himself scarce." **c)** *youth.* Someone who gets away with murder. *Uno beccato ad alleggerire la profia del portafoglio e non punito, è l'archetipo dello scarafone!* "Someone gets caught relieving his teacher of her purse, and doesn't get punished—that's what they mean by getting away with murder."

SCARICÀRE, *vt., rude.* (Lit., to unload.) To leave a romantic/sexual partner one is no longer interested in. *M'ha scaricata per telefono, il coglione!* "That shithead, he dumped me over the phone!"

SCÀRPE, *f. pl., N., crim.* (Lit., shoes.) **Fare/Levare le scarpe.** (Lit., to take someone else's shoes off.) To steal the tires from a car. *Quartiere bene un corno! Hanno fatto le scarpe alla mia macchina ieri notte!* "Nice neighborhood my ass! They stole the tires from my car last night!"

SCARPÉTTA, *f., C.* **Fare la scarpetta.** To clean up a dish, especially the sauce, with a piece of bread. *Non gli hanno* *insegnato che alle cene eleganti non si fa la scarpetta?* "Didn't they teach him that you don't mop up your plate at elegant dinners?"

SCARPINÀRE, *vi.* **a)** *slang.* To get away. *Hanno scarpinato dalla porta-finestra sul retro.* "They sneaked away through the French doors in the back." **b)** *youth.* **Scarpinare un branco.** To walk for a long time. *Mi ha fatto scarpinare un branco per cercare un vecchio disco di Frank Sinatra.* "She made me walk for miles looking for an old Sinatra record."

SCÀRSO, *adj., youth.* (Lit., scarce.) **1.** Said of someone who is not up to date. *Adele? Scarsa, non sa neanche chi sono gli U2.* "Adele? Out of touch. She doesn't even know who U2 is." **2.** Said of a poorly endowed girl. *Lui dice che Barbara è una bomba a letto? Non si direbbe, scarsa com'è.* "He says Barbara is a bombshell in bed? You wouldn't believe it, she's such a stick."

SCARTÒFFIA, *f., youth.* (Lit., paper; red tape.) School books and notebooks. *Dieci chili di scartoffie mi devo portare ogni mattina. Io chiedo i danni al Provveditorato.* "I have to carry ten kilos of books and notebooks every morning. I'll sue the school board."

SCASSACÀZZI, *m./f., C., rude.* (Lit., ballbuster.) Annoying and nagging person. *Vito è uno scassacazzi, non devi credere a tutte le sue storie lacrimevoli.* "Vito is a professional whiner. Don't believe all his tearful stories."

SCASSAMÌNCHIA, *m./f., C., rude. See* **scassacazzi.**

SCASSÀRE, *vt.* (Lit., to loosen; to force.) To annoy; to bore. *E non scassare, che qui si sta lavorando sul serio.* "Don't be a bore. There are people working here."

SCÀTOLE, *f. pl.* (Lit., boxes.) Testicles. **Rompere le scatole/Stare sulle scatole.** Euphemism for **rompere i > coglioni/rompere le palle.**

SCAVÀLCO, *m., C., crim.* (Lit., climbing over.) A burglary/robbery carried out by climbing over a window or balcony. *È caduto dal terzo piano mentre faceva uno scavalco: ingessato da capo a piedi.* "He fell while trying to break into a fifth-story apartment. He's in a cast from head to toe."

SCAVÀRSI, *vi. pronom., N.* (Variation of "cavarsi di mezzo," to get out of someone's way.) To rid someone of one's presence. *Ho capito che vuoi star solo, adesso mi scavo.* "I see you want to be alone. I'll get out of your way."

SCAZZÀRE, *vi., N., rude.* (From > **cazzata** plus "s.") *See* **cazzeggiare.**

SCAZZÀRSI, *vi. pronom., rude.* (Antonym of > **incazzarsi.**) **1.** To get bored; to lose interest. *Mi sono scazzato di 'sto cantante. Me ne vado.* "I've had enough of this singer. I'm leaving." **2.** To calm down. *Lui s'incazza e poi si scazza, non ti preoccupare.* "He blows up and then he cools down. Don't worry." **3.** To argue. *Si scazzano di nuovo? Ma non stavano per partire per la loro seconda luna di miele?* "Are they bickering again? Weren't they about to leave for their second honeymoon?" **4.** To have to deal with an annoying situation/person. *Mi prendeva in giro, adesso è lui che si scazza con l'impresario.* "He was teasing me before. Now he's the one who has to hassle with the builder."

SCAZZÀTO, *adj.* (From > **scazzarsi, 1.** Lit., without penis.) Bored; listless; in a bad mood. *Che t'hanno fatto sul lavoro che sei così scazzato?* "What did they do to you at work? You're so crabby."

SCÀZZO, *m., youth.* (From > **scazzarsi.**) **1.** Quarrel; fight. *C'è stato un megascazzo tra vetero-fascisti e vetero-comunisti fuori dalla scuola.* "There was an all-out fight between old fascists and old communists outside the school." **2.** Boredom. *Che scazzo il viaggio in Scozia! Pioveva sempre.* "Our trip to Scotland was a pain in the neck. It rained all the time." **3.** Trouble; difficult situation. *Io però t'ho aiutato quando hai avuto quello scazzo finanziario.* "I, however, did help you financially when you were in that fix."

SCÈNDERE, *vi., N.* (Lit., to come down.) **Scendere dall'albero/dal pero/dal trespolo.** (Lit., to climb down the tree/the pear tree/the perch.) To lower one's sights; to get off one's high horse. *Tu in quel ristorante non ci vai perché ci va il popolino? Ma scendi dal pero!* "You don't go to that restaurant because the clientele is too down to earth? Come off it!"

SCHÉGGIA, *f., youth.* (Lit., splinter.) **a)** *crim., S.* A car tire. *Traffica in schegge "usate," come le chiama lui.* "He deals in 'used' tires, as he calls them." **b)** *youth.* **Essere una scheggia.** (Lit., to be a splinter.) To be very fast. *Hai già fatto tutte le commissioni? Sei una scheggia!* "Are you back from your errands? You're fast!"

SCHEGGIÀRE, *vi., N., youth.* (From > **scheggia, b.**) To go at very high speed; to flee. *Il cartello dice che la piscina è solo per gli ospiti dell'albergo? Alla peggio dobbiamo scheggiare.* "The sign says the swimming pool is only for hotel guests? If worst comes to worst we'll have to scram."

SCHIÀNTO, *m., youth.* (Lit., splitting.) **Uno schianto.** Marvelous person or thing. *La sua donna? Uno schianto.* "His girlfriend? A blast."

SCHIAVETTÓNI, *m. pl., C., crim.* Handcuffs. *Sarò un agnello, giuro, ma risparmiatemi gli schiavettoni.* "I'll be a good boy, I promise, but please don't make me wear the handcuffs."

SCHIFÌO, *m., S.* (Lit., repugnance, in southern dialects.) **A schifio.** To hell; to rack and ruin; badly. *A schifio finisce, perché Don Ciccio non vuole pagare la mazzetta!* "We'll all go to rack and ruin because Don Ciccio doesn't want to pay protection money!"

SCHIODÀRE, *youth.* (Lit., to remove nails.) **1.** *vt.* To get someone out of trouble. *L'ho schiodato da un brutto pasticcio. In cambio ho avuto . . . la sua eterna riconoscenza.* "I got him out of serious trouble. All I got in exchange was . . . his eternal gratitude." **2.** *vt.* To cough up. *Schioda un po' di lira per la broda, se no il concerto te lo scordi.*

"Cough up some money to fill the tank, otherwise forget the concert." **3**. *vt*. To leave (the person one is dating). *Vorrei schiodarlo, poi mi fa pena e tiro avanti.* "I'd like to send him packing. Then he starts whining, so I keep him." **4**. *vi., C.* To be very attracted to. *A te schiodano di più le bionde o le brune?* "Are you pulled by blondes or brunettes?"

SCHIODÀRSI, *vr., youth*. (From > **schiodare**.) **1**. To split; to go away. *Beh, se non vi decidete io mi schiodo.* "Well, if you don't make up your minds, I'm going to split." **2**. To change habits. *A trent'anni, mio fratello vive ancora in casa; non si schioderà mai.* "At thirty my brother still lives at home. He'll never change."

SCHIODÀTO, *adj., youth*. (From > **schiodare**.) **1**. Without a sexual/sentimental partner. *Tutti i miei amici sono schiodati come me. Potremmo fondare un ordine religioso.* "All my friends are single like me. We could found a religious order." **2**. Back on one's feet. *Non pensavo che essere mollato da quella stronzetta mi avrebbe fatto sentire così schiodato.* "I never thought that being dumped by that little bitch would get me back on my feet so fast."

SCHIZOFRENÌA, *f., youth*. (Lit., schizophrenia.) Anxiety; nervousness. *Va soggetta ad attacchi di schizofrenia da matepatia. Niente di grave.* "She is subject to anxiety attacks due to math phobia. Nothing serious."

SCHIZZÀRE. (Lit., to squirt.) **a)** *vi., slang, rude*. **1**. To urinate. *I ragazzi facevano la gara a chi schizzava più lontano.* "The boys competed to see who could pee the farthest." **2**. To ejaculate. *Chiede a tutte di farlo schizzare. Patetico.* "He asks every girl to make him shoot off. He's pathetic." **b)** *youth*. **1**. *vi*. To run away. *Ti richiamo più tardi, adesso devo schizzare.* "I'll call you back later. I must run now." **2**. *vi*. To behave in an extravagant, excited, hyper way. *Schizza un po', sai, ed è anche un po' bamba; non pericoloso, però.* "He's a bit schizo, you know, a bit of a dimwit. But he's not dangerous." **3**. *vt*. To leave one's sexual/sentimental partner. *See* **schiodare**

3. c) *vi., narc.* To lose it because of the influence of hallucinogenic drugs. *Si fa delle mega dosi, poi schizza da far paura.* "She does megacubes of acid, right? Then she freaks out. It's real scary."

SCHIZZÀTO, *adj.* (From > **schizzare.**) **a)** *youth.* **1.** Left by one's partner or ignored by one's peer group. *Non so perché, ma lei è una che resta lì schizzata mentre gli altri si divertono.* "I don't know why, but she always stays in a corner while everyone else is having a ball." **2.** Anxious; nervous; hyper. *È schizzata perché il medico vuole fare altri esami.* "She's antsy because her doctor wants to do some more tests." **b)** *narc.* Under the influence of narcotics. *Ultimamente l'ho visto meno schizzato; dici che ne sta venendo fuori?* "It seems to me he's been less stoned lately. Do you think he's kicking the habit?"

SCHÌZ(Z)O, *adj., youth.* (Contraction of "schizofrenico," schizophrenic.) Nervous; anxious. *Ma no, sto bene, sono solo un po' schizo.* "I feel fine, really, just a little antsy."

SCHÌZZO, *m.* (Lit., spurt.) **a)** *slang.* **1. Schizzo anticipato.** Premature ejaculation. *Cesare ha il problema dello schizzo anticipato, lei vuole portarlo dal medico.* "Cesare goes off too fast. She wants to take him to the doctor." **2.** Shot of liquor in coffee. *Partiva col primo schizzo a metà mattina. Alle tre del pomeriggio era praticamente andato.* "He had his first shot around midmorning. By three in the afternoon he was gone." **b)** *youth.* **1.** Insignificant and worthless person or thing. *Irene esce con quello schizzo perché può farne quello che vuole.* "Irene goes out with that twit because she can wrap him around her little finger." **2.** A small quantity. *Questa fetta di torta deve bastare per tutti: perciò, uno schizzo a testa.* "That slice of cake must do for all of us. So just a little bit each, OK?" **c)** *narc.* Drug injection. *Ancora uno schizzo, dai, l'altro non l'ho sentito neppure!* "One more shot, come on, I didn't even feel the first one."

SCIACQUÉTTA, *f., C.* Bimbo. *La zona è piena di sciacquette. Carine, ma dopo un po' ti stufano.* "There are lots of bimbos around here. They're cute, but you tire of them quickly."

SCICCÓSO/SCICCHETTÓSO, *adj., C.* (Italianization of the French "chic.") Excessively elegant. *Si atteggiava a dandy, tutto sciccoso e con l'aria annoiata.* "He played the dandy, which meant he wore great clothes and a bored expression on his face."

SCÌMMIA, *f.* (Lit., monkey.) **a)** *slang.* Vagina. *Mi ha schiodata perché non gli interessa più la mia scimmia. E me l'ha pure detto!* "He dumped me because he grew tired of my pussy. And he told me in so many words!" **2.** Drunkenness. *See* **sbornia. b)** *narc.* **1.** A bad experience with drugs. *S'è preso uno spaghetto con un paio di scimmie, così ha deciso di piantarla con la roba.* "He had a couple of bad trips, so he decided to quit dope." **2. Scimmia in spalla.** English "monkey on one's back," i.e., almost complete addiction to narcotics. *L'han trovata morta? Beh, era un po' che aveva la scimmia in spalla.* "They found her dead? Well, she had had a monkey on her back for quite some time." **c)** *youth.* Depression. *Va dallo strizzacervelli perché ha la scimmia cronica.* "He's seeing a shrink because he's chronically down."

SCIÒLTO, *adj., C., youth.* (Lit., loose, untied.) Said of one who does not want to make serious commitments. *Io con te ci esco anche, ma t'avverto, sono una tipa sciolta.* "You want a date with me? You've got a date. But I like my freedom."

SCIROCCÀTO, *adj., C., youth.* (From "scirocco," sirocco.) Extravagant, bizarre (as if under the influence of the scirocco wind). *Visto? Non salutano più. Sono tutti sciroccati.* "See that? They don't even say hello anymore. They're wacko."

SCIROPPÀRSI, *vt. pronom., youth.* (From "sciroppo," syrup.) To keep a boring person company; to put up with a boring thing. *Mentre mi sciroppavo sua nonna, Ida le cuccava la grana.* "While I was playing the good child with her grandma, Ida stole her money."

SCLÈRO, *f., youth. See* **arterio, 2.**

SCÒGLIO, *m., C.* (Lit., marine rock.) Ugly girl. *See* **cozza.**

SCOGLIONÀRSI, *vi. pronom., rude.* (Lit., to lose one's balls.) To get bored; to get annoyed. *Se continui a dargli del traditore lui si scogliona e ti tradisce sul serio.* "If you go on accusing him of cheating on you, he'll get fed up and he'll really do it."

SCOGLIONÀTO, *adj., rude.* (From > **scoglionarsi.**) **1.** Bored; annoyed. *Peppino è scoglionato di natura, non farci caso.* "Don't mind Peppino. He's chronically bored." **2.** Unlucky; negative. *Avevo appena abbassato la capotte che si è messo a piovere. Non sono scoglionato?* "As soon as I put down the convertible roof it began to rain. I have lousy luck, don't I?"

SCOPÀRE. (Lit., to sweep.) **1.** *vt.* To possess sexually. *L'ho scopata tre volte, un dopo l'altra, e non m'ha neanche detto grazie.* "I fucked her three times—bam-bam-bam—and she didn't even say 'thanks.'" **2.** *vi.* To have sex. *Non scopano più, ma pare non gliene importi a nessuno dei due.* "They don't sleep together anymore, but neither of them seems to care."

SCOPÀTA, *f.* (From > **scopare.**) Sexual intercourse. *Lei non era tipo da una scopata e via, era un tipo di cui innamorarsi perdutamente.* "She wasn't the kind of woman you sleep with once. She was the kind you fall desperately in love with."

SCOPATÌNA, *f.* (From > **scopata.**) A quickie. *Non aveva mai fatto una scopatina in treno. Perché no? Un'esperienza nuova.* "She had never had a quickie on a train. Why not? It would be a new experience."

SCOPATÓRE, *m.* (From > **scopare.**) A man who has a very active sexual life. *Non capisco come si sia fatto la fama di grande scopatore. Con me è stato un disastro.* "I don't understand how he became known as a great stud. With me he was a flop."

SCOPATRÌCE, *f.* (From > **scopare.**) A woman expert in the arts of love. *Gli assicurarono che Grazia era una grande scopatrice, che lo avrebbe aiutato a superare le sue inibizioni.* "They swore Grazia was great at sex, that she would help him overcome his inhibitions."

SCOPAZZÀRE, *vi.* (From > **scopare.**) To have an active and easy-going sexual life. *Sai, d'estate si scopazza, ma d'inverno, con il freddo, il lavoro, si conclude poco.* "See, in summer you swing a lot, but during the long winter months you work a lot and don't do it much."

SCOPERCHIÀRE, *vt., youth, rude.* (Lit., to take the lid off.) To undress someone completely in order to have sex. *L'ha scoperchiata ed è rimasto a bocca aperta: era troppo, troppo bona, dice.* "He took her clothes off and stood there in awe; she was such a knockout, he says."

SCOPERÉCCIO, *adj.* (From > **scopare.**) **1.** Said of a person who shows sexual proclivity and prowess. *Sai, a volte queste tipe scoperecce sono una gran delusione.* "You know, sometimes the swinging types are a disappointment." **2.** Said of a thing/situation that has sexual potential. *La luna piena, il mare, il caldo: il potenziale scopereccio mi sembra alto.* "The full moon, the sea, warm weather: ideal conditions for intense sexual activity."

SCOPICCHIÀRE, *vi.* (From > **scopare.**) **1.** Not to refrain from occasional, including adulterous, sexual encounters. *Hanno scopicchiato per qualche mese, poi il marito è tornato ed è finito tutto.* "They got it on now and then for a few months, then her husband came back and it was all over." **2.** To have sex rarely and badly. *A sessant'anni si lamenta perché scopicchia solo più, dice lui.* "He complains, because at sixty he doesn't do it as much as he used to."

SCOPPIÀRE, *vi., youth.* (Lit., to blow up.) **1.** To reach the end of one's rope. *Ho studiato talmente tanto per il compito di latino che alla fine scoppiavo.* "I worked so hard preparing for my Latin test I almost died." **2.** To ejaculate. *Gli è bastato guardare quel film per scoppiare.* "He got off just by watching that movie."

SCOPPIÀRSI, *youth.* (Lit., to get blown up.) **1.** *vt. pronom.* To waste; to squander. *Ti sei scoppiato tutto, anche i soldi del biglietto di ritorno? Sei matto.* "You even squandered the money for your return ticket? You're loony." **2.** *vr. recipr.* To stop being a couple/dating each other. *Si sono scoppiati un'altra volta? Si rimetteranno insieme, vedrai.* "They split? They'll get together again, you'll see."

SCOPPIÀTO, *adj.* (From > **scoppiare.**) **a)** *slang.* Exhausted; beat. *"Allora, facciamo che siamo pari a tennis?" "Sì, sono scoppiata."* "'Well, shall we declare this tennis game a draw?' 'Yes, I'm shot.'" **b)** *youth.* **1.** Not thinking straight anymore. *Va in giro dicendo che lei è omo. È scoppiato.* "He's spreading around the rumor that she's gay. He's gone apeshit." **2.** Out-of-date person/thing. *"Dici che questa gonna è scoppiata?" "Positivo. Va il lungo ormai."* "'Are you telling me this skirt is out?' 'Roger. Long skirts are in now.'" **3.** Without a sexual/sentimental partner. *Che fai il sabato sera adesso che sei scoppiata?* "Now that you're single again, what do you do on Saturday nights?" **c)** *narc.* Enslaved to drugs. *Ottimo cliente per il nostro spacciatore: è scoppiato di brutto.* "Great client for our local pusher. He's hooked."

SCÒRFANO, *m., S., youth.* (Lit., scorpion fish.) A very ugly person, especially female. *Anche gli scorfani, poverini, hanno diritto a un po' di su e giù.* "Even dogs, poor things, are entitled to a little fun."

SCOR(R)ÉGGIA, *f., N., rude.* **a)** *slang.* Fart. *Facevano a gare di scorreggia!* "They had a who-farts-the-loudest competition!" **b)** *youth.* **Andare a scorreggia.** To be outstanding; to be doing great. *Va a scorreggia in tutto: donne, soldi, tutto!* "He's a wizard in everything he does: women, money, you name it!"

SCOR(R)EGGIÓNA, *f., N., youth.* (From > **scorreggia, a.**) Motorcycle. *Se mi ammettono a quella università privata il matusa mi regala una scorreggiona megagalattica!* "If they admit me into that private university, my old man will buy me a motorcycle that's out of this world!"

SCÒRTICO, *m., C.* (Probably from Latin "scorticum," prostitute.) Small apartment/room used only for sexual encounters. *Devo trovare uno scortico in fretta, altrimenti Tamara me la scordo.* "I have to find a love nest quickly. Otherwise I can forget about Tamara."

SCRÀUSO, *adj., C., youth.* Unprepared; worthless. *Perché ti accontenti di uno scrauso come Mario?* "Why do you put up with a twit like Mario?"

SCRÒFANO, *m., youth. See* **scorfano.**

SCROSTÀRSI, *vr., youth.* (Lit., to remove oneself as if one were a scab.) To move; to go away (because one's presence is not desired). *Scrostati che puzzi. Non lo sai che esistono le docce?* "Keep away from me; you stink. Don't you know there are such things as showers?"

SCÙCIO, *m., C., crim.* (From > **scucire.**) Theft performed by cutting the victim's bag or clothes. *"I tuoi pantaloni sono rotti dietro." "Oh, no, m'hanno fatto uno scucio!"* "'Your back pocket is torn.' 'Oh, no! They cut it to swipe my wallet.'"

SCUCÌRE, *vt.* (Lit., to unstitch.) **1.** To steal; to get something by illegal means. *Le ho scucito la collana a teatro.* "I stole her necklace at the theater." **2.** To fork over. *Scuci, scuci, non fare finta di niente come al solito.* "Come on, fork over some money, instead of looking the other way, as usual."

SCÙFFIA, *f., N.* (Lit., capsizing.) **Prendersi una bella scuffia.** To fall head over heels in love with someone. *Da quando si è preso una bella scuffia per la vichinga è al settimo cielo.* "He's been on cloud nine ever since he fell in love with the Viking beauty."

SCÙLO, *m., youth. See* **disculo.**

SDÀTO, *adj., C., youth.* (Composed of "dato," given, plus "s.") Out-of-fashion, used a lot, seen around, and therefore uninteresting. *Le Timba? Sdate!* "Timberland shoes? They are out!"

SDERENÀTO, *adj., C.* (Composed of "reni," kidneys, and "s.") **1.** Worn-out, exhausted. *Che roba il trasloco! Sono completamente sderenato.* "I'm so tired after moving. I'm beat!" **2.** In bad shape, out of kilter. *Questi cassetti non si chiudono più, sono tutti sderenati.* "These drawers don't close anymore. They're all out of kilter."

SÉCCHIA, *m./f.,* **SECCHIÓNE,** *m.,* **SECCHIÓNA,** *f., N., youth.* Excessively zealous student, beloved by his/her teachers; a nerd. *Non è quella gran cima, sai, più che altro è una secchiona.* "She isn't such a genius, you know; she's really a nerd."

SÉCCO, *adj.* (Lit., dry.) **1. A secco.** Without resources: money, gasoline, women, dope, etc. *Sono a secco, a secco di tutto: soldi, donne, mezzo di trasporto.* "I'm left with nothing, really nothing: no money, no women, no means of transportation." **2. Fare secco qualcuno.** (Lit., to make someone dry.) To kill someone. *Dov'è finito il corpo? Sei sicuro di averlo fatto secco?* "Where did the body go? Are you sure you iced him?"

SEDÉRE, *m.* (Lit., buttocks.) *See* **culo a3,** meaning luck.

SÉGA, *f., rude.* (Lit., saw.) **a)** *slang.* **1.** Male masturbation. **Farsi/Spararsi/Tirarsi una sega.** To masturbate. *Tira seghe, ecco cosa fa chiuso nel cesso per ore.* "He jacks off, that's what he does locked for hours in the bathroom." **2.** Nothing. *Ma cosa vuoi spiegargli la differenza tra memoria RAM e memoria ROM. Non capisce una sega.* "Why are you trying to explain to him the difference between RAM memory and ROM memory? He doesn't understand scratch." **3.** Worthless person, especially in the expression: **Una mezza sega.** *Non avrai paura di quella mezza sega?* "You aren't afraid of that twit, are you?" **b)** *youth.* **Fare sega:** *See* **segare, b1.**

SEGÀRE, *N.* (Lit., to saw.) **a)** *slang.* **1.** *vi.* To run away. *Se hanno segato è perché avevano la coscienza sporca.* "They must have run away because they had a dirty conscience." **2.** *vt.* To get rid of; to sack. *Il partito l'ha segato per salvare la coalizione.* "The party sacked him to save the coalition." **3.** *vt.*, *rude*. To possess sexually. *See* **scopare. b)** *vi.*, *youth*. **1.** To play hooky. *Abbiamo segato e poi dove siamo finiti? Al museo!* "We played hooky and where did we end up? In the museum!" **2.** To be stimulating, captivating. *Sto video sega, perché non lo guardi?* "This video is a blast, why don't you watch it?"

SEGÀTA, *f.* (From > **sega.**) Stupid action or speech; trifle. *Fa un mucchio di segate, ma mai niente di veramente infame.* "He behaves silly, but he never does anything really evil."

SEGATÙRA, *f.*, *crim.* (Lit., sawdust.) A cigarette made by mixing cigarette butts. *È così mal ridotto che si fa le segature!* "He's so down and out he has to smoke cigarette butts."

SEGHÌNO, *m.*, *youth*. (From > **sega.**) **1.** Inexperienced and clumsy attempt at male masturbation. *Le he spiegato cosa doveva fare, ma alla fine è venuto fuori un seghino.* "He showed her what she had to do, but all he got was a lousy hand job." **2.** A student who plays hooky systematically. *Tu ovviamente non c'eri, ma il kaiser ha detto che i seghini verranno segati tutti a giugno.* "You weren't there, as usual. The principal announced that all hooky players will be held back at the end of the year."

SEICÈNTO, *f.*, *crim.*, *rude*. (Lit., six hundred.) Passive male homosexual (because his "motor" is in the back, as in the old FIAT 600). *La vedi quella seicento? Mi ha salvato la vita l'altra sera.* "See that queer over there? He saved my life the other night."

SEMINÀRIO, *m.*, *crim.* (Lit., seminary.) Prison. *Lo chiamano seminario perché quando sei dentro devi pregare molto per salvare la pelle.* "They call prison the 'seminary,' because when you're in you have to pray a lot to save your hide."

SÈNZA SPERÀNZA, *idiom, adj., youth.* (Lit., hopeless.) Boy or girl who, being unattractive, clumsy, and unpleasant, has no hope of finding a partner. *Cosa deve fare uno senza speranza come lui secondo te? Uccidersi?* "What should a hopeless guy like him do? Kill himself?"

SERENÀTA, *f., C., crim.* (Lit., serenade.) Break-in and robbery carried out at night. *Una volta le serenate erano facili. Adesso non più, con tutte le luci alogene nei giardini.* "Nighttime break-ins used to be easy. Not anymore, with all the halogen lights they put in gardens."

SESSANTANÒVE, *m.* (Lit., sixty-nine.) Reciprocal oral sex. *Lui era altissimo e lei piccola piccola: il sessantanove non gli veniva molto bene.* "He was very tall, and she very short: not ideal for doing sixty-nine."

SET-ÌGLIA, *f., youth.* Family. (Pun on the etymology of the word "famiglia," where "fam," taken as an abbreviation of "fame," hunger, is replaced with "set," abbreviation of "sete," thirst.) *"Quanti siete nella tua set-iglia?" "Cinque, incluso il cane."* "'How many in your family?' 'Five, including the dog.'"

SFANGÀRE, *vt., C.* **1. Sfangar(ci) qualcosa.** To get/earn something for oneself despite the odds; to come out ahead. *Senza faticare tanto, ho sfangato dieci milioni.* "Well, I raked in ten million without even doing much." **2. Sfangarla.** To have a close shave; to get out of a bad situation unscathed. *L'ha sfangata, ma la macchina è dal rottamaio.* "He made it by the skin of his teeth, but his car is at the junkyard."

SFÀTTO, *adj.* (Lit., undone.) **a)** *slang.* Worn out after a night of debauchery. *Mamma, se è sfatta, chissà cos'avrà combinato ieri notte!* "Gee, she looks like a mess. She must have had some night!" **b)** *narc. See* **fatto, a.**

SFAVÀRSI, *vi. pronom., youth.* To get bored. *Io mi sfavo, tu ti sfavi, lei si sfava. Ma che ci stiamo a fare qui?* "I'm bored, you're bored, she's bored. What are we doing here?"

SFÌGA, *f., youth.* (Lit., the condition of being cuntless.) **1.** Bad luck. *Ci hanno soffiato sotto il naso gli ultimi due biglietti. Che sfiga!* "They snatched the last two tickets out from under our nose. What a piece of bad luck!" **2.** A prolonged period of bad luck. "*Come va a sfiga di questi tempi?*" "*Non me ne parlare, una megasfiga!*" "'How are you doing in the bad luck department these days?' 'Don't remind me. Never been so unlucky in my whole life.'"

SFIGÀTO, *adj., youth.* (From > **sfiga.**) **1.** A male who doesn't have access to the female sexual organ; a male who seems unable to find a girlfriend. "*Sei ancora sfigato?*" "*Non più. Esco con Cinzia.*" "'Still no sex?' 'Things have changed. I'm going out with Cinzia.'" **2.** Unlucky. *Se ti impresto il walkman, te lo rubano di nuovo. Sei troppo sfigato.* "If I lend you my Walkman, they'll steal it again. You have too much bad luck." **3.** Ugly, unpleasant, inconvenient, referring to a thing. Also in the superlative form, **sfigatissimo.** *Uh, che coda allo skilift! Le piste più sfigate le trovi sempre tu.* "What a line at the ski lift! You're good at choosing the worst slopes."

SFILÀRE, *vt.* (Lit., to take off.) **a)** *crim.* **Sfilare il sacco.** (Lit., to remove the sack.) To steal a wallet. *Ho sfilato un sacco bello rigonfio e cosa ci ho trovato dentro? Buoni sconto!* "I snatched a nice, fat wallet, and what did I find inside? Discount coupons!" **b)** *youth.* To get something through cunning and dexterity. *Hanno sfilato il testo del compito di greco al prof. Che colpo!* "They swiped, copied, and returned the text of the Greek in-class test! What a feat!"

SFINOCCHIÀTO, *adj., C.* Badly done; sloppy. *Quelli del comune avrebbero ripulito i giardinetti: guarda che lavoro sfinocchiato.* "This is what the city means by cleaning the public parks: look what a sloppy job they did."

SFITÌNZIA, *f., youth.* A girl, especially a follower of the > **paninari** style. *Che ti aspetti da una sfitinzia? Che le interessino i problemi sociali?* "Did you expect that a with-it, upper-class girl would take an interest in social issues?"

SFIZIÓSO, *adj., S.* (From "sfizio," whim.) Pleasant, unusual, attractive. *Il tessuto di quella sacca imita la carta di* *giornale. Sfizioso!* "A backpack made with a fabric that looks like newspaper! Cool!"

SFLANELLÀRE, *vi., youth.* (From > **flanella.**) To neck. *See* **pomiciare.**

SFÓTTERE, *vt.* (From > **fottere.**) To make fun of someone. *Piantala di sfotterla per come balla. Mica sei Nureyev!* "Stop making fun of the way she dances. You're not exactly Nureyev!"

SFOTTITÙRA, *f.* (From > **sfottere.**) Making fun of someone. *Io bbb-balbet-ttt-to, ma tu-uuu hai rot-ttto con l-le-ee tue sfot-tt-titure!* "I st-tt-ammer-rr, yessss, but I'-I've had enough of-fff you te-ee-asing mm-me!"

SFROCETÀTO, *adj., C.* (From "froge," nostrils.) Excessive; brazen; immoderate. *Tre milioni s'è preso per quel lavoretto. Ammazza, se è sfrocetato!* "Three million lire he got for that little job. He's greedy!"

SFRUCULIÀRE, *vt., S.* To provoke someone through malicious allusions; to make fun of someone. *Se lo sfruculiate ancora un po' con la faccenda che sua moglie avrebbe un amante, lui tira fuori la lupara.* "If you go on provoking him about his wife's supposed affair, he'll draw his gun and shoot you."

SGALLETTÀTA, *f., C.* Bimbo. *Si era messo con Marika, anche se aveva la fama di sgallettata.* "He started dating Marika, even if she had a reputation for being a bimbo."

SGAMÀRE, *C.* **a)** *slang.* **1.** *vi.* To intuit; to get the drift; to get wise. *"Dov'è finito il nostro pollo?" "Hmm, secondo me ha sgamato."* "'Have you seen our chicken?' 'No, I'm afraid he got wise.'" **2.** *vt.* To catch in the act. *Li ho sgamati che stavano per bucarmi i copertoni.* "They were trying to slash my tires, but I caught them red-handed." **b)** *vt., youth.* To stare at someone with interest. *L'ho dovuta sgamare per molto tempo prima che si degnasse di accorgersi della mia presenza.* "I stared at her for a long time. Finally she acknowledged my presence."

273

SGAMÓNE, *m., C.* (From > **sgamare, a1.**) Someone with good intuition. *Come ha fatto a capire cosa volevamo fare? Che sgamone!* "How could he know what we were up to? He's a wizard!"

SGANASCIÀRSI (PER LE/DÀLLE RISÀTE), *vi. pronom., C.* (From "sagnasciare," to dislocate one's jaw.) To double over. *L'ultimo film di Benigni mi ha fatto sganasciare dalle risate.* "The last Benigni movie was so funny I almost died laughing."

SGANASCIÓNE/SGANASSÓNE, *m., C.* Slap; punch. *Se ti trovo ancora a parlare con quei drogati, ti dò uno di quegli sganassoni!* "If I see you talking again with those drug-addicts, I'll whack you!"

SGANCIÀRE, *vt., youth.* (Lit., to unhook.) **1.** To pay; to fork over. *La multa l'abbiamo presa per colpa tua: mo' sganci.* "It was your fault we got the ticket. You fork it over now." **2.** To leave one's sentimental partner; to get rid of someone. *T'ha sganciata perché la gonna era un po' corta? Uno così, meglio perderlo che trovarlo.* "He dumped you because your skirt was a bit too short? Good riddance to bad rubbish!"

SGARRÀRE, *vi., S.* **1.** To lack precision. *Scusa, come fa un orologio al quarzo a sgarrare?* "Excuse me, but how can a quartz watch not keep the right time?" **2.** Not to comply with one's duties. *Quando c'è un casino sul lavoro, quei bastardi pensano subito che sia stato io a sgarrare.* "When there's trouble at work, those bastards immediately think I'm the one who's screwing up."

SGÀRRO, *m.* **a)** *S., crim.* An offense calling for the spilling of blood. *Ha commesso un altro sgarro: è un uomo morto.* "He's offended one big shot too many; he's a dead man." **b)** *N., youth.* Misfortune. *All'esame Lalla ha avuto uno sgarro bestiale.* "At the test, Lalla couldn't have had worse luck."

SGASÀRSI, *vi. pronom., youth.* (Lit., to let gas out.) **1.** To lose energy and enthusiasm. *È la terza volta che proviamo a passare quel crepaccio. Io mi sono sgasato.* "This is the third time we've tried to get through that crevasse. I'm out of gas." **2.** To calm down; to come off one's high horse. *E sgasati un po', che di gente che è andata sul Cervino ce n'è a migliaia!* "Stop bragging! Thousands of people have been to the top of the Matterhorn!"

SGASÀTO, *adj., youth.* (From > **sgasarsi.**) Depressed; listless. *Quel film di Fassbinder m'ha lasciato sgasato totale.* "I'm completely down after seeing that film by Fassbinder."

SGAS(S)ÀTA, *f., N.* **a)** *slang.* Sudden and violent acceleration. *Senti la sgassata? Arriva il bullo della zona.* "Do you hear them peel out? Our local bully is arriving." **b)** *youth.* **Darsi una sgassata:** *See* **sgasarsi, 2.**

SGOBBÀRE, *vi., N.* (From > **sgobbo.**) To work hard. *Ho sgobbato come una scema per finire in tempo e non mi hanno neanche detto grazie.* "I almost killed myself to finish in time, and they didn't even say thanks."

SGÒBBO, *m.* **a)** *slang.* Work. **Andare allo sgobbo.** To go to work. *Va allo sgobbo alle quattro di mattina.* "He goes to work at four in the morning." **Staccare dallo sgobbo.** To leave work. *Stacco presto dallo sgobbo stasera, vieni a fare una partita a biliardo?* "I'm leaving work early tonight. How about a game of pool?" **b)** *crim.* Theft. *Lo sgobbo non rende mica più come una volta: oggi vanno forte la droga, la prostituzione, cose così.* "Old-fashioned theft doesn't pay as much today as do drugs, prostitution, things like that."

SGOMMÀRE, *vi., youth.* (From "gomma," tire plus "s.") To burn rubber, to drive at high speed. *Prese la curva a cento all'ora, sgommando sull'asfalto caldo.* "He took the curve at a hundred kilometers an hour, burning rubber on the hot asphalt."

SGONFIÀRE, *vt., N.* (Lit., to deflate.) To annoy; to tire out. *M'avete sgonfiato con le vostre lamentele. Datevi un po' da fare, invece.* "You've worn me out with your whining. Why don't you get something done for a change?"

SGONFIÀRSI, *vi. pronom.* (Lit., to get deflated.) *See* **sgasarsi.**

SGRAFFIGNÀRE, *vt.* To steal something with cunning and dexterity; to take something on the sly. *Dove hai sgraffignato quel berretto? È figo!* "Where did you swipe that cap? It's cool!"

SGRÀNA, *m., C.* (From "sgranare," to eat a lot.) Pimp. *Lo sgrana vuole più soldi, ma i clienti io mica me li invento!* "My pimp demands more money, as if I could produce clients just like that."

SGROPPÀRE, *vi., C.* To work hard. *See* **sgobbare.**

SGURÀRE, *vt., N.* To clean thoroughly. *Hai sgurato bene quella pentola?* "Did you clean that pot well? It ought to shine."

SHAKERÀRSI, *vr., youth.* (Italianization of English "to shake.") To work up a sweat (especially when dancing). *Guarda come si shakera in pista il nostro bamba!* "Look, even our klutz is up there shaking like crazy!"

SIGNÓR, *m.,* **SIGNÓRA,** *f.* (Lit., Mr., Ms., Mrs.) Used as an adjective to mean excellent, outstanding. *Una signora lavapiatti, gliela raccomando personalmente.* "A superior dishwasher. I personally recommend it."

SIGNÓRA, *f.* (Lit., madam, lady.) **a)** *crim.* The madam of a brothel. *Nascondi quei soldi! Se ti vede la signora che non le dai tutto . . .* "Put that money away! If the madam gets the idea that you aren't giving her everything . . ." **b)** *narc.* **La bianca signora.** (Lit., the white lady.) Cocaine. *Tutti in bianco alla festa, e pronti a partire, per fare onore alla bianca signora.* "Everyone dressed in white at the party and was ready to take off, in honor of Snow White."

SIGNORÌNA, *f.* (Lit., Miss.) A prostitute in a brothel. *Era giovane, timida, vestita modestamente, eppure faceva la signorina da Louise.* "She was young, shy, and modestly dressed, and yet she was one of Louise's girls."

SILÌCIO, *m., youth.* (Lit., silicon.) **1.** A tough guy. *Non* *andrei a protestare per il ferro: il Bindi è un silicio.* "I wouldn't complain about that motorcycle. Bindi is a tough customer." **2.** An indestructible thing. *Io vorrei cambiare il televisore, ma quello che abbiamo è un silicio.* "I'd like to change our TV set, but the one we have is indestructible."

SÌMILE, *m./f., youth.* (Lit., alike.) A youth who wears imitation brand or designer clothes. *Se senti lui, porta solo roba autentica, ma per me è un simile.* "If you listen to him, he only wears genuine designer clothes, but in my opinion they're knockoffs."

SINGLE, *Eng., adj., m./f., youth.* Without a sexual/sentimental partner. *"Single stasera?" "Ahimé sì, come ogni altra sera."* "'Single tonight?' 'Oh yes, like every other night.'"

SIRÌNGA, *f., narc.* (Lit., syringe.) Drug injection. *No, un'altra siringa no, me ne sono fatta una due ore fa.* "No, I don't want another hit. I did one two hours ago."

SIRINGÀRE, *vt., N., crim.* (Lit., to syringe.) To rob; to cheat. *See* **fregare.**

SIRINGÀRSI, *vr., narc.* (Lit., to syringe oneself.) To inject a drug, especially heroin. *Pensa, si è siringato persino al matrimonio di sua sorella!* "Can you believe it? He shot up even at his sister's wedding."

SKÀZZO, *m., youth. See* **scazzo.**

SKEGGIÀRE, *vi., youth. See* **scheggiare.**

SKIZZÀRE, *vt., youth. See* **schizzare.**

SLAMÀRE, *vi., N., youth.* To be good at picking up girls. *Slama solo quando è fatto.* "He's good at picking up girls only when he's stoned."

SLAMPADÀTO, *adj., N., youth.* (From "lampada," lamp.) A person who gets tanned with an infrared lamp. *Uh, se sei slampadato! Sembri un'aragosta appena cotta.* "You got yourself quite some tan in that salon! You look like a lobster right out of the pot."

SLAPPÀRE, *vt., N.* (From "slappa," tongue.) To eat everything to the point of licking the plate. *Hai slappato tutto? Ma non eri a dieta?* "You ate everything, to the last crumb? Weren't you on a diet?"

SLEGÀRE, *vt., youth.* (Lit., to untie.) **1.** For something to have a disinhibiting effect. *Hai bisogno di qualcosa che ti sleghi, poi vedrai che la situazione sembrerà meno brutta.* "If you loosen up, you'll see that the situation will look less dreary." **2.** *rude.* To deflower a girl. *Non ha mai slegato nessuna?* "He has never popped anyone's cherry, has he?"

SLÉGO, *m., youth.* (From > **slegare.**) Anything exciting that helps someone to loosen up. *Che slego ti andrebbe? Una corsa col carro? Una fumata?* "What makes you loosen up? A ride in the car? A smoke?"

SLÈPPA, *f., N.* **1.** A lot. *"Posso prendere un po' di queste mele?" "Sì, sì, ne ho una sleppa."* "'Can I take some of these apples?' 'Yes, sure, I've got a heap of them.'" **2.** Slap; punch. *Gliene han date una tale sleppa che gli è venuta la commozione cerebrale.* "They gave him such a thrashing he got a concussion." **3.** Penis. *Lui lo chiama affettuosamente "la mia sleppa." In effetti, non esagera.* "He affectionately calls it 'my big thing.' He isn't wide off the mark."

SLIMONÀRE, *vi. See* **limonare.**

SLINGUÀRE, *vi., N.* (From "lingua," tongue, plus "s.") **a)** *slang.* To lick (also sexually). *Lei gli disse chiaro e tondo che lui era solo bravo a slinguare.* "She told him in so many words that he was only good as a clit-licker." **b)** *youth.* To exchange deep kisses. *Hanno slinguato tutta la sera, ma non sono andati a letto.* "They French-kissed all evening, but they didn't sleep together."

SLOGGIÀRE, *vi.* (Lit., to leave a place, a dwelling.) To rid someone of one's presence. *Se non sloggiate dal cofano della mia Jaguar, ve la faccio vedere io!* "I warn you, get away from my Jaguar's hood, otherwise . . ."

SLUMÀRE, *vt., N., youth. See* **lumare.**

SLUPÀRE, *vt., youth.* (From "lupo," wolf, plus "s.") *See* **sbafare.**

SLURPÀTA, *f., youth.* (From English "to slurp.") **1.** Slurp. *Non vuoi del gelato? Neanche una slurpata?* "Would you like some ice cream? Not even a slurp?" **2.** Necking. *See* **limonata, a.**

SMACK, *Eng., m., youth.* A kiss with a smack. *Mi ha dato uno smack durante il funerale: si sono girati tutti!* "He gave me a smack during the funeral, which made everyone turn around."

SMADONNÀRE, *vi.* (From > **madonne,** meaning curse plus "s.") To curse; to swear. *Quando vide lo sbrego sulla fiancata dell'Alfa nuova fiammante si mise a smadonnare come un ossesso.* "When he saw the scratch along the side of his new Alfa, he began swearing like a trooper."

SMALTÌTA, *f., C., youth.* Scare, especially when the danger is over. *Gli skinhead hanno menato duro alla manifestazione contro il razzismo. Ci siamo presi una smaltita!* "Skinheads were beating people up at the demonstration against racism. We were scared shitless!"

SMAMMÀRE, *vi.* (Lit., to wean oneself.) To clear out; to go away. Used especially in the imperative: **Smamma!** Get lost! *La torta non è ancora pronta. Smamma!* "The cake isn't ready yet. Get lost!"

SMANAZZÀRE, *vt., N.* (From "mano," hand, plus "s.") For a man to feel a woman against her will. *Pensa che l'infermiere ha cercato di smanazzarla con il marito lì nel letto, malato!* "Would you believe it? That male nurse tried to feel her up while her husband was lying sick in bed!"

SMANDRAPPÀTO, *adj.* **1.** Said of a person who wears shabby and worn-out clothes. *Gira tutto smandrappato perché vuol far credere di essere senza un soldo.* "He walks around in rags because he wants everyone to believe he has zero money." **2.** Beat; exhausted. *Sono talmente smandrappato che non riesco neanche a tenere* *gli occhi aperti.* "I'm so worn out I can't even keep my eyes open."

SMANETTÀRE, *vi., youth.* (From "manetta," the throttle on a motorcycle, plus "s.") To accelerate repeatedly; to drive a motorcycle at the highest possible speed. *Puoi smanettare quanto vuoi, ma quella non è mica una Harley.* "You can rev it up as much as you want, it won't turn into a Harley."

SMAR(R)ONAMÉNTO, *m., N.* (From > **smar(r)onare, 2.**) Nuisance, especially one lasting for a long time (so that it "wears one's testicles out"). *Uno smarronamento, il corso di aggiornamento per insegnanti!* "The course for teachers was a long, boring nuisance."

SMAR(R)ONÀRE, *N.* (From > **marroni,** plus "s.") **1.** *vi.* To make a blunder. *Ti sei dato da fare con una che credevi vedova, e invece ha un bel maritone? Ma smarroni sempre!* "You came on to the widow who turned out to be happily married to a big guy? You blew it again!" **2.** *vt.* To bore; to annoy someone. *Mi hai veramente smarronato con la tua gelosia!* "I've had it with your jealousy!"

SMAR(R)ONÀTA, *f.* (From > **smar(r)onare**) **a)** *slang.* **1.** Blunder. *Gli hai detto che sua moglie era appena andata via con Umberto? Bella smarronata.* "You told him his wife had just left with Umberto? Nice blunder!" **2.** Unsuccessful criminal enterprise. *Bella smarronata ci siamo fatti: abbiamo assaltato un furgone portavalori vuoto!* "The greatest blunder in the history of crime: we tried to rob an empty bank van!" **b)** *youth.* Nuisance. *Il ripasso di latino è una smarronata, ma c'è di peggio nella vita.* "The Latin review session is a nuisance, but there's worse."

SMAR(R)ONÀTO, *adj., youth.* (From > **smar(r)onare, 2.**) Bored; cross. *Sto smarronato senza ragione, però sto smarronato.* "I'm cross. I have no reason to be, but I am."

SMENÀRE, *vt., N.* (From > **menare,** plus "s.") **1.** To pay; to spend; to lose (money). *Ho smenato un fottio di soldi per* *far riparare la macchina.* "I forked over a pile of money to have my car repaired." **2.** To deal in stolen goods *'Sti orecchini scottano. Puoi smenarli in fretta?* "These earrings are hot. Can you find a buyer for them quickly?'"

SMERDÀRE, *vt., rude.* (From > **merda,** plus "s.") **1.** To soil. *Ma che diavolo avete fatto ieri sera per smerdare la casa così?* "What the hell did you do last night to turn the house into such a pigsty?" **2.** To humiliate; to disgrace. *Ho gridato: "Ecco il beneamato della polizia!" Così l'ho smerdato davanti a tutti, il traditore!* "I shouted: 'Here's the darling of the cops!' Now his name is shit around here, the traitor!'"

SMICCIÀRE, a) *vt., C., slang.* To take a good look at. *Ma l'hai smicciata bene? Per me ha almeno cinquant'anni.* "Did you get a long, hard look at her? She must be at least fifty." **b)** *vi., N., youth.* **1.** To be lively, full of beans. *Andiamo a divertirci che stasera mi sento che smiccio.* "Let's go have some fun. I'm on a roll tonight." **2.** To clear out. *"Smicciate, quel tavolo da biliardo è prenotato."* "Scram! That pool table is taken."

SMINCHIÀRE, *vt., youth.* (From > **minchia,** plus "s.") **1.** To annoy; to be a nuisance. *See* **smar(r)onare. 2.** To break; to crumple; to crush. *Che t'ha fatto quello zaino per sminchiarlo così?* "Do you have something against that backpack? You're destroying it."

SMOCCÀRE, *vi., narc.* (From the English "to smoke.") To smoke cigarettes and/or hashish and marijuana. *"E lei, smocca?" "Oh, sì, da una vita."* "'Does she smoke?' 'Oh, yes, since forever.'"

SMOKE, *Eng., m., narc.* Joint; hashish; smoking. *"Hai smoke?" "No, me l'hanno fregato a scuola."* "'Do you have a smoke?' 'No, they stole all I had left at school.'"

SMOLLÀRE, *vt., N., youth.* (From > **mollare,** plus "s.") **1.** To give back. *Ehi, è ora che tu mi smolli il mio CD di Elton John.* "Hey, give me my Elton John CD back." **2.** To inflict. *See* **mollare, 2. 3.** To transmit a disease. *Non mi avrà mollato l'epa? Da qualche giorno mi vedo giallo.*

"Perhaps he gave me hepatitis. I don't like that yellow color of my face."

SMOLLÀRSI. (From > **mollare.**) **a)** *vi./vt. pronom., youth.* **1.** To go. "*Dove ti stai smollando?*" "*In nessun posto. Vagolo.*" "'Where are you going?' 'Nowhere in particular. I'm wandering about.'" **2.** To eat; to drink. *See* **allungarsi.** **3.** To steal. *Lei ha mollato lo zaino sulla panchina e io me lo sono smollato.* "She left her backpack on the bench and I lifted it." **b)** *vr., narc.* To do drugs. *Se vuoi quel lavoro non puoi più smollarti. Fanno il test anti-droga.* "If you want that job, no more dope. They test for drugs there."

SMÓNTA, *f., N., crim.* (From "smontare," to get off.) A theft performed on a bus or train, from which the perpetrator gets off ("smonta") as soon as possible. *Hanno messo un mucchio di pula in borghese sul cinquantanove. Niente più smonta per un po'.* "They put a lot of undercover cops on the number fifty-nine bus. No more on-and-off-the-bus thefts for a while."

SMUCINÀRE, *vi., C.* To rummage, thus messing things up. *I ladri hanno smucinato anche nel cesto della biancheria sporca.* "The burglars even rummaged through the laundry basket."

SNÌFFA, *f.* (Italianization of English "to sniff.") **a)** *slang.* Odor; stench. *Che sniffa in camera tua! Ma che ci fai là dentro?* "There's a horrible stench in you room. What are you doing in there?" **b)** *narc.* Cocaine. *Ottima sniffa, ma troppo cara.* "Great nose candy, but way too expensive."

SNIFFÀRE, *vt.* (Italianization of English "to sniff.") **a)** *slang.* **1.** To sniff. *Ma cos'hai da sniffare per tutta la casa?* "What's making you go sniffing all around the house?" **2.** To sense something fishy. *Ha sniffato che non volevamo includerlo nell'affare.* "He sensed that we didn't want him in on their deal." **3.** To sniff tobacco. *Maria Teresa sniffa. Le piacciono tanto le tabacchiere.* "Maria Teresa sniffs tobacco. She has a thing for snuff boxes." **b)** *narc.* To sniff cocaine. "*Sniffiamo?*" "*No, ho* *sniffato troppo ieri sera.*" "'How about sniffing with me?' 'No, I sniffed too much last night.'"

SÓFFIA, *m., N., crim.* (From > **soffiare, 2.**) Spy; police informer. *Se dici al soffia che il colpo si fa all'altra banca, lui la polizia la manda là.* "If you tell the weasel we're doing the robbery at the other bank, he'll send the police over there."

SOFFIÀRE, *crim.* (Lit., to blow.) **1.** *vt.* To steal with dexterity. *Mi han soffiato le chiavi della macchina. Non ho mai capito come abbiano fatto.* "They snatched my car keys. To this day I don't understand how they did it." **2.** *vi.* To tip off the police, the enemy, or the victim. *Quanti anni in meno mi date se soffio?* "How many years do you take off if I talk?"

SOFFIÀTA, *f.* (From > **soffiare, 2.**) Tip-off. *Bella soffiata. Non c'è nessuno qui!* "Great tip-off. There's no one here!"

SÒFFICE, *adj., youth.* (Lit., soft.) Said of a girl who is pleasantly well-endowed (but not too much). *Soffice la sbarbina! Dove l'hai pescata?* "Nice chick. Where did you pick her up?"

SÒFFOCO, *m., N.* (From "soffocare," to choke.) Sultriness; unbreathable air. *C'è troppo soffoco in questo bar. Andiamocene.* "This joint is full of smoke. Let's go."

SOGGETTÓNE, *m., youth.* (From "soggetto," person.) Daft, naive boy. *Non dirmi che Bobo non ha capito dove doveva andare. Che soggettone!* "Don't tell me Bobo didn't understand where he was supposed to go. What a doodle!"

SÒLA, *f., C.* (From Roman dialect word for "suola," sole.) **a)** *crim.* A swindle in which one does not share the loot with one's accomplice. *M'ha fatto la sola l'ultima volta. Se fossi in lui, me ne starei in Madagascar.* "Last time we worked together he cheated me out of my share. If I were him, I'd stay in Madagascar." **b)** *youth.* **Dare una sola/Prendere una sola.** To stand someone up; to be stood up. *Vedi, una donna ti dà una sola se tu sei il tipo* *da prenderla.* "See, a woman will stand you up, if you're the kind of man who goes around asking for it."

SOLÀRE, *adj., youth.* (Lit., solar.) **1.** Crystal clear. *"Allora hai capito cosa devi fare?" "Solare!"* "'So, do you know what you must do?' 'Roger!'" **2.** Intense, acute (feeling, desire). *Ho una voglia solare di vedere il mio ganzo.* "I can't wait to see my boyfriend."

SOLDÀTO, *m., crim.* (Lit., soldier.) The lowest rank in a mafia family. *Un soldato obbedisce sempre, capito?* "A soldier obeys all the time, capeesh?"

SOLIMÀNO, *m., youth.* (From "solo," by oneself, and "mano," hand.) Masturbation. *Fa solitari e solimani, ma vive contento.* "He plays solitaire and does his own hand-jobs. He's happy, though."

SOSPÌRO, *m., narc.* (Lit., sigh.) A puff from a marijuana joint. *Un sospiro a te e uno a me? O.K.?* "One puff for me and one for you. OK?"

SPACCABÀLLE, *m., N., rude.* See **rompiballe.**

SPÀDA, *f.* (Lit., sword.) **a)** *slang.* Penis. See **bastone. b)** *crim.* False key. See **bambola. c)** *narc.* A syringe needle. By extension, drug-addict. *La spada era piena di roba, ma non riusciva a trovare un ago neanche morto.* "The junkie had a lot of stuff, but he couldn't find a needle for the life of him." **c)** *youth.* A cool person. *Pietro? Una spada, ti puoi fidare.* "Pietro is cool, you can trust him."

SPAGHÉTTI, *m. pl., racist.* See **maccheroni.**

SPAGHÉTTO/SPÀGO, *m.* (Singular of "spaghetti.") Scare. *Quando mi sono vista quell'energumeno davanti al buio mi sono presa uno spaghetto!* "That goon popped up in front of me in the dark. I got such a scare!"

SPALLÓNE, *m., N., crim.* (From "spalla," shoulder.) Smuggler (who crosses the border carrying merchandise on his shoulders). *Negli anni sessanta la valle era percorsa dagli spalloni che portavano i soldi in Svizzera.* "In the 1960s, smugglers went up and down the valley carrying money into Switzerland."

SPAPARACCHIÀRSI/SPAPARANZÀRSI, *vr., S.* To sit down or lie down in a comfortable and relaxed position (implying that one has plenty of time to enjoy it). *Starsene spaparanzati su una sdraio a Miami Beach: quello sì che è vivere!* "To while one's time away lying on a chaise-longue in Miami Beach. That's the life!"

SPARÀRE. (Lit., to shoot.) **1.** *vi.* To fart. *Spara in continuazione, è impossibile averlo intorno.* "He farts all the time. It's impossible to have him around." **2.** *vt.* **Sparare (cazzate)/Spararle grosse.** (Lit., to shoot big ones.) To boast. *Le spara grosse: basta farci la tara.* "He's always shooting you a line. You should take it with a grain of salt."

SPARÀRSI, *vt. pronom.* (Lit., to shoot oneself.) **a)** *slang, rude.* **Spararsi una sega.** *See* **sega, a1. b)** *youth.* To do; to consume. **Spararsi un disco/un panino/una sigaretta.** To listen to a record/To eat a sandwich/To smoke a cigarette. *See* **allungarsi. c)** *narc.* **1. Spararsi in vena.** To inject heroin. *Lei dice che si spara in vena, mo io non le ho mai visto neanche un segno.* "She brags about mainlining, but I've never seen so much as a mark on her body." **2. Spararselo/la in vena.** To like someone so much that one would like to be able to inject oneself with him/her. *Non so cos'abbia di speciale, ma io Aldo me lo sparerei in vena.* "I don't know what's so special about Aldo, but if I could I'd take him intravenously."

SPARASÉGHE, *m./f., youth, rude.* (Lit., "hand-job shooter.") **1.** A boy who devotes himself to masturbation. *Fa lo sparaseghe da quando aveva undici anni—precoce, eh?* "He's been jacking off since he was eleven—precocious, wouldn't you say?" **2.** A girl expert in manual masturbation. *Fiorella non la dà, ma è notevole come sparaseghe.* "Fiorella doesn't give it to anyone, but her hand-jobs are super."

SPARÀTO, *adj.* (Lit., shot.) **a)** *youth.* As fast as lightning. Without thinking twice. *È partito sparato per non so dove e chi l'ha più visto?* "He ran away like lightning, destination unknown, and he's gone." **b)** *narc.* Intoxicated with narcotics. *Pensa te, risolve meglio i problemi di matematica quando è sparato.* "Would you believe it? He solves math problems better when he's stoned."

SPÀSTICO, *adj., N., youth.* (Lit., spastic.) Clumsy; incompetent; slow in the brain. *Dio, se sei spastico! Devi aprire la chiavetta della benza per avviare la moto!* "Jesus, you're slow! You have to open the gas tank before starting the motorcycle!"

SPAZZOLÀRE, *vt.* (Lit., to brush.) **1.** To eat voraciously, quickly, and thoroughly. *See* **slappare. 2.** To steal. *Non appena la signora uscì dallo scompartimento, i due le spazzolarono le valigie.* "As soon as the woman stepped out of the compartment, the two thieves lifted her luggage and ran away." **3.** To possess sexually. *Squittiscono, ma se le spazzoli bene non banfano più.* "They all protest at first, but if you fuck them well they get really quiet."

SPECCHIÉTTI, *m. pl., youth.* (From "specchio," mirror.) Eyeglasses. *Sfiziosi quegli specchietti di Versace!* "Those Versace glasses are really cool!"

SPEED, *Eng., f., narc.* **1.** Cocaine, amphetamine. *Per lui la speed è come la super per la macchina: fa girare meglio il motore.* "Speed is to him what super gasoline is to the car: it makes his engine work better." **2. Essere in speed.** To be euphoric, in a good mood. *Sono in speed, eh? Me lo dicono tutti.* "I'm on a roll, am I not? That's what everyone says."

SPEEDBALL, *Eng., f., narc.* Mixture of heroin and cocaine, taken by either injection or inhalation. *Mai provato una speedball? Galattica!* "Never tried a speedball? It's out of this world!"

SPEEDY, *Eng., adj., youth.* A man who ejaculates too soon. *Se racconta a tutte che sono uno speedy non le vedo più neanche col binocolo!* "If she tells all the women I come too fast, they won't come near me!"

SPENNÀRE, *vt.* (Lit., to pluck.) **1.** To have one's hair cut. *L'ha spennato mica male quel tosacani, no?* "His hairdresser sheared him real nice, didn't he?" **2.** To fleece. *M'hanno* *spennato al casinò: anche la fede gli ho lasciato.* "They fleeced me at the casino. I even left my wedding ring."

SPENNÀTO, *adj.* (From > **spennare, 2.**) Down and out. *Non vorrei dire, ma quand'è mai che lui non è stato spennato?* "Please, tell me a time when he wasn't broke."

SPERMÀTICO, *adj., youth.* (Lit., spermatic.) Horny. *Mani lunghe, sguardo spermatico: non t'avvicinare.* "Groping hands, horny eyes: don't go near him."

SPETAZZÀRE, *vi., N.* (From "peto," fart.) **1.** *rude.* To fart. *See* **sparare. 2.** To emit pollutants (motor). *Con i controlli di adesso, te la sequestrano una macchina che spetazza in quel modo.* "With today's clean-air standards they'll impound a car that spits poisons like yours."

SPINELLÀRE/SPINELLÀRSI, *vi., vi. pronom., narc.* (From "spinello," joint.) To take drugs by smoking a joint. *Ottavio ha i genitori che spinellano, è per quello che spinella senza problemi.* "Ottavio can smoke sticks all he wants. His folks do it too."

SPINÈLLO/SPÌNO, *m., narc.* (Lit., jointstick.) Hashish or marijuana cigarette. *Abbiamo provato tutti almeno uno spinello, no?* "We've all smoked at least one joystick, haven't we?"

SPOMPÀTO, *adj.* (Lit., unable to pump.) Beat; exhausted. *See* **scoppiato.**

SPOMPINÀRE, *vt., rude.* (From "pompino," blow job, plus "s.") To do a blow job on a male. *Lei dice di non farlo per soldi, ma se ti spompinazza, qualcosa in cambio glielo devi dare.* "She doesn't do it for money, she says, but if she gives you a blow job you'll have to give her something in return."

SPÓNDA, *f.* (Lit., bank.) **a)** *crim.* **Fare sponda.** (Lit., to shore up.) To pickpocket someone by pretending to have bumped into him/her casually. *"Mi scusi," le ho detto quando l'ho urtata, e intanto le ho fatto sponda.* "'Excuse me,' I said when I bumped into her, while snatching her wallet." **b)** *slang.* **Essere dell'altra spon-**

da. (Lit., to belong to the other shore.) To be a homosexual. *Mai visto in compagnia di una donna. Per me, è dell'altra sponda.* "I've never seen him with a woman. I think he goes the other way."

SPRANGÀRE, *vt., N., youth.* (Lit., to bolt.) To beat up someone with crossbars. *Quelli del gruppo animalista l'han sprangato perché usa animali per i suoi test.* "Some activists from the animalist group clubbed him because he uses animals for his tests."

SPRINT, *Eng., m.* To be lively, quick, dynamic. *Ha sprint, andrà lontano.* "She's got pizzaz; she'll go far."

SPROFÓNDO, *m., C.* (Lit., deep.) **Allo sprofondo.** In the boondocks. *Ma dove mi stai portando, allo sprofondo?* "Where are you taking me? To the boondocks?"

SPÙGNA, *f.* (Lit., sponge.) **1.** One who drinks alcoholic beverages in great quantity. *Vittoria ha vinto la gara dei grandi bevitori di vodka. È una di quelle spugne!* "The competition for greatest vodka drinker was won by Vittoria, who is what you'd call a sponge." **2.** A girl/woman who talks endlessly. *Ero seduta vicino alla spugna a cena, non ho aperto bocca per tutta la sera.* "I was seated next to that chatterbox at dinner. I couldn't get one word in."

SPUPAZZÀRE, *vt., C.* (From "pupa," doll, plus "s.") **1.** To cuddle someone excessively. *La spupazza da mane a sera, ma non basta mai.* "He spoils her rotten, but it's not enough for her." **2.** To entertain someone out of duty. *Piera me la sono spupazzata io tutta la sera, così voi vi siete divertiti.* "I got stuck with entertaining Piera all evening, while you had fun."

SPUTTANAMÉNTO, *m., rude.* (From > **sputtanare.**) Revelation of someone's sins, which causes one to lose his/her reputation. *È venuto fuori che il grande medico presentava come sue le ricerche dei suoi studenti: uno sputtanamento!* "It turns out that the great physician was plagiarizing his students' research: can't show his face anymore."

SPUTTANÀRE, *vt., rude.* (From "puttana," whore, plus "s.") To reveal someone's sins, which causes one to lose his/her reputation. *Se vuoi sputtanarlo, raccontalo a Irma: in mezz'ora lo sapranno tutti.* "If you want to make him lose face, tell that story to Irma. Everyone will know it in half an hour."

SPUTTANÀRSI, *vi. pronom., rude.* (From > **sputtanare.**) To behave so that one loses his/her reputation. *Si è sputtanata con lui una volte per tutte raccontandogli un sacco di palle sull'origine della sua ricchezza.* "When she lied to him about the source of her wealth, she lost all credit with him once and for all."

SPUTTANÀTO, *adj., rude.* (From > **sputtanare.**) Discredited. *In questa città Angelo è sputtanato. Deve ricominciare da un'altra parte.* "Angelo's name is shit in this town. He has to start all over again someplace else."

SQUADRÉTTA, *f., crim.* (Lit., small squad.) A group of prison guards who specialize in beating up inmates. *Non date fastidio a Nino, che è in buona con la squadretta.* "Don't annoy Nino. He's on good terms with the pig squad."

SQUAGLIÀRSI/SQUAGLIÀRSELA, *vi. pronom.* (From "squagliare," to melt.) To make oneself scarce; to vanish. *Io direi che è ora di squagliarsela: tra poco qui succede il finimondo.* "I think we'd better clear out. It won't take long before all hell breaks loose around here."

SQUAGLIÀTO, *adj., youth.* (Lit., melted.) Wasted; rotten (said of a person). *Mi hanno detto delle cose di Silvio! Veramente uno squagliato!* "They told me some ugly stories about Silvio. What a scumbag."

SQUÀLLOR, *m., youth.* (Contraction of "squallore," dreariness.) Debasement. *La palma dello squallor va alla festa da Donatella.* "The first prize for gloomy goes to Donatella's party."

SQUATTER, *Eng., m./f., polit.* Member of a hard-line 1990s anarchist, ecologist, alternative political movement. *Gli squatter hanno spaccato un mucchio di vetrine* *durante la manifestazione di sabato.* "The activists from the anarchist groups broke a lot of shop windows during the Saturday demonstration."

SQUÌLLO, *f.* (Lit., ring.) Prostitute. *Cinquecentomila m'ha ciulato quella squillo, per fare cosa poi!* "That call girl squeezed five hundred thousand lire out of me. And let's not talk of her performance!"

SQUÌNZIA, *f., youth.* (From the Emilia-Romagna dialect word "squézza," small, lively girl.) Young girl (especially if up-to-date, attractive, mischievous). *Carina la tua ragazza, ma un po' una squinzia, io ci starei attento.* "You've got yourself a nice girlfriend there, but a little pesky. I'd watch out."

SQUÌNZIO, *adj., youth.* Odd, crooked, peculiar. "*Vuoi provare il fritto di formiche rosse?*" "*E proviamolo. Meglio una cosa un po' squinzia che niente.*" "'Would you like to try some fried red ants?' 'Oh, well, OK. Something wacky is better than nothing.'"

STACCÀRE, *vi., C.* (Lit., to detach; to stop.) To finish one's work shift; to take some time off. *Stacco giovedì, così mi faccio il week-end lungo.* "I'm getting off on Thursday, so I'll have a long weekend."

STÀNGA, *f.* (Lit., bar.) A tall and lanky person. *Uh, che stanga la tua amica! Spero le piacciano gli uomini piccoli.* "Your friend is so tall! I hope she likes short men."

STÀRCI, *vi.* (Lit., to be/stay there.) To be sexually available. "*Dicono che ci stia.*" "*Dicono. Ma tu ci hai provato?*" "'They say she's available.' 'That's what they say. Have you tried?'"

STÀRE, *vi., youth.* (Lit., to be/stay.) To date. *Sta con lui da una vita, ormai sono simbiotici.* "They've been together for so long they've become symbiotic."

STÉCCA, *f.* (Lit., bar, picket, cue.) **a)** *slang.* **1.** One-thousand- and ten-thousand-lire banknote. *Ho solo due stecche. Bastano?* "I only have twenty thousand lire. Will that be enough?" **2. Fare stecca/Fare tutta stecca.** To work two shifts back to back. *L'ultima in fabbrica è che* *vogliono farci fare tutta stecca. Ma dove sono i sinda-cati?* "The latest smart idea the management has come up with is to make us work two shifts back to back. Where the hell are the trade unions?" **3.** A great billiard player. *Vuoi sfidarlo? Cattiva idea, come stecca è imbattibile.* "Do you want to challenge him? Bad idea, he's unbeatable at billiards." **b)** *crim.* **Lasciare la stecca.** To get out of jail. *Pino ha lasciato la stecca. Se vuoi, è disponibile.* "Pino is out of jail and is available. It's up to you." **c)** *narc.* Variable quantity of hashish or marijuana sold wrapped in aluminum foil. *Vuoi troppo per quella stecca, mica è d'oro!* "You want too much for that foil. It isn't gold!"

STECCÀRE, *vi.* **1.** To miscue. *Adesso ha il servizio. Per me stecca.* "It's his serve now. I think he'll blow it." **2.** To have sex. *See* **fare > canestro. 3.** To beat up. *See* **menare.**

STELLÀTO, *adj., C.* (Lit., starry.) **Essere/Stare stellato.** To be penniless. *Caschi male con me. Sto stellato.* "You came to the wrong address. I'm broke."

STÈNDERE, *vt.* (Lit., to spread.) **a)** *slang.* **1.** To hit a pedestrian with a vehicle. *Andava a centoventi sul lungofiume: ha steso una vecchietta.* "He was driving at a hundred and twenty kilometers an hour on the river drive. He ran over an old lady." **2.** To kill. *Ha pagato un killer perché stendesse suo marito.* "She paid a killer to have her husband knocked off." **3.** To leave speechless. *Mi ha dato una risposta che mi ha steso.* "Her answer blew me away." **b)** *youth.* To possess sexually. *Lei faceva tanto la smorfiosa, invece s'è lasciata stendere.* "She played hard to get for a while, but in the end she let him have his way with her."

STÉSO, *adj., C.* (Lit., spread out.) **1.** Exhausted. *Non voglio fare una gara con te. Sono steso.* "I don't want to race with you. I'm wiped out." **2.** Down and out. *Mi domandi come si sta stesi? Beh, non si ha più molto da perdere.* "You're asking me what life is like in the gutter? Well, you've got nothing to lose."

STIRÀRE, *vt., N., youth.* (Lit., to iron.) To hit with a vehicle. *L'han stirata, così ha una scusa per rifarsi il naso.* "They ran her over. Now she has an excuse to have her nose done."

STÌTICO, *adj., N./C.* (Lit., constipated.) **1.** Poorly done; insufficient. *Che tema stitico hai fatto.* "Is this your essay? Two measly pages?" **2.** Emotionally stingy; uptight. *Bruttino, stitico, non un genio. Ma ha una virtù che è una?* "On the ugly side, standoffish, not a genius. Does he have one single virtue?"

STOCCAZZÀRE, *vt., N., youth.* (From "toccare," to touch, plus "s.") To pat; to feel (usually unwanted by the recipient). *Il vantaggio di un locale buio è che puoi stoccazzare.* "The big advantage is that in a dark joint one can cop a feel."

STONÀTO, *adj.* (Lit., out of tune.) **a)** *slang.* Out of sorts. *Non mi hai fatto assolutamente niente: sono stonata oggi.* "You did nothing to me. It's just that today I'm out of sorts." **b)** *narc.* (From English "stoned.") Intoxicated with narcotics. *Mi capisci o sei troppo stonato?* "Am I getting through? No? You looked too stoned to me."

STOPPÀRE, *vt., youth.* (From English "to stop.") **1.** To stop. *Mettiti la cintura, che se no la polizia ci stoppa.* "Put on your seat belt, otherwise the police will stop us." **2.** To interrupt. *Se te l'ho già detto, stoppami.* "If I told you before, stop me." **3.** To hold someone back at the end of the school year. *Quello di italo voleva stopparmi, ma la corte marziale mi ha graziato.* "The Italian teacher wanted to hold me back, but the other teachers saved me."

STÒRIA, *f.* (Lit., story, history.) **a)** *youth.* **1.** Amorous relationship (of 1st through 5th degree, depending on the intimacy reached, 5th degree being nonorthodox sex.) *"Ha avuto una storia di quarto grado con lui." "Vuoi dire una storia di sesso." "Ah, ah, sesso."* "'She had a fourth-degree story with him.' 'You mean they had sex.' 'Yes, they did.'" **2.** Subject; matter. *Che storie ti fai?* "How are you doing?" **3.** Situation. *Io in quella storia lì non ci voglio più stare.* "I want out of that situation." **b)** *narc.* Drug traffic; drug taking. *Si fa solo storie di coca.* "She deals with drugs; only cocaine, though."

STÒRTA, *f., crim.* (Lit., crooked; bent.) Bad information (as opposed to > **dritta**). *E tu al caramba dagli una storta, intanto per un po' ti lascia in pace.* "Say something to the cop—anything—so he'll leave you alone for a while."

STÒRTO, *adj., youth.* (Lit., crooked; bent.) **1.** Incompetent (opposite of > **dritto**). *Per lui che è così storto, quel lavoretto al supermercato è una manna.* "For a good-for-nothing like him, that job at the store is a godsend." **2. Storto perso.** (Lit., irretrievably crooked.) Not all there; weird. *Di certo è storto perso, se sia anche peggio, non lo so.* "He's wacky. If he's anything worse than that, I don't know."

STORY, *Eng., f., youth.* See **storia, a).**

STÒZZA, *f., C.* A lot, especially of food. *Mangia 'na stozza di spaghetti, poi si lamenta che ingrassa.* "He eats a heap of spaghetti; then he complains because he's put on weight."

STRÀCCI, *m. pl.* (Lit., rags.) **1.** Clothes. *Lei li chiama "i miei stracci," ma è tutta roba firmata.* "She calls them 'my rags' but they are all designer clothes." **2.** *C.* Vegetables. *Una volta, se eri povero, mangiavi stracci, adesso sono di moda.* "Once upon a time, you ate vegetables if you were poor. Now they're in."

STRACCIAMÀNICI, *f., youth.* (From "stracciare," to tear, and "manico," meaning penis.) Sexually insatiable girl. *Veronica è una delizia, d'accordo, però è anche una stracciamanici.* "Veronica is a peach, agreed, but she's almost a nympho."

STRACÙLO, *m., C., rude.* (From "culo," ass, meaning luck, and the superlative prefix "stra.") Amazing and undeserved luck. *Hai beccato l'unico posto alla specialità di anestesiologia? Straculo, direi.* "You got the only slot in the anesthesiology internship program? You're obscenely lucky."

STRAFÀTTO, *adj., narc./youth.* (From "fatto," done, and the superlative prefix "stra.") Superlative degree of > **fatto,** in all its meanings.

STRAFOGÀRSI, *vr., C.* To eat like a pig. *Stava per morire, tanto s'è strafogato.* "He gobbled up so much food he almost died."

STRAFUGNÀRSI, *vr. rec., N.* (Lit., to rub against one another.) To neck. *See* **pomiciare.**

STRAFUGNÀTO, *adj., N.* Wrinkled; creased. *Non vieni al concerto con noi tutto strafugnato. Cambiati!* "You're not coming to the concert with us in those dirty clothes. Go and get changed!"

STRAPAZZÀRE, *vt.* (Lit., to ill-treat.) To fondle; to possess sexually. *L'ha strapazzata, certo, ma lei era consenziente. Di cosa si lamenta, adesso?* "He had his way with her, true, but she went for it. Why is she complaining now?"

STRÀPPO, *m., youth.* (Lit., tear.) Ride; lift. *Salta su che ti dò uno strappo.* "Jump in, I'll give you a ride."

STRAPPÓNA, *f., C.* (From "strappo," meaning vagina.) Sexually available girl/woman. *Era una nota strappona di borgata, con cinque figli da cinque uomini diversi.* "She was well known in the poor neighborhood: a broad with five children from five different men."

STRAVACCÀRSI, *vi. pronom., N.* To sprawl out. *Se ti chiamano per un colloquio di lavoro, per carità non stravaccarti sulla sedia.* "If you're called for a job interview, try not to sprawl all over the chair, please."

STRAVÒLTO. a) *youth.* **1.** *adj.* Exhausted. *See* **steso. 2.** *m.* Weird, peculiar person. *Non uscirei con Filippo, ha la fama di stravolto.* "I wouldn't go out with Filippo; he has a reputation as a wacko." **b)** *adj., narc.* Completely stoned. *Non l'ho mai vista stravolta fino a questo punto. Dici che devo chiamare il medico?* "I've never seen her so zonked out. Do you think I should call a doctor?"

STRÉPPA/STRÌPPA, *f., narc.* Heavy drugs. *Capisco che ti piaccia l'erba, ma perché la streppa? Ti fonderà il cervello.* "I understand you like grass, but why heavy shit? It'll fry your brain."

STRESS, *Eng., m., youth.* Boring, annoying thing or event. *Oltre a tutto il resto, anche un saggio di storia dobbiamo fare. Ti dico, uno stress.* "On top of everything else, we've been assigned a history essay. Let me tell you, it's too much."

STRIPPÀRE, *vi.* (From "strippa," meaning drug.) **a)** *youth.* To lose one's mind; to despair. *Non è ancora il caso di strippare: magari ti telefona domani.* "Don't freak out; not yet. He may call you tomorrow." **b)** *narc.* To take heavy drugs. *Strippa da poco, forse può uscirne.* "He hasn't been on heavy stuff for a long time; maybe he can still come off it."

STRIPPÀTO, *adj.* (From > **strippare.**) **a)** *youth.* Dazed; out of one's mind. *"Come mai è così strippato?" "Eh, sai, la sua ragazza si è uccisa."* "'How come he's in such a daze?' 'Well, you see, his girlfriend killed herself.'" **b)** *narc.* Stoned. *No, brigadiere, glielo giuro, non sono strippato, solo stanco.* "No, officer, I swear I'm not stoned, just tired."

STRÌSCIO, *m., youth.* (Lit., shuffle; scrape.) **Di striscio.** Casually; not in earnest. *La fila di striscio: se va va, se non va, pazienza.* "He's giving it a try with her. If it works out, fine; if it doesn't, it doesn't."

STRÌZZA, *f.* (From "strizzare," to squeeze.) Scare, fear. *See* **spaghetto.**

STRIZZACÀZZI, *f., C., rude.* (From "strizzare," to squeeze, and "cazzi," pricks.) Ugly and annoying girl. *Povera Bea, la considerano una strizzacazzi. Io non la trovo così antipatica.* "Poor Bea, they all think she's a pain in the neck and an eyesore. I don't find her so horrible."

STRIZZACERVÈLLI, *m./f., youth.* (From "strizzare," to squeeze, and "cervelli," brains.) Psychoanalyst; shrink.

Sono troppo sfatto, devo andare da uno strizzacervelli. "I'm so down. I must see a shrink."

STRONZÀGGINE, *f., youth, rude.* (From > **stronzo.**) **1.** Being a despicable person. *Come fai a dire che la stronzaggine può anche coesistere con l'intelligenza?* "How can you say that turdness and intelligence can be found in one and the same person?" **2.** Behavior typical of a despicable person. *Da quando in qua essere corretto con i prof è un sintomo di stronzaggine?* "Since when are you a turd if you behave correctly with your teachers?"

STRONZÀTA, *f., rude.* (From > **stronzo.**) **1.** Action and words typical of a despicable person. *Spii quei due che stanno pomiciando dietro il cespuglio? Che stronzata!* "You're peeping at those two necking behind the bush? What a turd!" **2.** Badly done thing. *Ha scritto un libro che è una vera stronzata.* "She wrote a really crappy book." **3.** Useless but amusing gadget. (Also in the diminutive **stronzatìna.**) *Beh, un bastone da passeggio a molla mi sembra . . . una stronzatina.* "Well, I think that a walking cane with springs is a stupid little gadget."

STRONZÉTTO, *m.,* **STRONZÉTTA,** *f., youth.* Ironic variation of > **stronzo.** *Fa la stronzetta perché ha dei begli occhi.* "She thinks she can get away with murder because of her beautiful eyes."

STRÓNZO, *m.,* **STRÓNZA,** *f.* (Lit., turd.) Turd. **a)** *slang, rude.* Despicable person. *Al cinema si diverte a sussurrare oscenità alle ragazze sedute nella fila davanti alla sua. Che stronzo!* "He has fun at the movies whispering obscenities to the girls seated ahead of him. What a turd!" **b)** *youth.* Used ironically and affectionately to mean "buddy." *Ehi, vecchio stronzo, come te la passi?* "Hey, motherfucker, how are things going for you?"

STRUCCÀRE, *vi., N.* To rummage. See **sfrucugliare.**

STRUMÉNTO, *m., C.* (Lit., instrument.) Penis. See **aggeggio.**

STRÙSCIO, *m., C./S.* (Lit., rubbing.) Leisurely evening walk along a town's main street. *Ormai, lo struscio è una cosa del passato, tranne che nei piccoli paesi.* "The evening promenade is now a thing of the past, except in small towns."

STURBÀRE, *vt., C.* (From "turbare," to trouble, plus "s.") To trouble deeply. *Dice che lo diverte travestirsi da donna, ogni tanto. A me sturba.* "He says he likes to dress up like a woman every now and then. That troubles me."

SU, *prep.* (Lit., on, over.) **a)** *crim.* **Fare su.** To steal; to swindle. *Ha lasciato la cassa aperta con due centoni in vista e io li ho fatti su.* "He left the cash register open, with two hundred thousand lire sitting there. So I picked them up." **b)** *slang.* **Fare su e giù.** (Lit., to go up and down.) To make love. *Niente di più rilassante che fare un po' su e giù.* "There's nothing more relaxing than a little roll in the hay."

SUCCHIÀRE, *vt.* (Lit., to suck on.) **1.** To consume too much fuel. *Una macchina degli anni sessanta succhia un casino, come no.* "A 1960s car is a gas guzzler, that's for sure." **2.** *rude.* To practice fellatio. *Gli disse chiaro e tondo che lei non lo succhiava.* "She told him in so many words that she doesn't suck it."

SUCCHIÒTTO, *m.* (Lit., pacifier.) **a)** *slang.* **1.** A kiss, especially on the neck, in which the skin is "sucked." *Come faccio ad andare in ufficio domani? Guarda che succhiotto!* "How can I show up at work with this hickey on my neck?" **2.** Blow job. *Quanto vuoi per un succhiotto?* "How much do you charge for a blow job?" **b)** *crim.* Prison. *Eh, dovrà ciucciarsi un bel po' di anni nel succhiotto.* "I'm afraid he'll have to spend several years in the slammer."

SÙGNA, *f., C.* **1.** Filth. *Che sugna che hai addosso! Lavati!* "Gee, you're filthy! Take a shower." **2.** Money. *Dici che chiedo troppa sugna? Vai da un altro.* "I'm asking for too much money, you say? Then go to someone else."

SUÒLE, *f. pl., crim.* (Lit., soles.) **1. Portare via le suole.** To run away. *Sono riusciti a portare via le suole appena in tempo.* "They managed to run away just in time." **2.** Policemen. *Senti? Solo le suole camminano così.* "Do you hear? Only cops walk like that."

SUPERCARROZZÀTA, *adj., f.* (From **"carrozzata,"** meaning well-endowed, and the superlative "super.") *See* **carrozzata.**

SUSÌNA, *f., C.* (Lit., plum.) Vagina. *See* **albicocca.**

SVACCAMÉNTO, *m., youth.* (From > **svaccare.**) Mental and physical listlessness that leads to idleness; sloth. *Da quando c'è la supplente, in classe c'è uno svaccamento generale.* "Ever since we got that substitute teacher we've all become real lazy."

SVACCÀRE/SVACCÀRSI, *vi./vi. pronom., youth.* To become listless, idle, slothful. *Volevano raccogliere fondi per i senzatetto. Hanno svaccato dopo due settimane.* "They wanted to raise funds for the homeless. They ran out of gas in two weeks."

SVACCÀTO, *adj., youth.* (From > **svaccare.**) Listless, lazy, indolent, slothful. *Neanche per un bel gallo ti daresti da fare? Sei proprio svaccata.* "You wouldn't even get into gear for a nice hunk? You're really lazy."

SVÀCCO, m. (From > **svaccare.**) **1.** Sloth; boredom caused by inactivity. *C'era un tale svacco al bar della spiaggia che si tagliava col coltello.* "There was so much boredom at the bar on the beach, you could cut it with a knife." **2.** Lack of sense of duty; sloth leading to noncompliance with one's duties. *Con lo svacco che c'era al museo, è già andata bene che abbiano rubato solo tre dipinti.* "Given the slothful attitude of the museum guards, it's surprising they stole only three paintings."

SVAGÀRE, *vi., C.* To get a hint; to get the drift. *See* **sgamare.**

SVÀMPA/SVAMPÓSA, *f., C., youth.* Cigarette. *Io mi faccio dieci svampose al giorno, non una di più.* "I smoke ten cigs a day, no more."

SVAMPÀRE, *vt., C.* To smoke. *"Svampi?" "No, ho smesso."* "'Do you smoke?' 'No, I stopped.'"

SVÀNZIGHE, *f. pl.* (From German "zwanzig," twenty.)

Money. *Non guardare quella macchina, tu non hai abbastanza svanzighe.* "Don't even look at that car; you don't have enough money."

SVÀPORA, *f., youth.* (Perhaps from "evaporare," to evaporate.) Cigarette. *"Socializzi una svapora?" "Mi spiace, le ho finite."* "'Can I have a cig?' 'Sorry, I have none left.'"

SVELTÌNA, *f.* (From "svelto," quick.) Furtive and quick sexual encounter. **Fare/Farsi una sveltina.** To have a quickie. *Con lei solo sveltine, mica ho capito perché.* "I don't know why, but she only likes quickies."

SVÈNTOLA, *f.* (Lit., slap.) **1.** Sexy girl, who knocks you down. *S'è messo con una sventola! Per quello non lo vedi più in giro.* "You should see the knockout he's going out with. That's why he's no longer around." **2.** Crush. *Ti sei presa una bella sventola per quell'agente di borsa. O ti piacciono i soldi?* "You've got a nice crush on that investment banker. Or is it the money?"

SVÈNTOLE, *f. pl.* **1.** Flappy ears. *Ha una testa piccola e due sventole grosse così.* "He's got a small head and two flappy ears this big." **2.** Big hands. *Se ti mena con quelle sventole ti stacca la testa.* "If he beats you up with those paws he'll cut your head off."

SVICOLÀRE, *vi., youth.* (Lit., to slip away.) **1.** To sneak away. *Uff, è stata una faticata, ma sono riuscita a svicolare.* "Gee, it was tough, but I managed to sneak away." **2.** To play hooky. *Non svicolerò mai più, lo giuro.* "I'll never skip classes again, I swear." **3.** To avoid an unpleasant duty. *Volevano far pulire a me il seminterrato, ma sono riuscita a svicolare.* "They wanted me to clean the basement, but I managed to get out of it."

SVIOLINÀRE, *vt.* (From "violino," violin, plus "s.") To flatter; to fawn over. *Ha sviolinato la profia tutto l'anno, ma non le è servito a niente.* "She buttered up her teacher all year, but it did her no good."

SVÒGLIA, *f., N., youth.* (From "voglia," desire, plus "s.") Lack of will; apathy. *Lasciami stare, m'è presa la svoglia.* "Let me be. I'm in an 'I-want-nothing' mood."

SWATTÀRE, *vt., youth.* (From "watt," the unit of power equal to one joule per second, plus "s.") **1.** To think; to devise. *Ho swattato un modo magnifico per non fare il compito.* "I came up with a splendid idea for skipping the class test." **2.** To explain. *Swattaci la tua pensata.* "Share your brilliant idea with us." **3.** To write. "*Cosa swatti?*" "*Un papiro che non spedirò mai.*" "'What are you composing?' 'A letter that will never be mailed.'"

TABACCHIÈRA, *f., S.* (Lit., snuff box.) **1.** Vagina. *Il modo più sicuro per non avere figli? Non aprire la tabacchiera.* "The surest way not to have children? Not to open the lady's snuff box." **2.** Buttocks. *Al maschio della specie interessa una bella tabacchiera perché è indice di buone capacità riproduttive.* "The male of the species is interested in a nice tush, because it is a sign of good reproductive capacities."

TACCÀRE, *vi., N.* (From "tacco," heel.) To walk. *Non taccare così svelto, che siamo in anticipo.* "Don't walk so fast. We're early."

TÀCCHE, *f. pl., N., youth.* (Lit., notches.) **Dare delle tacche a qualcuno.** To leave someone behind in the dust. *Ti vantavi di potermi dare delle tacche a ping-pong in qualunque momento: vuoi provarci adesso?* "You boasted you could beat me at table tennis anytime. Would you like to try now?"

TACCHINÀRE, *vt., N., youth.* (From > **tacchino.**) **1.** To court a girl insistently. *Vuoi che la tacchini io per te? Per chi mi hai preso? Per Cyrano?* "You want me to pursue her on your behalf? Who do you think I am, Cyrano?" **2.** To possess sexually. *Le ho detto che volevo tacchinarla, a momenti mi uccideva.* "I told her I wanted to sleep with her. She almost killed me."

TACCHÌNO, *m.* (Lit., turkey.) **a)** *slang.* Penis. *Sta facendo* *una cura ricostituente per ringalluzzire il suo tacchino.* "He's taking medication to bring some zap back into his bird." **b)** *narc.* **Tacchino freddo.** (English "cold turkey.") Chills resulting from drug withdrawal. *Ecco che arriva il tacchino freddo! Hai ancora roba?* "Here comes the cold turkey! Do you have any dope left?"

TAFANÀRE, *vt., youth.* (From "tafano," horsefly.) To annoy, to pester. *Mi ha tafanato tutto il giorno. Qualcuno mi dia un acchiappamosche!* "He's been pestering me all day. Someone give me a pesticide!"

TAGLIÀRE, *N., youth.* (Lit., to cut.) **1.** *vt.* To make a long story short. *Taglia e vieni al dunque.* "We got that part of the story. Give us the punch line." **2.** *vt.* To leave one's sentimental partner. *Beppe? L'ho tagliato.* "Beppe? I dumped him." **3.** *vt.* To play hooky. *Non dirmi che non hai tagliato ieri. T'ho visto al caffè sul fiume.* "Don't tell me you didn't skip class yesterday. I saw you at the café on the river." **4.** *vi.* To slip away so as to avoid an unpleasant situation. *Devo tagliare. Se quello mi vede mi concia per le feste.* "I'm off. If that guy sees me he'll knock me black and blue."

TAGLIÀTO, *adj., N., youth.* (Lit., cut.) Cut off by friends and by people in general. *Marco è stato tagliato fin da piccolo.* "Marco has been a loner ever since he was a kid."

TÀGLIO, *m.* (Lit., cut.) **a)** *slang.* **Dare/Darci un taglio.** To stop whining, complaining, etc. *Ve bè, quell'automobilista è stato prepotente, ma adesso dacci un taglio!* "OK, that driver was an idiot, but cut it out now!" **b)** *narc.* Mixture of two or more kinds of drugs. *Niente più tagli, mi fanno stare da cane.* "No more mixed stuff; it's really bad for me."

TÀLCO, *m., narc.* (Lit., talcum powder.) Cocaine. *Racconta a tutti che vende talco, come se la gente non sapesse cos'è.* "He tells everyone he sells talcum, as if people didn't know what that is."

TAMÀRRO, *m., youth.* **a)** *slang, racist.* Redneck; coming from southern Italy (from the Arabic "tammar," date seller). *Quel tamarro non corrisponde allo stereotipo. Interessante, eh?* "That wetback isn't true to stereotype. Interesting, isn't it?" **b)** *youth.* Clumsy, uncouth, tacky youth. *Se continui a frequentarlo diventerai un tamarro pure tu.* "If you hang around him any longer you'll become as cloddish as he is."

TAMBÙRO, *m., S.* (Lit., drum.) **a)** *crim.* Member of the Camorra, the organized crime group of Naples. *Suo cugino un tamburo? Ma se sembra tanto una brava persona!* "Her cousin a member of the Camorra? He looks like such a nice guy!" **b)** *slang.* **Suonarc il tamburo.** (Lit., to play the drum.) To have anal sex. "*Ha suonato il tamburo con lui, sai?*" "*L'ha convinta.*" "'Did she tell you they did it through the back door?' 'Yeah, he persuaded her to do it.'"

TÀMPA, *f., N., youth.* (From the Piedmontese for "buca," hole.) Blunder. *Ho detto che era la persona più avara che conoscessi e lei era proprio dietro di me. Una tampa!* "I said she was the stingiest person I knew. And she was standing right behind me. What a blunder!"

TAMPINÀRE, *vt., N.* (From the Spanish "tapín," paw.) **1.** To pester; to torment. *La tampina da mesi, ma non è ancora riuscito a farsi fare il prestito.* "He's been pestering her for months, but he hasn't got the loan yet." **2.** To court a woman annoyingly. *Ha tampinato anche te in ufficio? Che porco!* "He came on to you at work too? What a pig!"

TAMÙGNO, *adj., N., youth.* Tough, determined, skillful. *Se vuoi aggiustare tu la barca, chiedi aiuto a Tommaso. Lui sì che è tamugno coi motori.* "If you want to repair your boat, ask Tommaso for help. He's a wizard with engines."

TÀNA, *f.* (Lit., den, lair.) **a)** *slang.* **1.** Vagina. *Sta bene solo nella tana.* "Her pussy is the only place where he feels at home." **2.** Ass. *Stai parlando dell'altra tana. No, quella è vietata.* "You're talking about the other entrance. Access to that is forbidden." **3.** Contraction of > **puttana.** *Che tana quella! M'ha ciulato i soldi mentre dormivo.* "What a whore! She stole my money while I was sleeping." **b)** *youth.* One's own dwelling, or private room. *Figa la tua tana, te la sei messa su da sola?* "This place is really cool. Did you set it up all by yourself?"

TANÀTO, *adj., C., youth.* To fail when called on in class. "*Tanato?*" "*Tanato di brutto, in mate e in fisica.*" "'Zapped?' 'Brutally zapped, in math and physics.'"

TANFÀRE, *vi., youth.* (From "tanfo," stench.) **1.** To stink. *Tanfa sempre in questo modo lui?* "Does he always stink this bad?" **2.** To wear a perfume. *Da quando in qua tanfi?* "Since when do you wear perfume?"

TANGÈNTE, *n.* (Lit., tangent.) Money extorted as bribery or for protection. *Il primo ministro prendeva tangenti persino da alcuni governi stranieri.* "The prime minister took bribes even from some foreign governments."

TÀNTA, *adj., f.* (Lit., so much.) An opulently sexy girl. *La Mirella è tanta, tantissima!* "Mirella is foxy, and there's so much of her!"

TAPPÀRSI, *vr., youth.* (From > **tappo, a2.**) To dress up, or to try to. *Ma come ti sei tappata? Andiamo mica alla prima della Scala!* "Why did you get dolled up like that? We're not going to opening night at La Scala!"

TÀPPO, *m.* (Lit., cork, bottle cap.) **a)** *slang.* **1.** Short person. *Fa' un po' di posto al tappo, almeno vede qualcosa anche lui.* "Leave some room for shorty, so he can see something too." **2.** Coat. *Un tappo di velluto! Che sciccheria!* "A velvet coat! How chic!" **b)** *youth.* Diaphragm used as contraceptive. *Ti sei dimenticata di mettere il tappo? Cristo!* "You forgot your diaphragm? Shit!"

TÀRA, *f., N., youth.* (Lit., tare.) **1.** Serious nuisance; harassment. *Non posso venire con voi; ho una tara da risolvere.* "I can't come with you. I've got a problem that needs taking care of." **2.** Annoying person. *Devo vedermi con quel tara di Giacomo. Spero che sia l'ultima volta.* "I'm supposed to meet with Giacomo, that pain in the neck. I hope it will be the last time."

TARDÓNA, *f., rude.* (From "tardi," late.) Middle-aged woman who pretends to be much younger, and who is sexually available. *Allora, ti sei buttato con la tardona?* "So, did you give it a try with the old bag?"

TARGÀTO, *adj.* (Lit., carrying a license plate.) Recognized by everyone as belonging to someone/something. *Tamara è targata Nicola, non ti puoi neanche avvicinare.* "Tamara carries a label that says 'Nicola's.' You can't even get close."

TAROCCÀRE, *vt.* (From > **tarocco, a2.**) To falsify documents; to counterfeit. *Taroccava qualunque documento: un maestro nel suo genere.* "He could falsify any document; he was an artist in his genre."

TARÒCCO, *m.* (Lit., tarot card.) **a)** *crim.* **1.** A clandestine note sent out of prison. *Riuscì a passarle il tarocco durante il fugace abbraccio alla fine del colloquio.* "As he hugged her hastily in the prison meeting room, he managed to slide the note into her pocket." **2.** Swindle; cheat; counterfeited merchandise. *Le hanno appioppato un bel tarocco, ma lei continua a dire che il braccialetto è di oro puro a diciotto carati.* "They dumped a false piece on her, but she keeps on saying the bracelet is pure 18-karat gold." **b)** *N., youth.* Worthless. *Si fa consigliare da Vincenzo, così le rifilano sempre dei bei tarocchi.* "She listens to Vincenzo's advice, which means they always dump crap on her."

TARRÀTA, *f., youth.* (From > **tarro.**) Silly, vile, ugly deed or thing. *L'ha messa incinta contro la sua volontà? Dio, che tarrata!* "He got her pregnant against her will? My God, what a jerk!"

TÀRRO, *adj., youth.* (Perhaps contraction of > **tamarro.**) Any thing or person that triggers negative emotions; tacky; vile. *Non mi sorprende che Andrea gli abbia fatto le scarpe sul lavoro. È un tarro.* "I'm not surprised Andrea pulled the rug out from under him at work. He's a skunk."

TÀSCA, *f.* (Lit., pocket.) Buttocks. *"Gliel'ha messo in* *tasca.*" "*Letteralmente o metaforicamente?*" "'*Tutti e due, temo.*' 'He stuck it up his asshole.' 'Literally or metaphorically?' 'Both, I'm afraid.'"

TÀSCHE, *f. pl.* (Lit., pockets.) Euphemism for > **coglioni.**

TÀZZO/TAZZÓNE, *m., N., youth. See* **tarro.**

TEATRÌNO, *m., N.* (Diminutive of "teatro," theater.) **Fare dei teatrini.** (Lit., to do theater.) To pretend; to make a fuss. *Poi lei ha fatto uno sei suoi teatrini e lui ha ceduto.* "In the end, she made a fuss and he relented."

TÉLA, *f., N., youth.* (Lit., cloth.) **Fare tela.** To run away; to flee. *Dopo aver rotto il cancello quei ragazzacci hanno fatto tela, ma sappiamo chi sono.* "Those kids ran away after breaking the gate, but we know who they are."

TELÀRE, *vi., N., youth. See* **fare > tela.**

TENTÀCOLO, *m., youth.* (Lit., tentacle.) Human arm. *L'abbrancò con i suoi tentacoli e non la mollò più.* "He grabbed her with his tentacles and didn't let go."

TEPPÌSTA, *m., N., youth.* (Lit., hooligan.) A youth who is not integrated into a group/society at large. *Prima era un teppista, adesso che ha trovato lavoro fa l'amicone con tutti.* "He used to play the misfit. Since he found a job, he's everyone's buddy."

TERRÓNE/TERÙN, *m., N., racist.* (From Piedmontese for "terra," soil, earth.) **1.** An immigrant from southern Italy. *Sapessi quanti terroni sono arrivati in città dal sud negli anni cinquanta.* "A lot of clodhoppers emigrated from the south to the northern cities in the 1950s." **2.** Redneck. *Non si buttano i rifiuti nel fiume. È da terroni!* "You don't throw garbage into the river, period. That's for rubes."

TÉSO, *adj. youth.* (Lit., nervous, anxious.) Complicated, hard, important. *La mia storia con lui? Interessante, ma tesa.* "My affair with him? It's interesting, but not relaxing."

TESSERÀRSI, *vt. pronom., youth.* (Lit., to become member of an organization.) To repent (as a pun between the two Greek words "tessares," four, and "pente," five, which in Italian sounds like "pentirsi.") *Mi sono tesserata di non averle dato una mano col compito di latino.* "Now I'm sorry I didn't help her with the Latin test."

TÈSTA, *f.* (Lit., head.) **a)** *slang.* **1.** *rude.* Glans. **Testa di cazzo.** Prickhead. *Uno che è una testa di cazzo ragiona col cazzo anziché con la testa.* "If you're a prickhead, you think with your prick instead of your head." **2. Dare di testa.** Not to be all there; to have lost one's marbles. *Io ti racconto cosa è successo, ma tu promettimi che non darai di testa.* "I'll tell you what happened, but you have to promise you won't lose it." **3.** One hundred thousand lire. *"Quanto fa?" "Un testa a testa."* "'How much is it?' 'A hundred thousand lire each.'" **b)** *rude, youth.* **Mettere la testa a posto.** (Lit., to mend one's ways; to mature.) To practice oral sex. *Io le ho chiesto se metteva la testa a posto, ma lei ha detto di no.* "I asked her if she was available for a head job, but she refused."

TESTÓNE, *m.* (From > **testa, a3.**) *Vuole un testone per il motorino. Potabile, no?* "He wants one million lire for the moped. Reasonable, don't you think?"

TÉTTE, *f.* Female bosom. *Belle tette, bel culo, che vuoi di più?* "Nice tits, nice ass. What more do you want?"

TETTÓNA, *f.* (From > **tette.**) Girl/woman endowed with an opulent bosom. *"Che tettona!" "Sì, ma pare sia finta."* "'What tits!' 'Yes, but they say they're phony.'"

TILT, *Eng., m.* **Andare in tilt/Fare tilt.** (Lit., to tilt.) To lose it; not to function any longer. *Non ho dormito per una settimana per finire quel lavoro. Poi ho fatto tilt.* "I didn't sleep for a week so I could finish that job. Now I'm out of commission."

TILTÀRE, *vi.* (From the English "tilt.") *See* **andare in > tilt.**

TÌMBE, *f. pl., youth.* (Contraction of "Timberland," a brand of fashionable American shoes.) Shoes. *Pensavo che le timba fossero autentiche, invece no.* "I thought his Timberland shoes were authentic. Not so."

TÌPO, *m./f., N., youth.* (Lit., type, character, person.) **1.** Boy/girl. *Conosci quella tipa?* "Do you know that gal?" **2.** Girlfriend/boyfriend. *Hai una tipa?* "Do you have a girlfriend?"

TÌRA, *m., N., crim.* (From "tirare," to pull.) **Fare il tira.** To be a police informant. *Hanno scoperto che faceva il tira.* "They discovered he was a squealer."

TIRAMÉNTO, *m., N., rude.* (From "tirare," to pull.) **1.** Being horny; feeling attracted by someone. *Un tiramento generale, dopo quel film porno.* "Horniness all around, after we saw that porno movie." **2.** *N.* **Un tiramento de casso.** (Dialect for: *un tiramento di cazzo;* lit., having one's penis pulled.) Annoying, boring situation; waste of time. *Parlare di affari con quel pirla è un gran tiramento de casso.* "Talking business with that shithead is a fucking waste of time."

TIRAMISÙ, *m., youth/narc.* (From the name of a dessert that means "pull me up," "cheer me up.") Anything that is exciting. *Ho bisogno di un tiramisù. Sesso, musica, qualunque cosa.* "I need some zing. Sex, music, anything."

TIRÀRE. (Lit., to pull.) **a) 1.** *vt.* To be attractive. *Le bionde lo tirano un casino.* "Blondes do turn him on." **2.** *vi., rude.* To feel horny. *Gli tira sempre e comunque, non ce n'è una che lo soddisfi.* "He's horny all the time. No woman is good enough for him." **3.** *vi., N., rude.* **Tirare (il cazzo) a qualcuno.** (Lit., for someone's penis to be pulling.) For someone to like something. **Se ti tira (il cazzo).** *Se ti tira potremmo andare a fare una sgommata.* "If it gives you a kick, we could go for a ride." **b)** *youth.* **1.** *vt.* To smoke cigarettes. *Ne tira quaranta al giorno: candidato alla morte precoce.* "He smokes forty a day. He's a candidate for premature death." **2.** *vi.* To go; to go by. *"Dove tiri?" "Al bar, vieni?"* "'Where are you going?' 'To our usual joint. Do you want to come?'" **c)** *vi., narc.* To sniff cocaine. *Tira, tira, non vedi com'è conciato il suo naso?* "Of course he sniffs. Have you taken a good look at his nose?"

TIRÀRSELA, *vi. pronom., youth.* (From > **tirare.**) **1.** To spend time. *Te la tiri bene al mare?* "Are you having a good time at the beach?" **2.** To be in cahoots with. *Non se la tira più con quel giro, sono troppo pericolosi.* "He doesn't hang around with that gang anymore; they're too dangerous." **3.** To be on one's high horse. *Quando non se la tira è anche simpatica.* "When she isn't on her high horse, she's even nice."

TIRÀRSI, *vt. pronom., narc.* (From > **tirare.**) To take drugs. **Tirarsi il buco.** To inject heroin. *Non si tira più il buco. Fuma e basta.* "She doesn't shoot up anymore, but she still smokes."

TIRÀTA, *f.* (Lit., pull.) **a)** *slang.* Smoke puff. *Dopo due tirate le è venuto un attacco d'asma che non ti dico.* "After two drags she had an asthma attack. Scary, real scary." **b)** Cocaine inhaling. *"Vuoi una tirata?" "No, la coca no."* "'Would you like to sniff?' 'No, no coke for me.'"

TIRÀTO, *adj.* (Lit., pulled.) **1.** Stingy. *Era un uomo molto tirato, che le misurava anche i soldi della spesa.* "He was a stingy man, who even counted out her food-shopping money." **2. Tirato a lucido.** Dressed up. *Dove andiamo di bello tutti tirati a lucido?* "Where are you going, all dressed up like that?"

TIRÌNO, *m., N., youth.* A sound made by smacking one's lips together, which sounds like a kiss, addressed to a sexy girl/woman. **Fare un tirino/dei tirini.** *Tutte le volte che gli passo davanti quegli sciocchi mi fanno dei tirini.* "Every time I walk by them, those idiots make smacking noises at me from across the street."

TÌRO, *m.* (Lit., draught.) **a)** *slang.* **1.** A puff of tobacco or hashish. *È dai, fammi dare un tiro.* "Come on, let me have a drag!" **2.** Love affair. *Hanno avuto un tiro, ma è finito.* "They had an affair, but it's over." **3. Essere/Mettersi in tiro.** To dress up. *Dici che devo mettermi in tiro per la cena?* "What do you say? Should I dress up for dinner?" **4. In tiro.** Horny. *Vai in tiro anche quando guardi un film* *tragico? Ma è una malattia!* "You get horny even when you watch a tragic movie? You must have a disease!" **b)** *crim.* **Sparare il tiro.** To send warning signals to one's accomplices. *Hanno sparato il tiro, dobbiamo filare.* "They sent the signal, we'd better run."

TOCCÀRSI, *vr., rude.* (Lit., to touch oneself.) **1.** To masturbate. *Quando era piccolo credeva che a toccarsi si sarebbe ammalato!* "When he was a kid he believed he'd get sick if he played with himself." **2.** For a man to touch his genitals so as to fend off the evil eye. *Pensa com'è retrogrado, si tocca se un gatto nero gli attraversa la strada.* "He's so backward! He touches down there if a black cat crosses the street in front of him."

TÓCCO, *adj.* (Lit., touched.) Loony. *Lo vedo spesso ai giardinetti che parla da solo. Dev'essere un po' tocco.* "I often see him in the park, talking to himself. I think he's a bit loony."

TÒCCO, *m.* (Lit., piece.) A remarkable item. *Che tocco il tuo uomo!* "What a specimen of a man you've got!"

TOGÀRSI, *vr., youth.* (From "toga," toga, gown, robe.) To dress up; to dress fashionably. *"Ci hai messo tutto 'sto tempo a vestirti?" "Non mi sono vestito, mi sono togato."* "'Why did it take you so long to get dressed?' 'I didn't just get dressed; I dressed up.'"

TÒGO, *adj., youth.* (From the Hebrew "tov," good, and the German "tauglich," skillful.) Handsome; competent; outstanding; beautiful (said of a person or a thing.) *"Che ne dici di questo vestito?" "Togo."* "'Give me your honest opinion of this dress.' 'Cool.'"

TÓMBA, *f., crim.* (Lit., tomb.) Safe (because they look alike). *Hai richiuso la tomba? Almeno non se ne accorgono subito.* "Did you close the safe? At least they won't find out right away."

TOMBÌNO, *m., N., youth.* (Diminutive of "tomba," tomb.) **Fare un tombino a qualcuno. 1.** To inflict a humiliating defeat. *Se giochi a scacchi con lui, ti farà sicuramente un tombino.* "If you play chess with him, he'll blow you away for sure." **2.** To fail a student in an oral test. *Cosa stai a preoccuparti? Tanto lo sai già che quella di filo ti farà un tombino.* "What are you worrying about? You already know that the philosophy teacher will flunk you."

TÓNDI, *m. pl.* (Lit., dinnerware.) **Impagliare i tondi.** (Lit., to pack the dinnerware.) To flee. *Gli abusivi impagliarono i tondi subito prima che la polizia li sbaraccasse.* "The squatters fled before the police kicked them out."

TÓNNO, *m., N.* (Lit., tuna.) **a)** *slang.* Penis. *See* **pesce. b)** *youth.* Sucker. *Povero tonno, l'hanno lasciato seminudo sul bordo della strada.* "Poor sucker, they left him half-naked on the side of the road."

TOP, *Eng., m., youth.* **Al top.** At one's best. *Marco è proprio al top, professionalmente.* "Professionally, Marco is in top form."

TOPPÀRE, *vi.* (Contraction of "intoppare," to trip over.) **a)** *crim.* For criminals to screw up so badly that they get arrested. *I caramba sono stati fortunati: se i ladri non toppavano non li prendevano mica.* "The police were lucky. They caught the burglars only because they screwed up real bad." **b)** *youth.* To make a mistake. *Ho toppato con te, lo ammetto.* "I made a mistake with you, I'm sorry."

TORTÌNO, *m., youth.* (Mixture of "torta," cake, and "festino," small party.) **Fare un tortino.** (Lit., to make a small cake.) A party that turns into a small orgy. *Io a casa sua non ci vado. Ogni volta finisce che fanno un tortino.* "I'm not going to his place. Each of his parties turns into an orgy."

TOSACÀNI, *m./f., youth.* (Lit., dog clipper.) Barber; men's hairdresser. *Ma il tuo tosacani sa fare solo quel taglio lì?* "Is that the only cut your hairdresser knows how to do?"

TOSAPÈCORE, *m./f., youth.* (Lit., sheep fleecer.) Women's hairdresser. *Il mio tosapecore non vuole assolutamente farmi bionda.* "My hairdresser adamantly refuses to dye my hair blond."

TOSÀRSI, *vr., youth.* (Lit., to shear oneself.) To have one's hair cut. *Non la riconoscevo più. Dev'essersi tosata.* "I didn't recognize her. She must have had her hair cut."

TÒSSICO. (Contraction of "tossicomane," drug addict.) **a)** *m., narc.* Drug addict. *Guarda quel tossico, poveretto, ridotto a rovistare nei rifiuti.* "Look at that drug addict, poor thing, reduced to rummaging through garbage cans." **b)** *adj., youth.* Unpleasant; unattractive. *Si capisce che è sempre sola: è troppo tossica.* "It's not surprising she's always alone; she's a real drag."

TOSTÀRE, *vt., N.* (From > **tosto.**) To thrash someone. *Vuoi che te lo tostiamo? Un centone ti costa.* "You want us to beat him up? It'll cost you a hundred thousand lire."

TÒSTO. (Lit., tough.) **a)** *m., slang.* Penis. **b)** *adj., youth.* **1.** Hard, tough, aggressive. *Manda lei a protestare, che è una tosta.* "Why don't you send her to complain? She's a tough cookie." **2.** Turgid. Also in the superlative form, **tostissimo.** *Non puoi fargli un combino scopatorio? Ce l'ha tostissimo.* "Can't you find him a one-night stand? He's real horny."

TOT. (From Latin "so many.") **a)** *m., slang.* **Un tot.** A certain number/amount; a lot. *Ci vuole un tot di tempo per fare questo lavoro, rassegnati.* "It takes some time to get this job done. Take it easy." **b)** *adj., youth.* Big, great. *Ho una fame tot.* "I can't tell you how hungry I am."

TOTÀLE, *m., youth.* (Lit., total.) Summing it all up. *Totale, Marco e Luisa si sono piantati.* "Summing it all up, Marco and Luisa split up."

TÒZZO, *m., C., youth. See* **paninaro.**

TRÀCCIA, *f., C., youth.* (Lit., track, trail.) **Buttarsi sotto traccia.** (Lit., to throw oneself under the tracks.) To take the subway. *"Non sarai mica venuta a fette?" "No, mi sono buttata sotto traccia."* "'You didn't come on foot, did you?' 'No, I took the subway.'"

TRAM, *m.* (Lit., streetcar.) *See* **attaccarsi al tram.**

TRÀMPOLI, *m. pl.* (Lit., stilts.) **1.** Long and skinny legs.

Rallenta un po', io non ho mica i tuoi trampoli! "Slow down, my legs aren't as long as yours!" **2.** Female shoes with very high heels. *Come fa a non cadere da quei trampoli?* "How come she doesn't fall off those spikes?"

TRAMVÀTA/TRANVÀTA, *f., C., youth.* (From "tram," streetcar.) **1.** Violent clash. *Guardavo la pubblicità di Calvin Klein e ho dato una tramvata nel palo della luce.* "I was looking at the Calvin Klein billboard and I crashed into the light pole." **2.** Trick; swindle; cheat (also in a love affair). *Eliana? Buona quella! Mi sono preso una tramvata con lei!* "Eliana? That's a good one. She played a nice trick on me."

TRAPANÀRE. (Lit., to drill.) **a)** *vt., slang, rude.* To possess sexually. *L'ho trapanata tre volte e si lamentava ancora.* "I nailed her three times; she was still complaining it wasn't enough." **b)** *vi., youth.* To be very successful at picking up girls. *Trapana bene sulle piste da sci: bello, abbronzato, gran sciatore.* "He's good at picking up girls on ski slopes. He's handsome, tanned, a great skier."

TRÀPANO, *m.* (Lit., drill.) **a)** *slang.* Penis. *Dice che di me le interessa solo il trapano.* "She says the only part of my body that interests her is my drill." **b)** *youth.* One who is, or believes he is, a great stud. *Lascia a intendere di essere un gran trapano. Ci credi tu?* "He wants you to believe he's a great stud. Do you believe him?"

TRÀPPOLA, *f.* (Lit., trap.) **1.** Malfunctioning tool or vehicle. *La mia vecchia trappola parte solo a spinta.* "My old wreck starts only if you push it." **2.** Trick. *M'han venduto degli scarponi usati come nuovi: bella trappola.* "They sold me used boots as new. Nice trick." **3.** Vagina. *Con la sua bella trappola le è facile intrappolare noi, poveri ometti.* "She's got such a nice pussy it's easy for her to ensnare us, poor men." **4.** Prostitute. *Fa la trappola occasionale, non tira su molta grana.* "She turns tricks now and then, so she doesn't make much money."

TRAPPOLÀRE, *vt., N., youth.* (From > **trappola, 2.**) To scheme. *Perché ti sei chiuso dentro? Cosa stai trap-*

polando? "Why did you lock yourself inside? What are you scheming?"

TRÀVE, *m.* (Lit., beam.) Penis. *L'hanno soprannominato l'uomo-trave. Indovina perché.* "They nicknamed him the big-pole-man. You can guess why."

TRÈMENS, *adj.* (Latin "shaking," from the phrase "delirium tremens.") Delirious, raving, loony. *"Capisci che sta dicendo?" "Cosa vuoi che ci sia da capire, lei è tremens."* "'Do you understand what she's saying?' 'There's nothing to understand; she's raving nuts.'"

TRÈNO, *m., C., youth.* (Lit., train.) **Stare sotto i treni.** (Lit., to lie under a train.) To feel hopelessly trapped in a miserable situation. *I grigi stanno divorziando e mia sorella si buca. Sto veramente sotto i treni.* "My folks are getting divorced and my sister shoots up. I feel really trapped."

TRICHÈCO, *m., youth.* (Lit., walrus.) Obtuse, listless person. *Io ho cercato di far capire al tricheco che il meccanico lo stava fregando. Niente da fare.* "I tried to tell our friend the lamebrain that the mechanic was cheating him, but I didn't get through."

TRÌFOLA, *f., N.* (Lit., truffle, in northern dialects.) **1.** Vagina. *Le hai chiesto la trifola al vostro primo appuntamento, e lei se n'è andata. Comprensibile.* "You asked her for her pussy at your first appointment, and she left. Understandable." **2.** Girl, woman. **Andar per trifole.** (Lit., to look for truffles.) To go on an expedition aiming at having sex. *"Vuoi andar per trifole con questo tempo da lupi?" "No, grazie."* "'Do you want to go cruising on such a horrible night?' 'No, thanks.'"

TRIGÀRE, *vi.* (From > trigo.) To maneuver on the sly; to plot. *Han trigato, han trigato, fino a quando non sono riusciti a fregare la banca.* "They schemed and plotted, until they succeeded in ripping off the bank."

TRÌGO, *m.* (Contraction of "intrigo," intrigue, dirty trick.) **1.** Trick. **Fare dei trighi.** To plot dirty tricks. *In collegio,* *l'unico divertimento che avevamo era far dei trighi ai nostri compagni.* "When I was at boarding school the only fun thing we did was to play tricks on the other boys." **2.** Complicated mechanism or situation. *Non voglio sapere che trighi hanno in mente.* "I don't want to know what tricks they're plotting."

TRIP, *Eng., m.* **a)** *narc. Abbiamo in programma un trip da coca. Vuoi unirti a noi?* "We're planning to do some coke. Would you like to join us?" **b)** *youth.* Fixation. **Avere il trip di qualcosa.** To have a bee in one's bonnet. *Ha il trip della musica indiana.* "She has a fixation for Indian music."

TRÌPPA, *f., narc.* (From English > **trip.**) Any drug. *Hai trippa? Qualunque cosa, se no muoio.* "Do you have dope? Anything, otherwise I'll die."

TRIPPÀTA, *f., narc.* (From English > **trip.**) *Ha la trippata facile: le basta un po' di colla.* "She trips out easily. A little glue is enough for her."

TRÌSTE, *f., youth.* (Lit., sad.) **Fare una triste.** To cut a sorry figure. *Le sue tristi sono veramente da piangere.* "Her blunders are so terrible they'd make you cry."

TRÒIA, *f., rude.* (Lit., sow.) Whorish girl or woman. Also in the diminutive **troietta,** used for younger girls. *Si vede che è una troietta, non perderci la testa.* "You can see she's a little sow, so don't lose your mind over her."

TROIÀIO, *m., rude.* (Lit., pigsty.) **1.** Filthy dwelling. *"Che troiaio!" "Non lo pulisci mai?" "Mai."* "'This is a pigsty! Do you ever clean it?' 'No, never.'" **2.** Joint frequented by whores and/or shady characters. *Gran barman in quel troiaio.* "A lot of harlots and goons in that joint; great bartender too."

TROIÀTA, *f., rude.* (From > **troia.**) *See* **porcata.**

TROMBÀRE. (From "tromba," meaning penis.) **a)** *vt., slang, rude.* To possess sexually. *M'ha trombata, ma quella è stata la prima e l'ultima volta.* "He banged me, but that was the first and last time." **b)** *youth.* **1.** *vt.* To hold a student back at the end of the school year. *Temeva la trombassero, invece l'hanno risparmiata.* "She was afraid they would hold her back, but instead they spared her." **2.** *vi.* To function perfectly. *Questo motoscafo tromba che è un piacere!* "This motorboat flies!"

TROMBÀTA, *f., rude.* (From > **trombare, a).**) *See* **ciulata,** in all its meanings.

TROMBÀTO, *adj., rude.* (From > **trombare, a).**) *See* **ciulato,** in all its meanings.

TRÓMBE, *f. pl.* (Lit., trumpets.) **1.** Ears. *Ehi, apri le trombe, ti sto parlando.* "Listen to me, I'm talking to you!" **2. Avere le trombe.** To pout. *Madamigella ha le trombe, come al solito.* "The princess is sulking, as usual."

TRONÀRE, *vt.* (Contraction of "intronare," to deafen.) **a)** *slang.* **1.** To deafen. *Quella musica mi ha tronato completamente.* "That music stunned me completely." **2.** To cheat; to defeat; to eliminate. *Ha avuto un colloquio per quel posto di lavoro in banca, ma l'han tronato.* "He interviewed for a job at the bank, but they threw him out." **b)** *youth.* To run into another car. *Ero fermo al semaforo, quando quello dietro di me mi ha tronato.* "I was stopped at a red light when the guy behind me rammed into me."

TRÓNCO, *m.* (Lit., trunk.) **a)** *slang.* Penis. *See* **trave. b)** *youth.* **Un tronco.** A girl endowed with a beautiful body. *Dopo tanti mesi di solitudine Pietro si è trovato un bel tronco.* "After several months of solitude, Pietro found himself a knockout girl."

TRÒNO, *m.* (Lit., throne.) Toilet seat. *Ancora sul trono? C'è qualcun altro qui che ha bisogno del cesso.* "Are you still on the throne? There are others here who need the bathroom."

TRÒPPO, *adv., youth.* (Lit., too much.) A lot, extraordinarily, unbelievably. *Troppo giusta, sei, da non crederci.* "You're so with it, it's unbelievable."

TRÙCCA, *f.* **a)** *youth.* Story, news, affair. *Sai l'ultima* *trucca a proposito di Antonella?* "Have you heard the latest gossip about Antonella?" **b)** *narc.* Cigarette made with narcotic substances. *Queste non sono sigarette, sono trucche.* "These aren't cigarettes, they're joints."

TRÙCIDO, *m., C.* (Perhaps a mixture of "truce," grim, and "sudicio," filthy.) Redneck; filthy and disgusting person. *Sull'autobus si è creato il vuoto intorno a quel tizio: un trucido incredibile.* "There were ten empty seats around that guy on the bus: he was such a filthy slob!"

TRUSCHÌNO, *m., N.* (Lit., surface gauge, a tool used in the mechanical industry.) Agreement on the sly; plot. *Fanno degli strani truschini; meglio non indagare.* "They're cooking up something strange; better not to ask what."

TRUZZÀTA, *f., N., youth.* (From > **truzzo.**) Action or enterprise typical of a tacky and uncouth person. *Non saluta, non ringrazia, non scuce una lira: una truzzata dopo l'altra.* "He never says hello, he never says thanks, and never offers to pay for anything. He behaves like a turd."

TRÙZZO, *m.,* **TRÙZZA,** *f., N., youth.* (From the Lombard "truzzà," to pretend, to counterfeit.) An uncouth and provincial youth who dresses and behaves with no style. *Non me ne fa un baffo della sua opinione, è una tale truzza.* "I couldn't care less what she thinks. She's such a rube."

TÙBO, *m., N.* (Lit., pipe.) **1.** Penis. *Ha un tubino, non un tubo.* "He has a weenie, not a stick." **2.** A liter of wine. *Non ciucciarti tutto il tubo da solo!* "Don't chug that bottle all by yourself!" **3.** *rude.* Passive male homosexual. *Vattene, i tubi qui dentro non ce li vogliamo!* "Go away! We don't want any faggots in here!" **4. Un tubo.** Nothing. *Non ha capito un tubo? Normale.* "He understood zilch? Normal for him, isn't it?"

TUMORÀTA, *f., youth, rude.* (Lit., showing tumors.) Ugly, almost repulsive girl. *Bella non è, d'accordo, ma non è poi quella tumorata che dicevate.* "OK, she isn't a beauty, but she isn't the eyesore you described to me."

TÙRCO, *adj.* (Lit., Turkish.) **a)** *slang.* **Cose turche.** Unspeakable things. *Dovevi vedere la città dopo che ci sono passati i tifosi della squadra ospite. Hanno fatto cose turche.* "You should have seen the town after the fans of the visiting team raided it. They did unspeakable things." **b)** *narc.* (Mistranslation of "turkey," tacchino, as in the phrase "cold turkey.") Stoned. *E chi lo capisce più quando è turco?* "Who can follow his rambling when he's stoned?"

UAU!, *interj., youth.* (Phonetic transcription of English "wow!") Exceptional! Remarkable! Awesome! *Uau, che figona!* "Wow, what a foxy lady!"

UCCELLATÓIO, *m., youth.* (Lit., place made up with nets and traps to capture birds.) Whorehouse; brothel. *Hanno aperto un uccellatoio nella zona. Vuoi provarlo?* "They've opened a brothel nearby. Do you want to try it?"

UCCÈLLO, *m.* (Lit., bird.) **1.** Penis. *"Se mi tradisci ancora una volta,"* gli ha detto, *"ti chiudo l'uccello in gabbia e butto via la chiave."* "'If you cheat on me one more time,' she told him, 'I'll lock your bird in a cage and throw away the key.'" **2.** Blockhead. *Se lo capisce l'uccello, lo capiscono tutti.* "If that prick understands it, everyone will."

ÙLTIMO A SAPÉRE, *idiom, youth.* (Lit., the last to know.) Saint Joseph, the Virgin Mary's husband, supposedly the last to know of her pregnancy. *Chi fa l'ultimo a sapere alla recita natalizia?* "Who plays St. Joseph at the Christmas play?"

ULTRÀ, *m./f., youth.* (Lit., extremist.) Soccer fans who support their team by violent attacks against the other team's fans. *"Gli ultrà sono un po' spariti."* *"Eh, già, i club non li finanziano più."* "'There are fewer hooligans at soccer games.' 'Well, the clubs don't finance their operations any more.'"

ULULÀTA, *f., youth.* (Lit., howling session.) Political demonstration (where people howl their slogans). *Bella ululata sabato: le signore bene erano tutte terrorizzate.* "Nice howling at the demonstration last Saturday. All the upper-class ladies were scared shitless."

UNCINÀTO, *adj., narc.* (Translation of English "hooked.") Intoxicated with narcotics. *È uncinato perso, chi lo sgancia più?* "He's completely hooked; no one can get him off."

ÙNGERE, *vt.* (Lit., to grease.) **1.** To beat up. *Vuoi ungerlo? Che t'ha fatto?* "You want to massage him? What did he do to you?" **2.** To bribe. *Allora, è stato unto l'onorevole?* "We said we'd grease the representative's palm. Has that been done?"

ÙNGHIA, *f., C.* (Lit., nail.) **1. Pagare sull'unghia.** To pay cash on the spot. *Mi han fatto pagare dieci milioni sull'unghia per la macchina. Sono spennato.* "I had to fork over ten million lire cash for the car. I'm broke." **2. Essere/Stare a unghia.** To be penniless. *Stanno a unghia, anche se cercano di salvare le apparenze.* "They're left with zero money, even though they keep up appearances."

UP, *Eng., m., narc.* High. **Mandare in up.** (Lit., to send upward.) To have a positive effect. *Solo la cenere mi manda veramente in up.* "Only the white lady gives me a high."

UP AND DOWN, *idiom, youth.* (Translation of the Italian phrase "su e giù.") Sexual intercourse. *Fanno up and down tre volte la settimana, caschi il mondo.* "They have sex three times a week, no matter what."

URBÀNO, *m.* (From the phrase "vigile urbano," city traffic policeman.) Traffic policeman. *Dillo all'urbano che quello zozzone ti perseguita.* "Tell the policeman that that pig is stalking you."

ÙVA, *f., crim.* (Lit., grapes.) Blood. *Quei bastardi gli hanno spremuto un bel po' d'uva ieri sera.* "Those bastards squeezed a lot of blood out of him last night."

UVA, *f., youth.* (Lit., ultraviolet light.) Tanning lamp. *Ha un'UVA megalattica in casa, per quello sembra un dattero anche a Natale.* "She's got a powerful tanning lamp at home, that's why she looks like a date even at Christmas."

VACÀNZA, *f., crim.* (Lit., vacation, holiday.) **Essere in vacanza.** (Lit., to be on vacation.) To do time. *Tre anni di vacanza s'è beccata per quel furto.* "She got three years for that robbery."

VÀCCA, *f.* **a)** *N., slang.* **1.** *rude.* (Lit., cow.) Whorish woman. *Pupetta è una vacca, suo marito ne ha viste di cotte e di crude.* "Pupetta is a bitch; you wouldn't believe what her husband has had to endure." **2.** (From the silk industry, in which "vacche" are the silkworms that rot.) **Andare/Finire in vacca.** To go to rack and ruin. *Eravamo partiti benissimo con quell'affare, ma è finito tutto in vacca.* "Our business started out great. Now it's all gone to rack and ruin." **b)** *C., youth.* **A vacca.** Haphazardly; for no reason; for silly reasons. "*Perché è andato in Austria per tre mesi?*" "*E chi lo sa, fa tutto a vacca.*" "'Why did he go to Austria for three months?' 'Who knows? He does things like that, without thinking.'"

VACCÀTA, *f.* (From "vacca," cow.) *See* **cazzata, porcata, stronzata.**

VA E VIÈNI, *idiom.* (Lit., come and go.) Sexual intercourse. **Fare va e vieni.** To have sex. *Senti? Sono i vicini che stanno facendo di nuovo va e vieni.* "Can you hear? It's our neighbors who are pumping again."

VAFF!, *interj.* (Lit., "va' a fare . . ." go and . . .) *See* **vaffanculo.**

VAFFANBÀGNO, *interj.* (Lit., "go take a bath.") *See* **vaffanculo.**

VAFFANCÙLO, *rude.* (Contraction of the expression "Va' a fare in culo," up your ass.) **1.** *interj. Vaffanculo!* "Piss off!" **2.** *m.* Insult. *Quando c'è Pino, i vaffanculo si sprecano.* "When Pino is around, there are insults for everyone."

VANGÈLO, *m.* (Lit., gospel.) **a)** *crim.* Criminal file. *In questura c'è un vangelo su di lui che tiene due cassetti.* "At police headquarters his rap sheet fills two drawers." **b)** *youth.* Karl Marx's *Das Kapital. È uno dei pochi che ha letto tutto il vangelo dalla prima pagina all'ultima.* "He's one of the few who have read *Das Kapital* cover to cover."

VÀSCA, *f., N., youth.* (Lit., tub.) **Fare la vasca.** To stroll up and down a town's main street with one's friends, at sunset or on the weekend, when everyone else is there too. *Non abbiamo niente di meglio in programma che fare la vasca?* "We've got no better plan than strolling up and down Main Street?"

VASELÌNA, *f., crim.* (Lit., vaseline.) **1.** The police (because of their habit of > **ungere, 1,** i.e., beating up people in custody). *La vaselina è andata giù pesante con Tonio.* "The police went at it a bit too harshly with Tonio." **2.** Thrashing. *Un'altra vaselina così e ci rimango secco.* "Another thrashing like this one and I'll kick the bucket."

VÈCCHIO, *m.*, **VÈCCHIA,** *f., youth.* (Lit., the old one.) Father/Mother. **I vècchi.** Parents. *I vecchi vanno a svernare al mare. Che pacchia!* "My old folks will winter at our beach house. Great!"

VÉDOVA, *adj., youth.* (Lit., widow.) A girl who has been left by her boyfriend. *Secondo me Olga, che era rimasta vedova, ha finito il lutto.* "I have the impression that Olga, who was ditched by her boyfriend, is no longer in mourning."

VÉDOVA NÉRA, *idiom, f., narc.* (Translation of the English "black widow.") Black capsules containing amphetamines. *Quella non è una caramella al caffè, è una vedova nera.* "That's not coffee candy, it's black widow."

VEGETÀLE, *m., youth.* (Lit., vegetable.) Listless, boring person. *Leonardo era troppo . . . gasato, così adesso esci con quel vegetale di Giorgio?* "Leonardo was too . . . pumped up, so now you're going out with Giorgio? That vegetable?!"

VÉLA, *f., youth.* (Lit., sail.) **1. Fare vela.** (Lit., to set sail.) To flee; to play hooky. *Le piace il rischio: fa vela e poi gironzola intorno alla scuola.* "She likes to skirt danger. She skips classes but hangs around the school." **2. Andare a vela.** (Lit., to sail.) To be homosexual. *Che posto noioso! Vanno tutti a vela.* "What a boring place! They're all gay."

VELÀTA, *f.* (From "velarsi," to wear a veil.) To be a closet homosexual. *Tientelo per te, ma Danilo è una velata.* "Just for your information—Danilo is a closet queen."

VÉNA, *f., narc.* (Lit., vein.) **Spararsi in vena.** *See* **Spararsi.**

VENÌRE, *vi.* (Lit., to come.) To ejaculate (for a man); to reach orgasm (for a woman.) *Il loro obiettivo era di venire sempre, ma sempre, insieme.* "Their aim was to come together each and every time."

VERDÓNE, *m.* (From "verde," green.) **1.** A dollar bill. *In questo paese puoi compare di tutto se hai dei verdoni.* "Provided you've got green stuff, you can buy anything you want in this country." **2.** Money. *Niente verdoni? Niente merce.* "No green stuff? No merchandise."

VERDÙRA, *f.* (Lit., vegetables.) **a)** *slang.* Vagina. *Ehi, ragazzo, non vuoi un po' di verdura?* "Hey, lover-boy, don't you want some cake?" **b)** *youth.* Passive male homosexual (because the most common term for homosexual, > **finocchio,** is the name of a vegetable). *Lo sai, vero, che quella è la spiaggia dove vanno le verdure?* "You're aware that's the beach where the fruits go, aren't you?"

VERTEBRÀTO, *m., youth.* (Lit., vertebrate.) Human being. *Dice che preferisce il suo gatto ai vertebrati: più affidabile.* "He says he prefers his cat to humans: he's more reliable."

VESTITÌNO, *m., youth.* (Lit., small dress.) Condom. *Se non ti metti il vestitino, con te non ci gioco.* "If you don't wear your raincoat, I won't play with you."

VÉTRI, *m. pl., youth.* (Lit., glasses.) Eyeglasses. *Se lavi i vetri magari qualcosa vedi.* "If you clean your glasses you may be able to see something."

VIAGGIÀRE, *vi.* (Lit., to travel; to go on a trip.) **a)** *youth.* **1.** To have sex easily and frequently. *A quanto pare, in Svezia ha viaggiato un casino.* "It seems he did a lot of swinging during his trip to Sweden." **2.** To live, to get by. *Viaggia, niente di più.* "She gets by, nothing better than that." **b)** *narc.* **1.** To take drugs. *Viaggia con l'ero da molti anni.* "He's been doing smack for years." **2.** To be under the influence of drugs. *Non mi piace come sta viaggiando.* "I don't like the way his trip is going."

VIÀGGIO, *m., narc.* (Lit., trip.) A trip under the influence of drugs. **Farsi un viaggio.** (Lit., to go on a trip.) To take drugs. *Beh, hai trovato i soldi per il viaggio o devo cuccarli alla vecchia?* "So, did you find the money for the trip, or do I have to lift it from my old lady?"

VICHÌNGA, *f.* (Lit., Viking.) A blonde and tall tourist from northern Europe. *Passa l'estate a Rimini a cuccare vichinghe.* "He spends every summer in Rimini picking up Vikings."

VILLEGGIATÙRA, *f., crim.* (Lit., vacation.) *See* **vacanza.**

VINAVÌL, *m., narc.* (Lit., brand name of a kind of white glue.) Drug cut with harmful substances. *È schiattata per un'overdose di vinavil.* "She overdosed on some strange mix and kicked the bucket."

VIOLÌNO, *m.* (Lit., violin.) **a)** *slang.* Ham. *Cos'hai trovato in dispensa? Un violino?* "What did you find in the pantry? A ham?" **b)** *youth.* Overly zealous and flattering student. *Se glielo chiede il violino, magari la lupa ci lascia uscire prima.* "Let's get the nerd to ask the Latin teacher. Maybe she'll let us go early." **c)** *crim.* Submachine gun. *Sei tu che hai il violino? Ho un lavoro per te.* "You're the guy with the submachine gun, right? I have a job for you."

VÌTA, *f.* (Lit., life.) A long time. *Non parlo più con loro da una vita.* "I haven't talked to them in ages."

VITÈLLA, *f., C., crim.* To be sentenced to life in prison. *Non gli han dato la vitella solo perché la vittima era un cravattaro.* "They didn't give him life without parole just because the victim was a fleecer."

VOGÀRE, *vi.* (Lit., to row.) *See* **remare.**

VOLÀNTE, *f.* (Lit., flying.) The police emergency squad. *La volante dei miei stivali! Sono arrivati mezz'ora dopo.* "Emergency squad my foot! They arrived half an hour later."

VÓLPE, *m., C.* (Lit., fox.) **a)** *slang.* **Mangiare pane e volpe.** *See* **pane. b)** *crim.* Policeman. *La volpe non ha fiutato niente, vai liscio.* "The cop didn't smell anything, go easy."

VOLPÌNO, *m.,* **VOLPÌNA,** *f.* (Lit., small fox.) The opposite of cunning. Silly. *Eh, che volpina Samanta a lasciarsi scappare che sapeva di loro due!* "Samanta let it out that she knew of their affair. What a fox!"

WANTED, *Eng., adj., youth.* Wanted by someone who has unfriendly intentions. *Non vengo in quel bar: sono wanted.* "I'm not going to that bar. I'm wanted by some goons there."

WATT, *f., youth.* (Lit., the unit of power equal to one joule per second.) A brilliant idea. *Allora, 'sta watt, te la fai venire o no?* "Well, what about that brilliant idea you were talking about?"

WEEKENDÀRE, *vi., youth.* (Italian verb formed with the English "weekend.") To spend the weekend. *Weekendano sempre a Cortina: più da paninari di così!* "They spend every weekend in Cortina. That's typical of the with-it crowd."

WHISKY, *Eng., m., youth.* Gasoline. *Whisky di puro malto si ciuccia 'sta Porsche.* "This Porsche guzzles a lot of super."

WOW! *Eng., interj., youth.* See **uau!**

WURSTEL, *German, m., youth.* Listless and spineless person. *Sentite, tiriamo a sorte chi si deve sorbire il würstel.* "Look, let's pull straws to see who has to put up with that weenie."

YELLOW, *Eng., m., narc.* LSD tablet, yellow in color. *O yellow o niente. Scegli.* "Either yellow sunshine or nothing. You choose."

YUPPIE/YUPPY, *Eng., m./f.* Yuppie. *Regola numero uno se vuoi fare lo yuppie: solo vino d'annata a minimo cinquantamila la bottiglia.* "Rule number one if you want to be a yuppie: only vintage wine, at least fifty thousand lire a bottle."

ZÀMPA, *f.* (Lit., paw.) Hand. *Giù le zampe! La torta è per la festa.* "Get your paws off that cake! It's for the party."

ZAMPÀRE, *vt.* (From > **zampa.**) To grab; to steal. *Il ragazzo ha zampato la radio ed ha telato.* "The kid lifted the radio and ran."

ZANÀRO, *m., N.* (From the name of the Zanarini bar in Bologna.) The same as > **paninaro.**

ZAPPÀRE, *vi., N., youth.* (Lit., to hoe.) To annoy. *Mamma, se zappi!* "Gee, you can be a pain in the neck!"

ZÉLLA, *f., C.* Filth. *Complimenti, ti daremo il primo premio come produttore di zella.* "Congratulations, the first prize for filth production goes to you."

ZÈUS, *m., youth.* (The Greek god Zeus.) God. *Orco Zeus, che sfiga!* "Darn, I'm really unlucky."

ZÌA, *f., N.* (Lit., aunt.) Passive male homosexual. *Lui ha una bella zia, ma non la porta molto in giro.* "He lives with a beautiful queen, but doesn't take her out much."

ZÌGO, *m., youth.* Outstanding, top, exceptional. *Potrei fare la Vasaloppen oggi: sono allo zigo!* "I could do the Vasaloppen cross-country race today; I feel zingy!"

ZIGRINÀRE, *vi., youth.* (From "zigrino," a tool that "mills," or "knurls" metal.) To have sexual intercourse. *Zigrini con Andrea o con Massimo?* "Are you doing it with Andrea or with Massimo?"

ZÌI, *m. pl., N.* (Lit., uncles.) **a)** *crim.* Policemen. *Sono arrivati gli zii. Devo andare via con loro, temo.* "The cops are here. I'm afraid I must go with them." **b)** *narc.* Members of the narcotics squad. *Vedi quei quattro che fanno finta di comprare roba? Tutti zii.* "Do you see those four guys pretending to buy dope? All vice."

ZIMÀRRO, *m., youth.* (Perhaps from "zimarra," worn-out cloak.) Unpleasant and rough person, not in tune with the style of middle-class youths. *È uno zimarro, ma ha già fatto più soldi di tutti noi.* "He's not with it at all, but he's already made more money than any of us."

ZÌNNE/ZÌZZE, *f. pl., C.* Tits. *S'è fatta ridurre le zinne di due taglie. Che oca!* "She had her tits reduced two sizes. What a goose!"

ZÌO, *m.* (Lit., uncle.) Euphemism for "Dio," God, used in curses. *Zio cane, che casino!* "Darn, what a mess!"

ZÒCCOLA, *f., S., rude.* (Lit., sewer rat.) Low-level prostitute. *Con quei soldi lì ti paghi solo una zoccola.* "With that kind of money, you'll only get a cheap whore."

ZOMBI(E), *m.* (From English "zombie.") **1.** Old-fashioned, traditional person. *Quello zombie di suo cugino vuole sposare una vergine.* "Her cousin is such a nerd he wants to marry a virgin." **2.** Living dead. *Mamma, sembri uno zombi, sei sicura di star bene?* "Gee, you look like a zombie, are you sure you're all right?"

ZOMPÀRE, *vi., C.* To jump onto a woman with whom one wants to have sex. *Alle donne, gnugnu, non si zompa addosso come fai tu.* "You don't pounce on women that way, you twit!"

ZÒPPO, *adj., m., youth.* (Lit., lame.) A boy who has no success at picking up girls. *Tutti zoppi a quella festa. Una pizza!* "All nerds at that party. A bore!"

ZÙCCA, *f., N.* (Lit., pumpkin.) **1.** A million lire. *Conta, conta le zucche, che tante così tutte insieme non le vedrai tanto presto.* "Count your millions. You won't see that many together for a long time." **2.** Head. *Ma che zucca* *che hai—grande e vuota.* "What a noggin you have—big and empty!"

ZÙCCHERO, *m., narc.* (Lit., sugar.) Cocaine; heroin. *Si tiene su con lo zucchero, ma incomincia a risentirne.* "He keeps on going thanks to the white stuff, but it's beginning to show."

3 Foreign Language Series From Barron's!

The **VERB SERIES** offers more than 300 of the most frequently used verbs. The **GRAMMAR SERIES** provides complete coverage of the elements of grammar. The **VOCABULARY SERIES** offers more than 3500 words and phrases with their foreign language translations. Each book: paperback.

Helpful Guides for Mastering a Foreign Language

2001 Idiom Series

dispensable resources, these completely bilingual dictionaries in four major European languages present the most frequently used idiomatic words and phrases to help students avoid stilted expression when writing in their newly acquired language. Each book includes illustrative sentences. Each feature is easy to locate and designed with clarity in mind.

2001 French and English Idioms, 2nd
0-8120-9024-1 $16.95, Can $23.95

2001 German and English Idioms
0-8120-9009-8 $16.95, Can $23.95

2001 Italian and English Idioms
0-8120-9030-6 $16.95, Can $24.50

2001 Japanese and English Idioms
0-8120-9433-6 $16.95, Can $23.95

2001 Russian and English Idioms
0-8120-9532-4 $21.95, Can $31.95

2001 Spanish and English Idioms
0-8120-9028-4 $14.95, Can $21.00

201 Verb Series

The most commonly used verbs are presented alphabetically and in all their forms, one to a page, in each of the many foreign languages listed here. Features of this series include discussions of participles, punctuation guides, listings of compounds, the phrases and expressions often used with each verb, plus much more!

201 Arabic Verbs
0-8120-0547-3 $13.95, Can $17.95

201 Dutch Verbs
0-8120-0738-7 $14.95, Can $21.95

201 Modern Greek Verbs
0-8120-0475-2 $11.95, Can $15.95

201 Polish Verbs
0-8120-0577-5 $16.95, Can $24.50

201 Swedish Verbs
0-8120-0528-7 $16.95, Can $24.50

201 Turkish Verbs
0-8120-2034-0 $14.95, Can $21.000

501 Verb Series

Here is a series to help the foreign language student successfully approach verbs and all their details. Complete conjugations of the verbs are arranged one verb to a page in alphabetical order. Verb forms are printed in boldface type in two columns, and common idioms using the applicable verbs are listed at the bottom of the page in each volume.

501 English Verbs
0-7641-0304-0 $14.95, Can $19.95

501 French Verbs, 4th
0-8120-9281-3 $14.95, Can $21.95

501 German Verbs, 3rd
0-8120-0284-2 $14.95, Can $19.95

501 Hebrew Verbs
0-8120-9468-9 $18.95, Can $27.50

501 Italian Verbs
0-7641-1348-8 $14.95, Can $21.00

501 Japanese Verbs, 2nd
0-7641-0285-0 $16.95, Can $23.95

501 Latin Verbs
0-8120-9050-9 $16.95, Can $23.95

501 Portuguese Verbs
0-8120-9034-9 $16.95, Can $24.50

501 Russian Verbs
0-7641-1349-6 $16.95, Can $24.50

501 Spanish Verbs, 4th
0-8120-9282-1 $14.95, Can $21.00

Books may be purchased at your bookstore, or by mail from Barron's. Enclose check or money order for total amount plus sales tax where applicable and add 18% for postage and handling (minimum charge $5.95). All books are paperback editions. New York, New Jersey, Michigan, and California residents add sales tax. Prices subject to change without notice. Visit our website at: www.barronseduc.com

Barron's Educational Series, Inc. • 250 Wireless Boulevard, Hauppauge, NY 11788
In Canada: Georgetown Book Warehouse, 34 Armstrong Avenue, Georgetown, Ont. L7G 4R9

(#33) R 5/05